Ideas and Identities:

The Life and Work of Erik Erikson

D1520948

Ideas and Identities:

The Life and Work of Erik Erikson

ROBERT S. WALLERSTEIN

and

LEO GOLDBERGER

Editors

International Universities Press, Inc.
Madison, Connecticut

Library of Congress Cataloging-in-Publication Data

Ideas and identities : the life and work of Erik Erikson / Robert S. Wallerstein, Leo Goldberger, editors.
    p.   cm.
    Chiefly papers originally presented at the symposium "Ideas and Identities" on the life and work of Erik Erikson held on January 15, 1995, at the Conference Center of the University of California, San Francisco, and sponsored by the San Francisco Psychoanalytic Institute and Society and the San Francisco Foundation for Psychoanalysis.
    Includes bibliographical references and index.
    ISBN 0-8236-2445-5
    1. Erikson, Erik, H. (Erik Homburger), 1902—Congresses.
2. Psychoanalysts—United States—Biography—Congresses.
3. Psychoanalysis—Congresses.   I. Wallerstein, Robert S.
II. Goldberger, Leo.
BF 109. E7I33   1997
150.19'5'092—DC21   97-30053
                                                    CIP

Manufactured in the United States of America

To the memory and the impact of Erik Erikson,
from his grateful colleagues and friends.

Contents

Acknowledgments

We are deeply grateful to the contributors who allowed their articles to appear in this volume celebrating the memory of Erik Erikson and his wide-ranging legacy. A special note of thanks to Joan Erikson* for allowing us to reprint several of her late husband's classic articles that were copyrighted in his name—and to Kai Erikson for facilitating the permission to reprint "The Galilean Sayings and the Sense of 'I' " from the *Yale Review*. To the Austen Riggs Center, Stockbridge, MA, and its medical director, Edward Robert Shapiro, we express our thanks for the use of Norman Rockwell's wonderful drawing of Erikson. The drawing, completed in the 1950s while Erikson still worked at Riggs, hangs in the entrance hall of the Center and has become emblematic of the Center's Erik H. Erikson Institute. Finally, we wish to thank Martin Azarian, the publisher, and Margaret Emery, the editor-in-chief, of International Universities Press for their generous help and encouragement in bringing this volume to fruition.

Robert S. Wallerstein, M.D.
Leo Goldberger, Ph.D.

Thanks to the authors and the editors of *Psychoanalysis and Contemporary Thought* for permission to reprint the following papers which were first published in Volume 19, No. 2, 1996

*We were saddened to learn of Joan Erikson's death, which occurred on August 3, 1997.

of the journal: "Erik Erikson and the Temporal Mind," by Marcia Cavell; "Erik Erikson as Social Scientist," by Neil J. Smelser; "Erik Erikson's Contribution Toward Understanding Religion," by Walter H. Capps; "Erik H. Erikson on Bodies, Gender, and Development," by Elizabeth Lloyd Mayer; "Entering History: Erik Erikson's New Psychological Landscape," by Robert Jay Lifton; "Erikson, Our Contemporary: His Anticipation of an Intersubjective Perspective," by Stephen Seligman and Rebecca Shahmoon Shanok.

"The Dream Specimen of Psychoanalysis" was first published in *The Journal of the American Psychoanalytic Association*, 2:2–56, 1954, and is reprinted by permission.

"The Problem of Ego Identity," first published in *The Journal of the American Psychoanalytic Association*, 4:56–121, 1956, also appeared in *Identity and the Life Cycle*, published by International Universities Press, 1958, and is reprinted by permission.

Erik Erikson's paper "The Nature of Clinical Evidence," first published in *Daedalus*, 87:65–87, 1958, also appeared in *Insight and Responsibility*, New York: Norton, 1964, and is reprinted by permission of Joan M. Erikson.

"The Galilean Sayings and the Sense of 'I'," was first published in *The Yale Review*, Spring, 1981, and is reprinted by permission.

Lawrence J. Friedman's chapter, "Erik H. Erikson's Critical Themes and Voices: The Task of Synthesis," was first published in *American Cultural Critics*, edited by David Murray, Exeter, U.K.: University of Exeter Press, 1995, and is reprinted by permission.

Contributors

Walter H. Capps, Ph.D. is Professor of Religious Studies and Chair of the Department of Religious Studies at the University of California, Santa Barbara

Marcia Cavell, Ph.D. is Visiting Associate Professor, Department of Philosophy, University of California, Berkeley

Lawrence J. Friedman, Ph.D. is Professor of History at Indiana University

Leo Goldberger, Ph.D. is Professor of Psychology, New York University and former Director of its Research Center for Mental Health

Robert Jay Lifton, M.D. is Distinguished Professor of Psychiatry and Psychology, City University of New York at John Jay College and the Graduate School. He is the Director of its Center for Violence and Human Survival

Elizabeth Lloyd Mayer, Ph.D. is Training and Supervising Analyst, San Francisco Psychoanalytic Institute; Associate Clinical Professor, Department of Psychiatry, University of California, San Francisco, School of Medicine; and Associate Clinical Professor, Department of Psychology, University of California, Berkeley

Stephen Seligman, D.M.H. is Clinical Professor of Psychiatry at the Infant–Parent Program, San Francisco General Hospital–University of California, San Francisco. He is on the faculty of the Psychoanalytic Institute of Northern California, and is an Affiliate Member and Visiting Instructor at the San Francisco Psychoanalytic Institute

Rebecca Shahmoon Shanok, M.S.W., Ph.D. is Director of the Early Childhood Group Therapy Service and Training Programs of the Child Development Center, Jewish Board of Family and Children's Services, and is in private practice in New York City

Neil J. Smelser, Ph.D. is Director, Center for Advanced Study in the Behavioral Sciences, Stanford, California

Robert S. Wallerstein, M.D. is Professor Emeritus and former Chairman of the Department of Psychiatry, University of California, San Francisco, School of Medicine, and a Training and Supervising Analyst, San Francisco Psychoanalytic Institute

1.

Erik H. Erikson, 1902–1994: Setting the Context

ROBERT S. WALLERSTEIN, M.D.

Erik Erikson was born in Frankfurt, Germany on June 15, 1902 and died in a nursing home in Harwich, Massachusetts, on Cape Cod, on May 12, 1994. Of that life of close to 92 years, spanning almost our entire twentieth century, it can be unhesitatingly asserted that, after Freud, no single psychoanalyst has had a more profound impact on our twentieth-century culture and world than he. Indeed very few analysts have reshaped psychoanalytic perspectives to the extent that he did.

As a psychoanalyst, Erikson's contributions have been monumental. He extended the developmental stages—first elaborated by Freud across the childhood years—to encompass the entire life span through adolescence, adulthood, and into aging and senescence; his conception of the psychosocial developmental process broadened Freud's psychosexual developmental ladder and embedded each individual development in its social and historical context; and he conceptualized the interlocking of these sequential life stages, both temporally, through the mutual cog-wheeling, the fitting together, over the succession of generations, and also laterally, in interaction with the sociohistorical surround, for each individual at a unique place in society and in history. Best known is his elaboration

1

of the concept of the crystallization of ego identity with the ever-present possibility of identity crisis and risk of identity diffusion in the life stage of adolescence, with its hopefully saving adolescent moratorium. It was this which made Erikson so much a culture hero and quasi-cult figure to generations of American youth, especially during the youth rebellions of the turbulent sixties.

These massive achievements have been expressed in a succession of fourteen books, of which the most significant and best known include the very first, *Childhood and Society* (1950), which made Erikson an instant household name in both the psychoanalytic world and the wider culture as well; *Young Man Luther* (1958a) and *Gandhi's Truth* (1969), which helped establish the nascent fields of psychohistory and psychobiography, inextricably linked ever since with Erikson's name; and onto the final coauthored *Vital Involvement in Old Age* (1986), a return to the then 80-year-old parents of the children originally chronicled in *Childhood and Society,* for a reconsideration of their entire life spans into their experience of old age in our time. What can readily be overlooked in this overview of Erikson's professional oeuvre is his towering position as a psychoanalytic clinician and educator as well as theorist; his famous 1954 paper, the "Dream Specimen of Psychoanalysis"—originally presented as a seminar to the candidates of the San Francisco Psychoanalytic Institute in 1949, and reprinted in this volume—is arguably the most important paper on dream analysis since Freud's *Interpretation of Dreams* in 1900.

It has been indeed the special fortune of the San Francisco Bay Area psychoanalytic community, where the scientific symposium honoring and celebrating Erikson's life and work around which this volume has been organized took place, that Erikson spent two major periods of his life in our midst, more time than anywhere else in the world. Born of a Jewish mother and an unknown Danish father, Erikson was brought up in the home of a Jewish pediatrician stepfather, in Karlsruhe, Germany. He took on the identity of an itinerant artist in an adolescent *Wanderjahr* across Europe—his own moratorium. He then obtained his first job, recommended by his boyhood friend

Peter Blos, who had preceded him there, as a teacher in the progressive private preschool and school established by Dorothy Burlingham in Vienna for her own four children and the children of other analysts and analysts in training. There Erikson was analyzed by Anna Freud (not without the wry regret expressed once to me that it should have been by Sigmund Freud) and received his psychoanalytic training in the Vienna Institute. And there he met, and in 1930 married, Joan Serson, a Canadian woman studying in Vienna, a very talented dancer and artist. She was later also an author in her own right, as well as coauthor of Erik's last book, and lifelong a helpful editor of his many books and articles.

In 1933 with the situation in Central Europe ominously darkening for psychoanalysis and especially for its Jewish cohort, Erik and his family came to the United States. Over the decade of the thirties he had an appointment at Harvard and then at Yale, and did his anthropological field work along with the anthropologist Scudder Mekeel with the Sioux Indians in the Dakotas, and then along with Alfred Kroeber with the Yurok in Northern California, all later to be written up in *Childhood and Society*. The decade of the forties, Erik's first stay in the San Francisco Bay Area, was spent as a professor in the famed psychology department at the University of California, Berkeley (UC Berkeley), and as one of the founding members and teachers in the San Francisco Psychoanalytic Institute. He was also a cofounder, together with his Jungian analyst friend and colleague, Joseph Wheelwright, of the Veterans Clinic created by the newly formed Mount Zion Hospital Department of Psychiatry, designed to address the psychiatric needs of the returning war veterans. That decade in California was unhappily brought to a close when Erikson, along with a cluster of most distinguished colleagues in the UC Berkeley Psychology Department, all resigned their positions rather than take the McCarthy-era loyalty oath that the University then required.

Erik spent the next decade, of the fifties, perhaps his most productive and certainly his most renowned clinical years, at the Austen Riggs Center in Stockbridge, Massachusetts, recruited by Robert Knight to work with him and the brilliant galaxy gathered in that small clinical center, including among others David Rapaport, Roy Schafer, Merton Gill, and Margaret Brenman. It was a decade of intense clinical involvement, as therapist, supervisor, and teacher, with the economically affluent but severely disturbed adolescents and young adults who were privileged to bring their treatment needs to that private psychiatric sanatorium in a small New England village. Erik counterposed that experience to his regular consulting visits to the Western Psychiatric Institute in Pittsburgh, observing the same play of psychopathology among economically deprived urban inner-city youth. The subsequent decade of the sixties was Erik's storied teaching period as a Harvard professor, giving his famed life cycle and life development courses, spreading his influence at the time throughout the academic university world, and even more widely, into the culture at large.

Upon Erik's retirement from Harvard in the early seventies, I was able, as Chief of the Department of Psychiatry at Mount Zion Hospital in San Francisco, and on the basis of substantial grant support that I could secure from Philip Hallen, Director of the Maurice Falk Medical Fund, to offer both Erik and his wife Joan—whom my wife, Judy, and I had gotten to know well when Erik and I had spent a Fellowship year together in 1964–1965 at the Center for Advanced Study in the Behavioral Sciences at Stanford, California, where we were privileged to participate in a small group to whom Erik regularly read drafts of chapters of his coming Gandhi book for critical comments—part-time positions in our department. At Mount Zion Erik was a central inspiring teacher of almost mythic proportions to our student cohorts in the various mental health professions in our training programs, with psychiatric residents, child psychiatry fellows, clinical psychology pre- and postdoctoral interns, postmaster's psychiatric social work interns, and students in the clinical training years in our then newly created Doctor of Mental Health program. Joan was senior consultant to our psychiatric inpatient and day hospital activities programs, developing further the kind of creative arts activities program for the psychiatrically ill that she had pioneered in the fifties at Austen Riggs. Erik and Joan participated with us in this manner until they left in 1987 to return to Cambridge, where an Erikson Center for academic and life studies was established under the auspices of Harvard University. The more than a decade and a half of living in Marin County and working at Mount Zion Hospital was the longest period that Erik and Joan had lived in one place since they first came to the United States in 1933. Together with the decade of the forties in Berkeley, it made the Bay Area the place that they called home for a longer period than anywhere else in the world. Erik's final days, after the period back in Cambridge with the Erikson Center at Harvard, were spent peacefully in a nursing home in Harwich, Massachusetts, on Cape Cod, close to his beloved Cotuit, where for several decades he and Joan had had a summer home on the beach.

It was on the basis of this long period of work in our midst, and together at Mount Zion, and as a close friend of the Eriksons over the thirty-year span since we were Fellows together in the sixties at the Center for Advanced Study at Stanford where we had adjacent studies and became good professional and family friends, that I undertook, after Erik's death, to organize an all-day symposium commemorating and celebrating the life and work of Erik Erikson, under the title "Ideas and Identities." This symposium, jointly sponsored by the San Francisco Psychoanalytic Institute and Society, and the San Francisco Foundation for Psychoanalysis, took place from 9:00 A.M. to 5:00 P.M. on January 15, 1995, at the Conference Center of the University of California, San Francisco. The proceedings of that symposium made up the bulk of Volume 19, Number 2, of the journal *Psychoanalysis and Contemporary Thought* (1996), and that material is the core around which this much expanded volume has been constructed. It contains both additional historic commentary as well as reprints of several of Erik's landmark clinical and theoretical contributions to our discipline and to its understanding of our world. It is to the design of this present volume, developed in close collaboration with Leo Goldberger, Ph.D., editor-in-chief of *Psychoanalysis and Contemporary Thought*, that I now turn.

The intent of the day-long 1995 symposium was to present six scientific talks, three in the morning and three in the afternoon, which would, in ensemble, comprehensively portray the full range of Erik's vast tapestry of contributions within psychoanalysis. The intent was to expand from that center, into the whole array of cognate disciplines of intelligence of the human mind; of issues of growth and development over the life cycle; of identity struggles and crystallizations; of psychohistory and psychobiography; of the psychoanalytic interface with the social sciences and with studies of religion; and, more broadly conceived, the impact of psychoanalytic thought upon contemporary philosophy, and, in its widest sense, upon our twentieth-century culture at large.

For these scientific presentations I was able to secure the commitment of a group of truly distinguished scholars in each of the six demarcated domains of inquiry, all but one of whom, Marcia Cavell, had known Erik personally and had worked with him over varyingly substantial and meaningful periods of time. The six, in order of their presentations, an order followed in this book, were as follows: (1) Marcia Cavell, Ph.D., a philosopher on the faculty at UC Berkeley, a longtime scholar of psychoanalysis as well, both as a student and a faculty member in earlier years at the Columbia University Center for Psychoanalytic Training and Research, and the author, in 1993, of a book, *The Psychoanalytic Mind: From Freud to Philosophy,* who spoke on Erik's contributions to the relationship of psychoanalysis to philosophy and to modern thought, under the title "Erik Erikson and the Temporal Mind"; (2) Neil J. Smelser, Ph.D., a longtime distinguished sociologist and the first University Professor from the social sciences at UC Berkeley, also a trained psychoanalyst, and currently the Director of the Center for Advanced Study in the Behavioral Sciences at Stanford, California, who spoke on Erik's contributions to the social sciences, under the title "Erik Erikson as Social Scientist"; (3) Walter Capps, Ph.D., Professor of Religious Studies at the University of California, Santa Barbara, and the organizer himself, years before, of a symposium assessing Erik's contributions to the study of religious thought and religious leaders in which Erik had been a central participant, who spoke on Erik's contributions to the study of religion, under the title "Erik Erikson's Contribution Toward Understanding Religion"; (4) Elizabeth Lloyd Mayer, Ph.D., a Training and Supervising Analyst at the San Francisco Psychoanalytic Institute and on the faculty of the Department of Psychology at UC Berkeley, who has carried out extended empirical studies of play constructions of young boys and girls within the model advanced originally by Erik in his 1950 seminal book, *Childhood and Society,* who spoke on Erik as a developmentalist in his specific concerns with gender and sexual development and identity, under the title "Erik Erikson on Bodies, Gender, and Development"; (5) Robert J. Lifton, M.D., Director of the Center on Violence and Human Survival at the City University of New York, longtime collaborator with Erik in psychohistorical inquiry via the "Wellfleet Conferences" on Cape Cod each summer, and author of numerous books essaying to comprehend the hurtful and demonic phenomena of our times—Chinese brainwashing, the horrors of the Vietnam conflict, the psychology of the Nazi concentration camp doctors, and the unspeakableness of Hiroshima and nuclear devastation—who spoke on Erik's contributions to psychohistory and psychobiography, under the title "Entering History: Erik Erikson's New Psychological Landscape"; and, last, (6) Kai Erikson, Ph.D., Erik's older son, distinguished Professor of Sociology at Yale University and past president of the American Sociological Association, who spoke on a major conception, that of pseudospeciation, which Erik had contributed to our efforts to understand the phenomena of human conflict, aggression, and the carnage of war, under the title "On Pseudospeciation."

The first five of these six scientific presentations at the symposium are presented in this volume in their temporal order, and under their symposium titles, immediately after this introductory chapter. Unfortunately, Kai Erikson has felt unable to have his polished manuscript available within the time frame of our publication schedule, and ideally, that paper will be published subsequently as a separate fitting addendum to this symposium grouping. Prior to the scientific papers of the symposium morning, there were brief welcoming remarks by Katherine MacVicar, M.D., President of the San Francisco Psychoanalytic Institute and Society, and by Mark I. Levy, M.D., President of the San Francisco Foundation for Psychoanalysis, followed by an introductory statement by me, as the symposium organizer, giving a brief biographical statement on Erik's life and work, followed by an outline of the program for the day. This statement was titled "Erik Erikson: 1902–1994," and its biographical content has been incorporated into this present chapter. Throughout the day I then introduced each speaker in turn, emphasizing his or her particular warrant for the assigned topic, and the nature of each one's personal and professional relationship to Erik and his work.

The morning session was ended by a forty-minute video excerpt from a weekend Freud–Jung symposium held in 1974, shortly after the publication of the Freud–Jung correspondence, under the auspices of the Friends of Langley-Porter (a support group for the Langley-Porter Institute, the psychiatric hospital under the management of the Department of Psychiatry of the University of California, San Francisco). The weekend Freud–Jung symposium, preserved on videotape, featured Erik Erikson, representing Freudian psychoanalysis, and his longtime friend and colleague, Joseph Wheelwright, the central figure in the C. G. Jung Institute in San Francisco, representing Jungian analysis. They spoke separately as well as having a joint discussion about the meaning and implications of the Freud–Jung interchanges of letters. At one point Erik, after making a point concerning Freud's meanings in a particular sequence, turned to Wheelwright, remarking, "*You'll* have to speak for *your* client!" What was presented at our symposium from the one two decades earlier was Erik's forty-minute talk on that occasion, a very moving evocation of Erik as a vital, living presence (as he had been as a 70-year-old) at our symposium—especially poignant for those in the audience who never had had the opportunity to see and hear him personally.[1]

[1]Our entire symposium was videotaped and edited into three two-hour tapes which contain all the scientific presentations, my introductory and concluding statements, the Erikson talk on videotape, and the musical presentation at the end of the day. These tapes are available for purchase

After the Erikson video presentation, the meeting adjourned for a close to two-hour luncheon break. There was an informal lunchtime session, which I chaired, at which various individuals, analysands, supervisees, friends, and colleagues of Erik's from his San Francisco periods as well as from the time at Riggs and then at Harvard, had an opportunity to informally present reminiscences and impressions. There were a total of nine speakers during this period: Daryl de Bell, Peyton Jacob, Maurice Marcus, Hildegard Berliner, Beulah Parker, Robert Rubenstein, Ilse Jawetz, John McGovern, and Margaret Brenman. Their talks were not recorded; they did portray a rich and illuminating range of relationships and a diversity of enduring impacts on this group of people, all of whom had been fortunate enough to have had significant personal relationships with Erik. These informal talks and personal reminiscences are not included in this volume, nor are they on the symposium videotapes.

In the symposium afternoon, the three scientific talks by Elizabeth Lloyd Mayer, Robert J. Lifton, and Kai Erikson were given, after which I, in concluding the day-long proceedings, read two documents. The first was Erik's "Mr. Erikson's Conviction," given at the hearing on June 1, 1950, before the University of California, Berkeley, Committee on Privilege and Tenure, explaining why he could not sign the McCarthy era-inspired Loyalty Oath required at that time of all its faculty and staff, and be able at the same time in good conscience to continue as a teacher of psychology to the University's students. This document had moved me deeply when it had been distributed by Karl Menninger to the professional staff of The Menninger Foundation in February 1951. Though that was years before I came to know Erik personally (which was not until 1964), and though I knew him only as the admired author of *Childhood and Society* (1950), I had somehow kept and cherished this document over the subsequent four-and-a-half decades and retrieved it from my files to read on this occasion.

---

through the San Francisco Foundation for Psychoanalysis, 2420 Sutter Street, San Francisco, CA 94115.

It is as stirring an affirmation of the meaning of freedom of intellect and freedom of inquiry as I have ever been privileged to see. That text is the first, chronologically, in the sequence of writings by Erikson in this volume.

It should be remarked in this connection that of more than twenty members of the American Psychoanalytic Association and candidates at the San Francisco Psychoanalytic Institute then teaching at the University of California, the majority signed the required loyalty oath under protest. Norman Reider, then an Assistant Clinical Professor of Psychiatry at UC San Francisco refused and was not reappointed. Erik Erikson, as Professor of Psychology and Lecturer in Psychoanalysis at UC Berkeley, refused, was reappointed anyway, but resigned nonetheless.

Following that statement, I also read to the symposium assembly President Bill Clinton's letter from the White House, dated May 13, 1994—the day after Erik's death. It was a very warm and persuasively insightful letter reflecting a real awareness of Erik's place in advancing human understanding and expressing real sadness and feeling for Erik's loss. This document (with the kind permission of Joan Erikson) is also published here. Joan Erikson, who came to California to attend the symposium, was invited by me to the podium to make whatever remarks she wished as the final statement of the day before the concluding musical performance. She had earlier indicated that she would like the opportunity to say her own final words, but when she came to the podium she felt so moved by the spirit and the feelings of the day that she could only say, in the line from *My Fair Lady*, "I could have danced all night."

The last formal event of the day, ending the afternoon, as the videotape of Erik's Freud–Jung talk had ended the morning, was a performance of part of a cantata composed by Maia Aprahamian, a Marin County composer and a warm friend of the Eriksons, in honor of their fiftieth wedding anniversary in 1980, titled *The Life Cycle: A Cantata Based on the Eight Stages*. This half-hour performance was given by a group of seventeen instrumentalists and singers, from the San Francisco Chamber Singers, and was conducted by the composer. In addition to the choral group, audience participation was elicited at intervals indicated in the score. The musical performance is recorded as part of the three-tape video recording of the symposium.

The day's events concluded with an hour-long cheese, cake, fruit, and wine celebration and reception in the hall outside the auditorium. I felt the symposium to be, in terms of the almost uniformly high caliber of the scientific presentations, the best professional meeting that I ever remembered attending in a single day as well as the most eloquently moving and inspiring tribute to the genius of a single man in which I had ever participated. It was just this conjunction of reactions that was also conveyed to me during the reception period by many of those who attended. These same sentiments were also communicated in the larger than usual number of notes of congratulation and appreciation that I later received as organizer and chairman of the symposium. I will only quote from one of the letter writers, Robert Lifton, a symposium participant and an individual whom I had never thought of as disposed to hyperbole. He wrote two letters, one on January 18, in the immediate wake of the symposium: "Dear Bob, My warm congratulations once more on the Erikson conference. The more I reflect on it, the more profound the whole day becomes for me. Yours was not only a labor of love but a very wisely and sensitively conceived enterprise. . . ." And in a subsequent letter, almost a month later, Lifton added: "Even truly wonderful conferences like the one you created require a recovery time—so I hope that by now you have recovered enough to realize what an extraordinary achievement that gathering was." I cite this, as one testament out of many, to the impact that that symposium had on those who attended, and it is of course this, both the content and also the spirit, that we wish to portray in this volume built around the symposium proceedings.

But this book does not stop with the end of the symposium day. It contains six additional contributions, four of them specially selected papers of Erik's. These were chosen to reflect the range and catholicity of Erikson's monumental contributions, to psychoanalysis in its core but more widely as well to the psychoanalytic illumination of vital dimensions of the human

condition, where he more than any other psychoanalyst since
Freud has made so marked a contribution. I should here state
the warrant we have felt for each of these inclusions (arrayed
in chronological order) in turn.

I have called "The Dream Specimen of Psychoanalysis"
(1954) arguably the most important single paper on dream
analysis since Freud's dream book in 1900. Freud's revolutionary conception at the turn of the century was that the manifest
dream, as remembered and represented by the dreamer, no
matter how seemingly irrational, strange, or nonsensical its content, could be imbued with highly specific and personal meanings in the ongoing emotional life of the dreamer if only the
elaborate transformations of the "dream work" (the dreamer's
defensive mental operations) could be psychoanalytically un-
done to reveal the hidden (unconscious) latent meanings, the
cluster of coalescing "dream thoughts" that united current
(perhaps only latent) mental preoccupations with guiding reso-
nances from the psychic conflicts of earlier (infantile) times.
This signal insight of Freud's led to the exploration of a vast
realm of hitherto ununderstood mental activity and the rein-
serting of it into the extended understanding of the psychic
economy of the patient in psychoanalysis. It thereby became for
Freud and his followers a major vehicle of the psychoanalytic
treatment process—the dream as "the royal road to the unconscious." However, a less happy, but perhaps inevitable, consequence of the extended "dream analysis" introduced by Freud
was the tendency to bypass or ignore the knowledge of the
dream life and of the dreamer that could be gleaned from
equally intensive scrutiny of the manifest dream itself.

It is this imbalance in the work (and art) of dream interpretation that Erikson's dream paper so successfully corrected,
through the device of taking for his text Freud's famous Irma
dream, that Freud himself had somewhat fancifully declared to
be the dream that was dreamt (at least in part) to enable him
to unveil the mystery of the dream itself. In his own long exege-
sis of this dream, a dream that is known by every psychoanalyst,
Erikson offered a series of linked observations and propositions: (1)He said that with modern (as of 1954 but probably

even more so as of today) advances in the avenues of psychoanalytic exploration, the centrality of dream analysis as practiced in Freud's day has gradually dwindled away and is in danger of being lost, and that this may well be to the detriment, rather than the gain, of full psychoanalytic understanding. He said that the art of "picking from a patient's daily dream productions whatever dream fragments, symbols, manifest images, and latent dream thoughts support the prevalent trend of interpretations" (Erikson, chapter 8, this volume, p. 122) should be earned through "advanced practice" rather than freely assumed by neophyte analysts as seems to be now so often the case. (2) He said too that the value and reward of a revived systematic dream interpretation can be vastly enhanced by equally intense attention to the so-called "superficial," the surface of the dream, its manifest content and its form(s). Erikson both outlined an array of "manifest configurations" that characterize every dream—sometimes by paradoxical absence —and also illustrated how much additional mileage could be extracted from the analysis of the Irma dream by explicit attention to each of these manifest configurations in turn. (3) And he noted that different levels of latent meaning could be elucidated in the Irma dream using this approach—even in the absence of confirming revelatory responses of the dreamer —meanings far beyond the professional meanings that Freud himself drew (and offered in the dream book) from the unhappy preoccupations of his then current life. These included psychosexual meanings that reverberated with Freud's revealed childhood conflicts, religious meanings of conversion and confirmation, touching on Freud's position as a Jew in an (anti-Semitic) Catholic world, and sociocultural meanings linked to the child-rearing practices prevalent in his time and place. It is such considerations that led Erikson ineluctably to the statement; "On closer inspection, then, the radical differentiation between a manifest and a latent dream, while necessary as a means of localizing what is 'most latent,' diffuses in a complicated continuum of more manifest and more latent items which are sometimes to be found by a radical disposal of the manifest configuration, sometimes by a careful scrutiny of it"

(p. 150). It is this corrected imbalance and expanded legacy of what is possible in dream interpretation that Erikson has bequeathed to us and it is presented in this volume as one of his landmark contributions to the theory and practice of psychoanalysis.

The next paper, reprinted here, from only two years later, is "The Problem of Ego Identity" (1956), the first and fullest elaboration of Erikson's best known—certainly in the wider intellectual world outside psychoanalysis that he has touched—theoretical conception. This paper was at the time regarded as so central to Erikson's overall conceptual edifice and so critical to the evolution of our psychoanalytic under-standings of the developmental process, that it was reprinted three years later (1959) as one of the three chapters in the monograph *Identity and the Life Cycle,* Erikson's effort at a full exposition of his conception of the (psychosocial) life develop-mental process originally presented in far less systematic form in his *Childhood and Society* (1950).

I have elsewhere presented (Wallerstein, 1997) my own reconsideration of this central Eriksonian conception, built around two propositions I developed. The first was, how and why, despite Erikson's increasing influence upon and accep-tance by our intellectual culture at large, just through such conceptions as identity crystallization and adolescent morato-rium, he was simultaneously being marginalized from the main stream of our evolving psychoanalytic metapsychology (at least in America) where his conceptions, like identity, did not easily fit into the then dominant ego psychological metapsychology paradigm. The second was how this then accounted for the continuing neglect of Erikson's forerunner contributions to the contemporary major shift in the prevailing psychoanalytic theoretical paradigm in the direction of the relational, the in-terpersonal, the intersubjective, and the constructivist, which can all be brought together under the rubric of a shift from the objective and natural science posture of a "one body" intra-psychic psychology to the subjective and interactive posture of a "two-body" interpersonal psychology. What I develop in my 1997 paper is the closeness of Erikson's conceptualizations, like that of identity, to the currently evolving conceptions of the self (in interaction with "objects"). This is a closeness on which Erikson himself remarked more than once, and it is one of the fundaments of the newly evolving (self and object) relational paradigm. Yet Erikson's life work in this arena has once again been neglected and not credited either for its forerunner role or its real, indeed much better fit, into these contemporary conceptualizations of psychoanalytic theorizing.

It is in the 1956 paper that Erikson's understanding of the conception of identity, identity crystallization, negative identity, identity confusion (and diffusion), and the adolescent moratorium are spelled out at their fullest and most systematic. The number of facets of the identity conception that he elaborated are manifold. I will mention a few (not necessarily in logical order): (1) The concept of identity is both a legitimate part of the psychoanalytic theory of the ego (and of the prevailing American ego psychology) and is simultaneously in its core, psychosocial, thus confirming the individual identity both from within and from without, from the wider sociocultural surround. (2) Identity formation is more than the summation of the accumulating identifications of the growing-up years, an evolution that is indeed more than the sum of its parts, though with all the parts playing their formative role. (3) Identity is but one major conception, and one developmental crystallization in its age-appropriate place in adolescence. It is set, however, within an overarching progressive conceptualization of the total human life cycle with its sequentially evolving normative tasks and struggles, with forerunner appearances in prior life stages as well as consequent ramifications into subsequent stages. (4) The psychosocial, epigenetically unfolding developmental sequencing over the postulated eight major stages of the human life cycle dovetails congenially with the psychosexual developmental ladder that Freud propounded for childhood development, perhaps even up to adolescence. (5) Whatever the turmoil and struggle of adolescence, it is still a normative stage and crisis, not an affliction. (6) For those adolescents who do fall pathologically into the more severe regressions of true identity diffusion, a therapeutic design can and should be fashioned that embeds the dyadic psychotherapeutic encounter of the consulting room within a therapeutic hospital and hospital community as a planfully institutionalized world between the overbearing pressures of the actual outer world and the fantastic inner world.

The third paper of Erikson's to be reprinted here is "The Nature of Clinical Evidence" (1958b), published originally in the scholarly journal *Daedalus,* not generally read by psychoanalysts, but reprinted subsequently as one of the six chapters in Erikson's widely read book, *Insight and Responsibility* (1964). Like the dream specimen paper, it is an exposition of Erikson's *clinical* thinking, and with important implications as well for the testing of evidence in clinical research into the psychoanalytic treatment process. And like the ego identity paper, this one also resonates in a strikingly congenial manner with the current psychoanalytic emphases on subjectivity, participant interacting involvement, and hermeneutic perspectives, though again written well in advance of the emergence of these contemporary emphases.

The focus of the paper is on how the psychoanalytic clinician assesses the clinical data of the consulting room in order to arrive at valid and meaningful clinical judgments. This is a process, which, though grounded in the time-honored procedures of clinical medicine, necessarily relies—in the absence of the more "objective" data of the physical examination and the laboratory procedures of modern medicine—much more heavily on the "subjectivity" of the clinician judge. Erikson has added the qualifier to this, "disciplined subjectivity" of which he says, "there is a core of *disciplined subjectivity* in clinical work—and this both on the side of the therapist and of the patient—which it is neither desirable nor possible to replace altogether with seemingly more objective methods" (p. 249). And he has prefaced this on the immediately preceding page with the statement that "Indeed there is no choice but to put subjectivity in the center of an inquiry into evidence and inference in such clinical work as I am competent to discuss"

(p. 248)—a statement very much at home in relation to contemporary psychoanalysis.

From there Erikson went on to point to the methodological parallels between the history gathering of the psychoanalytic therapist and the tasks and procedures of the professional historian. He leans here on the work of R. G. Collingwood, quoting that historian's statement of the essence of the historical process as one " 'in which the past, so far as it is historically known, survives in the present' " (p. 249). But Erikson draws back from a complete parallelism when he asserts only of the psychotherapist that, "in his sphere one makes history as one records it" (p. 251)—though those with Collingwood's philosophic posture might not accept this distinction. Where the two would agree wholeheartedly is on Erikson's assertion of the historical relativity of all psychotherapy, illustrated by his comparison of his own conception of mental illness with that of an old Indian shaman woman (pp. 250–251).

The bulk of Erikson's paper is occupied, like the dream specimen paper, with the detailed analysis of a dream of one of his young adult patients, presumably from the Austen Riggs Center, declared by the patient to be the most disturbing dream of his life. After the many pages of elaboration of the multiple layers of meaning discerned in the dream, much akin to the tour de force of the dream specimen paper, Erikson turned to the elucidation of the central task of his paper, the search for reliable confirmation of his interpretations via the use of his *"disciplined* subjectivity." "The proof of the correctness of our inference does, of course, not always lie in the patient's immediate assent. . . . Rather, the proof lies in the way in which the communication between therapist and patient 'keeps moving,' leading to new and surprising insights and to the patient's greater assumption of responsibility for himself" (p. 269), in itself neither a surprising nor a novel conclusion. But from there he went on to the quite up-to-date 1990s conclusion—albeit voiced in the mid-1950s—that there are "two main therapeutic agents . . . the insight gained into the pathogenic past, and the convincing presence of a therapeutic relationship which bridges past and future" (p. 270). And in the statement that "only by playing my role as a new person in his present stage of life can I clarify the inappropriateness of his transferences from the past" (p. 272), we find the counterpart of Balint's contemporaneous writings, in Britain, about the "New Beginning," as well as the forerunner of Loewald's subsequent writings, in America, of the new object relationship established between analyst and analysand. All these are reasons enough to mark out this lucid exposition and spirited defense of the nature (and the claimed credibility) of the inferential process in clinical psychoanalytic work as one of Erikson's most signal contributions to our clinical thinking and again a linking point to so much contemporary psychoanalytic thinking.

The last of this sequence of four papers by Erikson being reprinted here is the last paper I know him to have written on his famous (and favorite) theme of psychohistorical and psychobiographical exploration, "The Galilean Sayings and the Sense of 'I'." It is a complex interweaving of the sayings and parables of Jesus in his itinerant Galilean wandering and preaching to the farmers and fisherfolk before his final fateful entry into Jerusalem, along with the development in each growing individual of what Erikson calls here the Sense of "I" (and also later of "We"), which we more fashionably call today the development of the sense of personal agency (or what Erikson himself had much earlier designated as identity formation).

From personal conversations I gathered from Erik that this paper on Jesus was part of a much larger life project. His first (and monumental) foray into this psychobiographical and psychohistorical realm was the biographical *Young Man Luther: A Study in Psychoanalysis and History,* published in 1958, the story of the resolution and the transcending of a personal life and identity crisis in the young monk. This occurred through Luther's offering a new path through the social and moral crisis of religious faith in his historic time, which resonated through the countless hearts in the western world that shared with Luther the social, if not necessarily the personal, anguish that reflected their collective and shared place in space and time. The second and equally ambitious opus in this unfolding program was *Gandhi's Truth: On the Origins of Militant Nonviolence,* published in 1969. It was an exploration of Gandhi's personal midlife crisis in South Africa before his return to India. Back in India Gandhi then undertook to alter profoundly the relations between classes and between castes, between the many categories of rulers and ruled. He did this by a transcendent call to the power of nonviolence, militantly pursued, to overcome tempting recourses to violence as a response to human conflict, again both submerging and transcending intrapersonal conflicts and crises in shared social and societal resolutions.

Of this book, Erik once said facetiously to me that he had been mischievously tempted to call it *Middle-Aged Mahatma,* which he would then plan to follow with *Old Man Ben-Gurion.* This was at the time when the cocreator of the modern state of Israel with its ingathering of Jews in their own nation-state from the almost two millennium long worldwide Diaspora, had retired to be philosopher-sage and moral gadfly to the new nation from his retirement home in Sde Boker, his kibbutz in the Negev desert. The Ben-Gurion project never materialized—Erik was then in his seventies—and Erik's attention shifted from the son of contemporary Israel, carved out of modern Palestine, to that other, Jesus of Bethlehem, product of ancient Palestine, who succeeded so mightily in transforming our world. But the full book-length portrait of Jesus also never got written. What did emerge was the one paper, reproduced here, a template for that larger undertaking, which was published in the spring of 1981 in *The Yale Review,* at that time edited by Erik's son Kai. Since this is no doubt among the least known to the psychoanalytic world of all of Erik's writings, having been published in a journal not readily accessed by psychoanalysts, and as far as I can ascertain never before reprinted in any collection, I felt it especially warranted to bring the paper to this monograph.

By way of commentary on this paper, I offer two quotations from it. The one (p. 308) states the familiar Eriksonian identity theme in less familiar language: "I have already mentioned the importance for basic trust of the early feeding situation of the human infant, including that meeting of eye to eye which, it is increasingly clear, is an important source of the sense of *I*—and

of a primal *We*"—an explanation of that part of the paper's
title that refers to issues of identity formation (and malforma-
tion). The other and more extended quotation states the thematic linkage, as Erik perceived it, between the active
development of the personal I in each of us and what Jesus
held forth as the task to which he called all of humankind:

> [T]o be active (as well as central, continuous, and whole), or at
> any rate not to feel inactivated (or peripheral and fragmented)
> is one of the most essential dimensions of a sense of *I*. I would
> consider Jesus' emphasis on the patient's [the lame and the ill
> whom Jesus healed] propensity for an active faith, then, not only
> a therapeutic "technique" applied to incapacitated individuals
> but an ethical message for the bystanders as part of a population
> which at that time must have been weakened in its sense of
> being the master—or unsure of a faith that could promise to
> become master—of its collective fate. And as for the enduring
> meaning of this saying let me here note that this orientation
> reasserted itself in the history of psychotherapy with Freud's
> decision to make the hysterical patient *work* for recovery by let-
> ting his or her own inner voice direct "free associations" in
> search of the underlying conflicts instead of merely submitting
> to hypnosis [pp. 300–301].

I trust that I have here given both sufficient context and justification for the inclusion of this essay, addressing as it does Erikson's interests in history and biography and religion all
together.

Following the condolence letter from President Clinton
addressed to Joan Erikson upon Erik's death, are two additional
papers, not part of the Erikson symposium. One is a psychoanalytic effort to relocate Erikson and his oeuvre in relation to
the current interpersonal, relational, and intersubjective trends
that are transforming the governing postulates of contemporary psychoanalysis. The other is a psychoanalytically informed
historian's overview assessing Erikson's voice as a major American cultural critic of our century. In my brief statement of the
basis for including Erikson's ego identity paper in this volume
I have already noted that despite having an impact on our world

culture and our intellectual life greater than that of any analyst since Freud, Erikson's work never found its proper integration into the then-dominant (at least in America) ego psychological metapsychology paradigm architected by Hartmann and his collaborators. In fact, over time, Erikson became progressively marginalized and gradually less remarked upon within the mainstream of psychoanalytic theory and practice. It is this marginalization that I tried to account for in my 1994 essay. This was in terms of an awkwardness of fit between Erikson's psychosocial and epigenetic developmental conceptions—his intergenerational cogwheeling of our sequentially unfolding life cycles, and his central concepts of identity, identity formation, and identity diffusion—and the tripartite structuralizations of the dominant ego psychology constructs, centered around impulse–defense configurations and the manifold compromise formations amongst the various contending psychic instances. Yet just because of Erikson's efforts to accommodate his conceptions to the ego structural theory language dominant in his day, they have not for the most part been drawn upon, or even recognized, as vital forerunners to so much of today's relational and interpersonal psychoanalytic thinking.

It is this psychoanalytic limbo into which Erikson's life work, magisterial as it is, has fallen, that I feel accounts for the otherwise so puzzling phenomenon that whereas the gradually infiltrating object relational, interpersonal, intersubjective, phenomenological, and other subjectivistic renderings of psychoanalytic phenomena, with their central theoretical place for concepts of self and object (and identity), all succeeded in so transforming American analysis over recent years, Erikson's own very major contributions in this overall arena have not systematically been credited, but have continued to be relatively neglected as but remnants of the era of the ego psychology and structural language.

In a significant effort at rectifying this vastly undeserved neglect, Seligman and Shanok in their paper reexamine four aspects of Erikson's "way of looking at things" in order to elaborate the many convergences and potentials that arise when Erikson's theorizing is approached in light of the current relational, interpersonal, and intersubjective psychoanalytic orientations. The four major themes that they single out for this reconsideration are Erikson's identity concept as a potentially interactional and dialectical conception spanning the entire life course; his reorientation of the role of infantile sexuality and the role of the body in the psychosocial developmental process—that is, his theory of "zones, modes and modalities"; his epigenetic developmental model that anchors the developmental process within and in relation to the temporal particularities of the sociohistorical surround; and, finally, his methodological approach to clinical and to psychobiographical and psychohistorical material. This contribution by Seligman and Shanok makes Erikson and his work highly contemporary indeed, and therefore represents both a very appropriate and timely current perspective, and, hopefully, a forward-looking clarion call to stimulate further efforts to maintain the influential contemporaneity of Erikson's life and work.

The final paper in this volume is by Lawrence J. Friedman. Professor of History at Indiana University, and an Erikson scholar, who is currently preparing an authorized biography of Erik Erikson for which he has extensively interviewed the family members and many of Erik's friends and colleagues. He interviewed me at length and we have had substantial exchanges subsequently by mail and telephone. He was asked whether he could prepare a chapter-length biographical statement for this volume. Instead, he offered a recently published chapter, "Erik H. Erikson's Critical Themes and Voices: The Task of Synthesis," from a volume titled *American Cultural Critics* (1995). This article, from the standpoint of the intellectual as a cultural critic, assesses Erikson's place as a major influence on American culture and American intellectual life across the second half of the twentieth century and seemed a fitting close to this volume. Within this framework Friedman sees Erikson as being most influential in shifting psychoanalytic attention (or at least some portion of psychoanalytic attention) toward social concerns in "three general topical areas—the nature of American society, the premises and applications of psychoanalysis, and the elements of the human life-cycle—that attracted much of his attention from the 1930s to the 1980s" (Friedman, 1995, (p. 355).

The critique of American culture—compared both implicitly and explicitly to the totalitarian tragedies of Germany and Russia—was stated in essays already written in the 1930s and 1940s, which became chapters for *Childhood and Society* (1950). On the one hand Erikson's vision, as an immigrant to America from ravaged Europe, was ebulliently optimistic. He saw an America full of energy and imbued with an openness to diverse ethnic and cultural groupings, all amalgamating into what Erikson conceived as a more inclusive, panhuman identity. Yet Erikson also had apprehensions, "about the intensity of American economic competitiveness, the country's work ethic, and its allegiance to productive efficiency over more enduring human values" (p. 356). And he became increasingly fearful for his adopted land with the rise of McCarthyism (which as we have seen had led to his own extrusion from academia), the Vietnam war, the intensification of the nuclear arms race, and the escalating racial polarization in America. All this played a role, no doubt, in his development of the concept of "pseudo-speciation" as such an increasingly destructive mechanism in human affairs.

In his comparable (implicit) critique of psychoanalysis as a "movement" and itself a culture, Erikson never considered an overtly rebellious or deviationist role, and he often lamented, in conversations with me, the marginalized role to which he felt himself to have been unfairly consigned by the psychoanalytic establishment. Rather, he subtly but significantly sought—with some degree of success but never as much as he hoped—to shift the focus of psychoanalytic concerns from pathography and ego weakness, to ego strengths and resiliences, from case histories, seen as templates upon which to map out remedial psychotherapeutic strategies, to life histories, with all their potential for guided growth and change. And all this would be aided and abetted by all the supports that the society and culture could muster at its best. And for this, the therapeutic community created at the Austen Riggs Center in the 1950s with the psychotherapeutic work that Erikson (and

the others) were engaged in, and the kind of nontherapy creative arts and activities program developed by Joan Erikson,
stood as an invaluable blueprint. In all this Erikson added impressive support to the culture and personality movement as
represented by his anthropology colleagues, Ruth Benedict,
Gregory Bateson, and Margaret Mead, and to the kind of configurational perspective in this realm, similar to what he had
assembled for intrapsychic and therapeutic purposes in his seminal paper on dream analysis in the clinical realm.

Erikson's eight-stage human life-cycle concerns, perhaps
his most enduring contribution to psychoanalysis, were developed with considerable assistance from Joan. Here Erikson
both went beyond Freud in elaborating his developmental perspective over the entire life span into old age and senescence,
and also massively shifted emphasis away from (or beyond) the
purely psychosexual to the far broader psychosocial, with the
concomitant shift as well from just neurotic vulnerabilities to
ego strengths and potentials. With this altered focus he could
confront the task (and crisis) inherent in each life stage not just
from the standpoint of the potential for faulty or traumatized
deformation but also from the standpoint of successful resolution, of achieved *virtues,* and of sustaining societal rituals. In
this sense the psychosocial developmental process contains a
strongly ethical dimension, for which in turn Erikson has been
criticized as a psychoanalytic moralist.

All these are the dimensions developed at greater length
in Friedman's chapter in which he makes no bones about the
fact that Erikson, more artist and humanist than scientific
scholar, is often unsystematic and annoyingly vague, with the
three long-term areas of concern into which Friedman has divided his overview never logically well joined or folded into
one another. But that after all is Erikson, as Friedman rightly
asserts, and his plea to his readers is not to try to reduce Erikson
or to fit the corpus of his life work into a falsely logical and
systematic framework.

A last word on the several photographs that are included
in this book. The lengthwise portrait of Erik and Joan dancing
(at my daughter Amy's wedding) is from my personal collection

of photographs. All the others, of Erik at several stages in his own life cycle—from the early Professor of Psychology at UC Berkeley in the forties, unfamiliar, yet with clear resemblance to the Erik we know, to the more recent (and very familiar) mature sage, Erik Erikson, almost an icon of our contemporary culture—and of the musicians performing at our Erikson symposium are from the collection of Daniel Benveniste, Ph.D., a psychoanalytic psychologist in the San Francisco Bay Area, who has devoted himself to the historical archival study of psychoanalysis in our community.

This entire volume is, I trust, both a faithful and evocative presentation of our January 15, 1995 symposium commemorating and celebrating the life and work of Erik Erikson, and also, far more broadly, a fitting tribute to the profound impact of a great psychoanalytic genius upon not only the science and profession to which he devoted his lifetime, but, more broadly, upon the whole wider twentieth century world culture of which the psychoanalytic way of thinking has become an integral part. I hope that it also conveys that a man born at the turn of our century, whose life spanned almost its entirety, is still, as we are coming close to a new century, in full resonance with the vanguard of our evolving discipline.

I want to add as a final very personal note a paragraph from the brief biographical statement that I made in my introductory remarks at the January 1995 Symposium in San Francisco:

> Through all the time in our midst, many of us came to know Erik very well indeed, in all his greatness, his nobility, his gentleness, and his genuine compassion for all human beings and for all the vicissitudes of the human condition. He and Joan played a very singular and intimate role in the life of my own family, and with our children, as I know that he did with some other close family friends and colleagues. We all miss him profoundly. In my own active adult and professional lifetime, I have been fortunate enough to have worked closely with two individuals I feel to have been authentic geniuses. Erik was one of them. I loved Erik.

REFERENCES

Erikson, E. H. (1950), *Childhood and Society*. New York: W. W. Norton.

——— (1954), The dream specimen of psychoanalysis. *J. Amer. Psychoanal. Assn.*, 2:5–56.

——— (1956), The problem of ego identity. *J. Amer. Psychoanal. Assn.*, 4:56–121.

——— (1958a), *Young Man Luther: A Study in Psychoanalysis and History*. New York: W. W. Norton.

——— (1958b), The nature of clinical evidence. *Daedalus*, 87:65–87. (Orginally presented as a contribution to an interdisciplinary symposium on "Evidence and Inference" at MIT in 1957.) Reprinted in *Insight and Responsibility*. New York: W. W. Norton, 1964, pp. 47–80.

——— (1969), *Gandhi's Truth: On the Origins of Militant Nonviolence*. New York: W. W. Norton.

——— (1981), The Galilean sayings and the sense of "I." *The Yale Review*, Spring:321–362.

——— Erikson, J. M., & Kivnick, H. Q. (1986), *Vital Involvement in Old Age: The Experience of Old Age in Our Time*. New York: W. W. Norton.

Friedman, L. J. (1995), Erik H. Erikson's critical themes and voices: The task of synthesis. In: *American Cultural Critics*, ed D. Murray. England: University of Exeter Press, pp. 173–191.

Wallerstein, R. S. (1997), Erikson's concept of ego identity reconsidered. *J. Amer. Psychoanal. Assn.*, 45. In press.

2.

Erik Erikson and the Temporal Mind

MARCIA CAVELL, Ph.D.

It was my misfortune to have known Erik Erikson only through his writings, which I first discovered as a graduate student in the fifties. Years later, I used *Childhood and Society* in the first course I taught on Freud for philosophers. Erikson gave more texture than Freud did, I felt, to the idea that the mind has a history.

Very few psychoanalysts have had much influence on philosophy: Freud, of course; Melanie Klein, a little; in other countries, though in this one hardly at all, Lacan. Perhaps the neglect of Erikson is due to some of the very qualities many of us appreciate in him most, his disdain for jargon, the breadth of his interests, and the fact that he cared more—or so it seems to me—for the life lived than for theory. Yet those of us who were psychoanalytically minded were influenced by Erikson early on, in something like the way that once you have seen the snow scenes of Breughel, they cast their light over every winter day. Having with great pleasure reread a few of Erikson's books over the last few months, I will outline here what I see now in some of the questions that have interested us both, and what I see also as Erikson's contribution to them.

Erikson's life theme was the nature of identity, specifically human identity. Like Freud, he knew it is not a timeless Platonic essence that somehow settles itself into a human body, but a process of growth. Yet more than Freud, Erikson was interested in adulthood, the happy outcome of this process. To my knowledge he is the only psychoanalyst who extensively explored Freud's casually said but seriously meant remark that psychic health is the ability to love and work. Erikson's life stories of Gandhi and Luther show these abilities as ways of dealing with universal conflicts that result in a wholeness of the self rather than divisions within the self, in the capacity to embrace an ever-widening community as part of that wholeness, and in the kind of freedom from the past that releases one for commitment to the future.

This is the first thing that struck me in my rereading, the way Erikson pitched identity between past and future, but I was struck also by Erikson's account of a childhood stage that precedes love and work and prepares the way. I have in mind the stage he calls autonomy versus shame and doubt. Why, I wondered, should these negative conditions be the other face of self-rule, or freedom? What do shame and doubt have to tell us about what it is to be or to have a human self in the first place? What do they tell us about autonomy?

In the following I will sketch a picture of the mind that shows the essential connections between these things, since Erikson was pointing to something like this configuration in his various discussions of identity although he would not have put it as I will. So I am less offering an interpretation of what he said than taking it up in the spirit of a dialogue which I wish he were able to pursue with me.

Given how fond we are of talk about the self, it is remarkable that the concept enters Western thought for the first time in the seventeenth century. Of course, similar concepts had been around for a long time, like mind and the mental, rational animal, person, psyche, and soul. But the self, as the entity referred to by the word *I* and as therefore characterized by the subjective, inner view that seems so crucial to the mental, was a discovery of Descartes. Erikson (1962, p. 183) refers to Descartes' famous *cogito* argument, "I think therefore I am," as marking the end of medieval philosophy. It is true that Descartes had one foot in the Old World, but with the *cogito* he staked out the New, setting generations of philosophers the task of understanding how to think about this self with its peculiarly inner perspective. We are still at it. Without Descartes there would be, just to name a few, no Hume, Kant, Hegel, Brentano, Husserl, Wittgenstein, Heidegger, or Freud.

The thinking that concerned Descartes included not only believing but also desiring, willing, regretting, rueing, feeling guilty about, and so on, through the list of psychological attitudes. He explicitly included many of them, and above all, doubt. For he was in search of a method of sorting the true from the false, and he thought if he could discover something indubitable he would have made a start.

As we know, he found it in the very act of doubting. The one thing I cannot doubt is the existence of the doubter, myself. So whatever other knowledge we can have begins, Descartes held, with self-knowledge of this sort. His next question was, What is this self whose existence I know through first-person thought? I will call this the question of first-person identity.

Descartes was distinguishing, as philosophers have after him, between two different kinds of questions we can ask about who we are. The first notes that I have a special epistemological position to those of my own thoughts that are conscious. It is not that I know them infallibly, as perhaps Descartes believed, but that my relation to them is different from my relation to your thoughts. Those I know from your behavior and by inference. My own I know, it seems, immediately and on no basis of evidence. Why this is puzzling, and how to solve the puzzle, are questions I will not attempt to answer here. Even so, we can go some way toward answering the question of first-person identity by considering the nature of first-person thought.

The second sort of question asks about aspects of ourselves that need not be knowable in a special first-person way; in fact, they need not be mental states at all. A description of a person's talents and character traits, his unrememberable past and his so-called ego strengths, his IQ, his physical liabilities, his family history, are all answers to this second sort of question. For lack of a better term I will call it the question of empirical identity.

Luther's words, "Here I stand, I can do no other," implicitly answer yet a third sort of "Who am I?" question. We can state it like this: What do I stand for? What are the things, if any, that I really care about? What are my principles and my values? What am I doing with my life? I think it is often the third question that bothers us when we confess to ourselves that we do not know who we are, and the third question that takes us to love and work as adult human activities. Both the second and the third questions presume first-person thinking, however, and about this thinking doubt can teach us a lot.

To forestall misunderstanding, I will first mention some ways in which many of us think Descartes was seriously wrong. Among others, he was wrong to think that mind might exist without body, that we could know what we think independently of any knowledge of other minds and the external world, that there can be such a thing as subjectivity without intersubjectivity. Yet in giving doubt the importance he did he was onto some very interesting things: the conceptual links between doubt and self-consciousness, and the complexity of skills that the capacity for doubt presupposes. Doubt of the sort Descartes had in mind, or that Luther would have expressed had he worried that his challenge to the Church might be misguided, does not presuppose the doubter's belief in the existence of God, or in the possibility of infallible knowledge.

1. The capacity for doubt does presuppose that the doubter grasps the distinctions between truth and falsity, right and wrong, between objective and subjective. Someone who can doubt must sometimes be able to say of himself, "I believe that such-and-such is the case, but is it true?" A grasp of these distinctions is equally a precondition for having thought of the sort I am talking about. Doubt and belief, doubt and thought, come together; for to believe that something is the case, and to know one believes it, is also to know that how things seem to me may not be how things seem to you, and that neither may be how they are. This is what it means to have a belief of the sort I have in mind. Of course all kinds of creatures, and things like thermostats as well, can respond in highly discriminating ways to the environment. Some people call that having thoughts. If it is, then I am referring to thought in a more sophisticated sense.

2. Doubt presupposes that the thinking in question is propositional in character, or best expressible in propositions like "The earth is flat" (or round), "There is a unicorn in the garden," or "I am angry with Mary." Not all of a thinking creature's thoughts must be of this nature, but some must be, for only such thoughts allow for doubt, or reflections such as "It seems to me that the earth is flat, but perhaps I am mistaken," "Maybe I misjudge the creature in the garden," and "I wonder why I'm so angry with Mary." Reflections like these are crucial to being a moral agent, and also a psychoanalytic patient.

We call these attitudes self-reflective, and they are. But the phrase is misleading in suggesting a stance of passive observation toward what we think. I observe that you must be angry from what you say and do. I can observe that I am angry as well. But more typically, in thinking, "I am angry," though it may be true that I am, the very thinking it in this explicitly conscious, first-person mode allows me to take various attitudes toward my anger. Someone who knows some of the time that she believes or values x is capable of assessing her own beliefs and values.

Mental attitudes form a holistic web in which any mental state is related to the others in ways that are causal and also, to some extent, rational. This is true of thoughts of which we are unaware, as well as of ones that are fully conscious. The latter, however, put me in a position to draw the connections more tightly between one thought and its neighbors. Some thoughts are rejected; others are qualified; in the process I take new attitudes toward myself as the one who has these thoughts. Much of this shifting takes place spontaneously, some of it consciously and with effort. In either case, the assessment that consciousness affords may result in a new state of mind. One distinctive characteristic of self-knowledge, then, is that it is not merely reportorial but has consequences for the knower as agent. I described doubt as an activity, above, to emphasize this practical aspect of thinking.

3. Finally, doubt presupposes that the doubter grasps the meaning of "I"—which is an intricate matter. To begin with, one must know that "I" said by me refers to me, but also to anyone else, when said by him. Its reference shifts along lines similar to "here" and "there," "now" and "then," also "I" and "you," "I" and "me." "I" is an indexical expression whose meaning, like these other indexicals, depends for its reference on the particular conditions of its utterance.

Knowing the meaning of "I" comes with knowing also—implicitly knowing—that if the sentence "I am sad," said by me at a given time, is true, then the sentence "Marcia Cavell is sad," said by anyone else, is also true. The reason both statements must be true if one is, is that they refer to the same entity. There are not two entities, a ghostly thing some people have called the transcendental ego and a human body that may or may not have a mind. There is only one entity, regarded from two points of view, yours and mine. We learn to discriminate mental content, our own included, only in an intersubjective field.

Particularly with regard to the third point, I have developed Descartes's remarks about doubt in ways he would not have, since I think that first-person thought presumes time and an interpersonal world. Having my own mind and knowing something about yours are interdependent. In my view, even acquiring the concept of an object requires two persons, "lassoing" an object through communing about it together, and thereby giving it a public, objective status.

I can bring out the temporal dimension of the mind by contextualizing my discussion of the grammar of the first-person in a way that reveals its home in the family romance. To learn the use of "I" is to learn one's way around a complex affective and social map on which people can occupy the same position in space at different times; the same person can be sometimes angry and sometimes glad; I can be sad now but know now that I may be happy later, and so on. The map is learned through the body's ability to move through space and time, and the spirit's ability to tolerate emotional conflicts of various kinds. So it is a map that is necessarily constructed through presence and absence, joy and mourning, love and loss.

In "The Problem of Ego Identity," Erikson (1956) writes: "Linguistically as well as psychologically, identity and identification have common roots" (this volume, p. 185). He goes on to ask: "Is identity, then, the mere sum of earlier identifications, or is it merely an additional set of identifications?" (this volume, p. 185). I don't think it is merely either one. If I am right about what sort of thing a self is, then nothing less than an account of what first-person thinking presupposes will tell us about identity. Identification plays an important role in this account, since it holds that a first-person perspective comes only with knowing that others have one as well. Learning that just is a form of identification. "The implicit conclusion that an individual ego could exist against or without a specifically human[1] environment," Erikson (1956) rightly says, "is senseless" (this volume, p. 227).

What, then, is a self? Many philosophers have held that in being aware I am thinking any particular thought I apprehend not only what I think, but also the "I" in question. They have thought of beliefs or desires themselves as a kind of object which the introspective eye, turned inward, beholds; they have assumed that there must be another kind of object, one that, impossibly, is the very same with the self that is doing the seeing.[1] Yet this object is mysteriously elusive, they grant, always just beyond my experience and even my intellectual grasp.

There are a number of confusions here that I will not try to untangle. Instead let me summarize my discussion of doubt in order to suggest an answer to the question of first-person identity. The answer I suggest makes identity complex, but not mysterious. What I refer to when I say "I" is this embodied creature who has all the holistically interrelated thoughts that distinguish me from other creatures like me. A self just is a creature that can speak of itself reflexively as itself, with everything this presupposes in the way of a shared, intersubjective world and communication with other persons whom we know

[1]No allusion to Heinz Kohut is intended.

as creatures in many ways like ourselves. In virtue of the capacity for self-reflexive thought, a self is an agent who can take various attitudes toward his own thoughts and activities, including the attitude of responsibility, the root of which word is, interestingly, *respondeo,* or "I answer."

" 'God gave [man] a mind and a memory, and the rudiments of an identity,' " Erikson (1962, p. 183) says, quoting Augustine. I say that any creature with a mind and a memory has by virtue of that fact the rudiments of an identity, and is someone who can speak of itself as a self.

The developmental sequence that Erikson outlines begins of course not with autonomy versus shame and doubt but with an earlier stage he calls trust versus distrust. An infant does not have a mind from the beginning; nor is there some magic moment at which we can say, "Aha, Now mind is here!" But a lot is going on for infants from the beginning that prepares the way. In view of the mind's interpersonal character, it makes sense to suppose with Erikson that interpersonal experiences around the issue of trust versus distrust affect what sort of an I-sayer the child will become and so the quality of his later actions, whether he engages the world with authority or retreats from it in doubt and despair.

Erikson called shame and doubt the downside of autonomy. He was surely right that they can cripple initiative; yet in giving them the importance he did, he was also, I think, noticing their positive role in the advent of the mind. I see the connection between shame and the mental this way: as an object in the world one is hostage to the world. If knowledge of one's self as an I-sayer is necessarily bound up with knowledge of others as occupants of the world that the map of I-saying draws, then these others are occupants to whom one knows one is as visible as they are to oneself. People have written about the importance of children's discovery that they can sometimes keep their thoughts to themselves. Perhaps not enough has been written about an equally important experience in the making of the mind, the discovery that others may know things about me of which I am ignorant. Shame is the essential expression of our awareness that both literally and metaphorically, each of us has a back as well as a front. You see me as I may not want to be seen; you may discover motives of mine that are not yet clear to me. This is knowledge that may be vital to one's welfare, but it is not a comfortable knowledge.

My earlier discussion of the essential links between doubt and the mind may have made clear that the nature of thinking opens us to peculiar kinds of anxiety. On Descartes' view, the mind is dependent only on God, and it is able, through His beneficence, to have certain knowledge about some things. Most of us now think instead that the mind is dependent on history, the world, and other minds, that there is no such thing as certainty and no such thing as the self or the ego, if by that one means some indivisible entity, behind my thoughts and directing them. (In one of its senses, at least, consciousness is essentially the same as self-consciousness; for when I am conscious of thinking that you seem sad, I can know I am having this thought. The only object before me, however, is not myself but you. This is just one way that what we call the self cannot be captured as an isolated entity, a fact of which Lacan makes heavy weather: we exist as selves only through a complex relationship with the world.) Grounded as it is in the painful facts that we might be wrong and that there is little we can know for sure, the capacity for doubt bears witness to our finitude, which it takes a certain capacity for trust to tolerate with grace. In the absence of trust, doubt can function not as a call to act on reflection but as a paralysis of the will. This is the downside of doubt, the threat to autonomy Erikson describes.

We have considered shame and doubt, the self, and the nature of mind. How does autonomy come in? To answer that I turn to a man Erikson takes as one of its finest exemplars. In the last chapter of *Young Man Luther*, Erikson (1962) recounts the events in Luther's life with which we are most apt to be familiar: his nailing of the 95 theses on the door of the Wittenberg church, the papal bull excommunicating him in 1521, and Luther's subsequent appearance before the Diet of Worms. In describing this last event Erikson does not mention that Luther was given the chance to recant his writings and that in view of the gravity of recantation, he asked for a day to reflect.

The request granted, Luther appeared the following afternoon to give a speech before a large crowd.

He distinguished between his pedagogical works for which he should not be asked to apologize, and the violence of his polemic, for which he did; as for the rest, he said he would recant if convinced of his error either by the Bible or by reason. Otherwise he could not go against his conscience, which was bound by the word of God to speak the truth as he saw it. He concluded, or so legend has it, by declaring, "Here I stand. I can do no other."

Luther believed that reason inheres in every mind. Because it does, he held that the individual can speak to God directly, without the intermediary of the Church. It was of course this assertion of the autonomy of human reason that the Church found intolerable, and this assertion that Luther could not gainsay without betraying his own mind and with it everything he valued. Erikson reads Luther's act on that fateful day as a paradigm case of something he calls a "strong sense of identity," of which "faith, conviction, authority, indignation," he says, are all attributes. I might also call it the identity of integrated agency.

Any creature who can think first-person thoughts is an agent who forms intentions on which he sometimes acts. Every agent is able to consider some of his beliefs and desires in the light they shed on each other. In the process he may come to feel that some of the things he wants he does not approve of himself for wanting, that some are not compatible with other things he wants, that some look less desirable when he thinks about them a little harder. Such a process instances rationality, which as I remarked earlier, is an essential tie in the network that is a mind.

A child of 5 can see that if he wants to buy a present for his mother with money he has saved, and that he has enough for the yellow ribbon but not for the box of candy, then he will have to settle for the ribbon, or earn some more money, or reconsider the matter. This child is reasoning about values, and in his reasoning the rudiments of Luther's autonomous act are present. What is lacking is its complexity. In 1521, Luther was a 38-year-old man, a man who had disciplined himself for years to think hard about what he believed and valued. He had formed both a coherent set of values and a coherent picture of the self he wanted to be, and he was fortunate enough to have the courage to act in accord with what he thought.

Autonomy, the word Erikson aptly chooses to name the stage at which shame and doubt come into play, means freedom, literally: the condition of self-rule. A long tradition in philosophy analyzes freedom as a condition available only to rational creatures. That seems right. For if we were to say simply that freedom is doing what one wants, we would quickly have to add that not just any wants will do. The compulsive hand-washer does what he in some sense wants, but it is not the right kind of wanting; there is some problem, furthermore, about just who he is.

The split self, or the divided self, thinks one thing in one part of his mind, and another in another part. He feels conflict that he does not avow. Or more accurately, he does not know what he thinks or wants or feels, not necessarily because it is repressed, but because he has not made it explicitly conscious and thought it through. When he acts it is apt to be with a sense of inner compulsion or outer constraint.

Luther's "constraint," if we can call it that, consisted in the fact that having reviewed in his mind all the relevant considerations, his will was single-minded. He could do no other, not because he was constrained by a force beyond or within but alien to his will, but because there was nothing else which, everything considered, he really wanted to do or to be. To consider all the relevant factors and to act in accord with one's best judgment, is to act rationally. To do what one wants, when wanting has been in this way refined by reason, is to act autonomously. Erikson calls the penultimate chapter of *Young Man Luther* "Meaning It," and what interests him, as it does me, is the state of a person of whom we can say, "He means what he says," or "He knows his own mind." Though this sort of self-knowledge depends on first-person thinking, it signals a degree of autonomy that many of us do not have.

There is a seeming paradox about autonomy that perhaps goes some way toward explaining why acts like Luther's are the exception rather than the rule. Thinking by nature acknowledges values and laws, like reason itself, that partly because they are not one's own creation make claims on one's assent. Thus, conflicts about dependency versus independence belong with the issues of autonomy versus shame and doubt, initiative versus guilt. The one who is able to love and work must accept the risks and demands that come with greatly valuing something that exists outside himself. He posits goals that may be completed not at all, and if at all, by others. He makes himself vulnerable to fortune. In doing so, however, he feels himself an agent in a story much wider than his own. His sense of himself grows firmer as the community with which he identifies grows larger. The seeming paradox, then, is that the degree of autonomy that Erikson calls the strong sense of identity comes only with acknowledging dependencies of certain kinds, just those dependencies that ground first-person thought.

When Freud wrote about the self he used the term *das Ich*, "the I." Though "ego" is an imposition by the translators of *The Standard Edition*, they were not necessarily wrong to give Freud's highly ambiguous concept a less personal name than he did, for Freud tended to lump together many different kinds of things that can be said about the mind, all the way from structures of learning and behavior, of which one could never be conscious, to fully conscious avowals.

Concerned as he rightly was to deny the equation between mind and consciousness, Freud was preoccupied with what is earlier than consciousness, hidden behind it, or working even according to entirely different laws. So he neglected precisely *das Ich* and failed to deliver his promised essay on consciousness. Because he lacked a theory of first-person thinking, he lacked a view of identity that could comprehend such things as responsibility, the capacity for change that is a response to explicit self-evaluation, and a commitment to the future. It is not surprising, then, that Freud had a great deal to say about impediments to love and work, but not much about love and work themselves.

There is a multitude of other meanings that the word *identity* may have. I doubt there is just one concept here, but a great many. Erikson tended to move among them without signaling the differences, which makes both for a lack of clarity and a richness in his writing. I have not referred to, for example, self-image, conscious or unconscious, nor one's identity *as* a girl or a boy, and, say, a poet, a rebel, a witch, or a Sioux. Instead I have concentrated on the concepts that I believe are central to the subject of the self, and central also in Erikson's work. How the meanings I have slighted are related to these central concepts will have to be elaborated elsewhere.

In conclusion, I will return to the idea of self-consciousness as a genuine form of knowledge, and with it to telling stories. When I say I am angry, am I stating a fact about myself, evincing a bit of "theoretical" self-knowledge? Or am I expressing myself? Or am I, as some think, constituting my state of mind in the very act of speaking it, shaping the person I am going to be?

Some philosophers think we must select one of these options. I do not think this is so. When I tell you that I will scream if you play that record another time, I may be speaking truly even as I lose my temper and threaten you. Every speech act does many things simultaneously. Just as confusing as this ambiguity, moreover, are the relations between the following: (1) knowledge of what I *do* believe; (2) determining what I *ought*—as a rational creature—to believe; and (3) the effect on myself of my own second-order mental attitudes.

Typically we figure out the practical question of what we ought to believe about x by looking to that part of the world where x might be: Has Mary treated me unjustly? Is there a unicorn in the garden? A Third World War on the horizon? The practical question is constrained by the truth—as one can best determine it—since belief, unlike imagination, is thus constrained. So even the practical question does not leave us much choice. Then once I have determined what to believe about x, knowledge of my beliefs about x is possible since I have a belief to be known; but because knowledge follows so close on the heels of practice, the fact that there is this knowledge may be obscured.

We sometimes can prize the factual and the practical questions apart, however, by considering occasions on which the latter have already been decided, as with beliefs we had in the past. Of course, we may not know what we once believed, and may not have known even then. Nevertheless, there is sometimes a fact of the matter that can in principle be discovered.

Neither determining what to believe nor knowing about my beliefs is yet constitutive of myself. My own activity plays a role in both, but it is too small to be interesting. Self-constitution enters in a bigger way with those self-evaluating attitudes that I discussed above. If I truly come to think my anger with Mary is unjustified, that thought reverberates across the entire holistic network of my mental states. I may no longer be angry with Mary, and other attitudes closely related to my anger may also change. In this way one's self-interpretations take oneself in hand to a serious extent. Luther's "Here I stand" was presumably a declaration, a promise, a warning, a bit of theoretical and empirical self-knowledge, a practical reassessment of the truth as he saw it about many things, and the outcome of a self-reflective process that shaped the self he was to be.[2]

Long before the idea of narrative became fashionable, Erikson was showing us, in his own wonderful narratives, how the distinctively human self is partially given and partially constructed out of what it is given; that we are creatures who to some extent achieve our own identities, both by the way we construe our beginnings and by what we do; and finally, that the story of our lives is a story in which, necessarily, history and other people play important parts. These are some of the ideas that are well captured in the conceit of the self as a protagonist in a story one tells oneself.

But it is easy to draw from this a false moral. One can mistake the fact that no knowledge is ever final for the different idea that truth is a concept we should give up. One can think that because self-consciousness has a constructive function, therefore it does not have one that is also truth-telling. One

[2]I owe the distinctions in these last three paragraphs to Richard Moran (1988).

might consider in this context the difference between making up a story and making up one's mind (Frankfurt, 1988). When I genuinely make up my mind about something, some nascent value or commitment may emerge. Making up one's mind is thus like making up a story in that something new appears. But I cannot make up my mind unless I know something about the mind I am making up. So it is not like making up a story, in that there are limits on what one can say. The category of the usefully coherent cannot replace that of the true.

Among the things psychoanalysts want for their patients is that they be able to acknowledge their limitations, what they have said and done, what they believe and feel and want; that sometimes they will remember what happened, or investigate what is the case, rather than fantasize about it; that they not deny the value to them of someone they have loved and lost. None of these attitudes is intelligible unhinged from the concepts of truth and telling the truth. With this I believe Erik Erikson would also have agreed.

REFERENCES

Erikson, E. (1956), The problem of ego identity. *J. Amer. Psychoanal. Assn.*, 4:56–121.
———— (1962), *Young Man Luther.* New York: W. W. Norton.
Frankfurt, H. (1988), Identification and wholeheartedness. In: *The Importance of What We Care About.* Cambridge, U.K.: Cambridge University Press, pp. 159–177.
Moran, R. (1988), Making up your mind: Self-interpretation and self-constitution. *Ratio* (New Series), 1:135–151.

3.

Erik Erikson as Social Scientist

NEIL J. SMELSER, Ph.D.

My objective in this essay is to throw light on two questions. First, *was* Erik Erikson a social scientist? Second, what *kind* of social scientist was he? My short answer to the first question is "yes"; my short answer to the second question is "a very good one." I will organize my elaboration of that assessment under four headings:

- Erikson, the quintessential interdisciplinarian
- Some unresolved methodological issues in his interdisciplinary program
- Erikson's diagnosis of and verdict on Western, especially American, society
- Erikson's sociological idealism, which contains elements of positive utopianism

ERIKSON THE QUINTESSENTIAL INTERDISCIPLINARIAN

Erikson was, above all, a psychoanalyst, and it can be argued plausibly that his most enduring contributions are to psychoanalysis, in the form of his profound recasting of the psychosexual-social development of the individual person. But one cannot think of his contributions to knowledge without acknowledging immediately that he had many other intellectual

49

identities, and, more important, he brought these identities continuously into creative synthesis with one another.

His most notable interdisciplinary adventures were in anthropology and history. In *Childhood and Society* (Erikson, 1950), arguably his most influential work, he developed his revised scheme of psychosocial development in the full comparative context of the Sioux, the Yurok, Hitler's Germany, and Gorki's Russia. It is no exaggeration, either, to state that he can be regarded as inventor of modern psychohistory, embodied principally in his works on Luther (Erikson, 1958) and Gandhi (Erikson, 1969), but also in other works on Shaw, Jefferson, Christ, Einstein, and others. In these works Erikson was as much historian as psychoanalyst, and as much an integrator of the two as a practitioner of each—virtues which lend enormous credibility to this work.

Yet I find other disciplinary incarnations of Erikson as well. He was a lifelong artist—in his prepsychoanalytic avocation, as a student of the aesthetics of children's play, and a consistently "seeing" or "visual" type of person in his human observations. He was an economic historian. If one reads the several-page account of the industrial history of Ahmedebad (Gandhi's city) and forgets it was Erikson writing, one would find an economic historian plying his craft—from the standpoint of archival data cited, descriptive variables employed, causes invoked, and interpretative schemes used (Erikson, 1969, pp. 262–263). As a sociologist myself, I easily identified that dimension in Erikson as well. He was sensitive to the power of social stereotypes, as is clear from his comparison of the comparative social stereotyping of Ahmedebad and Pittsburgh (Erikson, 1969, p. 29). He was sensitive to the sociological significance of caste in India, race in America, occupational niche in Reformation Germany, gender and sexism in Victorian Vienna. Finally, as I hope to demonstrate, Erikson had at least a schematic sociological diagnosis of modern Western society.

Not only was Erikson many disciplinary persons; those persons were always conversing productively with one another in his work, as the following statements reveal:

- On his characterization of the volume *Childhood and Society*: "a psychoanalytic book on the *relation* of the ego to society" (1950, p. 16; emphasis added).
- On development: "The cogwheeling stages of childhood and adulthood are . . . truly a system of *generation* and *regeneration*—for into this system flow, and from this system emerge, those social attitudes to which the institutions and traditions of society attempt to give unity and permanence" (Erikson, 1964b, p. 152).
- On the identity process: It is located "*in the core of the individual* and yet also *in the core of his communal culture,* a process which establishes, in fact, the identity of those two identities" (Erikson, 1969, pp. 265–266).
- On the meshing of individual neurosis and social history: "Luther . . . was an endangered young man, beset with a syndrome of conflicts. . . . He found a spiritual solution. . . . His solution roughly bridged a political and psychological vacuum which history had created in a significant portion of Western Christendom. Such coincidence, if further coinciding with the deployment of highly specific personal gifts, makes for historical 'greatness' " (Erikson, 1958, p. 15).
- On psychohistory: "[It] is the study of individual and collective life with the combined methods of psychoanalysis and history" (Erikson, 1974, p. 13).
- On interdisciplinarity itself: "Only psychoanalysis and social science together can eventually chart the life cycle interwoven throughout with the history of the community" (Erikson, 1959a, p. 18).

In my estimation, this creative blending of perspectives to generate new insights and truth through integration is one of the keys to the understanding of Erikson's creativity.

Now, when a psychoanalyst—or any other kind of discipline-oriented scholar—makes such commitments to become more comparative, more historical, more developmental, and more incorporative of different analytic levels in his work, this necessarily generates a tension, a kind of disciplinary unease or discomfort. That tension arises from an inevitable pressure to relativize the universals of one's discipline. A simple example demonstrates this principle: in his theory of dreams, Freud posited a universal psychosexual meaning to certain symbols, such as water, snakes, and ovens with bread in them. As one moves through different cultural contexts and different eras of history, however, it becomes progressively more difficult to hold to this universal formulation, and more essential to qualify it through relativization or historicization.

Erikson did not escape this tension. In fact, he celebrated it by pointing out the necessity of making the concession to relativity and historicity. Some examples follow:

- On national character: "It will not do to call one nation psychiatric names. Every nation has *particular* regressive syndromes to which it is apt to revert to when safety and identity are threatened" (Erikson, 1945).
- On the universalism of neurosis: "It is not enough . . . to reduce [Gandhi's crisis with his father] to the 'Oedipus Complex' reconstructed in thousands of case histories as the primal complex. The oedipal crisis . . . must be evaluated as a part of man's over-all development. [It] may be called the *generational complex*" (Erikson, 1969, pp. 131–132).
- In a similar vein, Erikson reported a sympathy for the approach of an old shaman woman in Northern California, pointing to the value of her outlook and therapeutic methods *in the context of her society* (Erikson, 1964c).

In his biography of Erikson, Robert Coles noted this tendency. Erikson, he said, was suspicious of "wild" psychoanalyzing; that is the indiscriminate application of invariant psychoanalytic categories to persons, artistic productions, and historical events. "Erikson had literally tried to complicate things, and stop the wholesale transfer of psychoanalytic concepts to Indian tribes or German politicians or Russian novelists" (Coles, 1970, p. 165). Coles went on to suggest that one of Erikson's motives in selecting *identity* as a core integrating concept was to get away from culture-bound, less inclusive psychoanalytic categories in his studies of history, biography, and anthropology. Be that as it may, Erikson did make the move toward relativization and historicization, and in the process became less wild and less orthodox. While this move no doubt both charmed and disarmed many potential skeptics, it also involved him in some unresolved methodological problems, to which we now turn.

METHODOLOGICAL PROBLEMS IN ERIKSON'S INTERDISCIPLINARITY

One can speak only in positive terms about Erikson's effort to cross the bridges among disciplinary frameworks and between different levels of analysis. It must be recognized, however, that this is an exceptionally difficult kind of intellectual operation, and for that reason rarely undertaken. Furthermore, those who attempt these syntheses and face the difficulties are often drawn into intellectual resolutions that leave much to be desired.

What are the difficulties? They lie in the very nature of disciplinary, indeed disciplined, thought. In order to be disciplined, the investigator has to narrow the focus of inquiry to manageable proportions. The main way of doing this is to make two orders of assumptions about the world: (1) what order of reality is central and problematical, and (2) what order of reality is peripheral and nonproblematical. For example, in the first case the psychoanalyst typically has taken the inner psychological reality of impulse representation, conflict, defense, adaptation, and psychopathology as problematic; the economist typically has taken the realities of market interchange among individuals and organizations as the primary analytic focus. By contrast, for example, the psychoanalyst, as a rule, does not raise central, disciplined questions about the structure and functions of institutions or cataclysmic social changes, but, at best, takes them into account as features of the patient's psychic environment, thus preserving the analytic focus on the individual; the economist, as a rule, takes individual tastes and social institutions as "given," thus permitting him or her to proceed with a certain degree of analytic neatness and simplicity.

It should be evident from this brief characterization that this analytic simplification is both necessary and theoretically powerful, but at the same time oversimplifying and distortive of the totality of reality. Furthermore, what one disciplinary specialist takes as peripheral the other takes as central, and vice versa. To ask that one take the other's as *also* and *simultaneously* central is to invite a disciplined thinker to desert his or her creative simplifications and enter into the messy, multivariable, more realistic world but at the same time sacrifice the analytic power associated with his or her own discipline.

Despite the difficulties of venturing outside disciplinary boundaries, scholars sometimes undertake to do so. It is not an overstatement to say that, in most cases, they do so badly. Typically they employ one of two closely related strategies, each of which soon becomes unproductive and illegitimate. The first is to argue by *analogy*; simply stated, this is to assert that processes at one level are like those at another—the person or society is a machine, the society is an organism, the group has a mind, the institution of marriage functions like any economic market, and so on. The second is to argue by *reduction*; simply stated, this is an attempt to translate, without loss, all statements at one analytic level into statements regarding the operations of variables at another level. Examples of reductionism are explaining mental phenomena in exclusively physiological terms, thus reducing the former to the latter, or, with Marx and Engels, explaining the state exclusively as the servant of the dominant ruling class, thus robbing it of independent analytic significance.

I will dismiss the questionable strategies of analogy and reduction, largely because Erikson himself rejected them as antithetical to his whole intellectual mission. There is a third strategy that, to my mind, offers most promise. It goes as follows: to preserve the analytic gains of disciplinary simplification by retaining distinctive levels of analysis, but to relax systematically the parameters (the "givens") and to trace the ramifications of that relaxation—for example, to have the economists' envision motivational givens other than economic maximization, and trace the ramifications of these variations for economic behavior and the functioning of markets (for a development of this strategy for psychoanalysis and the other social sciences, see Wallerstein and Smelser, 1969).

I mention this analytic strategy partly as a way of high-lighting what Erikson did *not* do as a social scientist. Erikson was certainly cognizant of and interested in theoretical issues, both in psychoanalysis and in the social sciences, but I would submit that he was not interested in the systematic theoretical formulation of those issues, with an accompanying attention to the logical structure of theory, the production of systematic hypotheses, rigorous testing of those hypotheses under con-trolled conditions, and all the rest. Rather, I would also submit, he was predisposed—through his own aesthetic predilections and through his thoroughgoing clinical training—to take an alternative approach, an approach that was individually and historically specific. As is well known, Erikson focused on the innovative, creative, generation-shaping, historically trans-forming individual—Luther, Gandhi, Jefferson, Martin Luther King (in passing), and others—and treated them in terms of the intersection of their biographies with their historical eras. These historical eras also were specific: the Reformation, colo-nial India, the transition from late colonial to early republican America, and the civil rights revolution. So, in the end, Erikson stayed with the mode of the "life history" and the "case his-tory," though he regarded these as "no longer manners of speaking" (Erikson, 1974), in that individual biography and historical reality were always in interaction with one another. In a word, Erikson's approach, even to interdisciplinarity, was consistently and always in the clinical mode.

The inevitable shortfall of this mode, of course, lies in its lack of generalizability. It remains forever rooted in the specific individual and the specific historical era. As far as general for-mulations are concerned, they are just that—*general*. For exam-ple, momentous historical transitions occur under conditions when there is a decisive meshing among individual neurosis, a political and psychological vacuum generated by previous so-cial change, and "highly specific personal gifts." These condi-tions are quite nonspecific, and Erikson never went further in attempting to identify them in generic terms that would be identifiable in a variety of historical settings—that is, as principles.

The same methodological problem appears elsewhere in Erikson's work, though in different garb. This has to do with the generalizability of his "stages of life" scheme beyond the Western historical context. On the one hand, Erikson formulated the scheme in very general if not universal terms—basic trust, initiative, guilt, intimacy, generativity, despair, and so on. On the other hand, in illustrating the *social* side of some of the stages, he linked that side to institutions that are distinctively Western, if not American, in reference. For example, in *Childhood and Society*, Erikson (1950) remarked that in the industry versus inferiority phase, "the inner stage seems all set for 'entrance into life,' except that life must first be school life"; schools, of course, are not found in all societies. And in the identity versus role confusion stage in adolescence, he spoke of the power of "cliques and crowds," and of "falling in love," which are, evidently, like adolescence itself, somewhat modern and Western-looking. Once again, the tension between universal reference and cultural specificity appears.

Erikson experienced this issue directly in his seminar in Ahmedebad. He found there what he diplomatically described as Indians' nonacceptance of his developmental scheme on account of its evident inapplicability to Indian religious, historical, and contemporary conceptions of development. He himself made a heroic effort to reconcile the evident cultural differences. But in the end he found only a general point of comparability:

> It would be fruitless to compare these [Western and Indian] schemes point for point. What is more important is the principle which makes them comparable at all—that is, the epigenetic principle according to which in each stage of life a given strength is added on to a widening ensemble and re-integrated at each later stage in order to play its part in a full cycle—if and where fate and society permit [Erikson, 1969, p. 38].

But we must pause here and ask what is being done. Faced with obvious cross-cultural noncomparability, the temptation is—and Erikson gave in to it—to move in a *general* direction, so that what was noncomparable becomes comparable through inclusion. But in that operation the whole scheme loses applicability through its very generalization. What we witness is the tension between comparability and specificity of formulation. Erikson struggled with but did not resolve that tension, but if it will help matters any, it is also true to say that none of us ever has.

A DIAGNOSIS OF WESTERN, ESPECIALLY AMERICAN, SOCIETY

The preceding material has demonstrated that Erikson was a keen observer of society, as well as an original thinker with respect to the multiple linkages between individual and society. In addition, it is possible to extricate from Erikson's writings a recurrent set of ideas about the contemporary Western world. I will emphasize here the tension between alienation and admiration on the one hand, and between negative and positive utopian elements in his thought. Needless to say, we will also find a mixture of both description and evaluation, of both neutrality and ideological commitment.

There are evident reasons to suspect that, in his own development, Erikson had tendencies to distance himself from his own society, to be correspondingly alienated, and to search continuously for his own identity. He says as much. Writing in 1964, he described himself as a young man: "an artist . . . which can be a European euphemism for a young man with some talent, but nowhere to go" (Erikson, 1964a, p. 2; see also Erikson, 1970). Elsewhere he referred to "my generation of alienated youth in Europe" (1969, pp. 10–11), without actually confessing—but strongly suggesting—that he belonged to that generation. Furthermore, there was a certain consistency in his alienation. Not only did he exhibit that general distance from society in his youth, but he also refrained from unalienating himself by joining groups of alienated German youths—groups that sometimes had sinister overtones (Coles, 1970, p. 16).

The second circumstance contributing to Erikson's sense
of alienation and preoccupation with identity was his experience as an immigrant to America, a discontinuity that fed into
already ambiguous identities—German or Danish, Jewish or
non-Jewish. Again there are no secrets here; Erikson tells us
that his status as an immigrant focused him on the problem of
identity (Erikson, cited in Evans, 1967, p. 29), and he added
that his migration from East to West in the United States accentuated this preoccupation.

Be all that as it may, one discovers in Erikson's writings a
certain idealization of the simplicity and complexity of the
West's (and America's) past and corresponding disen-
chantment with the present, modern world. At one moment
he contrasted primitive tribes with modern civilizations. In the
former, people "have a direct relation to the sources and
means of production . . . to [children], body and environment,
childhood and culture [and] . . . are all one world." In our
times, however, "[the] expansiveness of civilization, together
with its stratification and specialization, force children to base
their ego models on shifting, sectional, and contradictory pro-
totypes" (Erikson, 1959a, p. 22). On another occasion he noted
that while the agricultural and mercantile stages of development generated their own distinctive forms of alienation, under conditions of contemporary industrialization, "man turns
other men and himself into tools, and the machines he runs
into machinery which runs him . . . the *technological* world of
today is about to create kinds of alienations too strange to be
imagined" (1964c, pp. 104–105). For America, Erikson had an
evident nostalgia for its early years: "the first self-made nation,
creating itself out of immigrants who came from all the pseudo-
species of the world and converged here" (K. Erikson, 1973,
p. 121). But America, like the rest of the modern world, seemed
to have gone haywire in its pace of change. It had fallen victim
to a kind of "quantitative overreach" (K. Erikson, 1973, p.
121):

How can we really grasp, in one lifetime—to speak only of what
America has wrought—Hiroshima, the moon landings, or, for

that matter, our moral malaise at the height of our mechanized power of destruction? And . . . how few of us can feel sufficiently in touch with a sufficiently significant number of human beings to be activated by and to activate them, insulated as many of us are in compartments within the gigantic networks of long-range mobility, of industrial complexes, and telecommunication [Erikson, 1974, pp. 80–81].

To move to specifics, what were the precise features of modern, industrial, technological civilization that Erikson regarded as alienating? The following appear in his commentaries:

- *Mechanization*: "Industrial man's attempt to identify with the machine as if it were a new totem animal leads him into a self-perpetuating race for robot-like efficiency, and yet also the question as to what, when all adjustments are made, is left of a human 'identity' " (Erikson, 1964c, p. 105).
- *Technological overdevelopment*: After mentioning Hiroshima and the landing on the moon, Erikson (1966) concluded that "[America] overreached its own comprehension of itself." He went on to express the hope that change "could yet become part of a planned world fit for a wider identity and a new adulthood on earth, but not by way of the cosmic coercion of gadgetry . . ." (p. 501).
- *Institutional decay*: Erikson speaks of "*anxieties* aggravated by the decay of existing institutions which have provided the historical anchor of an elite's identity" (Erikson, 1964d, p. 204).
- *The danger of totalitarianism*: "Technological centralization today can give small groups of . . . fanatic ideologists the concrete power of totalitarian state machines . . ." (Erikson, 1959c, p. 159).
- *Pseudospeciation and the possibility of world-destruction*: "[Is man] destined to remain divided into . . . 'pseudo-species' forever playing out one (necessarily incomplete) version of mankind against all the others until, in the glory of the nuclear age, one version will have the power and the luck to

destroy all others just moments before it perishes itself?"
(Erikson, 1970, p. 24).

It was this last possibility that held out the greatest dread
for Erikson. It was a version of the "cultural lag" theory of
social change: the human cultural tendency to bond into mutually antagonistic groups has failed to evolve into a recognition
that man is one species, and because of the development of
technology, that tendency now threatens the very existence of
the human race. "[Man] may not only blow himself up with
an atom bomb, but he may . . . poison his woods and water at
home now, and outer space in the future. He may also create
a way of life for himself which personality and organism cannot
bear (even if specialized organisms and personalities survive)
and which the generational process cannot bear" (Erikson,
cited in Evans, 1967, p. 109).

Such is the negative portrait that Erikson painted of our
technological, complex, and divided society. In connection
with that portrait, the following paradox has come to my mind:
If one examines the content of the portrait, it is remarkably
similar to the composite portrait painted by the mass society
theorists of the 1940s and 1950s—Emil Lederer, Hannah Ar-
endt, Erich Fromm—who stressed the depersonalization and
institutional erosion of modern society. It is also similar to the
ideas of the theorists of the critical school or Frankfurt school,
Adorno, Horkheimer, Herbert Marcuse, and later Jürgen Habermas, who stressed the oppressive and humanly destructive
effects of technology, bureaucracy, and mass communication.
I cannot find any significant particulars of difference between
these schools of thought and Erikson's diagnosis.

The paradox is this: Why was Erikson never really assimi-
lated to these schools, especially to the radical, neo-Marxist left
represented by the critical school? It is clear that he was not.
But why? I venture the following three hypotheses for consideration.

   1. Erikson made a different use of psychoanalysis than did
      the mass society and critical schools. Erikson remained

a psychoanalyst as such, though he modified that field fundamentally in a social direction. The critical theorists in particular *relied* on psychoanalysis, but they regarded it as a liberating, indeed critical, mode of thought, which could, much as Marxist thought did, unmask the contradictions of the modern West. The critical theorists, especially Marcuse, actively *rejected* psychoanalysis on the grounds of its individualist bias; that is, they claimed that psychoanalysis located social problems on the individual and thus excused society, whereas, in their reality, the sickness of society lay with the society itself.

2. Social class, the central preoccupation of the Marxist tradition, scarcely figured in Erikson's theoretical formulations. He was sensitive to class in society, as we have seen. But he left it out of his diagnosis of society. In his characterization of pseudospeciation he argued that "in all his past man has based much of his identity on mutually exclusive group identities in the form of tribes, nations, castes, religions, and so on" (Erikson, 1970, p. 24). But there is no mention of class or class warfare, the central proposition of his like-minded, left-minded contemporaries.

3. Most important, in my mind, is the fact that the phenomenon of oppression, the hallmark of all Marxist and neo-Marxist derivatives, did not figure centrally in Erikson's characterization of modern industrial society. He would notice it; for example, he pointed out that systems based on "suppression, exclusion and exploitation" generate evil self-images on the part of those dominated, a version of the phenomenon of identification with the aggressor (Erikson, 1959a, p. 31). But there was no systematic incorporation of oppression in Erikson's characterization of modern life, and this, I would argue, placed him in a different arena from other social critics who shared so much of his negative view of that life.

Utopian Elements in Erikson's Thought

I have just laid out the essentials of Erikson's negative utopia, as these appeared in his diagnosis of contemporary society. These ingredients are a materialistic fetishism, worship of technique, bureaucracy, and social complexity; an instrumentalization and depersonalization of human relations; alienation and despair; directionlessness; loss of identity; and an irrational pseudospeciation, irrational because it is likely to become the instrument of the destruction of humanity, when combined with the nuclear technology at hand.

At the same time, we also discover vivid elements of a positive utopia recurring in Erikson's writings—elements that also help explain his wide appeal as a thinker in the twentieth century. This utopia was not systematically laid out; he took some of it from earlier periods in history, some from other societies, and some from the future. A number of themes touch on the idea of harmony:

- *The psychological harmony provided by proper identity:* "The key problem of identity . . . is . . . the capacity of the ego to sustain sameness and continuity in the face of changing fate. But fate always combines changes in inner conditions, which are the result of ongoing life stages, and changes in the milieu, the historical situation. Identity connotes the resiliency of maintaining essential patterns in the processes of change" (Erikson, 1964c, pp. 95–96).
- *The harmony of the social and the psychological:* "only by maintaining, in its institutionalized values, meaningful correspondences to the main crises of ego development, does the society manage to have at the disposal of its particular group identity a maximum of the conflict-free energy accrued from the childhood crises of a majority of its young members" (Erikson, 1959c, p. 155). Elsewhere he noted desirability of "fit" between institutions and phases of psychosocial development; for example, between religion and basic trust, and between legality ("law and order") and autonomy (Erikson, 1959b, pp. 64–65, 73–74).

- *On the harmony between maleness and femaleness:* Erikson held
  excessive masculinity to be responsible in part for some of
  the ills of our time. The dominant male identity is, he said,
  "based on a fondness for 'what works' and for what man can
  make, whether it helps to build or to destroy" (Erikson,
  1968, p. 262). He saw women's identity as a counterforce:
  "Maybe if women would only gain the determination to represent publicly what they have always stood for . . . they might
  well add an ethically restraining, because truly supranational,
  power to politics in the widest sense" (Erikson, 1968, p. 262).
  In another context he regarded Gandhi's rejection of British
  colonialism as a kind of rejection of Western masculinity,
  and he wrote, with evident admiration, of Gandhi's mix of
  maleness and femaleness, as well as the "basic bisexuality"
  of Indian civilization (Erikson, 1969, p. 44).
- *On the harmony among generations:* "The utopia of today . . . is
  based on a reduction in the number of births *and* a new
  ethic based on a greater awareness of what each generation
  owes to the next. . . . All over the world today there is more
  of a sense . . . that whatever is going to happen to the next
  generation is our problem today" (Erikson, cited in Evans,
  1967, pp. 109–110).

But Erikson's greatest preoccupation, I believe, was with
the evils of pseudospeciation and the potential of that warped
system of identity for world destruction. His antidote was for a
transformation of identity in a universal direction. He saw in
Freud's writings on eros "the implication that [the future] demands an all-human adulthood" (Erikson, 1982, p. 95). For
Erikson, the realization of this means a true utopia. It would
give "[man] a chance to act as an adult *and* as a knowing
participant in one human specieshood . . . this would overcome
pseudo- (or quasi-) speciation; that is, the splitting into imaginary species that has provided adult rejectivity with a most moralistic rationalization of the hate of otherness" (Erikson, 1982,
p. 95). Thus, in the end, Erikson emerges as kind of panhuma-
nist, an advocate of the universalization of human identity,

which alone can provide the basis for realization of maturity and an ethic of mutual acceptance and love.

CONCLUSION

I have used the word *utopian* to characterize both the negative and positive elements of Erikson's diagnosis of society. That use is deliberate, and for two reasons. The term both reflects his outlook and possesses elements of unrealism. Erikson's diagnosis of the contemporary West is certainly selective, one-sided, and short on specifics; his view is the subject of continuous debate between cultural pessimists and cultural optimists; that debate, moreover, has not been and will not be finally resolved. His hopes for a harmonious, universally inclusive, and ethical world seem likewise simple and unrealizable, given the apparently irreducible evidence of the potential for human conflict and destruction.

Yet, in the very last analysis, to leave the judgment at that would be wrong. In the end we have to respect, admire, envy, and love Erikson for his ideals. Like the world leaders who fascinated him and commanded his attention, Erikson led the way in elevating us to levels of thought and hope that we, on our mundane own, are almost never capable of attaining. He will live in future generations not only for the brilliance of his thought but also for his spiritual elevation. For both of those we owe him eternal gratitude.

REFERENCES

Coles, R. (1970), *Erik H. Erikson: The Growth of His Work.* Boston: Little, Brown.

Erikson, E. H. (1945), A memorandum to the Joint Committee on Post War Planning. In: *A Way of Looking at Things: Selected Papers from 1930 to 1980, Erik H. Erikson,* ed. S. Schlein. New York: Norton, 1987, pp. 366–374.

——— (1950), *Childhood and Society,* 2nd ed. New York: Norton, 1978.

———— (1958), *Young Man Luther: A Study in Psychoanalysis and History*. New York: Norton, 1962.

———— (1959a), Ego development and historical change. In: *Identity and the Life Cycle. Psychological Issues*, Monogr. 1. New York: International Universities Press, pp. 18–49.

———— (1959b), Growth and crises of the healthy personality. In: *Identity and the Life Cycle. Psychological Issues*, Monogr. 1. New York: International Universities Press, pp. 50–100.

———— (1959c), The problem of ego identity. In: *Identity and the Life Cycle. Psychological Issues*, Monogr. 1. New York: International Universities Press, pp. 101–166.

———— (1964a), The first psychoanalyst. In: *Insight and Responsibility*. New York: Norton, pp. 17–46.

———— (1964b), Human strength and the cycle of generations. In: *Insight and Responsibility*. New York: Norton, pp. 110–157.

———— (1964c), Identity and uprootedness in our time. In: *Insight and Responsibility*. New York: Norton, pp. 87–107.

———— (1964d), Psychological reality and historical actuality. In: *Insight and Responsibility*. New York: Norton, pp. 160–215.

———— (1966), Remarks on the "wider identity." In: *A Way of Looking at Things: Selected Papers from 1930–1980, Erik H. Erikson*, ed. S. Schlein. New York: Norton, 1978.

———— (1968), *Identity: Youth and Crisis*. New York: Norton.

———— (1969), *Gandhi's Truth: On the Origins of Militant Nonviolence*. New York: Norton.

———— (1970), Autobiographic notes on the identity crisis. In: *The Twentieth-Century Sciences: Studies in the Biography of Ideas*, ed. G. Holton. New York: Norton, 1972, pp. 3–32.

———— (1974), *Dimensions of a New Identity: The 1973 Jefferson Lectures in the Humanities*. New York: Norton.

———— (1982), *The Life Cycle Completed: A Review*. New York: Norton.

Erikson, K. T., Ed. (1973), *In Search of Common Ground: Conversations with Erik H. Erikson and Huey P. Newton*. New York: Norton.

Evans, R. I. (1967), *Dialogue with Erik Erikson.* New York: Harper & Row.

Wallerstein, R. S., & Smelser, N. J. (1969), Psychoanalysis and sociology: Articulations and applications. *Internat. J. Psycho-Anal.,* 50:693–710.

4.

Erik Erikson's Contribution Toward Understanding Religion

WALTER H. CAPPS, Ph.D.

I have selected three subject areas to illustrate the contribution Erik Erikson has made toward understanding the nature and function of religion. The first has to do with his concentration on the biographies of religious leaders, especially those who also qualify as intriguing personalities. Of course, one thinks here of Erikson's (1958) monumental study *Young Man Luther*, the book in which he exercised the analytical and interpretive methods of "psychohistory" to come to terms with the life of the Protestant reformer. Subsequently, Erikson (1969) published a companion volume, though rooted in another time and place, *Gandhi's Truth*, which carried the same interpretive techniques forward. Along the way, there were numerous additional religious personages to whom Erikson turned his attention. When he explained a bit about why these books had the tone and temperament they had, he said, "but you have to remember where we [always Joan was included] were when we wrote them." Some of the Gandhi material was composed in Assisi (wasn't the author also thinking about St. Francis?), and the Luther book was written in a fishing village overlooking Lake Chapala in Mexico. Of course, by dint of his own biography, Erikson was thinking of Soren Kierkegaard throughout his

67

life. Then there is the psychohistorical rendition of the life of
Martin Luther King, Jr., that was designed and started, but
never carried out. Throughout his career, Erikson made allusions to the life of Jesus of Nazareth, and gave numerous hints
as to how Jesus' life would be interpreted if psychohistorical
sensitivities and techniques were applied. As it turns out, Jesus
was the subject of the last study Erikson published, an essay on
the life of Jesus, published in 1981 in *The Yale Review*.[1]

Now, simply looking at this from the outside, without regard for the technical details involved, Erikson's approach to
the subject of religion is both distinctive and (can we say it?)
correct. Others who study the subject focus on institutions, belief systems, the phenomenology of religious experience, distinctive worldviews, or any number of other empirical factors
that certainly have their place and play a role. But who else has
concentrated such disciplined and methodological attention
on the lives of religious individuals, and not simply in some
hagiographical form (as in recalling "the lives of the saints"),
nor with deliberate devotional intentions, but, instead, because
the subject is interesting. And, I would add, there is no effective
way of coming to terms with the subject of religion without
addressing its influence on individual lives, the ways in which
individual lives and distinct moments of history become interdependent, and the intentionally cultural role assigned to or
assumed by these extraordinary religious personalities.

One could go much further with this kind of study than
has been accomplished to date. How about a psychohistorical
interpretation of the life, thought, and work of His Holiness,
the Dalai Lama, for example?[2] How about a similar study of the

[1] It is particularly gratifying to me that Erikson completed this essay, his
final published piece, so far as I know, for he told me on several occasions
that he had been thinking about the life of Jesus throughout his career.
Having underestimated the reaction to his study of Martin Luther, he wondered whether a study of Jesus would instigate a firestorm of reaction. As it
happened, the publication of his final essay went largely unnoticed. By then,
scholarly attention had turned to other matters. Of course, by 1981, the
scholarly interpretation of the life of Jesus had already accommodated the
Qumran and Nag Hammadi discoveries.

[2] In making this suggestion, I wish to call attention to the fact that psychohistorical analyses have been applied to Western figures rather exclusively,
and not to representatives of Asian religious and/or cultural traditions. In

current president of the Czech Republic, Vaclav Havel,[3] whose
very response to the breakdown of totalitarianism is thoroughly
informed by an attitude toward culture that has been shaped by
moral, religious, and spiritual values? In fact, were the primary
Erikson insight writ large, one could make a compelling case
that the religious traditions themselves can be approached as
extensions and exemplifications of the lives—indeed, the biographies—of their founders. It is time, for example, to approach Buddhism this way. There is no reason why Islam
cannot be approached in the same way, Confucius as well, numerous Hindu sages, numerous rabbis—indeed, the possibilities are immense. In sum, when Erik Erikson stepped into this
field, he created magnificent intellectual opportunities, only a
scant few of which have been pursued to date.

There is irony here, however. When Erikson (1958) published *Young Man Luther*, the scholarly community, for the
most part, missed the point. There were the predicted scholarly
debates about whether he had gotten Luther's story right, or
whether he was reading ontogenetic factors back in (For an
early discussion of this debate, see D. Capps, W. Capps, and
M. G. Bradford, 1977). Roland Bainton, Luther's semiofficial
biographer, was incensed, and refused to take Erikson's work
seriously (Spitz, 1977). There were others who made similar
denunciations. But, in a quiet voice, Erikson simply explained

---

my view, the life and work of Tenzin Gyatso, the Dalai Lama, would make a
very apt subject for psychohistorical interpretation given the fact that he is
not only regarded as one of the truly spiritual personages of our time but is
also the recipient of the Nobel Prize for Peace. I have taken some exploratory
steps in this direction in my essay "The Convergence of Religious and Political Perspectives," soon to be published in a collection of essays honoring
the Dalai Lama on the occasion of his sixtieth birthday (Capps, in press).

[3]Vaclav Havel, the President of the Czech Republic, is a particularly
fitting subject for this kind of analysis and interpretation, given the fact that
the "velvet revolution" in 1989, ending the domination of the Czechoslova-
kian people by the power of the Soviet Union, was initiated as a *cultural
revolution*, with Havel, one of the nation's leading writers, being regarded as
its prime instigator. Were this subject engaged in a psychohistorical manner,
the analyst would find considerable materials with which to work. The Havel
literature is already extensive, and includes such stellar pieces as *Letters to
Olga* (1988), and *Vaclav Havel or: Living in Truth* (1989), together with as-
sorted collections of speeches, essays, and letters.

that he wrote *Young Man Luther* to try to convince his colleagues in psychology to take history seriously. Every psychoanalytic interpretation, he urged, needed to be mindful of specific
historical circumstances. Oddly, though perhaps not surpris-
ingly, the firestorm came from theologians and church historians, perhaps out of academic turf considerations. But I
certainly trust that, in the long run, Erikson's voice will be
heard with even greater influence. The study of religion cannot
proceed without deliberate, disciplined concern for the influence of individuals—call them exemplary individuals—who
have given their traditions as much characterization as has occurred from any other source. The exceptionally intriguing
point that Erikson raised, that has still not been fully explored,
is still out there for inquirers to probe further: How does it
happen that some human beings are in social and cultural positions to assume this role? Why is the religious element so prominent, for example, in the recent revolution in South Africa?
And why is it chiefly manifest in the life and influence of individuals (such as Bishop Tutu), apart from whom such developments could hardly be explained? Certainly no matter how
deeply one wishes to pursue this matter, it has to do with the
psychological makeup of these individuals, their character, the
intricate way in which that makeup and their accommodation
of social and cultural forces become interdependent, or, more
precisely, are of one piece. Erikson's work both confirms and
teaches that there is no real, substantial, or enduring understanding of religion unless these matters are tended to. Instead
of being suspicious of *Young Man Luther, Gandhi's Truth*, and
the other studies that remain more embryonic than fully developed, one should approach them as pioneering efforts that
help set out a course for further intellectual work.

Second, Erik Erikson contributed toward increased understanding of religion by providing documentation and illustration of how individuals construct worldviews. Admittedly, this
sounds simplistic, but there is a particular point to be made.
Sigmund Freud himself had explored the relationship between
psyche and culture in such well-known studies as *Civilization
and Its Discontents* (1930), *Moses and Monotheism* (1939), *The*

Future of an Illusion (1927), and elsewhere, while many writers and theoreticians, influenced by Freud, pushed the psyche-and-culture tandem even further in their analyses of the manner in which Western culture is a product of collective neurosis or psychoses or of failed exchanges within psychological reality. But, to my knowledge, no one prior to Erik Erikson had undertaken to explain these matters in specific individual and historical terms. This brings us back to Erikson's studies of Luther, Gandhi, and the others, but from a slightly different vantage point. Erikson described the process by which individuals take what they have been given—in terms of genetic inheritance, natural endowment, and historical circumstance—and weave all of it together into some consistent whole, that is, if individuals meet successfully the sequence of challenges that constitute the human life cycle. The scholarship on this subject has been dominated by commentary on the dynamics of the human life cycle itself, and on the viability of the contrasting sets of possibilities that characterize each of the cycle's stages. My suggestion is that another aspect of this theory—and we have to recognize it as theory—deserves very serious consideration, and we can put it this way: The adoption of a worldview is not something that is done mechanically, as if one simply selects an "ism," a philosophy, or a religion from within a set of possibilities, like one might choose a particular automobile, or a certain brand of appliances. Rather, the adoption of a worldview involves highly selective, synthetic, constructive work in which a large set of differentiable, temperamental, and dispositional factors come into play, a large portion of which are probably never brought into full cognizance. Indeed, if one wanted to put this insight into formula, one would say that Immanuel Kant's now famous "apriori/synthetic judgments" are implicit in worldview construction, and much that is assigned to apriori status is of a psychological or, more exactly, psychogenetic nature.

Here Erikson can be credited with two very significant accomplishments. First, he recognized all of this to be the case, that is, that worldview construction involves the interdependent coordination of these various elements. Second, in some specific instances, he identified how the construction—or, better, the composition—came into formation. Clearly, here as elsewhere in Erikson's observations, a strong aesthetic element is present. Worldview construction, like the formation of personality, is thoroughly compositional. It is composed and stylized, as are cultures, as are personalities.

This is an important point, for several reasons. Today an increasing number of writers and scholars have been paying increasing attention to what might properly be called "ordinary life philosophy"—writers such as Studs Terkel, Taylor Branch, and, of course, Robert Coles, as well as others in the United States, and a growing number of writers and scholars in Europe, chiefly at Uppsala University in Sweden. Their intention is to trace the process by which "ordinary life philosophies" are composed, and they recognize this process, as we have indicated, to be highly selective, and, in most instances, syncretistic and individualized. Erikson was out ahead on this issue. His illustrative works on Luther, Gandhi, and the others stand as case studies in this emerging field, and the theory upon which he drew—as reflected in his studies of "the modalities of social life," "reflections on American identity," Native American conceptions of the supernatural, the brilliant chapter on "Toys and Reasons" in *Childhood and Society* (Erikson, 1950, chapter 6), and elsewhere—gives this emergent field of inquiry both direction and substance. In every instance, when Erikson theorized he had specific individuals in mind. Conclusion: To the extent that understanding of religion requires understanding of how human worldviews as well as lifeviews are constructed, Erik Erikson fully deserves to be regarded as a seminal theorist.

Third, there is a matter that has not been given much attention, and may not have been perceived as a subject of much importance so far as understanding of religion is concerned. I refer to the Vietnam War, or, more specifically, to a matter that belongs to the social, cultural, and psychological impact of that war. Within this frame, attention is called to the situation of veterans (particularly combat veterans) of the war, a significant number of whom tried to take up postwar life while experiencing what is most commonly referred to as posttraumatic stress disorder.

Once, many years ago, I had the privilege of addressing a Vietnam War veterans group, and I cited testimony other veterans had offered about the experience of returning home from the war. To establish boundaries and bonds, I read some passages from Philip Caputo's (1977) *A Rumor of War* and from lesser known veterans' autobiographical reflections. In the midst of these readings, I inserted a passage from the writings of Thomas Merton (1978), the late Trappist monk, in which he was describing the highs and lows of monastic experience, as experienced by the monk himself. In the course of this description, Merton wrote the following lines:

> I have become an explorer for you, a searcher in realms which you are not able to visit—except perhaps in the company of your psychiatrist. I have been summoned to explore a desert area of man's heart in which explanations no longer suffice, and in which one learns that only experience counts. An arid, rocky, dark land of the soul, sometimes illuminated by strange fires which men fear and peopled by spectres which men studiously avoid except in their nightmares. And in this area I have learned that one cannot truly know hope unless he has found out how like despair hope is.

I was not being deceitful or coy, but I read the passage to the veterans without providing anything close to full background on its author. This situation, however, was to be altered dramatically during the discussion period following. A significant number of veterans wanted to know more. Was the author of the provocative statement about hope and despair a veteran himself? In what branch of service did he serve? Had he been wounded? Had he experienced persistent psychological trauma? During the course of this discussion I came to recognize that the veterans had almost stumbled into an identifiable form of spiritual experience without being able to recognize or name it. And with some of them, over a longer period of time, when we have been able to read the writings, say, of St. John of the Cross concerning "the dark night of the soul" (with near textual equivalents in other religious traditions), I have heard them say, "yes, this is what we have experienced." They are referring to the experience of abject negativity, when nothing that one counted upon actually came to pass. Or, as one of them described it to me, "the land of Nod becomes the land of Not, and the angels are not on the side of angels any longer." There have been several fine studies of this phenomenon, initiated by Peter Marin's (1981) provocative essay, "Living in Moral Pain," and presented in book form by William Mahedy (1986), *Out of the Night: The Spiritual Journey of Vietnam Vets*, and, more recently, by Walter Davis (1994), *Shattered Dream: America's Search for Its Soul.*

After having probed this subject for more than two decades, including tracing the cultivation of readjustment and resocialization programs for veterans of the Vietnam War that have come to prominence in the United States during this period, I wish to pay tribute to Erik Erikson for providing the therapeutic theory. Of course, Erikson didn't devote himself specifically to this subject. Rather, the theoretical base and therapeutic instrumentation was developed by a gifted psychiatrist, Robert Jay Lifton, who repeatedly called Erikson "mentor" (Lifton, 1985, 1991). Lifton's theory, in large part, was influenced by Erikson. In fact, if you take the basic pattern respecting "identity and the life cycle," and probe it for the dysfunctionalisms that it identifies and exhibits, one gets very close to the point of view that became prevailing theory in veterans' readjustment work. Lifton's pioneering work on veterans (whom he described as being "neither victims nor executioners") and on survivors of war, together with much of the theory that became explicit in his study of "protean man," was thoroughly informed by Erikson's understanding of "identity confusion" in contrast to "identity achievement." When one considers all of this, one recognizes that Erik Erikson has contributed substantially to the healing that has come following the Vietnam War, healing that has been acknowledged to represent a spiritual quality.

So, in conclusion, I have selected three critical subject areas with which Erik Erikson has contributed to an understanding of the nature and function of religion. Without question, there are other frames of reference that could be probed, and considerably more analysis and interpretation could be directed to the frameworks selected. The truth is that Erikson's writings covered so much interpretive territory—from psychology and psychoanalysis to aesthetics, cultural studies, and narrative history—that the more one works with any part of it, the more clearly one sees the organic interrelationships and self-consistencies. There is religion in all of it. Perhaps the most profoundly religious factor of all is that, in so many ways, like the equations he studied, the psychoanalyst came to embody the insights he had identified. That is, his study of the human life cycle was reflected in his own stage-by-stage journey through life.

Here it is appropriate to point out that his description of the "eight stages" can be understood to belong to the same literary genre that includes such examples as John Bunyan's classic *Pilgrim's Progress* (1678), Joseph Campbell's *Hero with a Thousand Faces* (1956), and even the sequencing of aesthetic, moral, and religious modalities that informs the writings of Soren Kierkegaard. He became known to readers outside his field of specialization with his provocative and controversial study of Martin Luther. His final essay, as we have noted, was a description of the life of Jesus, as portrayed in the Gospel texts. The life stories of religious personages, coupled with interest in how such stories pertained to case/life histories of persons one might meet every day, was a sustained item of interest throughout his life. From this vantage point, Erikson's studies can be understood to start where William James' *Varieties of Religious Experience* (1900) leaves off.

Why this preoccupation with the subject of religion? Robert Lifton suggested that "Erikson recognized that religion was where many of the formative events (both historical and psychological) happen." As Erikson's extended analysis illustrated, the major events in life as well as the formative events in culture give evidence of religious connotation, and, as he asserted in his Jefferson Lectures (1974), historical awareness is sharpened by psychological insight. But his interest in the subject was not only analytical and theoretical. In addition, the one who connected life cycle with history, who spoke of ego and communality, who was forever offering astute commentary on "American identity," and even added fresh insight to our understanding of Thomas Jefferson, had a large stake in the outcome (Erikson, 1974). That is, he knew that the regression–progression polarities were reflective of both individual development as well as the course of human history. He understood, as he put it in the final chapter of his study of Gandhi, that "both religion and politics have made rituals out of man's basic need to confess the past in order to purge it, while psychoanalysis has clarified the way in which many kinds of imaginative productions are also confessions" (Erikson, 1969, p. 438). In other words, the various modalities, distinguishable to be sure, were all of one piece. Thus, when Erikson addressed the subject of religion, he concentrated on the quest for truth, and truth was always linked to integrity, and integrity to wholeness, and wholeness to "being well," or, as he put it sometimes, to "being all right." For each of his essays, the fundamental question was about whether integration of elements is possible. Thus, the positive resolution of the regression–progression polarity registers just as clearly in social, historical, and cultural terms as it does in individual psychological terms. Throughout he kept faith with the conviction that these several worlds were interrelated, that, as he put it frequently, "we cannot lift a case history out of history" (pp. 15–16). Elaborating on this point, he wrote in *Insight and Responsibility*: "Human strength, then, depends on a total process which regulates at the same time the sequence of generations and the structure of society. The ego is the regulator of this process in the individual" (Erikson, 1964, p. 152).

In the end, his work stands as testament to moral courage. The truth he enjoined is truth that owns its integrity in the positive, constructive integration of individual, social, and historical components. In my view, this is what effective religion aspires to be, too. I see him as one who significantly expanded our understanding of human challenge, while identifying the tools (the toys, the reasons) to meet this challenge. Even in religious terms—no, especially in religious terms—it would be difficult for anyone to give us more.

REFERENCES

Bunyan, J. (1678), *Pilgrim's Progress*. London: Oxford University Press, 1966.

Campbell, J. (1956), *Hero with a Thousand Faces*. New York: Merridan Books.

Capps, D., Capps, W., & Bradford, M. G., Eds. (1977), *Encounter with Erikson*. Missoula, MT: Scholars Press.

Capps, W. H. (in press), The convergence of religions and political perspectives.

Caputo, P. (1977), *A Rumor of War*. New York: Holt, Rinehart, & Winston.

Davis, W. (1994), *Shattered Dream: America's Search for Its Soul*. New York: Trinity Press International.

Erikson, E. H. (1950), Toys and reasons. In: *Childhood and Society*. New York: Norton, pp. 209–246.

——— (1958), *Young Man Luther: A Study in Psychoanalysis and History*. New York: Norton.

——— (1964), *Insight and Responsibility*. New York: Norton.

——— (1969), *Gandhi's Truth: On the Origins of Militant Nonviolence*. New York: Norton.

——— (1974), *Dimensions of a New Identity*. New York: Norton.

Freud, S. (1927), The future of an Illusion. *Standard Edition*, 21:1–56. London: Hogarth Press, 1961.

——— (1930), Civilization and Its Discontents. *Standard Edition*, 21:57–145. London: Hogarth Press, 1961.

——— (1939), Moses and Monotheism. *Standard Edition*, 23:1–137. London: Hogarth Press. 1964.

Havel, V. (1988), *Letters to Olga*, tr. P. Wilson. New York: Henry Holt & Co.

——— (1989), *Vaclav Hamel or: Living in Truth*, ed. J. Vladislav. Boston: Faber & Faber.

Lifton, R. J. (1985), *Home from the War: Vietnam Veterans: Neither Victims Nor Executioners.* New York: Basic Books.
———— (1991), Home from the war: The psychology of survival. In: *The Vietnam Reader,* ed. W. H. Capps. New York: Routledge, pp. 54–67.
Mahedy, W. (1986), *Out of the Night: The Spiritual Journey of Vietnam Vets.* New York: Ballantine.
Marin, P. (1981, November), Living in moral pain. *Psychol. Today,* pp. 71–80.
Merton, T. (1978), A letter on the contemplative life. In: *The Monastic Journey.* New York: Doubleday, pp. 218–223.
Spitz, L. W. (1977), Psychohistory and history. The case of young man Luther. In: *Encounter with Erikson: Historical Interpretation and Religious Biography,* ed. D. Capps, W. H. Capps, & M. G. Bradford. Missoula, MT: Scholars Press, pp. 38–66.

5.

Erik H. Erikson on Bodies, Gender, and Development

ELIZABETH LLOYD MAYER, Ph.D.

Erik Erikson was one of the most extraordinary psychoanalysts our field has seen. Central among his legacies was his profound understanding of the generativity that makes life, even after death, something ongoing. So it is his ongoing life—in particular the ongoing power of his writings and ideas—that I will focus on as I address his contributions to our understanding of bodies, gender and development. However, I want to focus on something else as well: the ongoing power not just of Erikson's *ideas* but also of his remarkable personal presence. The two, I think, are related: Erikson's presence was crucial to his quality as a teacher, thinker, and clinical psychoanalyst. I want to make a point of that because I think there are some interesting things to be learned from the way in which Erikson's particular personal presence contributed not just to the extent of his influence, but also, I believe, to the actual nature of the ideas he chose to develop. (I probably also make a point of it because I am aware psychoanalysts have sometimes tended toward finding Erikson's kind of personal presence a bit suspect, as having somehow questionably seductive rather than creative repercussions.)

The writer Angeles Arrien (1993) has identified the three kinds of power that define what shamanic societies all over the

79

world call "big medicine." The first is the power of knowledge and information. The second is the power of position and the willingness to take a stand. And the third is the power of presence or charisma. Erik Erikson had plenty of all three. I will try to explore how those combined aspects of who Erikson was, made for what I think can be called "big medicine" for psychoanalysis—his power of personal presence along with his power of knowledge and his willingness to take a stand.

My discussion will be focused on Erikson's work as it relates to the body and what he called modes of function, described for the first time in his *Childhood and Society* (the first edition of which appeared in 1950), particularly in that book's second chapter, "The Theory of Infantile Sexuality." That chapter is packed with contributions along the first two dimensions described by Arrien: It is filled with new knowledge and information, and it takes a very particular stand—not, incidentally, a common psychoanalytic stand in the 1940s—regarding the crucial importance of integrating the social, the cultural, the historical, and the biological into the psychoanalytic exploration of human experience. But I am not going to focus on that chapter's new knowledge nor on the particular stand Erikson took in it. Instead, I want to highlight the third of Arrien's dimensions: *personal presence*, and ways in which particular qualities of Erikson's personal presence helped determine, I think, the actual *content* of what he was writing about in *Childhood and Society*, and determined as well the nature of the particular medicine he brought to the way analysts were thinking about bodies and gender at the time *Childhood and Society* was published.

Like so many others, I had my first impressions of Erikson while he was teaching a large lecture course at Harvard. Even in that setting—and then later in a small seminar for residents and fellows at Mount Zion Hospital in San Francisco—I was struck by the quality that probably distinguishes most great teachers: the way in which Erikson's attention to anything or anybody suddenly imbued that thing or that person with a new and heightened sense of value. It was not that Erikson did or said anything to *grant* particular or new or explicit value.

Rather, the mere fact of his attention had a peculiarly effective
way of undercutting boredom, cynicism, or whatever else inter-
feres with apperceptive wonder and appreciation. Paul Roazen
has written about Erikson's determined optimism; perhaps optimism is part of what it was. I do not think I ever heard him
not curious, *not* certain that we would find something exciting
just around the corner if we kept looking. His enormous respect for the extent of human capacity had a galvanizing effect
on people and was, I think, at the heart of why his presence
galvanized and drew us. He brought out the best in what he
studied as well as in the people he studied with. That, to me,
was the essence of his charisma and lay at the root of his power
of personal presence.

Now when Erikson started conceptualizing how the early
experience of having a body related to the more general experience of being a person, this ability to discern value and identify
adaptive purpose helped, I believe, actually shape what he was
able to perceive. In particular, it shaped how he began reorient-
ing our entire field with regard to female sexuality. Despite his
firm grounding in Freud's early theory of female development,
the actual *observations* Erikson reported in chapter 2 of *Childhood and Society* constituted a radical challenge to the theory
he ostensibly embraced. It is very interesting to see how the
text unfolds, so I will spell it out.

He starts with theory: the theory that was eventually to
become his epigenetic theory of development over the life cycle. He explains how the oral and anal phases of development
incorporate zone-specific experiences (i.e., sucking and defe-
cating), which become elaborated into more general modes of
function (i.e., trust and autonomy). He then moves on to talk
about the genital phase, and he articulates the relation between
genital zone experiences and consequent modes of function
for both boys and girls. What follows is fascinating. Erikson
wrote this chapter during the late 1940s, when psychoanalytic
ideas about female development were firmly consolidated
around the notion that the girl was, to use Freud's familiar
phrase, "a little man"—a man *manqué*, a psychological male

whose body happened to be missing something crucial to male-ness. The work of Horney and Jones—the two who had, during the 1920s, significantly challenged the idea that femininity con-sisted primarily of lack—had gone pretty well underground, and would not be revived until Zilboorg and Stoller came along, some years later.

So Erikson proceeds, in *Childhood and Society,* to lay out a fairly standard 1940s description of female psychodynamics during the genital phase:

> Girls have a fateful experience at this stage, in that they must comprehend the finality of the fact that although their locomo-tor, mental and social intrusiveness is equally increased and as adequate as that of boys, they lack one item: the penis. While the boy has this visible, erectable, and comprehensible organ to attach dreams of bigness to, the girls' clitoris cannot sustain dreams of sexual equality [1950, p. 88].

This is hardly a radical rethinking of Freud's *Three Essays.* But here is what strikes me as really interesting. Having laid out that highly conventional position, Erikson adds a postscript:

> But we must add . . . a further development, namely, *a rudimen-tary generative mode*. . . we will present some evidence pointing to what a clinician knows and works by even if he does not always know how to conceptualize it, namely that boys and girls are differentiated not only by differences in organs, capacities, and roles, *but by a unique quality of experience. This is the result of the ego's organization of all that one has, feels, and anticipates.* It is never enough, then, to characterize the sexes by the way they differ from each other. . . . *Rather, each sex is characterized by a unique-ness which includes (but is not summed up by) its difference from the other sex* [1950, p. 91, emphasis added].

Without seeming to do so—certainly without *claiming* to do so—Erikson has, in that paragraph, radically redirected the cast of analytic thinking about female development. Gender, he says, has to be understood in terms of the experience of what one *is* and *has*—not just the experience of what one is not and has not. With that articulation, the girl can no longer be viewed as male *manqué*; she exists in the pervasive organization of her own female uniqueness.

But for Erikson this brief excursion into theory is prologue: He is merely setting the stage for the essential stuff of chapter 2—his famous observations of differences in the ways boys and girls configure space as they play. Those observations are by now familiar to most people. In brief, Erikson observed that girls tend to build and be attracted to enclosed spaces, while boys build and are attracted to tall, towerlike structures. Now the *latter* observation—his observation about boys—was certainly nothing new to psychoanalysts. Nor were its implications any surprise; phallic preoccupations had long been recognized as significantly organizing for boys. What *was* new were Erikson's observations of girls and the tilt of their implications. Girls' use of space in play was as consistently configured as boys', and was as consistently preoccupied with certain organizing features. However, those organizing features were very different from the ones that characterized boys' play. The girls he studied were not preoccupied with the phallus or with its lack, but they were fascinated—by and large *happily* fascinated—with internal spaces, entrances, and enclosing walls. While boys were intently focused on the dimension of *high-low*, girls' attention was centrally concerned with the dimension of *open-closed*. Erikson interpreted these differences as projections, in space, of organ modes that had both social and biological determinants, but that derived, at least in part, from children's experiences of their respective genital morphologies.

Some years after writing *Childhood and Society*, Erikson (1964) elaborated the observations he made there into "The Inner and Outer Space: Reflections on Womanhood." Then, in 1974, he was invited by a former student to take a retrospective look at his earlier reflections and to comment on the immediate public response they had generated. A published dialogue ensued: "Once More the Inner Space" (Erikson, 1974). By that time, Erikson's findings had become part of popular culture, and "inner space" had become a catchphrase for the feminine experience.

Now all this, retrospectively, may not sound very radical. Other than setting up an experimental situation in which he was able to make some new and rather captivating observations, did he really affect *theory*?

I think he did. I think those early observations of play provided a crucial background against which authors of the past forty-five years—the past twenty, in particular—have been reconceptualizing the entire span of female development, especially in terms of what is now called primary femininity. Erikson placed the experience of *valuing femaleness* at the center of how the girl organizes her sense of herself as gendered. This immediately distinguished his exposition of female psychology from the views of his colleagues to a degree that is almost hard to imagine nowadays.

However, it seems to me that Erikson's radicalism here was in a certain sense *inevitable*. What I described as the essential basis of Erikson's galvanizing presence seems to me to have *required* that he approach girls and women in a way that departed from the contemporary mainstream. He started from the simple position that, if one were female, femaleness would be experienced as valuable. The inevitable corollary was that he, a male observing females, would have to comprehend that experience of value. He left plenty of room for vicissitudes of that valuation and for the elaboration of attendant conflicts, but I think the notion of half the human race as human beings manqués must have struck Erikson as just plain inconceivable.

I want now to digress slightly in two directions. First, I want to suggest that being married to Joan Erikson, the notion of the female portion of the human race as human beings manqués must have hit Erikson as particularly inconceivable. He repeatedly acknowledged how her extraordinary sensibilities, particularly aesthetic, influenced his work in crucial ways. On top of that, he was confronted by her quintessential grace and loveliness on a daily basis for sixty years. I recall being especially impressed by Erikson's describing, sometime in 1974, how he regretted the early publication of his work on the life cycle, in which he had portrayed the eight stages of life as a linear sequence. Had he (he said) talked more to Joan about it early on, he would have understood what she had shown him later, when she transformed his eight-stage system into a weaving: a magnificently complex, two-dimensional series of interpenetrations and blendings of colors. She had chosen each color to represent a different stage, and they ran in series along both the warp and the weft, dramatically portraying how each issue of every developmental stage penetrates every other phase, each time lending its own particular hue. The central diagonal in which the same colors met served to highlight the special salience of one particular set of issues for that particular phase of life with which Erikson had originally associated it.

Then, also in 1974, while Erikson was writing the Jefferson Lectures which he had been invited to give, I recall his asking a group of students to describe what "the American dream" had represented in each of our different American backgrounds. I doubt that anything we said ever got into the Jefferson Lectures, but by the end of the discussion, I do know that we each found ourselves with a sense of newly discovered significance regarding our own uniquely individual histories as Americans. Erikson's terrific respect for the value to be realized in human experience was an extraordinary lens through which to investigate the world. Repeatedly, I believe, it functioned to reorient people's views of themselves as well as what they were studying in many spheres, female psychology not least among them.

So I do think there was a real link between who Erikson was—his characteristic attunement to what there was to value in people—and the actual content of his contributions to the study of female development.

I suggested earlier that it is almost hard to imagine nowadays exactly how radical his observations in *Childhood and Society* must have seemed at the time. On the other hand, I am not sure things are as altered as we might think—or as we might *like* to think. Specifically, research that investigates girls' early mental representations of gender is by no means extricated from the view that lack of a phallus is a more central organizer for girls than is their experience of the genitals they actually possess.

I realized this, for example, when I looked at Roiphe and Galenson's (1981) much-cited research—pretty much a psychoanalytic standard these days—on the early genital phase, which documents the existence of an early genital awareness commencing between fifteen and nineteen months of age. They report that awareness of genital difference is crucial for both boys and girls in determining the cast of the early genital phase. But the awareness of difference on which they focus is defined by the penis: its presence in boys and its absence in girls. They describe many examples of what they identify as genital-derivative play, examples in which they observe children's preoccupation with this particular anatomical distinction. Significantly, these examples have a consistent structure insofar as they all represent literally *male* genital-derivative play, that is, they refer to the presence or absence of a phallus. So it is in these terms—phallic terms—that Roiphe and Galenson define the experience of genital difference for both boys and girls. In fact, this is not at all surprising, since their formal guidelines for identifying genital-derivative play are themselves heavily tilted toward equating genital-derivative with *male* genital-derivative (e.g., placing phallic-shaped objects in the genital area, poking and thrusting with phallic-shaped objects, etc.).

However, in a brief footnote, Roiphe and Galenson mention Erikson's findings:

> With the emergence in our infants of urinary and then genital awareness, Erikson's (1950) descriptions of the sex differences in block play were amply confirmed as we recorded that girls were now building largely enclosed structures while boys began to pile tall towers as a projection onto the inanimate world of the sense of their own genital body image [p. 96].

Throughout the book describing their research, Roiphe and Galenson make no other mention either of Erikson's observations *or, even more striking, of their own* regarding the prevalence of enclosed-structures play in the girls of fourteen to sixteen months whom they studied. So what happened to those observations? In citing Erikson, Roiphe and Galenson apparently agree that this play was in fact genital-derivative—that is, *female* genital-derivative—but, having once noted the prevalence of such play, it disappears entirely from Roiphe and Galenson's account of how girls in their study manifested derivatives of apparent awareness of their own genitals.

Roiphe and Galenson's confirmation of Erikson's observations—but in much, much younger children—intrigued me. It particularly intrigued me that such an observation could be made but its implications ignored—implications, that is, regarding the possible components of girls' early genital awareness that have to do with representations of *having* female genitals, along with whatever representations develop about *not* having male genitals. So I began looking to see whether other, similar observations existed. And I discovered that, though those early findings of Erikson's had for years been widely cited by psychoanalysts, sociologists, educators, and psychologists, they had never, as far as I could tell, been formally replicated.

I therefore undertook a replication. (Actually, it was a replication of intent but not precisely of design, since I somewhat modified the structure of Erikson's original investigation, so that boys' and girls' responses could be more systematically compared.) I was particularly curious, based on Roiphe and Galenson's footnote regarding the predominance of enclosed-spaces play in girls of fourteen to sixteen months, to determine at what age the orientation toward enclosed spaces in girls might be identifiable. If primary femininity constitutes one significant developmental line toward female gender identity—as I believe most psychoanalysts would now agree it does—the question of how early and in what ways the girl begins to develop a mental representation of femaleness is a crucial one, and preoccupation with enclosed-spaces play would seem to be worth looking at as possible evidence of such a mental representation.

I will summarize a few of my findings, all of which were indeed strongly in line with Erikson's. (Further details of this study are described in Mayer, 1991.) One set came out of a simple matching task developed by my collaborator, Daphne de Marneffe, Ph.D., and me. We built three structures out of

FIGURE 5.1. Block structure configurations (Mayer, 1991).

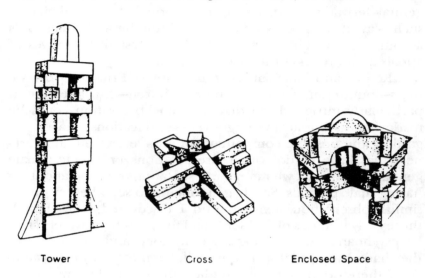

Tower   Cross   Enclosed Space

blocks. One corresponded to what Erikson described as his male configurations, one corresponded to his female configurations, and one was intentionally neutral with regard to the towerlike or enclosing attributes that defined the male and female configurations (see Fig. 5.1). We used a similar assortment of blocks for each configuration. I then met with forty-two children from kindergarten through sixth grade (we are currently undertaking the same investigation with preschool children), and asked them whether any one of the three block configurations would be more likely to "go with" a boy doll or a girl doll that lay on a tray near the structures. Next I asked the children a series of questions, including whether they liked one structure better than the others, as well as which they might have preferred when they were younger.

Dramatic results emerged. Twenty out of twenty-one girls promptly and unhesitatingly matched the girl doll with the enclosed space while fifteen of them matched the boy doll with the tower. Eighteen out of twenty-one boys matched the girl with the enclosed space, while sixteen of them matched the boy

TABLE 5.1.
Boy and Girl Dolls Matched with the Three Configurations

		Girl Doll	Boy Doll
Matched by Girls:			
Tower	(T)	0	15
Cross	(C)	1	5
Enclosed Space	(E)	20	1
	Total	21	21
Matched by Boys:			
Tower	(T)	1	16
Cross	(C)	2	4
Enclosed Space	(E)	18	1
	Total	21	21

doll with the tower (see Table 5.1). Seventeen out of twenty-one girls strongly preferred the enclosed space to the other two structures. Boys' preferences were not quite so straightforward, since a number of the boys emphasized that there was a difference between the structure they would prefer *now*, given their current ages, and the one they would have preferred when they were younger. Ten boys currently preferred the tower and drew no distinction between the structure they preferred now and the one they would have liked when younger. Another nine, for a total of nineteen out of twenty-one, stated that they would have liked the tower best when they were little, though they now preferred one of the other structures (see Table 5.2). Interestingly, this change of preference over time was reported by nine of the boys but only one of the girls. Even more interesting, all of the boys described similar reasons for their shifts away from preferring the tower: They talked about how, when they were little, they had not understood about how tall things could be hurt, or might be subject to danger. But since they had gotten older and understood about the problem of danger, they had stopped liking tall things quite so much. (So Freud lives—along, apparently, with something akin to what we are accustomed to calling male castration anxiety!)

TABLE 5.2
Preferences for the Three Configurations by Gender

		Girls	Boys	
			Now	When Younger
Tower	(T)	1	10	19
Cross	(C)	3	8	1
Enclosed Space	(E)	17	3	3
	Total	21	21	21

Of course, the really interesting thing about these findings involved the marvelously rich elaborations offered by the children as I asked them why they had matched the dolls as they did, why they liked one structure better than the others, or why their preferences had changed over time. A few samples of their comments follow, beginning with some of the girls.

GIRLS WHO PREFERRED ENCLOSED-SPACE CONFIGURATION (E)

Pam (age 5 years, 8 months; kindergarten)
ELM: Which do you like best?
Pam: This one (E).
ELM: And how come?
Pam: Because it looks more like a house. . . . Boys like towers and girls like houses. [Pam, when presented with the two dolls, had immediately matched the boy doll with the tower and the girl with the enclosed space.]
ELM: Why do boys like towers?
Pam: 'Cause they're masters. [Suddenly seems slightly embarrassed.] I can't think of anything.
ELM: No, you're giving very good answers; can you tell me some more—what do you mean, "masters"?

The dialogue extracts have been previously published in *Psychoanalytic Inquiry*, Volume 11, Number 4, pages 480–510 and are reprinted here with permission of the publisher.

Pam: Well, just *masters*, you know, people who tell other people what they can do. I can't *think* of anything [giggles]. . . .

ELM: Now, do boys like to be masters more than girls?

Pam: *I* think so.

ELM: How come? What do boys and girls think that makes them different that way?

Pam: I can't think . . . look, see there's only a *little* space to walk around in there (T) and there's *lots* of space to walk around in there (E).

Susan (age 6 years, 10 months; first grade)

Susan: [Points to (E) as her favorite.]

ELM: What do you like about it (E)?

Susan: I like it (E) because it looks like a palace. I like the shape, too . . . it is kind of special because it is kind of like a palace. . . . This (E) would be his [the boy doll's] least favorite. [Susan had matched the boy with the cross and the girl with the enclosed space.]

ELM: Now, how come?

Susan: Well, I don't know. It might look like a castle to them like it does to me. . . . Did you make these?

ELM: Yes, I did.

Susan: *All* of them?

ELM: Uh-huh.

Susan: *This* one (E) is *goo-ood*.

ELM: Thank you.

Susan: Did somebody else make one of them?

ELM: No, actually, I made them all. Does that surprise you?

Susan: Yes, you wouldn't find a boy in here (E).

ELM: You wouldn't?

Susan: Not in a palace.

ELM: Now, that is interesting. How come you wouldn't find a boy in there?

Susan: Well, he would be wearing playclothes and he wouldn't be in a castle if he was wearing playclothes. He could be *there* (C) because maybe there is a castle (E) and there is a place (C) where the boy next to

	the castle might play. But, see, the boy, he might not be invited [into E].
ELM:	I see. He would have to be invited?
Susan:	*Yes* [very decisive].

Nancy (age 8 years, 1 month; second grade)

Nancy:	I like *that* one (E).
ELM:	Okay, how come?
Nancy:	It's—it's—I think I like the design better than all of them and it's—I think it's built in a prettier way than some of the other ones. . . . My little brother would like that one (T) best. That one better than all the other ones. . . . I think he would feel that one was better than all of the other ones. [Nancy had previously matched the girl with the enclosed space and the boy with the tower].
ELM:	What do you think he would like about that (T)?
Nancy:	Well, it's taller than the other ones and he pretty much likes to build tall things and because he has some building blocks like this and he usually builds tall things like that. . . .
ELM:	Okay, does any one of the three seem fancier to you?
Nancy:	Well, to me it seems like that one (E) is fancier and that's why I pretty much like it. I like the shape and how it's really different than the other ones.
ELM:	And when you say "different," how do you mean, different?
Nancy:	Well, it has these different shapes. It has these different levels. You know, one (T) is taller and that (E) is kind of the medium one, I guess, and, um, well, it's just really interesting to me.

Ginger (age 10 years, 3 months; fourth grade)

| Ginger: | It (E) is neat, it's nice, it's like a room, it's enclosing kinda. . . . I remember when my neighbor was little he used to build tall towers and I used to build little rooms. 'Cause like tall towers—you know how kids are involved with airplanes—my neighbor was really |

into that, more than girls. But so many things have
changed since I was two: Lots of times boys and girls
have the same tastes now. [Ginger had matched the
girl with the enclosed space and the boy with the
tower.]

ELM: And the one you like best?
Ginger: This one (E).
ELM: How come?
Ginger: It's like an old Roman temple or something like that
and it's just a neat idea to have a little room . . . like
a real room that you would find somewhere like a
gazebo or something—um, the tall one (T), it's
like—it kind of looks too much like a rocketship. . . .

Rosa (age 11 years, 10 months; sixth grade)
ELM: Which do you like best?
Rosa: This one (E). I'd like to go into it, look out the
windows, sit on the windows, it's the nicest one to
go into. . . . it made me think of sort of an enclosed
space that you could look out and it was airy and it
just seemed like a girl more. . . . [Rosa had matched
the girl with the enclosed space and the boy with the
tower.] It looks more like a palace, girls like that
kind of stuff; you can go into it. . . . What *I* think is
that boys think that to be really high off the ground
is to be superior and this (T) just looks like something a boy would like . . . but when I first saw that
one (E), I thought right away that a girl would like
it because I guess 'cause girls just *would*, and it was
the one I liked too. . . . I'm a girl so that makes
sense. . . . I don't think girls are so interested in being the tallest.
ELM: Any other words you can think of about why you
liked that one (E)?
Rosa: The others just aren't as *interesting*.

A single example of a boy's response follows, since I am
particularly emphasizing girls and the way Erikson refocused

our observations of girls. This boy exemplifies the shift in preference from being younger to being older.

Barney (age 8 years, 6 months; second grade)

ELM: Which do you like best of the three?

Barney: I like this one (C).

ELM: How come?

Barney: Because as a little boy I started out liking ones better
like this (T) and, and, and I actually tried to put
them together sort of like this (T) and they just kept
falling down and I thought: This is not going to work,
they just kept falling down. Then I tried these (C)
and I thought they were just as fascinating but easier
to make. . . . this one (C) is kind of hard to notice
except it's neat how it's put together. This one (T)
you notice more . . . this one (E) is kind of simple
and it's, it's, it's, it's, *there* like it's *there* and there's
nothing else, except this one (T) is the biggest and
it's showing the most so it gets the most appreciation. . . . [Barney had matched the girl with the enclosed space and the boy with both the tower and the
cross, saying the boy went equally with each of them.]

ELM: Okay, does one of them seem fancier or more interesting to you than any other?

Barney: Well, from *my* point of view, the little one seems
more interesting. I also like the tallest one (T) because I *do* like to be good at things. I don't like to
be the *best* at things because I don't like to brag,
except I just don't like to be *bad* at things.

ELM: Now, you say you don't like to be best at things?

Barney: I *kind of* like to be best at things but I like to show it
not by bragging, but just doing it when I have to
because that's the way it happens.

ELM: And you think when you are feeling that way, not
bragging, you are just being good at things, then you
like that one (T)?

Barney: No, I still like this one (C) best because, because if
I had—I have strong feelings for that [being good

ELM:	at things] except if I had even *stronger* feelings about it, *then* I would like this one (T).
ELM:	I see.
Barney:	I like this one (C) because it's, it's not *bad*, but, it's, it's not bad but it's *good* and it's the size that I like.
ELM:	When you say even stronger feelings about it, you mean about being the best?
Barney:	Yes, if I had even stronger feelings about being the best. I'm not saying that I don't have that *little* feelings about it, I just don't have as much.
ELM:	Great, you are doing a wonderful job. Let's see Barney, you have one younger brother?
Barney:	There is Bill who is five, six years old . . . and then another brother. His name is Bobby—one and a half. He, *he* would like this one (T). He just likes to show off *all* the time. . . . he definitely likes to be the best or be tied at the best.

I want now to mention one pervasive aspect of the girls' associations that seems to me particularly in keeping with the challenge that Erikson's early findings posed to psychoanalytic theories of female development. It was noteworthy that, among almost all the girls I interviewed, the affective tone with which they responded to the enclosed space was highly positive. Not only did they strongly associate the enclosed space with femininity; they also strongly associated it with pleasure and with attractiveness. They were relaxed and happy—indeed, enthusiastic—as they pursued their thoughts about the enclosed space and its association with things female.

That observation, I believe, faces us with the question that Erikson raised for psychoanalysis when he reported his first findings concerning spatial orientation and gender in *Childhood and Society*. Are the origins of the pleasure with which girls respond to enclosed spaces to be found entirely in vicissitudes of an early depressive response to gender difference? Can we regard that pleasure simply as a defensive or compensatory strategy developed to deal with an early depressive reaction to being without a penis? Or may that pleasure point to a possible developmental line in which the experience of femininity is pleasurable from the beginning, and in which the perception of gender differences means, for the girls, valuing what she *has* in the way of femaleness, at the same time that she reacts to the discovery of what she *does not* have in the way of maleness? Obviously, I believe the latter possibility needs to be significantly taken into account, and Erikson did as well; that is why his early work posed such a radical challenge to psychoanalytic thinking about female development.

I would like at this point to return to Arrien's notion of what makes for a healer's effectiveness—that is, what makes for the capacity to effect "big medicine"—and my suggestion that the effectiveness of Erikson's healing influence, on people as well as ideas, derived from all three of the ingredients Arrien has identified: the power of knowledge, the willingness to take a stand, and the power of personal presence. I have focused especially on that last, because the particular power of Erikson's presence seemed to me to be closely interwoven with the quality of respect for human experience that enabled him to perceive things in new and fresh ways—including female psychology, with significantly healing influence for our ideas about gender.

But female psychology, really, is only a case in point. More generally, I believe there is something that does indeed constitute big medicine, in the respect for human capacity that infused the way Erikson involved himself with what he studied, as well as the people with whom he had contact. In fact, I believe we can extrapolate an extraordinarily powerful investigative paradigm from that very particular aspect of Erikson's legacy, a paradigm that is in itself big medicine for the way we structure our attempts to extend knowledge in our field or, for that matter, in any other. It is a paradigm which asserts that *the extent of our perceptive capacity critically hinges on the quality of relationship we have with the object of our investigation.* More specifically: Our perceptive capacities will be a direct function of our degree of respect for whatever it is we are investigating.

Barbara McClintock, the Nobel prize-winning geneticist, described what I see as her version of a similar principle when she was asked how she came up with her highly original discoveries. Scientific discoveries, she replied, happen when investigators get to know the thing they are studying so well (corn, in her case), that they actually feel what it is like to *be* that thing, when they develop what she called a *feeling for the organism*. Without that empathic involvement—*love,* she came pretty close to calling it—McClintock suggested that it was difficult, maybe impossible, to make really new or original discoveries in science. With it, on the other hand, new discoveries follow as a matter of course. Now McClintock devoted a lifetime to the study of one thing—corn, and getting to know corn very, very well. Erikson, in contrast, was quintessentially far-ranging in the many things he got to know, some in great depth, some only in passing. But Erikson's quality of respect for anything he got to know smacks, to me, of something akin to what McClintock articulated as the key to discovery making. Like the revolutionary impact of McClintock's discoveries regarding the transposition of genes for genetics, Erikson's discoveries—still, I believe, insufficiently appreciated by psychoanalysts for their originality, clinical relevance, and prescience—have a revolutionary import for our understanding of human beings.

Finally, I want to mention one more thing. Quite apart from the way in which this quality of respect for human capacity enabled Erikson to observe new things, that same quality of respect has an inevitably special relevance for us as psychoanalysts. Along with our power of knowledge and information, and along with our power of position and willingness to take a stand—forms of power which, as analysts, we habitually claim and utilize—the capacity to respect and value varieties of human experience is certainly the central determinant of our ability to help people, as well as to understand them. To that extent, Erikson remains an exemplar psychoanalyst.

REFERENCES

Arrien, A. (1993), *The Four-Fold Way.* New York: Harper Collins.
Erikson, E. H. (1950), *Childhood and Society,* 2nd ed. New York: Norton.

———— (1964), The inner and the outer space: Reflections on womanhood. *Daedalus*, 92:582–606.

———— (1974), Once more the inner space: Letter to a former student. In: *Women and Analysis*, ed. J. Strouse. New York: Grossman, pp. 320–340.

Mayer, E. L. (1991), Towers and enclosed spaces: A preliminary report on gender differences in children's reactions to block structures. *Psychoanal. Inquiry*, 11:480–510.

Roiphe, H., & Galenson, E. (1981), *Infantile Origins of Sexual Identity*. New York: International Universities Press.

6.

Entering History: Erik Erikson's New Psychological Landscape

ROBERT JAY LIFTON, M.D.

I will blend the conceptual and the personal in this paper as I think that is very much in Erik's spirit, and the best way to bring out what he has given us. We are all influenced by innovative people like Erik—by their ideas, of course—but also by how they live in and with those ideas.

The memories, the connections with Erik, extend for me over many places. I have strong images of our meetings, talks, and long walks in Stockbridge, in Wellfleet and Cotuit, in Cambridge, in New Haven, just about everywhere it seems. But I think it seems logical to begin with a Tiburon, California, story.

I was sitting with Erik in that pleasant little swimming pool that he and Joan had at their Tiburon house, and we were discussing one thing or another in a vague way, when he asked, with his own special tone of curiosity, "Bob, tell me something. Have you heard about these 'Jews for Jesus?' " I said, "Yes, I've heard of them Erik. They are a group of Jews who were born again in Christian fashion and are strongly attracted to Jesus." Then I thought I would be a little mischievous and asked him in turn, "Anyhow, Erik, which side are you on?" He then laughed a little, thought a little, and said, "Both, of course."

That answer was in keeping with Erik's sense of things, and also with one of my own little creations. I often shared with Erik my bird cartoons, which I do as a kind of avocation. They reflect absolutely no artistic talent, but they can express certain things more directly than other forms of writing. There is a particular example that seems relevant for that story of the swimming pool: a small, naive, enthusiastic bird looks up and says, "All of a sudden I had this wonderful feeling: 'I am Me!' " And a bigger, older, more skeptical, even jaundiced, bird looks down and says, "You were wrong." Erik was very fond of that one.

In my title I used the phrases "entering history" and "new psychological landscape." I chose those images because I wanted to bring out the imaginative reach of Erik's work. Again, I can best illustrate what I mean by a personal experience with his ideas. I have a very clear memory of an event that occurred in 1956. I was sitting on a couch, together with BJ, my wife, in a rented house in Georgetown in Washington, DC, where I spent one year working with David McK. Rioch after returning from the Far East. I picked up an issue of the *Journal of the American Psychoanalytic Association* and read Erik's essay "The Problem of Ego Identity" [see chapter 9]. I had just finished my research on Chinese and Westerners who had been put through Chinese communist "thought reform," or so-called "brainwashing," and without quite realizing it I was searching for the theoretical approach that would give me a deeper understanding of the process. I knew something about Erik's work, as I had read *Childhood and Society* earlier and had admired it greatly. But my response was different when I read this classic essay on identity. I had what could only be called a "eureka experience." The feeling I had was, "That's it!" "That's exactly right!" My transformative relationship with Erik had begun.

What I immediately sensed was that Erik's identity concept was a key to grasping what I had encountered. That was so, I believe, for two very simple reasons—simple now, but by no means simple at the time. There was first the clear principle of individual experience being associated with something much larger, indeed with the historical process itself. That principle informed Erik's entire essay. The second point was the sensitive dialectic of sameness and change. If you define identity as only inner sameness and continuity, you are missing half of it. The other half is the involvement of the self with some process of change, flux, newness. And I found Erik's work to be constantly immersed in precisely that dialectic.

So I could look at young Chinese who had been put through thought reform in terms of their sense of inner identity. That included all that had happened to them and to previous generations during the rush of Westernizing influence between the two world wars, whether that of John Dewey, or Bertrand Russell, or the influence of Christianity and then of Marxism and Communism. On top of all that came the thought reform process, which combined exhortation and coercion, always with the promise of renewal—but renewal or else, so to speak. Identity theory provided grounding for these varied currents, and enabled me to view the Chinese efforts at thought reform as seeking to convert young Chinese from an identity of the filial son—the central identity of patriarchal Confucian culture—to that of the filial Communist.

More generally, it became clear to me that what Erik was saying, as he did in all of his work, was that one simply cannot grasp individual experience—any individual experience—except in historical perspective. One needs that individual experience to understand what is going on at a particular moment of history. For instance, one could not understand the moment of Chinese history I was exploring without those individual interviews and their interpretation in terms having to do with identity. On the other hand, one could not grasp what was going on in those interviews—or in the lives of individual Chinese—without inwardly imagining the course of modern Chinese history. All this seems quite evident now, but I believe it was a revolutionary intellectual breakthrough at the time. What Erik was putting forward was a very significant change in psychological imagination. He was asking us to bring images of history to our psychological encounters, not only in wide-ranging research but in everyday psychological work as well. These historical images were to have equal standing with, say, those of sibling rivalry or the Oedipus complex—and self-consciously so, since we ourselves never function as tabula rasas. Further, this kind of psychohistorical imagination had to apply to therapists no less than researchers.

Now in Chinese thought reform, the process I was studying, the last significant act was the elaborate public denunciation of one's father. One denounced him specifically as a father but also—and this was the ultimate point—as a symbol of the old regime. As literally millions of young Chinese went about denouncing their fathers, we could witness a vivid and a painful example of individual and family acting on—and being acted upon by—the fierce currents of larger Chinese history. Identity theory provided the perspective needed for such an upheaval, and no one previously had thought of looking at individual people in the world in this way. A key phrase of Erik's—it is almost a mantra for this paper, as it was for his work—is his sentence: "We cannot lift a case history out of history" (Erikson, 1958, pp. 15–16).

What about Erik himself in all this? After reading that essay on ego identity, I felt I had to meet the man. A mutual friend, Fritz Redlich, was kind enough to arrange an introduction. I sent Erik a draft of a paper on Chinese thought reform, which seemed to fascinate him. He invited me to visit him at Stockbridge. Moved and thrilled, my first impression was an aesthetic one: Erik and Joan each made an exquisite appearance, framed by the soft beauty of their Stockbridge surroundings.

Almost from the moment of my arrival, we started walking. In fact, that seems to be what we did for most of that visit. Erik told me that Europeans tend to believe that good ideas emerge only when people are in motion. That made sense to me, though I was sufficiently awed by Erik at that moment that just about anything he said would have been equally convincing. In any case, the walking and the ideas did seem to blend. We must have walked around the town of Stockbridge about eight times. I was getting a bit tired. He was vigorous and strong. He was then in his mid-fifties and I was thirty.

He asked me a lot of questions about Chinese thought reform—about the conflicts in the people subjected to it, about the reformers themselves, about the Chinese Communist revolution. Although he asked them seemingly casually and often discursively, I could sense his focus and his intellectual intensity. More than many people realize, Erik was a rigorous and highly disciplined thinker while never narrowly disciplinary. In this case he wanted to imagine his way into Chinese thought reform because he found parallels in it with the struggles of Martin Luther in his training for the priesthood. He was immersed in such matters at the time and was just about to leave for Mexico, where he wrote his extraordinary psychobiography, *Young Man Luther.*

Then and later, we also talked a lot about his concept of totalism. And we discussed ways in which social movements called upon ideology for the promise of change, renewal, revitalization. Nobody in psychoanalysis was writing much about ideology, but for Erik it was a very general human need. It had to do with one's way of understanding self and world, and with one's response to or rejection of calls for upheaval. Ideology, above all, was inseparable from identity; there was always a tandem in Erik's work between the two. I learned to focus, in my own work, on ideology, broadly defined as central to human action. Americans tend to neglect it as a concept and negate it in themselves. We prefer to see ourselves as pragmatic and to more or less dismiss ideology as European stuff. But in fact it is universal stuff and, through Erik's early influence, came to infuse my work with a reach toward attachments and motivations beyond the personal.

During those early walks around Stockbridge, I also found myself back in Vienna with Erik. Vienna was very important for him to talk about while thinking about Luther, while thinking about Chinese thought reform. With his capacity for conveying multiple levels of experience, Erik evoked the Vienna environment as exciting and liberating and also, over time, suffocating. He in fact said to me that, even if he had not been forced to leave because of the rise of Hitler, he still would have, after a certain amount of time, *wished* to leave.

Erik was returning to his own historical experience as a way of associating to others' struggles with history—whether those of Luther or of the young Chinese I told him about. In connection with the latter, he had never been to China and had not read much about modern or contemporary China, but could immediately—intuitively and empathically—understand what I had struggled to grasp about the Chinese I had worked with. He was displaying his psychological and historical imagination, which gave rise to and was in turn deepened by his identity theory and sensitivity to ideology.

Everything had a context. That context was always highly significant for Erik, and here, too, he would find ways to make use of contexts important in his own life. Much has been written, some by Erik himself, about his elaborate identity struggles, and these struggles were very real and very serious over the course of his life. We know that he transformed them brilliantly into insight. But in the stress on his identity struggles, what was lost sight of was his capacity for self-conscious historical location in the process. He was always thinking historically about where he was, what he was doing, and what he was seeking. He would look back to different historical moments in his life and to the relationship of these personal moments to larger historical forces. From the beginning I came to think of Erik as a man with history in his bones. Of course, we all have history in our bones, but somehow Erik found access to that particular historical—or psychohistorical—bone marrow. He could touch it, articulate it, and interpret it with great conceptual meaning in ways that released and illuminated the history present in everybody's bone marrow.

What about his new model, what we can call his psychohistorical paradigm? I think it is most forcefully developed in *Young Man Luther*, which may indeed be his greatest book because it was so extraordinarily original. The model was in a way quite simple: It is that of the great man or great person in history. But everything resides in that operative word "in." Psychoanalysts have long had much to say about the great man, but in previous psychoanalytic generations the great man was almost never in history. For approaching the flow of history, psychoanalysts generally made use of Freud's two predominant models. One was the *Totem and Taboo* (1913) model, which is that of the sons rebelling against the fathers and eventually devouring the fathers. The second model for Freud was that of individual psychopathology, an approach that found intellectually disastrous expression in the Freud-Bullitt biography of Woodrow Wilson. These two Freudian paradigms could have their usefulness, but they tended to eliminate the very history they claimed to be studying.

Freud did say something else, however, that Erikson could seize upon. Concerning Moses, Freud (1939) wrote: "The great man influences his contemporaries in two ways: through his personality and through the idea which he puts forward" (p. 109). There Freud was beginning to enter into the historical process, though he did not carry these principles much further. How did Erikson extend and transform this model, which he surely did? He evoked Luther as himself a creation of the history of his time, who could in turn alter that history by means of his own extraordinary impact. Here we encounter a detailed, sensitive, often convoluted juxtaposition of the gifted individual person and his or her historical era. Painful struggles with individual conflicts parallel the collective struggles experienced by large numbers of people at a particular time and place. In the resolution of these conflicts—or partial resolution, as they are never fully mastered—the great person succeeds in illuminating those collective struggles, thereby providing for everyone certain forms of psychological or spiritual advance. In Luther's case, as Erikson understood it, that advance took the form of internalization of conscience, or "the meaning of meaning it." With Gandhi, it was the transformation of violence into nonviolence. Luther, like Gandhi, came "to lift his individual patienthood to the level of the universal one, and to try to solve for all what he could not solve for himself alone" (Erikson, 1958, p. 67).

As with all important work, the approach has value beyond its immediate applications. One can move from the great man or woman, as I have in most of my work, to a particular group of people acted upon by history, or themselves acting upon history, and explore their *shared themes*. To an extent, the great man emphasis is a product of nineteenth and earlier twentieth century European influences. A stress on shared themes probably emerges from late twentieth-century, particularly American, influences. In any case, the historical imagination that Erik introduced carries over to any such shared themes approach. This kind of historical imagination was crucial for me not only in my work on Chinese thought reform but in all of my other studies as well. That includes my work with Hiroshima survivors and their fearful struggles with the identity of the *hibakusha* or "explosion-affected person," having to do with their dreadful and tragic historical experience. Similarly, with Vietnam veterans, historical forces had much to do not only with their devastating war experience but also with their capacity for impressive individual change following that experience. They could undergo significant forms of change very rapidly, largely because currents in American life supported such change: for instance, in their struggles with violence and with macho forms of masculinity, and in their relationships with wives and girl friends and women in general. I could observe these changes over the course of the intensive, egalitarian, and ultimately healing "rap groups" with antiwar veterans during the early 1970s. One needed the kind of psychohistorical imagination Erik introduced for both facilitating and recognizing the resilience we encountered.

The shared psychohistorical themes model, then, extends the spirit of the great-person-in-history approach in coming to recognize that a particular group of people can illuminate a historical era. What is involved here is not only extending the psychological imagination into the historical process but understanding that psychological imagination to be itself largely formed by available historical influences.

Erik gave full and often playful expression of that historical imagination at our meetings over the years at Wellfleet, Massachusetts. In the early 1960s he and I began to talk of forming a group on psychology and history. It sometimes takes quite a while to convert thoughts into action, so in 1966 we had our first Wellfleet gathering. But that anticipated gathering had already entered into the architectural planning of the house for my wife and me, just then completed. We had two enormous

oak tables built into the renovated shack that became my study.
Our purpose, of course, was to provide lots of table space for
my work, but also a setting for the Wellfleet meetings that were
to occur.

Erik thrived at those meetings; he clearly enjoyed them.
He could speak very freely about work in progress and give
constant expression to his wonderfully discursive imagination.
Nothing in our discussions had to be complete or finished.
Though Erik tended to be meticulous in introducing ideas, he
could do so with much more freedom at Wellfleet than at other
places. He came every single year from 1966 until the mid-
1980s, when his health interfered. Throughout he was a loyal,
active, thoughtful participant. He was a very special person
there, as his ideas had been the original basis for the meetings.
There were lots of articulate, some might say overarticulate,
people at Wellfleet—almost everyone was a good talker. But
when Erik began to say something, everybody else was quiet.
People really listened. They knew they were encountering
something special. He brought up everything there: his work
on Luther, on Gandhi, on Jefferson and Einstein, on Jesus and
the sense of the "I," and later his work with Joan on adulthood
and old age.

There was always a certain sequence with Wellfleet—those
of you who knew Erik will recognize him in it. A few months
before the meeting I would call him up and say, "Erik, you
know Wellfleet is coming around. What would you like to talk
about this year?" He would say, "Oh, I don't know, Bob, I am
not really doing very much. I'm not sure I really want to talk
about anything." And I would say, "But Erik, I know people
would really like to hear you." And he would say, "But I think
maybe this year I would just like to sit back and listen." And I
would say, "Well Erik, if you were to make a few remarks, what
might you talk about?" And he would say, "Well I am doing a
little something about Jesus and the sense of the 'I.' It's nothing
much. And I haven't really worked out my ideas very well."
And I would say, "All right Erik, just present a few of your ideas
as beginning thoughts and people will respond, and they will
say things." And he would say, "I guess I can, but I don't want

to do it on the first day—maybe on the third." And I would say, "That's fine." So we would make a deal, and on the third day he would indeed present his ideas, would do it eloquently and loved doing so, and people would indeed respond intensely, and we felt ourselves to be participating in something profound and unique.

At the beginning of each of our Wellfleet meetings, we would have a go-round and people would describe all the wonderful things they had been doing for the last year or so and the equally wonderful things they were planning for the next year. But Erik would first take a deep breath and then say: "Here we are again. It's another year. We are back here at Wellfleet." He would say something like that every year, and I began to wonder why he always did. Then I realized that he was rendering the gathering a ritual. He was placing us in a certain time and space that we set aside every year—we would meet at about the same time with a lot of the same people. He was marking—that is, noting and acknowledging—the particular occasion as one in a series of occasions, all as a way of entering into the intellectual and psychological flow. I believe he was implying that if we were going to have the cosmic associations and explorations we always do at Wellfleet—something about the dunes and the sea encourages that, I believe—we ought to locate and anchor ourselves so to speak, in that particular time and place. Erik was always strong on the idea of rituals; he wrote about them and took them seriously as an issue in human behavior and a way of experiencing the world.

The historical immersion Erik advocated was by no means limited to large collective events. It was equally applicable—and this has been less appreciated—to immediate clinical situations. Consider that wonderful little vignette in *Childhood and Society*, entitled "Neurological Crisis in a Small Boy: Sam" (Erikson, 1950). We are given an elaborate mosaic that includes the conflicts of three generations of the boy's family, involvements in Jewish-Christian relations, and reflections on biblical struggles of family members and the influence of these struggles on Jewish life in general—all culminating in a particular clinical crisis. Erik was telling us that any individual person or "case" is just as much a part of history—must be understood in terms of history—as is a head of state or great religious leader. In the case of the "Small Boy Sam," that historical component extended from the Bible to the present and into the future. The point here is that Erik was more than just a clinician who entered into historical studies; he was a healer and thinker who showed us how clinical work could be permeated by an illuminating historical sensibility.

When I began my work in the late 1970s on Nazi doctors, I had already known Erik for more than twenty years, but from discussing that research with him I discovered him anew. Both at the Wellfleet meetings and during other long discussions he and I had about my impressions of Nazi doctors, I found his response to be stunning in its combination of excitement and nuanced observations. His enthusiasm for the work was related to his sense that it had particular historical importance. But I realize also that the work gave him an opportunity to reassert forms of knowledge related to his personal German cultural experience, a background that was inevitably suppressed, at least to a degree, over the course of reconstituting his life in America.

His impressions were manifold and lively, and he raised important questions for me. He said, "You know, when you speak to some of those Nazi doctors, you might make contact with their humanity." The comment made me a bit uncomfortable, but I came to realize that, while holding Nazi doctors responsible for what they did, he was emphasizing a principle of human complexity. It was similar to the idea, expressed by psychiatric clinicians, that schizophrenics are not necessarily schizophrenic twenty-four hours a day. That kind of observation helped me to realize that Nazi doctors were, for the most part, very ordinary men who had moved into evil, or had been socialized into evil. They did not have the mark of Cain on their foreheads. Erik told me I had earned the right to speak about the complexity even of Nazi doctors. That gave me courage, because precisely what upset many people about my work was its finding that Nazi doctors were quite ordinary and could frequently resemble the rest of us. That finding was consistent with the concept of "doubling" that I eventually evolved, the idea of a functional second self—in their case an Auschwitz self—relatively autonomous from the original self, as the means by which Nazi doctors adapted to evil. In that sense, like the schizophrenics I mentioned, a Nazi doctor was not a Nazi doctor twenty-four hours a day. And that overall perspective—of ordinariness and of shifting and contradictory behavior—enabled me, I believe, to grasp the more insidious kinds of psychological and ethical danger that Nazi doctors represented.

But in everything Erik did there was humor—and this was true even in his reflections on Nazi doctors. After we had talked at great length about genocide, about genocide as a world problem and a potential of many different nations and groups, not just Germans, he kind of leaned over to me with that naughty half-smile and said, "Don't tell anyone I said this, Bob, but I think that, in this case, the way that they did it, it had to be German." Here humor cleared the way for pinpointing what could be called a politically incorrect conviction with limited but significant applicability.

Indeed, his humor was so integral to his way of being that one had to see it as part of his worldview. He had a genius for lubricating just about any encounter with double takes, with odd and seemingly innocent forms of deflation, self-deflation, and also self-assertion. That is, he could be self-mocking to further his purposes. Consider a brief segment from a Wellfleet tape from the early 1980s, which I had occasion to listen to recently. He was making a presentation and came to a point he wished to emphasize concerning the mother-child connection, which he called the "primal order." He then added, "If you know a better word," and then paused, here you would expect someone to say, "then let me know it, and I'll consider using it." But, instead, he said, "If you know a better word . . . don't tell me. I like this term, 'primal order.' "

Another story about his humor very much involves Joan. Like almost everyone else one knows, I've sometimes had back problems. During one period that I was quite troubled by it, Joan generously promised to give me some help. Therefore, my wife and I took the hour drive from Wellfleet to Cotuit, where Joan was to give me my training exercises. She did just that, wonderfully—underwater exercises, outdoor exercises, indoor exercises. I felt energized and deeply grateful. She even extended her therapeutic eye to my ordinary movements, noting that my extremely quick way of getting up from a chair or sitting down again, insisting that I do such things more slowly. I said, "But Joan, I can't, I am a New York Jewish intellectual." She said, "Then you'll have to stop being that." As we were sipping our drinks and I was feeling no more back pain but only joy, I said, "Erik, I have something important to tell you. Joan just gave me these terrific exercises and I have to tell you now that I am going to transfer my transference from you to Joan." Erik paused, and I could observe something beyond his ordinary twinkle—more a look of deep mischief taking over—and I knew I was in trouble. "Ah" he said, "is that so? Do you mean the negative part or the positive part?"

At the time of his eightieth birthday, there were many parties for the Eriksons, and we had a small gathering for them at our house in Wellfleet. As a little present I gave Erik a bird cartoon. In this cartoon, one bird says, "An elf inside a wise man I can understand, but how can a wise man fit inside an elf?" And the second bird answers, "Eighty years of practice." I added to the card, "For Erik, the embodiment of elfhood, elfishness, and elfery"—that being, of course, a direct takeoff from his famous phrase in *Young Man Luther* concerning Luther's monkhood, monkishness, and monkery, and the significance of them all for psychoanalysis and the like. But the truth was that I felt there to be something fundamental about Erik's elfishness. You know, he was a big man, physically and intellectually, and yet he was an elf. He viewed things kind of sideways, as though he were a bit removed from human foibles. His mind dwelled on the edges of human experience, as though looking in from the outside with mischievous glances, being inside and outside that experience at the same time—all with a quality of visual and associative magic.

Erik's humor was also part of his sense of history. Everybody, he was telling us, has his or her own historical moments. You can do exciting things in extending those moments. But you are bound to them, there, in that place. You are vulnerable, we are all vulnerable. We can be defeated, and yet mostly we bungle through. That was the spirit of this humor and it was, for me, very powerful.

Now it has to be said that Erik was no saint. If described as one, he would surely not recognize himself and express disdain for the portrait. He could in fact be difficult, self-absorbed, inconsistent, and preoccupied in ways that could be hard for others to manage. He was an inveterate worrier, and his worries would worry other people. He was deeply committed to his ideas and could be uneasy when others would move in somewhat different directions. But his extraordinary capacity for empathy—and again that humor and humanity—would always come to the rescue.

For a few years at Wellfleet and elsewhere, he would grouse about my evolving work on the many-faceted or "protean" self, which was related to identity but also raised critical questions concerning identity. I was uneasy about that and he was uneasy. And then one day, again at Tiburon, he looked at me and said, "You know, I have been assigning your essay on the protean self to psychiatric residents in San Francisco. I think it is one of the most important things you have done." I was pleased and moved on many levels, among them my sense that he more than anyone could grasp what I was up to. I think he also ultimately understood that real mentorship was not the exact duplication of a mentor's work but rather the incorporation of the spirit of that work in evolving new directions.

What Erik did for younger people like myself coming into the field was not only to connect psychoanalysis and history but to connect psychoanalysis to the world. In that way he enabled us to enter, or reenter, psychoanalytic thought, and at the same time feel ourselves connected to the larger world. That was an extraordinary gift. Again, it seems like a logical perspective now, but it was anything but the established way at the time. He did what nobody in psychoanalysis had done before. It was nothing less than establishing a new dimension of reality, a different realm of psychological experience. I have no doubt that Erik was the most creative psychoanalytic mind since Freud.

Certain people are unique in the transformative power of their lives. Erik was such a person, both in transforming himself and in transforming others or enabling them to transform themselves. He drew upon chaos to bring about order and beauty in what he wrote and what he said. A person like Erik has to be profoundly missed, and we should be candid in saying so.

But I find solace in another image of Erik. It was a special moment that also occurred when Erik was eighty years old. We were walking down from his Cotuit home to the small inlet where we were going to swim—where Erik and Joan swam regularly. Erik suddenly stopped walking, waved his arm out toward the beautiful Cape scene, his eyes very bright despite the difficulties he was then having with them, and said to me: "You know, Bob, I never thought there would be all this—that I would be eighty years old and . . . able to swim." I understood immediately that he was talking about the great currents of his life, about the extraordinary flow of his journey from his beginnings, about all the unexpected developments, and all he had put together to make it work. I felt that he was saying, loud and clear, that he had lived a realized life. I hold on to that image—just as I hold on to the power of his work—in my deep sadness that he will not be coming to Wellfleet again, that I will never see before me the wise man inside the elf.

Wallace Stevens I think says these things more eloquently than I can: "Out of what one sees and hears / and out of what one feels / who could have thought to make so many selves / so many sensuous worlds."

REFERENCES

Erikson, E. (1950), A neurological crisis in a small boy: Sam. In: *Childhood and Society*. New York: Norton, pp. 21–34.
———— (1958), *Young Man Luther: A Study in Psychoanalysis and History*. New York: Norton, pp. 15–16.

Freud, S. (1913), Totem and Taboo. *Standard Edition*, 13:1–161. London: Hogarth Press, 1955.

——— (1939), Moses and Monotheism: Three Essays. *Standard Edition*, 23:3–137. London: Hogarth Press, 1964.

——— Bullitt, W. C. (1932), *Thomas Woodrow Wilson. Twenty-eighth President of the United States: A Psychological Study.* Boston: Houghton-Mifflin, 1967.

7.

A Conviction Born of Judiciousness

For distribution to
residents and other
staff members

DIV PROF ED
Winter VA Hospital
February 20, 1951

A CONVICTION BORN OF JUDICIOUSNESS

As an eloquent and courageous exemplification of the concept
of responsibility—of teacher to students—I here commend to
the staff and Fellows the following statement of position, made
by (Ex-Professor) Erik H. Erikson to the Committee on Privilege and Tenure of the University of California.

Karl A. Menninger, M.D.

MR. ERIKSON'S CONVICTION

Dear Sirs:

I deeply appreciate the privilege of a free hearing before a
committee of colleagues. With you I shall not play hide-and-
seek regarding a question which must be implicit in what you
wish to ask me and which must be explicit in what I shall have
to say: I am not and have never been a Communist, inside "the
party" or outside, in this country or abroad.

Because of my sincere appreciation of the position which
I now hold, I shall state (as freely and as briefly as I can) what
considerations and feelings have made it impossible for me in
good conscience to acquiesce in the latest form of "alternative
affirmation" which has been demanded.

115

I shall not go into matters which carry over from the issue of the special oath. But I may say that the constitutional oath still seems to me to cover admirably and fully my obligations to country, state, and job. I still resent being asked to affirm that I meant what I said when I signed the constitutional oath. One could accept such an additional affirmation wherever and whenever it might seem effective in a special emergency. To me, this contract is an empty gesture toward meeting the danger of infiltration into academic life of indoctrinators, conspirators, and spies. For a subversive person need not have a party card; a conspirator is not bound by declarations; a party member need not have a party card; a party member may be unknown to any but a few; a would-be commissar would not ask you for a hearing; and a fanatic indoctrinator may not feel that he lies when he says that he represents objective truth.

One may say, then, Why not acquiesce in an empty gesture, if it saves the faces of very important personages, helps to allay public hysteria, and hurts nobody? My answer is that of a psychologist. I do believe that this gesture which now saves face for some important people will, in the long run, hurt people who are much more important: the students. Too much has been said of academic freedom for the faculty; I am concerned about certain dangers to the spirit of the student body, dangers which may emanate from such "compromises" as we have been asked to accept.

For many students, their years of study represent their only contact with thought and theory, their only contact with men who teach them how to see two sides of a question and yet to be decisive in their conclusions, how to understand and yet to act with conviction. Young people are rightfully suspicious and embarrassingly discerning. I do not believe they can remain unimpressed by the fact that the men who are to teach them to think and to act judiciously and spontaneously must undergo a political test; must sign a statement which implicitly questions the validity of their own oath of office; must abrogate "commitments" so undefined that they must forever suspect themselves and one another; and must confess to an "objective truth" which they know only too well is elusive. Older people like ourselves can laugh this off; in younger people, however,—and especially in those most important students who are motivated to go into teaching—a dangerous rift may well occur between the "official truth" and those deep and often radical doubts which are the necessary conditions for the development of thought.

By the same token, the gesture of the contract will not allay public hysteria. I know that the general public at the moment indulges (as it always does when it is confronted with change) in a "bunching together" of all that seems undefinably dangerous: spies, bums, Communists, liberals, and "professors." A few politicians always thrive on such oversimplification, some out of simplicity, some out of shrewdness. But who, if the universities do not, will lead the countermove of enlightenment? Who will represent, in quiet work and in forceful words, the absolute necessity of meeting the future (now full of worse than dynamite) with a conviction born of judiciousness? If the universities themselves become the puppets of public hysteria, if their own regents are expressly suspicious of their faculties, if the professors themselves tacitly admit that they need to deny perjury, year after year—will that allay public hysteria?

If the Regents and the President had asked the faculty to join in a study of what Communism is—abroad, in this country, and on this campus—a study of what we need and can do about it, and what we need and can do against it; we all would have participated to the limit of our competency. Instead, the faculty was taken by surprise and hopelessly put on the defensive, in this most vital matter. This is a thoughtless, and if stubbornly pursued, a ruthless waste of human resources.

I realize that the University of California is a big place, with many purposes. In many departments the danger which I have outlined will not interfere with the finding and teaching of facts. Mine is a highly specialized place in an area of knowledge still considered rather marginal to true science. My field includes the study of "hysteria," private and public, in "personality" and "culture." It includes the study of the tremendous waste in human energy which proceeds from irrational fear and from the irrational gestures which are part of what we call "history." I would find it difficult to ask my subject of investigation (people) and my students to work with me, if I were to participate without protest in a vague, fearful, and somewhat vindictive gesture devised to ban an evil in some magic way—an evil which must be met with much more searching and concerted effort.

In this sense, I may say that my conscience did not permit me to sign the contract after having sworn that I would do my job to the best of my ability.

(Sgd) Erik H. Erikson
Professor of Psychology and Lecturer in Psychiatry

Berkeley, California, June 1st, 1950

A SHORT SUMMARY OF EVENTS

Prepared by the Committee for the Study of Several Issues
of the American Psychoanalytic Association

Every professor at the University of California used to take the following oath of office: "I do solemnly swear that I will support the Constitution of the United States and the Constitution of the State of California, and that I will faithfully discharge the duties of my office according to the best of my ability." In May, 1949, the Regents, without consultation with the faculty, added the following loyalty oath: "I do not believe in and am not a member of nor do I support any party or organization that believes in, advocates or teaches the overthrow of the United States government by force or violence." As a result of the protests of the faculty this loyalty oath was superseded on April 21, 1950 by the following contractual clause to be sworn to every year: ". . . and I also state that I am not a member of the Communist Party or any other organization which advocates the overthrow of the Government by force or violence and that

I have no commitments in conflict with my responsibilities with respect to impartial scholarship and free pursuit of truth."

Between May 15th and July 15th of 1950, all those who had refused to sign this special letter of acceptance (approximately 90) appeared for hearings before the Committee on Privilege and Tenure. None of them was found to be a Communist. Sooner or later all were recommended by the Committee for reappointment. On July 21, 1950, President Sproul recommended to the Board of Regents the reappointment of the nonsigners then cleared by the Committee on Privilege and Tenure. The Regents, by a majority of 11 to 9, reappointed the nonsigners. One Regent indicated an intent to move for reconsideration at the next meeting. From August 1st, 1950 on, the nonsigners failed to receive any salary for the new academic years or any letters of appointment. On August 25, 1950, Counsel for the Regents publicly advised them that the proposed revocation of appointments was contrary to state law. Governor Warren presiding, ruled accordingly, but an appeal from this ruling carried by a vote of 12 to 10. The Regents then by the same majority voted to revoke the appointments. President Sproul and Governor Warren voted with the minority; Admiral Nimitz, unable to attend, wired his opposition to the revocation. All Regents agreed that there was no charge of Communism. The dismissals were "a matter of discipline." The Regents voted that every nonsigner was to have a period of ten days within which to sign the special contract or to resign from the University as of June 30, 1950. On September 26th, 1950, the Academic Senate, Northern Section, adopted a resolution condemning the action of the Board of Regents in revoking the appointments of the nonsigners.

There were three issues involved: (1) After years of trial and testing, professors in the higher ranks have tenure, i.e., they are assured that they will not be subject to dismissal except on charges of incompetence or moral turpitude, judged by their colleagues. The breaking of these tenure agreements by dismissal of the nonsigners was regarded as destructive to the good name of the University. (2) Since the Middle Ages, universities have demanded self-government, namely, that no professor will be appointed except on faculty recommendation and no professor will be dismissed except with faculty consent. The action of the Regents was regarded as an infringement of the self-government. (3) The additional loyalty oath and contract clause was regarded by the nonsigners as an attempt at thought control and an insult to their dignity. This issue is best expressed in the enclosed letter by Mr. Erikson.

Of the more than 20 members of the American Psychoanalytic Association and candidates-in-training teaching at the University of California, the majority signed under protest. Dr. Norman Reider, M.D., Assistant Clinical Professor of Psychiatry, refused and was not reappointed. Erik H. Erikson, Professor of Psychology and Lecturer in Psychoanalysis, refused, was reappointed, but resigned.

8.

The Dream Specimen of Psychoanalysis

ERIK H. ERIKSON

I. ORIENTATION

Before embarking on advanced exercises in the clinical use of dream interpretation, it seems an attractive task to return, once more, to the "first dream ever subjected to an exhaustive interpretation." This, of course, is Freud's dream of his patient Irma (1900). While Freud has by no means published a full account of his exhaustive analysis, he, nevertheless, has offered this dream to his students as the original dream "specimen." For this reason (and for others, only dimly felt up to the time when Freud's letters to Fliess [1950] were published) the "Irma Dream" has imprinted itself on the minds of many as a truly historical document; and it seems instructive to discuss this dream once more with the specific purpose of enlarging upon some aspects of dream interpretation which we today, half a century later, would consider essential to an exhaustive analysis.

As we review in our minds the incidents of dream analysis in our daily practice and in our seminars and courses, it must

This chapter was first presented in 1949, in the form of two lectures, in the Seminar on Dream Interpretation of the San Francisco Psychoanalytic Institute. Somewhat enlarged after the publication of Freud's letters to Fliess.

121

be strikingly clear that the art and ritual of "exhaustive" dream analysis has all but vanished. Our advanced technique of psychoanalysis, with its therapeutic zeal and goal-directed awareness of ever-changing transference and resistances, rarely, maybe too rarely, permits that intellectual partnership, that common curiosity between analyst and patient which would take a good-sized dream seriously enough to make it the object of a few hours' concerted analysis. We know too well that patients learn to exploit our interest in dreams by telling us in profuse nocturnal productions what they should struggle and learn to tell us in straight words. And we have learned (or so we think) to find in other sources what in Freud's early days could be garnered only from dreams. Therefore, we feel that even a periodic emphasis on dreams today is wasteful and may even be deleterious to therapy. But let us admit that such restraint, more often than not, is a policy of scarcity rather than abundance; and that the daily choice of dream data, made necessary by such restraint, is more arbitrary and often whimsical than systematic. The truth is that the privilege of using choice and restraint in the interpretation of dreams must be earned; only sufficient regard, at least during the years of training, for the art of total dream analysis, brought up to date at each stage of the development of psychoanalysis, can help a candidate in psychoanalytic training to graduate to that much more advanced practice (now freely granted to beginners) of picking from a patient's daily dream productions whatever dream fragments, symbols, manifest images, and latent dream thoughts support the prevalent trend of interpretations. It stands to reason that a psychoanalyst can know which dream details he may single out for the purposes of the day only if, at least preconsciously, he has somehow grasped the meaning of the whole dream in relation to the course of the analysis and in relation to the course of the patient's life.

Such grasp can become a firm possession of the analyst's preconscious mental activity only if he has acquired by repeated exercise the potential mastery of the whole inventory of manifest leads, associational trends, and relevant life data which make up a whole dream. If he can learn this in his own analysis, so much the better. Some must learn it later, when dream analysis becomes the main vehicle of self-analysis. In the course of formal training, however, "exhaustive" dream analysis can best be studied in connection with those seminars, usually called "continuous," in which the study of the history of a whole treatment permits a thorough assessment of the inventory of forces, trends, and images in a patient's life including his dream life. I propose that we prepare ourselves for the task of this total analysis by taking up once more Freud's dream of his patient Irma.

To reinterpret a dream means to reinterpret the dreamer. Let me, therefore, discuss first the spirit in which we undertake such a reinterpretation.

No man has ever consciously and knowingly revealed more of himself, for the sake of human advance, than did Freud. At the same time, he drew firm lines where he felt that self-revelation should come to an end, because the possible scientific gain was not in proportion to the pain of self-exhibition and to the inconvenience of calumny. If we, in passing, must spell out more fully than Freud did certain latent dream thoughts suggested by him, we are guided by the consideration that the most legitimate didactic use of the personal data of Freud's life concerns a circumscribed area of investigation, namely, the dynamics of creative thought in general and, specifically, in psychoanalytic work. It seems to us that the publication of Freud's letters to Fliess points in this direction (1950).

In reviewing the dream of Irma, we shall focus our attention, beyond the fragmentary indices of familiar infantile and neurotic conflicts, primarily on the relation of this very dream to the moment in Freud's life when it was dreamed—to the moment when creative thought gave birth to the interpretation of dreams. For the dream of Irma owes its significance not only to the fact that it was the first dream reported in *The Interpretation of Dreams* (1900). In a letter sent to his friend Fliess, Freud indulges in a fancy of a possible tablet which (he wonders) may sometimes adorn his summer home. Its inscription would tell the world that "In this house, on July 24, 1895, the Mystery of the Dream unveiled [enthullte] itself to Dr. Sigm. Freud"

(1950). The date is that of the Irma Dream. Such autobiographic emphasis, then, supports our contention that this
dream may reveal more than the basic fact of a disguised wish
fulfillment derived from infantile sources; that this dream may,
in fact, carry the historical burden of being dreamed in order
to be analyzed, and analyzed in order to fulfill a very special
fate.

   This, then, is our specific curiosity regarding the dream of
Irma. We can advance this approach only in the general course
of demonstrating the dimensions of our kind of "exhaus-
tiveness" in the interpretation of dreams.

   But first, the background of the dream, the dream itself,
and Freud's interpretation.

II. THE IRMA DREAM, MANIFEST AND LATENT

The dreamer of the Irma Dream was a thirty-nine-year-old doctor, a specialist in neurology in the city of Vienna. He was a
Jewish citizen of a Catholic monarchy, once the Holy Roman
Empire of German Nationality, and now swayed both by liberal-
ism and increasing anti-Semitism. His family had grown rapidly;
in fact, his wife at the time was again pregnant. The dreamer
just then wished to fortify his position and, in fact, his income
by gaining academic status. This wish had become problematic,
not only because he was a Jew but also because in a recent
joint publication with an older colleague, Dr. Breuer, he had
committed himself to theories so unpopular and, in fact, so
universally disturbing that the senior co-author himself had dis-
engaged himself from the junior one. The book in question
(Studies on Hysteria) had emphasized the role of sexuality in
the etiology of the "defense neuropsychoses," i.e., nervous disorders caused by the necessity of defending consciousness
against repugnant and repressed ideas, primarily of a sexual
nature. The junior worker felt increasingly committed to these
ideas; he had begun to feel, with a pride often overshadowed
by despair, that he was destined to make a revolutionary discovery by (I shall let this stand) undreamed-of means.

It had occurred to Freud by then that the dream was, in fact, a normal equivalent of a hysterical attack, "a little defense neuropsychosis." In the history of psychiatry, the comparison of normal phenomena with abnormal ones was not new: the Greeks had called orgasm "a little epilepsy." But if hysterical symptoms, if even dreams, were based on inner conflict, on an involuntary defense against unconscious thoughts, what justification was there for blaming patients for the fact that they could not easily accept, nor long remember, and not consistently utilize the interpretations which the psychiatrist offered them? What use was there in scolding the patient, as Bernheim had done: "vous vous contre-suggestionez, madame?" "Defense," "transference," and "resistance" were the mechanisms, the concepts, and the tools to be elucidated in the years to come. It was soon to dawn on Freud that in order to give shape to these tools, a basic shift from physiologic concepts (to which he was as yet committed) to purely psychological ones, and from exact and sober medical and psychotherapeutic techniques to intuitive observation, even to self-observation, was necessary.

This, then, is the situation: within an academic milieu which seemed to restrict his opportunities because he was a Jew; at an age when he seemed to notice with alarm the first signs of aging, and, in fact, of disease; burdened with the responsibility for a fast growing family—a medical scientist is faced with the decision of whether to employ his brilliance, as he had shown he could, in the service of conventional practice and research, or to accept the task of substantiating in himself and of communicating to the world a new insight, namely, that man is unconscious of the best and of the worst in himself. Soon after the Irma Dream, Freud was to write to his friend Fliess with undisguised horror that in trying to explain defense he had found himself explaining something "out of the core of nature." At the time of this dream, then, he knew that he would have to bear a great discovery.

The evening before the dream was dreamed, Freud had an experience which had painfully spotlighted his predicament. He had met a colleague, "Otto," who had just returned from a summer resort. There he had seen a mutual friend, a young woman, who was Freud's patient: "Irma." This patient, by Freud's effort, had been cured of hysterical anxiety, but not of certain somatic symptoms, such as intense retching. Before going on vacation, Freud had offered her an interpretation as the solution of her problems; but she had been unable to accept it. Freud had shown impatience. Patient and doctor had thus found themselves in a deadlock which made a righteous disciplinarian out of the doctor and a stubborn child out of the patient: not a healthy condition for the communication of insight. It was, of course, this very kind of deadlock which Freud learned later on to formulate and utilize for a working through of resistance. At the time, Freud apparently had heard some reproach in Otto's voice regarding the condition of the patient who appeared "better, but not well"; and behind the reproach he thought to detect the stern authority of "Dr. M.," a man who was "the leading personality in our circle." On his return home, and under the impression of the encounter, Freud had written a lengthy case report for "Dr. M.," explaining his views on Irma's illness.

He had apparently gone to bed with a feeling that this report would settle matters so far as his own peace of mind was concerned. Yet that very night the personages concerned in this incident, namely, Irma, Dr. M., Dr. Otto, and another doctor, Dr. Leopold, constituted themselves the population of the following dream (1900, pp. 196–197).

> A great hall—a number of guests, whom we are receiving—among them Irma, whom I immediately take aside, as though to answer her letter, and to reproach her for not yet accepting the "solution." I say to her: "If you [du][1] still have pains, it is really only your own fault."—She answers: "If you [du] only knew what pains I have now in the throat, stomach, and abdomen—I am choked by them." I am startled, and look at her. She looks pale and puffy. I think that after all I must be overlooking some organic affection. I take her to the window

[1] German words in brackets indicate that the writer will question and discuss A. A. Brill's translation of these words.

and look into her throat. She offers some resistance to this, like a woman who has a set of false teeth. I think, surely she doesn't need them [sie hat es doch nicht notig].—The mouth then opens wide, and I find a large white spot on the right, and elsewhere I see extensive grayish-white scabs adhering to curiously curled formations which are evidently shaped like the turbinal bones of the nose.—I quickly call Dr. M., who repeats the examination and confirms it. Dr. M. looks quite unlike his usual self; he is very pale, he limps, and his chin is clean-shaven [bartlos]. . . . Now my friend, Otto, too, is standing beside her, and my friend Leopold percusses her covered chests and says: "She has a dullness below, on the left," and also calls attention to an infiltrated portion of skin on the left shoulder (which I can feel in spite of the dress). M. says, "There's no doubt that it's an infection, but it doesn't matter; dysentery will follow and the poison will be eliminated.". . We know, too, precisely [unmittelbar] how the infection originated. My friend, Otto, not long ago, gave her, when she was feeling unwell, an injection of a preparation of propyl. . . .propyls. . . .propionic acid. . . .trimethylamin (the formula of which I see before me, printed in heavy type). . . . One doesn't give such injections so rashly. . . . Probably, too, the syringe [Spritzed] was not clean.

I must assume here that Freud's associations to this dream are known to all readers, in all the literary freshness which they have in *The Interpretation of Dreams,* and in all the convincing planlessness of true associations, which, unforeseen and often unwelcome, make their determined entrance like a host of unsorted strangers, until they gradually become a chorus echoing a few central themes. Here I must select and classify.

Irma proves, first of all, to be the representative of a series of *women patients.* Freud remembers a number of *young women* in connection with the question whether or not they were willing to accept their therapist's "solution." Besides Irma, who we now hear is a rosy young *widow,* a *governess* comes to memory, also of youthful beauty, who had resisted an examination because she wanted to hide her false teeth. The dreamer remembers that it had been this governess about whom he had had the angry thought (which in the dream he expresses in regard to Irma), namely, *"Sie hat es doch nicht notig"* (incorrectly translated as, "She does not need them"). This trend of association establishes an analogy between women patients who will not accept solutions, who will not yield to examination, and who will not submit to advances, although their status promises an easy yielding: young widows, young governesses. Fifty years ago as well as today, suspicions concerning young women patients and especially "merry widows" found their way into medical wit, rumor, and scandal. They were accentuated at the time by the common but not officially admitted knowledge that the large contingent of hysterical women was starved for sexual adventure. On the sly it was suggested that the doctor might as well remove their inhibitions by deeds as well as words. It was Freud who established the fact that the hysterical patient transfers to the doctor by no means a simply sexual wish, but rather an unconscious conflict between an infantile wish and an infantile inhibition. Medical ethics aside, neither satisfaction nor cure could ensue from a sexual consummation of the transference.

But then other kinds of patients—men, women, and children—impose themselves on the dreamer's memory: *"good ones"* who fared *badly,* and *"bad ones"* who, maybe, were *better off.* Two hysterical ladies had accepted his "solutions" and had become worse; one had died. As to *obstreperous* patients, the dreamer must admit that he thinks of a very occasional patient, his own wife, and he must confess that even she is not at ease with him as the ideal patient would be. But are there any easy, any ideal patients? Yes, *children.* They do not "put on airs." In those Victorian days, little girls were the only female patients who undressed for examination matter-of-factly. And, we may add, children oblige the dream interpreter by dreaming simple wish fulfillments where adults build up such complicated defenses against their own wishes—and against the interpretation of dreams.

In speaking of his *men patients,* the dreamer is ruthless with himself and his memories. Years ago he had played a leading role in research which demonstrated the usefulness of cocaine for local anesthesia, especially in the eye. But it took some time to learn the proper dosage and the probable dangers: a dear friend died of misuse of cocaine. Other men patients come to mind, also *badly* off. And then there are memories concerning the *dreamer himself in his double role as patient and as doctor. He had given himself injections for swellings in the nose. Had he harmed himself?*

Finally the dreamer, apparently looking for a friend in his dilemma, thinks of his oldest and staunchest admirer, a doctor in another city, who knows all his *"germinating ideas,"* and who has fascinating ideas regarding the relationship of *nose and sexuality* and regarding the phasic aspect of conception; but, alas, he too has a *nasal affliction.* This faraway doctor is no other than Dr. Fliess, whom Freud at the time was consulting, confiding his emotions and his ideas, and in whom he was soon to confide his very self-analysis.

To state the case which Freud at the time wished to make we shall quote from his lengthy summary (1900, pp. 204–207).

The dream fulfills several wishes which were awakened within me by the events of the previous evening (Otto's news, and the writing of the clinical history). For the result of the dream is that it is not I who am to blame for the pain which Irma is still suffering, but that Otto is to blame for it. Now Otto has annoyed me by his remark about Irma's imperfect cure; the dream avenges me upon him, in that it turns the reproach upon himself. The dream acquits me of responsibility for Irma's condition, as it refers this condition to other causes (which do, indeed, furnish quite a number of explanations). The dream represents a certain state of affairs, such as I might wish to exist; *the content of the dream is thus the fulfillment of a wish; its motive is a wish.*

This much is apparent at first sight. But many other details of the dream become intelligible when regarded from the standpoint of wish fulfillment. I take my revenge on Otto. . . . Nor do I pass over Dr. M.'s contradiction; for I express in an obvious allusion my opinion of him: namely, that his attitude in this case is that of an ignoramus ("Dysentery will develop, etc."). Indeed, it seems as though I were appealing from him to someone better informed (my friend, who told me about trimethylamin), just as I have turned from Irma to her friend, and from Otto to Leopold. It is as though I were to say: Rid me of these three persons, replace them by three others of my own choice, and I shall be rid of the reproaches which I am not willing to admit that I deserve! In my dream the unreasonableness of these reproaches is demonstrated for me in the most elaborate manner. Irma's pains are not attributable to me, since she herself is to blame for them in that she refuses to accept my solution. They do not concern me, for being as they are of an organic nature, they cannot possibly be cured by psychic treatment.—Irma's sufferings are satisfactorily explained by her widowhood (trimethylamin); a state which I cannot alter.—Irma's illness has been caused by an incautious injection administered by Otto, an injection of an unsuitable drug, such as I should never have administered.—Irma's complaint is the result of an injection made with an unclean syringe, like the phlebitis of my old lady patient, whereas my injections have never caused any ill effects. I am aware that these explanations of Irma's illness, which unite in acquitting me, do not agree with one another; that they even exclude one another. The whole plea—for this dream is nothing else—recalls vividly the defense offered by a man who was accused by his neighbor of having returned a kettle in a damaged condition. In the first place, he said, he had returned the kettle undamaged; in the second place, it already had holes in it when he borrowed it; and in the third place, he had never borrowed it at all. A complicated defense, but so much the better; if only one of these three lines of defense is recognized as valid, the man must be acquitted.

Still other themes play a part in the dream, and their relation to my non-responsibility for Irma's illness is not so apparent. . . . But if I keep all these things in view they combine into a single train of thought which might be labeled: concern for the health of myself and others; professional conscientiousness. I recall a vaguely disagreeable feeling when Otto gave me the news of Irma's condition. Lastly, I am inclined, after the event, to find an expression of this fleeting sensation in the train of thoughts which forms part of the dream. It is as though Otto had said to me: "You do not take your medical duties seriously enough; you are not conscientious; you do not perform what you promise." Thereupon this train of thought placed itself at my service, in order that I might give proof of my extreme conscientiousness, of my intimate concern about the health of my relatives, friends and patients. Curiously enough, there are also some painful memories in this material, which confirm the blame attached to Otto rather than my own exculpation. The material is apparently impartial, but the connection between this broader material, on which the dream is based, and the more limited theme from which emerges the wish to be innocent of Irma's illness, is, nevertheless, unmistakable.

I do not wish to assert that I have entirely revealed the meaning of the dream, or that my interpretation is flawless. . . .

For the present I am content with the one fresh discovery which has just been made: If the method of dream-interpretation here indicated is followed, it will be found that dreams do really possess a meaning, and are by no means the expression of a disintegrated cerebral activity, as the writers on the subject would have us believe. *When the work of interpretation has been completed the dream can be recognized as a wish-fulfillment.*

We note that the wish demonstrated here is not more than preconscious. Furthermore, this demonstration is not carried through as yet to the infantile sources postulated later in *The Interpretation of Dreams.* Nor is the theme of sexuality carried through beyond a point which is clearly intended to be understood by the trained reader and to remain vague to the untrained one. The Irma Dream, then, serves Freud as a very first step toward the task of the interpretation of dreams, namely, the establishment of the fact that dreams have their own "rationale," which can be detected by the study of the "work" which dreams accomplish, in transforming the latent dream thoughts into manifest dream images. Dream work uses certain methods (condensation, displacement, symbolization) in order to derive a set of manifest dream images which, on analysis, prove to be significantly connected with a practically limitless number of latent thoughts and memories, reaching from the trigger event of the preceding day, through a chain of relevant memories, back into the remotest past and down into the reservoir of unconscious, forgotten, or unclearly evaluated, but lastingly significant, impressions.

Our further efforts, then, must go in two directions. First, we must spell out, for the Irma Dream, certain latent connections, which in *The Interpretation of Dreams,* for didactic reasons, are dealt with only in later chapters: here we think primarily of the dream's sexual themata, and their apparent relation to certain childhood memories, which in Freud's book follow the Irma Dream by only a number of pages. And we must focus on areas of significance which are only implicit in *The Interpretation of Dreams* but have become more explicit in our lifetime. Here I have in mind, first of all, the relationship of the latent dream thought to the dream's manifest surface as it may appear to us today after extensive studies of other forms of imaginative represensation, such as children's play; and then, the relationship of the dream's "inner population" to the dreamer's social and cultural surroundings.

I propose to approach this multidimensional task, not by an immediate attempt at "going deeper" than Freud did, but, on the contrary, by taking a fresh look at the whole of the manifest dream. This approach, however, will necessitate a brief discussion of a general nature.

III. Dimensions of the Manifest Dream

The psychoanalyst, in looking at the surface of a mental phenomenon, often has to overcome a certain shyness. So many in his field mistake attention to surface for superficiality, and a concern with form for lack of depth. But the fact that we have followed Freud into depths which our eyes had to become accustomed to does not permit us, today, to blink when we look at things in broad daylight. Like good surveyors, we must be at home on the geological surface as well as in the descending shafts. In recent years, so-called projective techniques, such as the Rorschach Test, the Thematic Apperception Test, and the observation of children's play, have clearly shown that any segment of overt behavior reflects, as it were, the whole store: one might say that psychoanalysis has given new depth to the surface, thus building the basis for a more inclusive general psychology of man. It takes the clinical psychoanalytic method proper to determine which items of a man's total behavior and experience are amenable to consciousness, are preconscious, or unconscious, and why and how they became and remained unconscious; and it takes this method to establish a scale of pathogenic significance in his conscious and unconscious motivations. But in our daily work, in our clinical discussions and nonclinical applications, and even in our handling of dreams, it has become a matter of course that any item of human behavior shows a continuum of dynamic meaning, reaching from the surface through many layers of crust to the "core." Unofficially, we often interpret dreams entirely or in parts on the basis of their manifest appearance. Officially, we hurry at every confrontation with a dream to crack its manifest appearance as if it were a useless shell and to hasten to discard this shell in favor of what seems to be the more worthwhile core. When such a method corresponded to a new orientation, it was essential for research as well as for therapy; but as a compulsive habituation, it has since hindered a full meeting of ego psychology and the problems of dream life.[2]

Let us, then, systematically begin with the most "superficial": our first impression of the manifest dream. After years of practice one seems to remember, to compare, and to discuss the dreams of others (and even the reports given to us of dreams reported to others) in such a matter-of-fact manner that one reminds himself only with some effort of the fact that one has never seen anybody else's dream nor has the slightest proof that it ever "happened" the way one visualizes it. A dream is a verbal report of a series of remembered images, mostly visual, which are usually endowed with affect. The

---

[2] "Formerly I found it extraordinarily difficult to accustom my readers to the distinction between the manifest dream-content and the latent dream-thoughts. Over and over again arguments and objections were adduced from the uninterpreted dream as it was retained in the memory, and the necessity of interpreting the dream was ignored. But now, when the analysts have at least become reconciled to substituting for the manifest dream its meaning as found by interpretation, many of them are guilty of another mistake, to which they adhere just as stubbornly. They look for the essence of the dream in this latent content, and thereby overlook the distinction between latent dream-thoughts and the dream-work. The dream is fundamentally nothing more than a special *form* of our thinking, which is made possible by the conditions of the sleeping state. It is the dream-work which produces this form, and it alone is the essense of dreaming—the only explanation of its singularity" [1900, pp. 466–467].

dreamer may be limited or especially gifted, inhibited or over-eager in the range of his vocabulary and in its availability for dream reports; in his ability to revisualize and in his motivation to verbalize all the shades of what is visualized; in his ability to report stray fragments or in the compulsion to spin a meaning-ful yarn; or in his capacity or willingness to describe the range of his affects. The report of a dream, in turn, arouses in each listener and interpreter a different set of images, which are as incommunicable as is the dream itself. Every dream seminar gives proof that different people are struck by different vari-ables of the manifest dream (or, as I would like to call them, by dream configurations) in different ways, and this by no means only because of a different theoretical approach, as is often hastily concluded, but because of variations in sensory and emotional responsiveness. Here early overtraining can do much harm, in that, for example, the immediate recognition of standardized symbols, or the immediate recognition of verbal double meanings may induce the analyst to reach a premature closure in his conviction of having listened to and "under-stood" a dream and of understanding dreams in general. It takes practice to realize that the manifest dream contains a wealth of indicators not restricted to what the listener happens to be receptive for. The most important of these indicators are, it is true, verbal ones; but the mere experiment of having a patient retell toward the end of an analytic hour a dream re-ported at the beginning will make it quite clear to what extent a verbal report is, after all, a process of trying to communicate something which is never completely and successfully rendered in any one verbal formulation. Each completed formulation is, of course, a complete item for analysis; and once told, the mem-ory of the first verbal rendering of a dream more or less re-places the visual memory of it, just as a childhood experience often retold by oneself or described by others becomes inextri-cably interwoven with the memory itself.

I pause here for an illustration, the shortest illustration, from my practice. A young woman patient of German descent once reported a dream which consisted of nothing but the image of the word S[E]INE (with the "E" in brackets), seen light against a dark background. The patient was well-traveled and educated and it therefore seemed plausible to follow the first impression, namely, that this image of a word contained, in fact, a play of words in a variety of languages. The whole word is the French river SEINE, and indeed it was in Paris (France) that the patient had been overcome with agoraphobia. The same French word, if heard and spelled as a German word, is SEHN, i.e., "to see," and indeed it was after a visit to the Louvre that the patient had been immobilized: there now existed a complete amnesia for what she had seen there. The whole word, again, can also be perceived as the German word SEINE, meaning "his." The letter "E" is the first letter of my name and probably served as an anchorage for the transference in the dream. If the letter "E" is put aside, the word becomes the Latin SINE, which means "without." All of this combined makes for the riddle "To see (E) without his . . . . in Paris." This riddle was solved through a series of free associations which, by way of appropriate childhood memories of a voyeuristic character and through the analysis of a first transference formation, led to the visual recovery of one of the forgotten pictures: It was a *Circumcision of Christ.* There she had seen the boy Savior without that mysterious loincloth which adorns Christ on the Crucifix—the loincloth which her sacrilegious eyes had often tucked at during prayers. (The dream word SEINE also contains the word SIN.) This sacrilegious and aggressive curiosity had been shocked into sudden prominence by the picture in the Louvre, only to be abruptly repressed again because of the special inner conditions brought about by the state of adolescence and by the visit to the capital of sensuality. It had now been transferred to the analyst, by way of the hysterical overevaluation of his person as a therapeutic savior.

The presence of meaningful verbal configurations in this dream is very clear. Less clear is the fact that the very absence of other configurations is equally meaningful. That something was only *seen,* and in fact focused upon with the exclusion of all other sensory experiences (such as spatial extension, motion, shading, color, sound, and, last but not least, the awareness of a dream population) is, of course, related to the various aspects of the visual trauma: to the symptom of visual amnesia, to an attempt to restore the repressed image in order to gain cure by mastery, and to a transference of the original voyeuristic drive onto the person of the analyst. We take it for granted that the wish to revive and to relive the repressed impulse immediately "muscles" its way into the wish to be cured. That the dream space was dark and completely motionless around a clear image was an inverted representation of the patient's memory of the trauma: an area with a dark spot in the center (the repressed picture) and surrounded by lively and colorful halls, milling crowds, and noisy and dangerous traffic, in bright sunlight. The lack of motion in the dream corresponds to the patient's symptoms: agoraphobia and immobilization (based on early determined defense mechanisms) were to end the turmoil of those adolescent days and bring to a standstill the struggle between sexual curiosity and a sense of sin. There was no time dimension in the dream, and there was none in the patient's by now morbid psychic life. As is often the case with hysterics, a relative inability to perceive the passage of time had joined the symptom of spatial avoidance, just as blind anxiety had absorbed all conflicting affects. Thus, all the omitted dimensions of the manifest dream, with the help of associations, could be made to converge on the same issues on which the one overclear dimension (the visual one) was focused. But the choice of the manifest dream representation, i.e., the intelligent use of multilingual word play in a visual riddle, itself proved highly overdetermined and related to the patient's gifts and opportunities: for it was in superior esthetic aspirations that the patient had found a possible sphere of conflict-free activity and companionship. In the cultivation of her sensitive senses, she could see and hear sensually, without being consciously engaged in sexual fantasies; and in being clever and witty she had, on occasion, come closest to replacing a son to her father. This whole area of functioning, then, had remained more or less free of conflict, until, at the time of accelerated sexual maturation and under the special conditions of a trip, sacrilegious thoughts in connection with an esthetic-intellectual endeavor had brought about a short-circuit in her whole system of defenses and reasonably conflict-free intellectual functions: the wish to see and feel esthetically, again, converged on sexual and sinful objects. While it is obvious, then, that the desublimated drive fragment of sacrilegious voyeurism is the force behind this dream (and, in this kind of case, necessarily became the focus of therapeutic interpretation) the total dream, in all of its variables, has much more to say about the relationship of this drive fragment to the patient's ego development.

I have temporarily abandoned the Irma Dream for the briefest dream of my clinical experience in order to emphasize the fact that a dream has certain formal aspects which combine to an inventory of configurations, even though some of these configurations may shine only by their absence. In addition to a dream's striving for *representability,* then, we would postulate a *style of representation* which is by no means a mere shell to the kernel, the latent dream; in fact, it is a reflection of the individual ego's peculiar time-space (Erikson, 1950a), the frame of reference for all its defenses, compromises, and achievements (Erikson, 1950b). Our "Outline of Dream Analysis" (Chart I), consequently, begins with an inventory of Manifest Configurations, which is meant to help us, in any given dream or series of dreams, to recognize the interplay of commissions and omissions, of overemphases and underemphases. As mentioned before, such an inventory, once having been thoroughly practiced, must again become a preconscious set of general expectations, against which the individual style of each dream stands out in sharp contour. It will then become clear that the dream life of some (always, or during certain periods, or in individual dream events) is characterized by a greater clarity of the experience of *spatial* extension and of motion (or the arrest of motion) in space; that of others by the flow or the stoppage of *time;* other dreams are dominated by clear *somatic* sensations or their marked absence; by a rich *interpersonal* dream life with an (often stereotyped) dream population or by a pronounced aloneness; by an overpowering experience of marked *affects* or their relative absence or lack of specificity. Only an equal attention to all of these variables and their configurations can help the analyst to train himself for an awareness of the varieties of manifest dream life, which in turn permits the exact characterization of a given patient's manifest dream life at different times of his treatment.

As for Part II of our "Outline" (Links between Manifest and Latent Material), the peculiar task of this paper has brought it about that the dreamer's associations have already been discussed, while some of the principal symbols still await recognition and employment.

IV. VERBAL CONFIGURATIONS

In the attempt now to demonstrate in what way a systematic use of the configurational analysis of the manifest dream (in constant interplay with the analysis of the latent content) may serve to enrich our understanding of the dream work, I find myself immediately limited by the fact that the very first item on our list, namely, "verbal configurations," cannot be profitably pursued here, because the Irma Dream was dreamed and reported in a German of both intellectual and colloquial sophistication which, I am afraid, transcends the German of the reader's high school and college days. But it so happens that the English translation of the Irma Dream which lies before us contains a number of conspicuous simplifications in translation, or, rather, translations so literal that an important double meaning gets lost. This, in a mental product to be analyzed, can be seriously misleading, while it is questionable that any translation could avoid such mistakes; in the meantime we may profit from insight into the importance of colloquial and linguistic configurations. Actually, what is happening in this translation from one language into another offers analogies with "translations" from any dreamer's childhood idiom to that of his adult years, or from the idiom of the dreamer's milieu to that of the analyst's. It seems especially significant that any such transfer to another verbal system of representation is not only accidentally to mistranslate single items, but to become the

CHART I: **OUTLINE OF DREAM ANALYSIS**

I. *Manifest Configurations*
Verbal
 general linguistic quality
 spoken words and word play
Sensory
 general sensory quality, range and intensity
 specific sensory focus
Spatial
 general quality of extension
 dominant vectors
Temporal
 general quality of succession time-perspective
Somatic
 general quality of body feeling
 body zones
 organ modes
Interpersonal
 general social grouping
 changing social vectors
 "object relations"
 points of identification
Affective
 quality of affective atmosphere
 inventory and range of affects
 points of change of affect
Summary
 correlation of configurational trends

II. *Links between Manifest and Latent Dream Material*
Associations
Symbols

III. *Analysis of Latent Dream Material*
Acute sleep-disturbing stimulus
Delayed stimulus (day residue)
Acute life conflicts
Dominant transference conflict
Repetitive conflicts
Associated basic childhood conflict
Common denominators
 "Wishes," drives, needs, methods of defense, denial, and distortion

CHART I: **OUTLINE OF DREAM ANALYSIS** (continued)

IV.   *Reconstruction*
      Life cycle
            present phase
            corresponding infantile phase
            defect, accident, or affliction
            psychosexual fixation
            psychosexual arrest
      Social process: collective identity
            ideal prototypes
            evil prototypes
            opportunities and barriers
      Ego identity and lifeplan
            mechanisms of defense
            mechanisms of integration

vehicle for a systematic misrepresentation of the whole mental product.

There is, to begin with, the little word *du,* with which the dreamer and Irma address one another and which is lost in the English "you." It seems innocent enough on the surface, yet may contain quite a therapeutic burden, a burden of counter-transference in reality and of special meaning in the dream. For with *du* one addressed, in those days and in those circles, only near relatives or very intimate friends. Did Freud in real life address the patient in this way—and (a much more weighty question) did she address the Herr Professor with this intimate little word? Or does the dreamer use this way of addressing the patient only in the dream? In either case, this little word carries the burden of the dreamer's sense of personal and social obligation to the patient, and thus of a new significance in his guilt over some negligence and in his wish that she should get well—an urgency of a kind which (as Freud has taught us since then) is disadvantageous to the therapeutic relation.

To enumerate other verbal ambiguities: there is a very arresting mistranslation in the phrase, "I think, surely she doesn't need *them,*" which makes it appear that the dreamer questions the necessity for Irma's false teeth. The German original, *"sie hat es doch nicht nötig,"* means literally, "she does not need *it,"* meaning her resistive behavior. In the colloquial Viennese of those days a richer version of the same phrase was *"das hat sie doch gar nicht nötig, sich so zu zieren,"* the closest English counterpart to which would be: "Who is she to put on such airs?" This expression includes a value judgment to the effect that a certain lady pretends that she is of a higher social, esthetic, or moral status than she really is. A related expression would be the protestation brought forth by a lady on the defense: *"Ich hate das doch gar nicht nötig, mir das gefallen zu lassen";* in English, "I don't need to take this from you," again referring to a misjudgment, this time on the part of a forward gentleman, as to what expectations he may cultivate in regard to a lady's willingness to accept propositions. These phrases, then, are a link between the associations concerning patients who resist "solutions," and women (patients or not) who resist sexual advances.

Further mistranslations continue this trend. For example, the fact that Dr. M.'s chin, in the dream, is *bartlos,* is translated with "clean-shaven." Now a clean-shaven appearance, in the America of today, would be a "must" for a professional man. It is, therefore, well to remember that the German word in the dream means "beardless." But this indicates that Dr. M. is minus something which in the Europe of those days was one of the very insignia of an important man, to wit, a distinctive beard or mustache. This one little word then denudes the leading critic's face, where the English translation would give it the luster of professional propriety: it is obvious that the original has closer relations to a vengeful castrative impulse on the part of the dreamer than the translation conveys.

Then, there is that little word *precisely* which will become rather relevant later in another context. In German one would expect the word *genau,* while one finds the nearly untranslatable *umittelbar* ("with a sense of immediacy"). In relation to something that is suddenly felt to be known (like the cause of Irma's trouble in the dream) this word refers rather to the degree of immediate and absolute conviction than to the precise quality of the knowledge; in fact, as Freud points out in his associations, the immediacy of this conviction really stood in remarkable contrast to the nonsensical quality of the diagnosis and the prognosis so proudly announced by Dr. M.

There remains the brief discussion of a play of words and of a most relevant simplification. It will have occurred to you that all the mistranslations mentioned so far (except "precisely") allude to sexual meanings, as if the Irma Dream permitted a complete sexual interpretation alongside the professional one—an inescapable expectation in any case.

The word play "propyl .... propyls .... propionic acid," which leads to the formula of trimethylamin, is so suggestive that I shall permit myself to go beyond the data at our disposal in order to provide our discussion of word play in dreams and in wit with an enlightening example. Freud associated "propyl" to the Greek word *propylon* (in Latin *vestibulum*, in German *Vorhof*), a term architectonic as well as anatomic, and symbolic of the entrance to the vagina; while "propionic" suggests *priapic*—phallic. This word play, then, would bring male and female symbols into linguistic vicinity to allude to a genital theme. The dream here seems to indulge in a mechanism common in punning. A witty word play has it, for example, that a mistress is "something between a mister and a mattress"—thus using a linguistic analogy to the principal spatial arrangement to which a mistress owes her status.

Finally, a word on the instrument which dispenses the "solution." The translation equips Dr. Otto with a "syringe" which gives the dream more professional dignity than the German original aspires to. The German word is *Spritze*, which is, indeed, used for syringes, but has also the colloquial meaning of "squirter." It will be immediately obvious that a squirter is an instrument of many connotations; of these, the phallic-urinary one is most relevant, for the use of a dirty syringe makes Otto a "dirty squirter," or "a little squirt," not just a careless physician. As we shall see later, the recognition of this double meaning is absolutely necessary for a pursuit of the infantile meaning of the Irma Dream.

The only verbal trend, then, which can be accounted for in this English discussion of a dream reported and dreamed in German induces us to put beside the interpretation of the Irma

Dream as a defense against the accusation of medical care-lessness (the dispensation of a "solution") and of a possible intellectual error (the solution offered to Irma) the suggestion of a related sexual theme, namely, a protest against the implication of some kind of sexual (self-) reproach.

In due time, we shall find the roots for this sexual theme in the dream's allusion to a childhood problem and then return to the dreamer's professional predicament.

We will then appreciate another double meaning in the dream, which seems to speak for the assumption that one link between the medical, the intellectual, and the sexual themes of the dream is that of "conception." The dream, so we hear, pictures a *birthday reception* in a great hall. "We receive" stands for the German *empfangen,* a word which can refer to conception *(Empfängnis)* as well as to reception *(Empfang)*. The dreamer's worries concerning the growth of his family at this critical time of his professional life are clearly expressed in the letters to Fliess. At the same time, the typical association between biological *conception* and intellectual *concept formation* can be seen in the repeated reference to "germinating ideas."

V. Interpersonal Configurations in the Dream Population

For a variety of reasons, it will be impossible to offer in this paper a separate discussion of each of the configurational variables listed in our "Outline." The medical implications of the sequence of *somatic* configurations must be ignored altogether, for I am not sufficiently familiar with the history of medicine to comprehend the anatomical, chemical, and procedural connotations which the body parts and the disease entities mentioned in the dream had in Freud's early days. The *sensory* configurations happen in this dream to fuse completely with the dreamer's *interpersonal* activities. Only once at a decisive point in the middle of the dream—there occurs a kinesthetic sensation. Otherwise, at the beginning as well as at the end of his dream the dreamer is "all eyes."

Most outstanding in his visual field, so it seems, is, at one time, Irma's oral cavity, and, at another, the formula trimethylamin, printed in heavy type. The infinite connotations of these

CHART II
Selected Manifest Configurations

I Interpersonal		II Affective	III Spatial	IV Temporal
The Dreamer	The Population			
1. WE are receiving	WIFE receives with him	Festive mood?	Spacious hall	Present
2. I take Irma aside	IRMA has not accepted the solution	Sense of urgency	Constricted to a "space for two"	Present
I reproach her		Sense of reproach		Past reaches into
3. I look at her	Complains, feels choked	Startle		Present, painful
4.	Looks pale and puffy			Present, painful
5. I think		Worry		Present, painful
6. I take her to window	Offers resistance	Impatience	Close to window	Present, painful
I look I think				
7.	THE MOUTH opens		Constricted to parts of persons	
8. I find, I see organic symptoms		Horror		
9. I quickly call Dr. M.	Dr. M. confirms symptoms	Dependence on authority		Present co-operative effort
10.	Looks pale, limps, is beardless			Present co-operative effort

CHART II (continued)

11.	OTTO, LEOPOLD, join examination	Present co-operative effort
12.	LEOPOLD point to infiltration	Present co-operative effort
13. I "feel" infiltration		
	Fusion with patient, Pain?	Future brighter
14.	Dr. M. gives nonsensical reassurance	Sense of reassurance
15. WE know cause of infection		Future brighter
16.	Conviction, faith	
	OTTO gave IRMA injection	Past guilt displaced
17.		
18. I see formula		
19. (judges)	Sense of righteousness	Present, satisfactory
20.	THE SYRINGE was not clean	Past, guilt localized

two items of fascination become clearer as we see them in a variety of dimensions.

The Irma Dream, to me, suggests concentration on the dreamer's interaction with the people who populate his dream, and relate this interaction to changes in his mood and to changes in his experience of space and time. The chart on pp. 144–145 lists contemporaneous changes in the dream's *interpersonal, affective, spatial,* and *temporal* configurations.

Given a diagrammatic outline, we have the choice between a horizontal and a vertical analysis. If we try the vertical approach to the first column, we find the dreamer, immediately after having abandoned the receiving line, preoccupied with an intrusive and coercive kind of examination and investigation. He *takes* the patient aside, reproaches her, and then *looks* and *thinks;* finally he finds what he is looking for. Then his activities of examining fuse with those of the other doctors, until at the end he again *sees,* and this time in heavy type, a formula. It is obvious, then, that investigation, in isolation or cooperation, is the main theme of his manifest activities. The particular mode of his approach impresses one as being *intrusive,* and thus somehow related to phallic.[3] If I call it a singularly male approach, I must refer to research in another field and to unfinished research in the field of dreams. Observations on sex differences in the play construction of adolescents (Erikson, 1951) indicate that male and female play scenes are most significantly different in the treatment of the space provided, i.e., in the structuring of the play space by means of building blocks and in the spatial vectors of the play activities. I shall not review the criteria here, because without detailed discussion a comparison between the task, suggested by an experimenter, of constructing a scene with a selection of building material and toys, is too different from the inner task, commanded by one's wish to sleep, to represent a set of images on the dream screen. Nevertheless, it may be mentioned that Dr. Kenneth Colby, in following up the possibility of preparing an analogous kind of psychosexual index for the formal characteristics of

---

[3] See the chapter "Zones, Modes, and Modalities" (Erikson, 1950a).

dreams, has found temporal suddenness, spatial entering, the sensory activity of looking, concern with authority, and a sense of ineffectuality, to be among the numerous items which are significantly more frequent in male dreams.[4] Dr. Colby has been able to isolate some such regularities in spite of the fact that the dream literature at the moment indulges in every possible license in the selection, description, and connotation of dream items. It seems to me that such studies might prove fruitful for research and technique, especially if undertaken in the frame of a standardized inquiry into the variables of dream experience, as suggested in our inventory of configurations. It is possible that the dream has hardly begun to yield its potentialities for research in personality diagnosis.

But now back to the "interpersonal" configurations, from which we have isolated, so far, only the dreamer's activities. If we now turn to the behavior of the dream population, it is, of course, a strangely intrapersonal social life which we are referring to: one never knows whether to view the cast of puppets on the dreamer's stage as a microcosmic reflection of his present or past social reality or as a "projection" of different identity fragments of the dreamer himself, of different roles played by him at different times or in different situations. The dreamer, in experimenting with traumatic reality, takes the outer world into the inner one, as the child takes it into his toy world. More deeply regressed and, of course, immobilized, the dreamer makes an autoplastic experiment of an alloplastic problem: his inner world and all the past contained in it becomes a laboratory for "wishful" rearrangements. Freud has shown us how the Irma Dream repeats a failure and turns to an illusory solution: the dreamer takes childish revenge on Otto ("*he* did it") and on Dr. M. ("he is a castrate and a fool"), thus appeases his anxiety, and goes on sleeping for a better day. However, I would suggest that we take another look at the matter, this time using the horizontal approach to the diagrammatic outline, and correlating the dream's changing interpersonal patterns with the dreamer's changing mood and perspective.

[4] According to a report presented to the Seminar on Dream Interpretation in the San Francisco Psychoanalytic Institute.

The dreamer, at first is a *part of a twosome,* his wife and himself, or maybe a family group, vis-à-vis a number of guests. "We receive," under festive circumstances in an opulent spatial setting. Immediately upon Irma's appearance, however, this twosomeness, this acting in concert, abruptly vanishes. The wife, or the family, is not mentioned again. The dreamer is suddenly *alone* with his worries, vis-à-vis a complaining patient. The visual field shrinks rapidly from the large hall to the vicinity of a window and finally to Irma's oral aperture; the festive present is replaced by a concern over past mistakes. The dreamer becomes active in a breathless way: he looks at the patient and thinks, he looks into her throat and thinks, and he finds what he sees ominous. He is startled, worried, and impatient, but behaves in a punitive fashion. *Irma,* in all this, remains a complaining and resistive vis-à-vis, and finally seems to become a mere part of herself: *"the mouth* opens." From then on, even when discussed and percussed, she does neither act nor speak—a good patient (for, unlike the proverbial Indian, a good patient is a half-dead patient, just alive enough to make his organs and complexes accessible to isolation and probing inspection). Seeing that something is wrong, the dreamer calls *Dr. M.* urgently. He thus establishes a *new twosome:* he and the "authority" who graciously (if foolishly) confirms him. This twosome is immediately expanded to include a professional group of younger colleagues, Dr. Otto and Dr. Leopold. Altogether they now form a small community: *"We know. . . ."*

At this point something happens which is lost in the double meaning of the manifest words, in the German original as well as in translation. When the dreamer says that he can *"feel"* the infiltrated portion of skin on the (patient's) left shoulder, he means to convey (as Freud states in his associations) that he can *feel this on his own body:* one of those fusions of a dreamer with a member of his dream population which is always of central importance, if not the very center and nodal point of a dream. The dreamer, while becoming again a doctor in the consenting community of doctors, thus at the same time turns into his and their *patient.* Dr. M. then says some foolish, nonsensical phrases, in the course of which it becomes clear that it had not been the dreamer who had harmed Irma, not at all. It is clear with the immediacy of a conviction that it was Dr. Otto who had infiltrated her. The dream ends, then, with Otto's professional and moral isolation. The dreamer (first a lonely investigator, then a patient, now a *joiner*) seems quite righteous in his indignation. The syringe was not clean: who would do such a thing? "Immediate" conviction, in harmony with authority, has clarified the past and unburdened the present.

The study of dreams and of culture patterns and ritualizations reveals parallels between interpersonal dream configurations and religious rites of conversion or confirmation. Let me repeat and underscore the points which suggest such an analogy. As the isolated and "guilty" dreamer quickly calls Dr. M., he obviously *appeals for help from higher authority*. This call for help is answered not only by Dr. M., but also by Dr. Leopold and Dr. Otto, who now, together with the dreamer, form a group with a *common conviction* ("we know"). As this happens, and the examination proceeds, the dreamer suddenly feels as if he were the sufferer and the examined, i.e., he, the doctor and man, fuses with the image of the *patient* and *woman*. This, of course, amounts to a surrender analogous to a spiritual conversion and a concomitant sacrifice of the male role. By implication, it is now *his* mouth that is open for inspection (passivity, inspiration, communion). But there is a *reward* for this. Dr. M. (symbolically castrated like a priest) recites with great assurance something that makes *no logical sense* (Latin, Hebrew?) but seems to be *magically effective* in that it awakes in the dreamer the *immediate conviction* (faith) that the causality in the case is now understood (magic, divine will). This common conviction restores in the dream a "*We*-ness" (congregation) which had been lost (in its worldly, heterosexual form) at the very beginning when the dreamer's wife and the festive guests had disappeared. At the same time it restores to the dreamer a *belongingness* (brotherhood) to a hierarchic group *dominated by an authority* in whom *he believes implicitly*. He immediately benefits from his newly won *state of grace:* he now has sanction for *driving the devil* into Dr. O. With the *righteous indignation* which is the believer's reward and weapon, he can now make *"an unclean one"* (a disbeliever) out of his erstwhile accuser.

Does this interpretation of the Irma Dream as a dream of conversion or confirmation contradict that given by Freud, who believed he had revenged himself on the professional world which did not trust him? Freud, we remember, felt that the dream disparaged Dr. M., robbing him of authority, vigor, and wholeness, by making him say silly things, look pale, limp, and be beardless. All of this, then, would belie as utterly hypocritical the dreamer's urgent call for help, his worry over the older man's health,[5] and his "immediate" knowledge in concert with his colleagues. This wish (to take revenge on his accusers and to vindicate his own strivings) stands, of course, as the dream's stimulus. Without such an id wish and all of its infantile energy, a dream would not exist; without a corresponding appeasement of the superego, it would have no form; but, we must add, without appropriate ego measures, the dream would not work. On closer inspection, then, the radical differentiation between a manifest and a latent dream, while necessary as a means of localizing what is "most latent," diffuses in a complicated continuum of more manifest and more latent items which are sometimes to be found by a radical disposal of the manifest configuration, sometimes by a careful scrutiny of it.

Such double approach seems to make it appear that the ego's over-all attitude in dream life is that of a withdrawal of its outposts in physical and social reality. The sleeping ego not only sacrifices sense perception and motility, i.e., its reactivity to physical reality; it also renounces those claims on individuation, independent action, and responsibility which may keep the tired sleeper senselessly awake. The healthy ego, in dreams,

---

[5] In another dream mentioned in *"The Interpretation of Dreams"* (1900), Freud accuses himself of such hypocrisy, when in a dream he treats with great affection another doctor whose face ("beardless, in actuality) he also alters, this time by making it seem elongated and by adding a yellow beard. Freud thinks that he is really trying to make the doctor out to be a seducer of women patients and a "simpleton." The German *Schwachkopf,* and *Schlemihl,* must be considered the evil prototype which serves as a counterpart to the ideal prototype, to be further elucidated here, the smart young Jew who "promises much," as a professional man.

quietly retraces its steps; it does not really sacrifice its assets, it merely pretends that, for the moment, they are not needed.[6]

I shall attempt to indicate this systematic retracing of ego steps in a dream by pointing to the *psychosocial criteria* which I have postulated elsewhere (Erikson, 1950a,b) for the ego's successive graduations from the main crises of the human life cycle. To proceed, I must list these criteria without being able to enlarge upon them here. I may remind the reader, however, that psychoanalytic theory is heavily weighed in favor of insights which make dysfunction plausible and explain why human beings, at certain critical stages, should fail, and fail in specific ways. It is expected that this theory will eventually make adequate or superior human functioning dynamically plausible as well (Rapaport, 1951; Kris, 1952b). In the meantime, I have found it necessary to postulate tentative criteria for the ego's relative success in synthesizing, at critical stages, the timetable of the organism, and the representative demands and opportunities which societies universally, if in different ways, provide for these stages. At the completion of infancy, then, the criterium for the budding ego's initial and fundamental success can be said to be a Sense of *Basic Trust* which, from then on, promises to outbalance the lastingly latent Sense of *Basic Mistrust*. Such trust permits, during early childhood, the critical development of a Sense of *Autonomy* which henceforth must hold its own against the Senses of *Shame* and *Doubt,* while at the end of the oedipal phase, an unbroken Sense of *Initiative* (invigorated by play) must begin to outdo a more specific Sense of *Guilt*. During the "school age," a rudimentary Sense of *Workmanship* and Work-and-Play companionship develops which, from then on, must help to outbalance the Sense of *Inferiority*. Puberty and Adolescence help the young person sooner or later to consummate the selective gains of childhood in an accruing sense of *Ego Identity* which prevents the lasting dominance of a then threatening Sense of *Role Diffusion*. Young adulthood is specific for a structuring of the Sense of *Intimacy* or else expose the

---

[6] See Ernst Kris' concept of a "regression in the service of the ego" (Kris, 1952a).

individual to a dominant Sense of *Isolation*. Real intimacy, in turn, leads to wishes and concerns to be taken care of by an adult Sense of *Generativity* (genes, generate, generation) without which there remains the threat of a lasting Sense of *Stagnation*. Finally, a Sense of *Integrity* gathers and defends whatever gains, accomplishments, and vistas were accessible in the individual's life time; it alone resists the alternate outcome of a Sense of vague but over-all *Disgust*.

This, of course, is a mere list of terms which point to an area still in want of theoretical formulation. This area encompasses the kind and sequence of certain universal psychosocial crises which are defined, on the one hand, by the potentialities and limitations of developmental stages (physical, psychosexual, ego) and, on the other, by the universal punctuation of human life by successive and systematic "life tasks" within social and cultural institutions.

The Irma Dream places its dreamer squarely into the crisis of middle age. It deals most of all with matters of *Generativity*, although it extends into the neighboring problems of Intimacy and of Integrity. To the adult implications of this crisis we shall return later. Here we are concerned with the dream's peculiar "regression." The doctor's growing sense of harboring a discovery apt to *generate new thought* (at a time when his wife harbored an addition to the *younger generation*) had been challenged the night before by the impact of a doubting word on his tired mind: a doubting word which was immediately echoed by self-doubts and self-reproaches from many close and distant corners of his life. At a *birthday* party, then, the dreamer suddenly finds himself *isolated*. At first, he vigorously and angrily asserts his most experienced use of one of the ego's basic functions: he examines, localizes, diagnoses. Such *investigation in isolation* is, as we shall see later on, one of the cornerstones of this dreamer's sense of *Inner Identity*. What he succeeds in focusing on, however, is a terrifying discovery which stares at him like the head of the Medusa. At this point, one feels, a dreamer with less flexible defenses might have awakened in terror over what he saw in the gaping cavity. Our dreamer's ego, however, makes the compromise of abandoning its positions and yet maintaining them. Abandoning independent observation the dreamer gives in to a *diffusion of roles: is* he doctor or patient, leader or follower, benefactor or culprit, seer or fumbler? He admits to the possibility of his *inferiority in workmanship* and urgently appeals to "teacher" and to "teacher's pets." He thus forfeits his right to vigorous *male initiative* and guiltily surrenders to the inverted solution of the oedipal conflict, for a fleeting moment even becoming the feminine object for the superior males' inspection and percussion; and he denies his sense of stubborn *autonomy*, letting *doubt* lead him back to the earliest infantile security: childlike *trust.*

In his interpretation of the Irma Dream, Freud found this trust most suspect. He reveals it as a hypocritical attempt to hide the dream's true meaning, namely, revenge on those who doubted the dreamer as a worker. Our review suggests that this trust may be overdetermined. The ego, by letting itself return to sources of security once available to the dreamer as a child, may help him to dream well and to sustain sleep, while promising revengeful comeback in a new day, when "divine mistrust" will lead to further discoveries.

VI. Acute, Repetitive, and Infantile Conflicts

I have now used the bulk of this paper for the demonstration of a few items of analysis which usually do not get a fair share in our routine interpretations: the systematic configurational analysis of the manifest dream and the manifest social patterns of the dream population. The designation of other, more familiar, matters will occupy less space.

Our "Outline of Dream Analysis" suggests next a survey of the various segments of the life cycle which appear in the dream material in latent form, either as acutely relevant or as reactivated by associative stimulation. This survey leads us, then, back along the path of time.

The most immediately present, the *acute dream stimulus* of the Irma Dream may well have been triggered by discomfort caused by swellings in nose and throat which, at the time, seem

CHART III
OUTLINE OF DREAM ANALYSIS

Analysis of Latent Dream Material
Acute sleep-disturbing stimulus
Delayed stimulus (day residue)
Acute life conflicts
Dominant transference conflict
Repetitive life conflicts
Associated basic childhood conflicts
Common denominators
"Wishes," drives, needs, methods of defense, denial, and distortion

---

to have bothered the usually sound sleeper: the prominence in the dream of Irma's oral cavity could be conceived as being codetermined by such a stimulus, which may also have provided one of the determinants for the latent but all-pervading presence in the dream of Dr. Fliess, the otolaryngologist. Acute stimulus and *day residue* (obviously the meeting with Dr. Otto) are associated in the idea as to whether the dreamer's dispensation of solutions may have harmed him or others. The *acute life conflicts* of a professional and personal nature have been indicated in some measure; as we have seen, they meet with the acute stimulus and the day residue in the further idea that the dreamer may be reproachable as a sexual being as well.

Let us now turn to matters of childhood. Before quoting, from *The Interpretation of Dreams*, a few childhood memories, the relevance of which for the Irma Dream are beyond reasonable doubt, I should like to establish a more speculative link between the dream's interpersonal pattern and a particular aspect of Freud's childhood, which has been revealed only recently.

I must admit that on first acquaintance with regressive "joining" in the Irma Dream, the suggestion of a religious interpretation persisted. Freud, of course, had grown up as a member of a Jewish community in a predominantly Catholic culture: could the overall milieu of the Catholic environment have impressed itself on this child of a minority? Or was the described configuration representative of a basic human proclivity which had found collective expression in religious rituals, Jewish, Catholic, or otherwise?

It may be well to point out here that the therapeutic interpretation of such patterns is, incidentally, as violently resisted
as is any id content (Erikson, 1953). Unless we are deliberate
and conscious believers in a dogma or declared adherents to
other collective patterns, we dislike being shown to be at the
mercy of unconscious religious, political, ethnic patterns as
much as we abhor sudden insight into our dependence on
unconscious impulses. One might even say that today when,
thanks to Freud, the origins in instinctual life of our impulses
have been documented and classified so much more inescapably and coherently than impulses rooted in group allegiances,
a certain clannish and individualist pride has attached itself to
the free admission of instinctual patterns, while the simple fact
of the dependence on social structures of our physical and
emotional existence and well-being seems to be experienced
as a reflection on some kind of intellectual autonomy. Toward
the end of the analysis of a young professional man who stood
before an important change in status, a kind of graduation, a
dream occurred in which he experienced himself lying on the
analytic couch, while I was sawing a round hole in the top of
his head. The patient, at first, was willing to accept almost any
other interpretation, such as castration, homosexual attack
(from behind), continued analysis (opening a skull flap), and
insanity (lobotomy), all of which were indeed relevant, rather
than to recognize this dream as an over-all graduation dream
with a reference to the tonsure administered by bishops to
young Catholic priests at the time of their admission to clerical
standing. A probable contact with Catholicism in impression-
able childhood was typically denied with a vehemence which
is matched only by the bitter determination with which patients
sometimes disclaim that they, say, could possibly have observed
the anatomic difference between the sexes at any time in their
childhood, or could possibly have been told even by a single
person on a single occasion that castration would be the result
of masturbation. Thus, infantile wishes to belong to and to
believe in organizations providing for collective reassurance
against individual anxiety, in our intellectuals, easily join other
repressed childhood temptations—and force their way into

dreams. But, of course, we must be prepared to look for them in order to see them; in which case the analysis of defenses gains a new dimension, and the study of social institutions a new approach.

The publication of Freud's letters to Fliess makes it unnecessary to doubt any further the possible origin of such a religious pattern in Freud's early life. Freud (1950) informs Fliess that during a most critical period in his childhood, namely, when he, the "first-born son of a young mother," had to accept the arrival of a little brother who died in infancy and then the advent of a sister, an old and superstitiously religious Czech woman used to take him around to various churches in his home town. He obviously was so impressed with such events that when he came home, he (in the words of his mother) preached to his family and showed them how God carries on ("wie Gott macht"): this apparently referred to the priest, whom he took to be God. That his mother, after the death of the little brother, gave birth to six girls in succession, and that the Irma Dream was dreamed during his wife's sixth pregnancy, may well be a significant analogy. At any rate, what the old woman and her churches meant to him is clearly revealed in his letters to Fliess, to whom he confessed that, if he could only find a solution of his "hysteria," he would be eternally grateful to the memory of the old woman who early in his life "gave me the means to live and to go on living." This old woman, then, restored to the little Freud, in a difficult period, a measure of a sense of trust, a fact which makes it reasonably probable that some of the impressive rituals which she took him to see, and that some of their implications as explained by her, appear in the Irma Dream, at a time when his wife was again expecting and when he himself stood before a major emancipation as well as the "germination" of a major idea. If this is so, then we may conclude that rituals impress children in intangible ways and must be sought among the covert childhood material, along with the data which have become more familiar to us because we have learned to look for them.

For a basic childhood conflict more certainly reflected in the Irma Dream, we turn to one of the first childhood memories reported by Freud in *The Interpretation of Dreams* (1900, p. 274):

> Then, when I was seven or eight years of age another domestic incident occurred which I remember very well. One evening before going to bed I had disregarded the dictates of discretion, and had satisfied my needs in my parents' bedroom, and in their presence. Reprimanding me for this delinquency, my father remarked: "That boy will never amount to anything." This must have been a terrible affront to my ambition, but allusions to this scene recur again and again in my dreams, and are constantly coupled with enumerations of my accomplishments and successes, as though I wanted to say: "You see, I have amounted to something after all."

This memory calls first of all for an ethnographic clarification, which I hope will not make me appear to be an excessive culturalist. That a seven-year-old boy "satisfies his needs in his parents' bedroom" has sinister implications, unless one hastens to remember the technological item of the chamber pot. The boy's delinquence, then, probably consisted of the use of one of his parents' chamber pots instead of his own. Maybe he wanted to show that he was a "big squirt," and instead was called a small one. This crime, as well as the punishment by derisive shaming, and, most of all, the imperishable memory of the event, all point to a milieu in which such character weakness as the act of untimely and immodest urination becomes most forcefully associated with the question of the boy's chances not only of ever becoming a man, but also of amounting to something, of becoming a "somebody," of *keeping what he promises*. In thus hitting the little exhibitionist in his weakest spot, the father not only followed the dictates of a certain culture area which tended to make youngsters defiantly ambitious by challenging them at significant times with the statement that they do not amount to much and with the prediction that they never will. We know the importance of urinary experience for the development of rivalry and ambition, and therefore recognize the memory as doubly significant. It thus becomes clearer than ever why Dr. Otto had to take over the severe designation of a dirty little squirt. After all, he was the one who had implied that Freud had promised too much when he said he would cure Irma and unveil the riddle of hysteria. A youngster who shows that he will amount to something is "promising"; the Germans say he is *vielversprechend,* i.e., he promises much. If his father told little Freud, under the embarrassing circumstance of the mother's presence in the parental bedroom, that he would never amount to anything, i.e., that the intelligent boy did not hold what he promised—is it not suggestive to assume that the tired doctor of the night before the dream had gone to bed with a bitter joke in his preconscious mind: yes, maybe I did promise too much when I said I could cure hysteria; maybe my father was right after all, I do not hold what I promised; look at all the other situations when I put dangerous or dirty "solutions" in the wrong places. The infantile material thus adds to the inventory of the doctor's and the man's carelessness in the use of "solutions" its infantile model, namely, exhibitionistic urination in the parents' bedroom: an incestuous model of all these associated dispensations of fluid.

But it seems to me that this memory could be the starting point for another consideration. It suggests not only an individual trauma, but also a pattern of child training according to which fathers, at significant moments, play on the sexual inferiority feelings and the smoldering oedipal hate of their little boys by challenging them in a severe if not viciously earnest manner, humiliating them before others, and especially before the mother. It would, of course, be difficult to ascertain that such an event is of a typical character in a given area or typical for a given father; but I do believe that such a "method" of arousing and testing a son's ambition (in some cases regularly, in some on special occasions) was well developed in the German cultural orbit which included German Austria and its German-speaking Jews. This matter, however, could be properly accounted for only in a context in which the relation of such child-training patterns could be demonstrated in their relation

to the whole conscious and unconscious system of child training and in their full reciprocity with historical and economic
forces. And, incidentally, only in such a context and in connection with a discussion of Freud's place in the evolution of civilized conscience could Freud's inclination to discard teachers
as well as students (as he discards Dr. O. in his dream after
having felt discarded himself) be evaluated. Here we are primarily concerned with certain consequences which such a cultural milieu may have had for the son's basic attitudes: the
inner humiliation, forever associated with the internalized father image, offered a choice between complete submission, a
readiness to do one's duty unquestioningly in the face of changing leaders and principles (without ever overcoming a deep
self-contempt and a lasting doubt in the leader); and, on the
other hand, sustained rebellion and an attempt to replace the
personal father with an ideological principle, a cause, or, as
Freud puts it, an "inner tyrant."[7]

Another childhood memory, however, may illuminate the
personal side of this problem which we know already from
Freud's interpretation of the Irma Dream as one of a vengeful comeback.

> I have already said that my warm friendships as well as my enmit-
> ies with persons of my own age go back to my childish relations
> to my nephew, who was a year older than I. In these he had the
> upper hand, and I early learned how to defend myself; we lived
> together, were inseparable, and loved one another, but at times,
> as the statements of older persons testify, we used to squabble
> and accuse one another. In a certain sense, all my friends are
> incarnations of this first figure; they are all *revenants*. My nephew
> himself returned when a young man, and then we were like
> Caesar and Brutus. An intimate friend and a hated enemy have
> always been indispensable to my emotional life; I have always

---

[7] As pointed out elsewhere (Erikson, 1950a), Hitler, also the son of an
old father and a young mother, in a corresponding marginal area, shrewdly
exploited such infantile humiliation: he pointed the way to the defiant destruction of all paternal images. Freud, the Jew, chose the way of scholarly
persistence until the very relationship to the father (the Oedipus complex)
itself became a matter of universal enlightenment.

been able to create them anew, and not infrequently my childish idea has been so closely approached that friend and enemy have coincided in the same person; but not simultaneously, of course, nor in constant alternation, as was the case in my early childhood [1900, p. 451].

This memory serves especially well as an illustration of what, in our "Outline," we call *repetitive conflicts,* i.e., typical conflicts which punctuate the dreamer's life all the way from the infantile to the acute and to the outstanding transference conflicts. The fact that we were once small we never overcome. In going to sleep we learn deliberately to return to the most trustful beginning, not without being startled, on the way, by those memories which seem to substantiate most tellingly whatever negative basic attitude (a sense of mistrust, shame, doubt, guilt, etc.) was aroused by the tiring and discouraging events of the previous day. Yet this does not prevent some, in the restored day, from pursuing, on the basis of their very infantile challenges, their own unique kind of accomplishment.

VII. TRANSFERENCE IN THE IRMA DREAM

Among the life situations in our inventory, there remains one which, at first, would seem singularly irrelevant for the Irma Dream: I refer to the "current transference conflict." If anything, this dream, dreamed by a doctor about a patient, would promise to contain references to countertransference, i.e., the therapist's unconscious difficulties arising out of the fact that the patient may occupy a strategic position on the chessboard of his fate. Freud tells us something of how Irma came to usurp such a role, and the intimate *du* in the dream betrays the fact that the patient was close to (or associated with somebody close to) the doctor's family either by blood relationship or intimate friendship. Whatever her personal identity, Irma obviously had become some kind of key figure in the dreamer's professional life. The doctor was in the process of learning the fact that this made her, by definition, a poor therapeutic risk for him.

But one may well think of another kind of "countertransference" in the Irma Dream. The dreamer's activities (and those of his colleagues) are all professional and directed toward a woman. But they are a researcher's approaches: the dreamer takes aside, throws light on the matter, looks, localizes, thinks, finds. May it not be that it was the Mystery of the Dream which itself was the anxious prize of his persistence?

Freud reports later on in *The Interpretation of Dreams* (1900) that one night, having exhausted himself in the effort of finding an explanation for dreams of "nakedness" and of "being glued to the spot," he dreamed that he was jumping light-footedly up a stairway in a disarray of clothes. No doubt, then, Freud's dreams during those years of intensive dream study carry the special weight of having to reveal something while being dreamed. That this involvement does not necessarily interfere with the genuineness of his dreams can be seen from the very fact, demonstrated here, that Freud's dreams and associations (even if fragmentary and, at times, altered) do not cease to be fresh and almost infinitely enlightening in regard to points which he, at the time, did not deliberately focus upon.

In our unconscious and mythological imagery, tasks and ideals are women, often big and forbidding ones, to judge by the statues we erect for Wisdom, Industry, Truth, Justice, and other great ladies. A hint that the Dream as a mystery had become to our dreamer one of those forbidding maternal figures which smile only on the most favored among young heroes (and yield, of course, only to sublimated, to "clean" approach) can, maybe, be spotted in a footnote where Freud writes, "If I were to continue the comparison of the three women I should go far afield. Every dream has at least one point at which it is unfathomable; a *central point*, as it were, connecting it with the unknown." The English translation's "central point," however, is in the original German text a *Nabel*—"a navel." This statement, in such intimate proximity to allusions concerning the resistance of Victorian ladies (including the dreamer's wife, now pregnant) to being undressed and examined, suggests an element of transference to the Dream Problem as such: the Dream, then, is just another haughty woman, wrapped in too many mystifying covers and "putting on airs" like a Victorian lady. Freud's letter to Fliess spoke of an "unveiling" of the mystery of the dream, which was accomplished when he subjected the Irma Dream to an "exhaustive analysis." In the last analysis, then, the dream itself may be a mother image; she is the one, as the Bible would say, to be "known."

Special transferences to one's dream life are, incidentally, not exclusively reserved for the author of *The Interpretation of Dreams*. In this context I can give only a few hints on this subject. Once a dreamer knows that dreams "mean" something (and that, incidentally, they mean a lot to his analyst), an ulterior *wish to dream* forces its way into the *wish to sleep by way of dreaming*. That this is a strong motivation in dream life can be seen from the fact that different schools of dynamic psychology and, in fact, different analysts manage to provoke systematically different manifest dreams, obviously dreamed to please and to impress the respective analysts; and that members of primitive societies apparently manage to produce "culture pattern dreams," which genuinely impress the dreamer and convince the official dream interpreters. Our discussion of the style of the Irma Dream has, I think, indicated how we would deal with this phenomenon of a variety of dream styles: we would relate them to the respective cultural, interpersonal, and personality patterns, and correlate all of these with the latent dream. But as to the dreamer's transference to his dream life, one may go further: in spurts of especially generous dream production, a patient often appeals to an inner transference figure, a permissive and generous mother, who understands the patient better than the analyst does and fulfills wishes instead of interpreting them. Dreams, then, can become a patient's secret love life and may elude the grasp of the analyst by becoming too rich, too deep, too unfathomable. Where this is not understood, the analyst is left with the choice of ignoring his rival, the patient's dream life, or of endorsing its wish fulfillment by giving exclusive attention to it, or of trying to overtake it with clever interpretations. The technical discussion of this dilemma we must postpone. In the meantime, it is clear that the first dream analyst stands in a unique relationship to the Dream as a "Promised Land."

This, however, is not the end of the transference possibilities in the Irma Dream. In the letters to Fliess, the impression is amply substantiated that Freud, pregnant with inner experiences which would soon force upon him the unspeakable isolation of the first self-analysis in history—and this at a time when his father's death seemed not far off—had undertaken to find in Fliess, at all cost, a superior friend, an object for idealization, and later an (if ever so unaware and reluctant) sounding board for his self-analysis. What this deliberate "transference" consisted of will undoubtedly, in due time, be fully recorded and analyzed. Because of the interrelation of creative and neurotic patterns and of personal and historical trends in this relationship, it can be said that few jobs in the history of human thought call for more information, competence, and wisdom. But it furthers an understanding of the Irma Dream to note that only once in all the published correspondence does Freud address Fliess with the lone word *Liebster* ("Dearest"): in the first letter following the Irma Dream (August 8, 1895). This singular appeal to an intellectual friend (and a German one at that) correlates well with the prominence which the formula for Trimethylamin (a formula related to Fliess' researches in bisexuality) has in the dream, both by dint of its heavy type and by its prominent place in the play of configurations: for it signifies the dreamer's return to the act of independent observation—"I see" again.

The Irma Dream, then, in addition to being a dream of a medical examination and treatment and of a sexual investigation, anticipates Freud's self-inspection and with it inspection by a vastly aggrandized Fliess. We must try to visualize the historical fact that here a man divines an entirely new instrument with unknown qualities for an entirely new focus of investigation, a focus of which only one thing was clear: all men before him, great and small, had tried with every means of cunning and cruelty to avoid it. To overcome mankind's resistance, the dreamer had to learn to become his own patient and subject of investigation; to deliver free associations to himself; to unveil horrible insights to himself; to identify himself with himself in the double roles of observer and observed. That this, in view of the strong maleness of scientific approach cultivated by the bearded savants of his day and age (and represented in the dreamer's vigorous attempts at isolating and localizing Irma's embarrassing affliction), constituted an unfathomable division within the observer's self, a division of vague "feminine yielding" and persistent masculine precision: this, I feel, is one of the central meanings of the Irma Dream. Nietzsche's statement that a friend is a lifesaver who keeps us afloat when the struggling parts of our divided self threaten to pull one another to the bottom was never more applicable; and where, in such a situation, no friend of sufficient superiority is available, he must be invented. Fliess, to a degree, was such an invention. He was the recipient of a creative as well as a therapeutic transference.

The "mouth which opens wide," then, is not only the oral cavity of a patient and not only a symbol of a woman's procreative inside, which arouses horror and envy because it can produce new "formations." It is also the investigator's oral cavity, opened to medical inspection; and it may well represent, at the same time, the dreamer's unconscious, soon to offer insights never faced before to an idealized friend with the hope that (here we must read the whole dream backwards) *wir empfangen:* we receive, we conceive, we celebrate a birthday. That a man may incorporate another man's spirit, that a man may conceive from another man, and that a man may be reborn from another, these ideas are the content of many fantasies and rituals which mark significant moments of male initiation, conversion, and inspiration (Kris, 1952b); and every act of creation, at one stage, implies the unconscious fantasy of inspiration by a fertilizing agent of a more or less deified, more or less personified mind or spirit. This "feminine" aspect of creation causes tumultuous confusion not only because of man's intrinsic abhorrence of femininity but also because of the conflict (in really gifted individuals) of this feminine fantasy with an equally strong "masculine" endowment which is to give a new and original form to that which has been conceived and carried to fruition. All in all, the creative individual's typical cycle of moods and attitudes which overlaps with neurotic mood swings (without ever coinciding with them completely) probably permits him, at the height of consummation, to identify with father, mother, and newborn child all in one; to represent, in equal measure, his father's potency, his mother's fertility, and his own reborn ideal identity. It is obvious, then, why mankind participates, with pity and terror, with ambivalent admiration and ill-concealed abhorrence, in the hybris of creative men, and why such hybris, in these men themselves, can call forth all the sinister forces of infantile conflict.

VIII. CONCLUSION

If the dreamer of the Irma Dream were the patient of a continuous seminar, several evenings of research work would now be cut out for us. We would analyze the continuation of the patient's dream life to see how his inventory of dream variations and how his developing transference would gradually permit a dynamic reconstruction of the kind which, in its most ambitious version, forms point IV of our "Outline":

CHART IV
Reconstruction

Life cycle
    present phase
    corresponding infantile phase
    defect, accident, or affliction
    psychosexual fixation ·
    psychosexual arrest
Social process: collective identity
    ideal prototypes
    evil prototypes
    opportunities and barriers
Ego identity and lifeplan
    mechanisms of defense
    mechanisms of integration

In the case of the Irma Dream, both the material and the motivation which would permit us to aspire to relative completeness of analysis are missing. I shall, therefore, in conclusion, select a few items which will at least indicate our intentions of viewing a dream as an event reflecting a critical stage of the dreamer's life cycle.

As pointed out, the Irma Dream and its associations clearly reflect a crisis in the life of a creative man of middle age. As the psychosocial criterion of a successful ego synthesis at that age I have named a *Sense of Generativity*. This unpretty term, incidentally, is intended to convey a more basic and more biological meaning than such terms as *creativity* and *productivity* do. For the inventory of significant object relations must, at this stage, give account of the presence or absence of a drive to create and secure personal children—a matter much too frequently considered merely an extension, if not an impediment, of genitality. Yet any term as specific as *parental sense* would not sufficiently indicate the plasticity of this drive, which may genuinely include works, plans, and ideas generated either in direct connection with the task of securing the life of the next generation or in wider anticipation of generations to come. The Irma Dream, then, reflects the intrinsic conflict between the partners and objects of the dreamer's intimate and generative drives, namely, wife, children, friends, patients, ideas: they all vie for the maturing man's energy and commitment, and yet none of them could be spared without some sense of stagnation. It may be significant that Freud's correspondence with Fliess, which initiates an *intellectual intimacy* of surprising passion, had begun a few months after Freud's marriage: there are rich references to the advent and the development of the younger generation in both families, and, with it, much complaint over the conflicting demands of family, work, and friendship. Finally, there is, in the material of the Irma Dream, an indication of the problem which follows that of the generative conflict, namely, that of a gradually forming *Sense of Integrity* which represents man's obligation to the most mature meaning available to him, even if this should presage discomfort to himself, deprivation to his mate and offspring, and the loss of friends, all of which must be envisaged and endured in order not to be exposed to a final *Sense of Disgust and of Despair*. The fact that we are dealing here with a man of genius during the loneliest crisis of his work productivity should not blind us to the fact that analogous crises face all men, if only in their attachments and allegiances to trends and ideas represented to them by strong leaders and by coercive institutions. Yet again, such a crisis is raised to special significance in the lives of those who are especially well endowed or especially favored with opportunities: for the "most mature meaning available to them" allows for deeper conflict, greater accomplishment, and more desperate failure.

A discernible relationship between the dreamer's acute life problem and the problems left over from corresponding infantile phases has been indicated in [Freud's] chapter VI. Here I shall select two further items as topics for a final brief discussion: psychosexual fixation and arrest; collective identity and ego identity.

In our general clinical usage we employ the term *fixation* alternately for that infantile stage in which an individual received the relatively greatest amount of gratification and to which, therefore, his secret wishes persistently return and for that infantile stage of development beyond which he is unable to proceed because it marked an end or determined slow-up of his psychosexual maturation. I would prefer to call the latter the point of *arrest,* for it seems to me that an individual's psychosexual character and proneness for disturbances depends not so much on the point of fixation as on the *range* between the point of fixation and the point of arrest, and on the *quality* of their interplay. It stands to reason that a fixation on the oral stage, for example, endangers an individual most if he is also arrested close to this stage, while a relative oral fixation can become an asset if the individual advances a considerable length along the path of psychosexual maturation, making the most of each step and cultivating (on the very basis of a favorable balance of basic trust over basic mistrust as derived from an intensive oral stage) a certain capacity to experience and to exploit subsequent crises to the full. Another individual with a similar range but a different quality of progression may, for the longest time, show no specific fixation on orality; he may indicate a reasonable balance of a moderate amount of all the varieties of psychosexual energy—and yet, the quality of the whole ensemble may be so brittle that a major shock can make it tumble to the ground, whereupon an "oral" fixation may be blamed for it. Thus, one could review our nosology from the point of view of the particular field circumscribed by the points of fixation and arrest and of the properties of that field. At any rate, in a dream, and especially in a series of dreams, the patient's "going back and forth" between the two points can be determined rather clearly. Our outline, therefore, differentiates between a point of psychosexual fixation and one of psychosexual arrest.

The Irma Dream demonstrates a great range and power of pregenital themes. From an initial position of phallic–urethral and voyeuristic hybris, the dreamer regresses to an oral–factual position (Irma's exposed mouth and the kinesthetic sensation of suffering through her) and to an anal–sadistic one (the elimination of the poison from the body, the repudiation of Dr. Otto). As for the dreamer of the Irma Dream (or any individual not clearly circumscribed by neurotic stereotypy), we should probably postpone any over-all classification until we have thought through the suggestions contained in Freud's first formulation of "libidinal types." In postulating that the ideal type of man is, each in fair measure, narcissistic *and* compulsive *and* erotic, he opened the way to a new consideration of normality, and thus of abnormality. His formulation does not (as some of our day do) focus on single fixations which may upset a unilinear psychosexual progression of a low over-all tonus, but allows for strong conflicts on each level, solved by the maturing ego adequate to each stage, and finally integrated in a vigorous kind of equilibrium.

I shall conclude with the discussion of ego identity (Erikson, 1950a,b, 1953). This discussion must, again, be restricted to the Irma Dream and to the typical problems which it may illustrate. The concept of identity refers to an over-all attitude (a *Grundhaltung*) which the young person at the end of adolescence must derive from his ego's successful synthesis of postadolescent drive organization and social realities. A sense of identity implies that one experiences an over-all sameness and continuity extending from the personal past (now internalized in introjects and identifications) into a tangible future; and from the community's past (now existing in traditions and institutions sustaining a communal sense of identity) into foreseeable or imaginable realities of work accomplishment and role satisfaction. I had started to use the terms *ego identity* and *group identity* for this vital aspect of personality development before I (as far as I know) became aware of Freud's having used the term *innere Identität* in a peripheral pronouncement and yet in regard to a central matter in his life.

In 1926, Freud sent to the members of a Jewish lodge a speech in which he discussed his relationship to Jewry and discarded religious faith and national pride as "the prime bonds." He then pointed, in poetic rather than scientific terms, to an unconscious as well as a conscious attraction in Jewry: powerful, unverbalized emotions *(viele dunkle Gefühlsmächte)*, and the clear consciousness of an inner identity *(die klare Bewusstheit der inneren Identität)*. Finally, he mentioned two traits which he felt he owed to his Jewish ancestry: freedom from prejudices which narrow the use of the intellect, and the readiness to live in opposition. This formulation sheds an interesting light on the fact that in the Irma Dream the dreamer can be shown both to belittle and yet also temporarily to adopt membership in the "compact" majority of his dream population. Freud's remarks also give added background to what we recognized as the dreamer's vigorous and anxious preoccupation, namely, the use of *incisive intelligence* in *courageous isolation*, the strong urge to investigate, to unveil, and to recognize: the Irma Dream strongly represents this ego-syntonic part of what I would consider a cornerstone of the dreamer's identity, even as it defends the dreamer against the infantile guilt associated with such ambition.

The dream and its associations also point to at least one "evil prototype"—the prototype of all that which must be excluded from one's identity: here it is, in the words of its American counterpart, the "dirty little squirt," or, more severely, the "unclean one" who has forfeited his claim to "promising" intelligence.

Much has been said about Freud's ambitiousness; friends have been astonished and adversaries amused to find that he disavowed it. To be the primus, the best student of his class through his school years, seemed as natural to him ("the first-born son of a young mother") as to write the *Gesammelten Schriften*. The explanation is, of course, that he was not "ambitious" in the sense of *ehr-geizig:* he did not hunger for medals and titles for their own sakes. The ambition of uniqueness in intellectual accomplishment, on the other hand, was not only ego-syntonic, it was ethno-syntonic, almost an obligation to his people. The tradition of his people, then, and a firm inner identity provided the continuity which helped Freud to overcome the neurotic dangers to his accomplishment which are suggested in the Irma Dream, namely, the guilt over the wish to be the one-and-only who would overcome the derisive fathers and unveil the mystery. It helped him in the necessity to abandon well-established methods of sober investigation (invented to find out a few things exactly and safely to overlook the rest) for a method of self-revelation apt to open the floodgates of the unconscious. If we seem to recognize in this dream something of a puberty rite, we probably touch on a matter mentioned more than once in Freud's letters, namely, the "repeated adolescence" of creative minds, which he ascribed to himself as well as to Fliess.

In our terms, the creative mind seems to face repeatedly what most men, once and for all, settle in late adolescence. The "normal" individual combines the various prohibitions and challenges of the ego ideal in a sober, modest, and workable unit, well anchored in a set of techniques and in the roles which go with them. The restless individual must, for better or for worse, alleviate a persistently revived infantile superego pressure by the reassertion of his ego identity. At the time of the Irma Dream, Freud was acutely aware that his restless search and his superior equipment were to expose him to the hybris which few men must face, namely, the entry into the unknown where it meant the liberation of revolutionary forces and the necessity of new laws of conduct. Like Moses, Freud despaired of the task, and by sending some of the first discoveries of his inner search to Fliess with a request to destroy them (to "eliminate the poison"), he came close to smashing his tablets. The letters reflect his ambivalent dismay. In the Irma Dream, we see him struggle between a surrender to the traditional authority of Dr. M. (superego), a projection of his own self-esteem on his imaginative and far-away friend, Fliess (ego ideal), and the recognition that he himself must be the lone (self-) investigator (ego identity). In life he was about to commit himself to his "inner tyrant," psychology, and with it, to a new principle of human integrity.

The Irma Dream documents a crisis, during which a medical investigator's identity loses and regains its "conflict-free status" (Hartmann, 1939; Rapaport, 1951). It illustrates how the latent infantile wish that provides the energy for the renewed conflict, and thus for the dream, is imbedded in a manifest dream structure which on every level reflects significant trends of the dreamer's total situation. Dreams, then, not only fulfill naked wishes of sexual license, of unlimited dominance and of unrestricted destructiveness; where they work, they also lift the dreamer's isolation, appease his conscience, and preserve his identity, each in specific and instructive ways.

REFERENCES

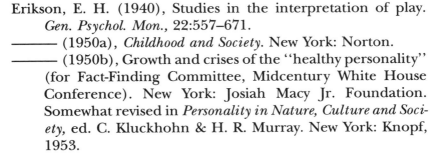

Erikson, E. H. (1940), Studies in the interpretation of play. *Gen. Psychol. Mon.*, 22:557–671.

——— (1950a), *Childhood and Society*. New York: Norton.

——— (1950b), Growth and crises of the "healthy personality" (for Fact-Finding Committee, Midcentury White House Conference). New York: Josiah Macy Jr. Foundation. Somewhat revised in *Personality in Nature, Culture and Society*, ed. C. Kluckhohn & H. R. Murray. New York: Knopf, 1953.

——— (1951), Sex differences in the play constructions of preadolescents. *Amer. J. Orthopsychiat.*, 21:667-692.

——— (1953), Identity and young adulthood. Presented at the 35th Anniversary of the Institute of the Judge Baker Guidance Center in Boston, May.

Freud, S. (1900), The Interpretation of Dreams. In: *The Basic Writings of Sigmund Freud,* tr. A. A. Brill. New York: Modern Library, 1938.

———— (1914), On the history of the psychoanalytic movement. In: *Thc Basic Writings of Sigmund Freud.* New York: Modern Library, 1938.

———— (1926), Ansprache an die Mitglieder des Vereins B'nai B'rith. *Gesammelte Werke,* Vol. 161. London: Imago, 1941.

———— (1950), *Aus den Anfängen der Psychoanalyse.* London: Imago.

Hartmann, H. (1939), Ichpsychologie und Anpassungs-problem. *Internat. Ztschr. f. Psychoanal. u. Imago,* 24:62–135.

Kris, E. (1952a), On preconscious mental processes. *Psychoanal. Quart.,* 19:540-560. Also in *Psychoanalytic Explorations in Art.* New York: International Universities Press.

———— (1952b), On inspiration. *Internat. J. Psycho-Anal.,* 20:377–389, 1939. Also in *Psychoanalytic Explorations in Art.* New York: International Universities Press.

Rapaport, D. (1951), *Organization and Pathology of Thought.* New York: Columbia University Press.

9.

The Problem of Ego Identity

ERIK H. ERIKSON

INTRODUCTION

In a number of writings (1946, 1950a, 1951, 1953) I have been using the term *ego identity* to denote certain comprehensive gains which the individual, at the end of adolescence, must have derived from all of his preadult experience in order to be ready for the tasks of adulthood. My use of this term reflected the dilemma of a psychoanalyst who was led to a new concept not by theoretical preoccupation but rather through the expansion of his clinical awareness to other fields (social anthropology and comparative education) and through the expectation that such expansion would, in turn, profit clinical work. Recent clinical observations have, I feel, begun to bear out this expectation. I have, therefore, gratefully accepted two opportunities offered me to restate and review the problem of identity. The present paper combines both of these presentations. The question before us is whether the concept of identity is essentially a psychosocial one, or deserves to be considered as a legitimate part of the psychoanalytic theory of the ego.

First a word about the term *identity*. As far as I know Freud used it only once in a more than incidental way, and then with a psychosocial connotation. It was when he tried to formulate his link to Judaism, that he spoke of an "inner identity"

["... die klare Bewusstheit der inneren Identität" (1926)] which was not based on race or religion, but on a common readiness to live in opposition, and on a common freedom from prejudices which narrow the use of the intellect. Here, the term *identity* points to an individual's link with the unique values, fostered by a unique history, of his people. Yet, it also relates to the cornerstone of this individual's unique development: for the importance of the theme of "incorruptible observation at the price of professional isolation" played a central role in Freud's life [see chapter 8]. It is this identity of something in the individual's core with an essential aspect of a group's inner coherence, which is under consideration here: for the young individual must learn to be most-himself where he means most to others—those others, to be sure, who have come to mean most to him. The term *identity* expresses such a mutual relation in that it connotes both a persistent sameness within oneself (self-sameness) and a persistent sharing of some kind of essential character with others.

I can attempt to make the subject matter of identity more explicit only by approaching it from a variety of angles—biographic, pathographic, and theoretical; and by letting the term *identity* speak for itself in a number of connotations. At one time, then, it will appear to refer to a conscious *sense of individual identity;* at another to an unconscious striving for a *continuity of personal character;* at a third, as a criterion for the silent doings of *ego synthesis;* and, finally, as a maintenance of an inner *solidarity* with a group's ideals and identity. In some respects the term will appear to be colloquial and naïve; in another, vaguely related to existing concepts in psychoanalysis and sociology. If, after an attempt at clarifying this relation, the term itself will retain some ambiguity it will, so I hope, nevertheless have helped to delineate a significant problem, and a necessary point of view.

I begin with one extreme aspect of the problem as exemplified in the biography of an outstanding individual—an individual who labored as hard on the creation of a world-wide *public identity* for himself, as he worked on his literary masterpieces.

I. Biographic: G.B.S. (70) on George Bernard Shaw (20)

When George Bernard Shaw was a famous man of seventy, he was called upon to review and to preface the unsuccessful work of his early twenties, namely, the two volumes of fiction which had never been published. As one would expect, Shaw proceeded to make light of the production of his young adulthood, but not without imposing on the reader a detailed analysis of young Shaw. Were Shaw not so deceptively witty in what he says about his younger years, his observations probably would have been recognized as a major psychological achievement. Yet, it is Shaw's mark of identity that he eases and teases his reader along a path of apparent superficialities and sudden depths. I dare to excerpt him here for my purposes, only in the hope that I will make the reader curious enough to follow him on every step of his exposition (Shaw, 1952).

G.B.S. (for this is the public identity which was one of his masterpieces) describes young Shaw as an "extremely disagreeable and undesirable" young man, "not at all reticent of diabolical opinion," while inwardly "suffering . . . from simple cowardice . . . and horribly ashamed of it." "The truth is," he concludes, "that all men are in a false position in society until they have realized their possibilities and imposed them on their neighbors. They are tormented by a continual shortcoming in themselves; yet they irritate others by a continual overweening. This discord can be resolved by acknowledged success or failure only: everyone is ill at ease until he has found his natural place, whether it be above or below his birthplace." But Shaw must always exempt himself from any universal law which he inadvertently pronounces; so he adds: "This finding of one's place may be made very puzzling by the fact that there is no place in ordinary society for extraordinary individuals."

Shaw proceeds to describe a crisis (of the kind which we will refer to as an *identity crisis*) at the age of twenty. It is to be noted that this crisis was not caused by lack of success or the absence of a defined role but by too much of both:

> I made good in spite of myself, and found, to my dismay, that Business, instead of expelling me as the worthless imposter I

was, was fastening upon me with no intention of letting me go. Behold me, therefore, in my twentieth year, with a business training, in an occupation which I detested as cordially as any sane person lets himself detest anything he cannot escape from. In March 1876 I broke loose.

Breaking loose meant to leave family and friends, business and Ireland, and to avoid the danger of success without identity, of a success unequal to "the enormity of my unconscious ambition." He granted himself a prolongation of the interval between youth and adulthood, which we will call a *psychosocial moratorium*. He writes: ". . . when I left my native city I left this phase behind me, and associated no more with men of my age until, after about eight years of solitude in this respect, I was drawn into the Socialist revival of the early eighties, among Englishmen intensely serious and burning with indignation at very real and very fundamental evils that affected all the world." In the meantime, he seemed to avoid opportunities sensing that "Behind the conviction that they could lead to nothing that I wanted, lay the unspoken fear that they might lead to something I did not want." This *occupational* part of the moratorium was reinforced by an *intellectual* one:

> I cannot learn anything that does not interest me. My memory is not indiscriminate; it rejects and selects; and its selections are not academic. . . . I congratulate myself on this; for I am firmly persuaded that every unnatural activity of the brain is as mischievous as any unnatural activity of the body. . . . Civilization is always wrecked by giving the governing classes what is called secondary education. . . .

Shaw settled down to study and to write as he pleased, and it was then that the extraordinary workings of an extraordinary personality came to the fore. He managed to abandon the *kind* of work he had been doing without relinquishing the work *habit:*

> My office training had left me with a habit of doing something regularly every day as a fundamental condition of industry as

distinguished from idleness. I knew I was making no headway unless I was doing this, and that I should never produce a book in any other fashion. I bought supplies of white paper, demy size, by sixpence-worths at a time; folded it in quarto; and condemned myself to fill five pages of it a day, rain or shine, dull or inspired. I had so much of the schoolboy and the clerk still in me that if my five pages ended in the middle of a sentence I did not finish it until the next day. On the other hand, if I missed a day, I made up for it by doing a double task on the morrow. On this plan I produced five novels in five years. It was my professional apprenticeship. . . .

We may add that these five novels were not published for over fifty years; but Shaw had learned to write as he worked, and to wait, as he wrote. How important such initial *ritualization of his worklife* was for the young man's inner defenses may be seen from one of those casual (in fact, parenthetical) remarks with which the great wit almost coyly admits his psychological insight: "I have risen by sheer gravitation, too industrious by acquired habit to stop working (*I work as my father drank*)" [emphasis added]. He thus points to that combination of *addictiveness* and *compulsivity* which we see as the basis of much pathology in late adolescence and of some accomplishment in young adulthood.

His father's "drink neurosis" Shaw describes in detail, finding in it one of the sources of his biting humor: "It had to be either a family tragedy or family joke." For his father was not "convivial, nor quarrelsome, nor boastful, but miserable, racked with shame and remorse." However, the father had a

> [H]umorous sense of anticlimax which I inherited from him and used with much effect when I became a writer of comedy. His anticlimaxes depended for their effect on our sense of the sacredness (of the subject matter). . . . It seems providential that I was driven to the essentials of religion by the reduction of every factitious or fictitious element in it to the most irreverent absurdity.

A more unconscious level of Shaw's oedipal tragedy is represented—with dreamlike symbolism—in what looks like a
screen memory conveying his father's impotence:

> A boy who has seen "the governor" with an *imperfectly wrapped-
> up goose under one arm* and *a ham in the same condition under the
> other* (both purchased under heaven knows what delusion of
> festivity) *butting* at the garden wall in the belief that he was
> *pushing open the gate,* and *transforming his tall hat to a concertina*
> in the process, and who, instead of being overwhelmed with
> shame and anxiety at the spectacle, has been so *disabled by merri-
> ment* (uproariously shared by the maternal uncle) that he has
> hardly been able to rush to the rescue of the hat and pilot its
> wearer to safety, is clearly not a boy who will make tragedies of
> trifles instead of *making trifles of tragedies*. If you cannot get rid
> of the family skeleton, you may as well make it dance.

It is obvious that the analysis of the psychosexual elements
in Shaw's identity could find a solid anchor point in this
memory.

Shaw explains his father's downfall with a brilliant analysis
of the socioeconomic circumstances of his day. For the father
was "second cousin to a baronet, and my mother the daughter
of a country gentleman whose rule was, when in difficulties,
mortgage. That was my sort of poverty." His father was "the
younger son of a younger son of a younger son" and he was
"a downstart and the son of a downstart." Yet, he concludes:
"To say that my father could not afford to give me a university
education is like saying that he could not afford to drink, or
that I could not afford to become an author. Both statements
are true; but he drank and I became an author all the same."

His mother he remembers for the "one or two rare and
delightful occasions when she buttered my bread for me. She
buttered it thickly instead of merely wiping a knife on it." Most
of the time, however, he says significantly, she merely "accepted me as a natural and customary phenomenon and took
it for granted that I should go on occurring in that way." There
must have been something reassuring in this kind of imperson-
ality, for "technically speaking, I should say she was the worst

mother conceivable, always, however, within the limits of the
fact that she was incapable of unkindness to any child, animal,
or flower, or indeed to any person or thing whatsoever. . . ."
If this could not be considered either a mother's love or an
education, Shaw explains:

> I was badly brought up because my mother was so well brought
> up. . . . In her righteous reaction against . . the constraints and
> tyrannies, the scoldings and browbeatings and punishments she
> had suffered in her childhood . . . she reached a negative atti-
> tude in which having no substitute to propose, she carried do-
> mestic anarchy as far as in the nature of things it can be carried.

All in all, Shaw's mother was "a thoroughly disgusted and
disillusioned woman . . . suffering from a hopelessly disappoint-
ing husband and three uninteresting children grown too old
to be petted like the animals and the birds she was so fond of,
to say nothing of the humiliating inadequacy of my father's
income."

Shaw had really three parents, the third being a man
named Lee ("meteoric," "impetuous," "magnetic"), who
gave Shaw's mother lessons in singing, not without revamping
the whole Shaw household as well as Bernard's ideals:

> Although he supplanted my father as the dominant factor in the
> household, and appropriated all the activity and interest of my
> mother, he was so completely absorbed in his musical affairs that
> there was no friction and hardly any intimate personal contacts
> between the two men: certainly no unpleasantness. At first his
> ideas astonished us. He said that people should sleep with their
> windows open. The daring of this appealed to me; and I have
> done so ever since. He ate brown bread instead of white: a star-
> tling eccentricity.

Of the many elements of identity formations which ensued
from such a perplexing picture, let me single out only three,
selected, simplified, and named for this occasion by me.

1. THE SNOB

"As compared with similar English families, we had a power of derisive dramatization that made the bones of the Shavian skeletons rattle more loudly." Shaw recognizes this as "family snobbery mitigated by the family sense of humor." On the other hand, "though my mother was not consciously a snob, the divinity which hedged an Irish lady of her period was not acceptable to the British suburban parents, all snobs, who were within her reach (as customers for private music lessons)." Shaw had "an enormous contempt for family snobbery," until he found that one of his ancestors was an Earl of Fife: "It was as good as being descended from Shakespeare, whom I had been unconsciously resolved to reincarnate from my cradle."

2. THE NOISEMAKER

All through his childhood, Shaw seems to have been exposed to an oceanic assault of music making: the family played trombones and ophicleides, violincellos, harps, and tambourines—and, most of all (or is it worst of all), they sang. Finally, however, he taught himself the piano, and this with dramatic noisiness.

> When I look back on all the banging, whistling, roaring, and growling inflicted on nervous neighbors during this process of education, I am consumed with useless remorse. . . . I used to drive (my mother) nearly crazy by my favorite selections from Wagner's Ring, which to her was "all recitative," and horribly discordant at that. She never complained at the time, but confessed it after we separated, and said that she had sometimes gone away to cry. If I had committed a murder I do not think it would trouble my conscience very much; but this I cannot bear to think of.

That, in fact, he may have learned to get even with his musical tormentors, he does not profess to realize. Instead, he compromised by becoming—a music *critic*, i.e., one who *writes about* the noise made by others. As a critic, he chose the *nom de plume* Corno di Bassetto—actually the name of an instrument which nobody knew and which is so meek in tone that "not even the devil could make it sparkle." Yet Bassetto became a sparkling critic, and more: "I cannot deny that Bassetto was occasionally vulgar; but that does not matter if he makes you laugh. Vulgarity is a necessary part of a complete author's equipment; and the clown is sometimes the best part of the circus."

3. THE DIABOLICAL ONE

How the undoubtedly lonely little boy (whose mother listened only to the musical noisemakers) came to use his imagination to converse with a great imaginary companion, is described thus: "In my childhood I exercised my literary genius by composing my own prayers . . . they were a literary performance for the entertainment and propitiation of the Almighty." In line with his family's irreverence in matters of religion, Shaw's piety had to find and to rely on the rockbottom of religiosity which, in him, early became a mixture of "intellectual integrity . . . synchronized with the dawning of moral passion." At the same time it seems that Shaw was (in some unspecified way) a little devil of a child. At any rate, he did not feel identical with himself when he was good: "Even when I was a good boy, I was so only theatrically, because, as actors say, I saw myself in the character." And indeed, at the completion of his identity struggle, i.e.,

> When Nature completed my countenance in 1880 or thereabouts (I had only the tenderest sprouting of hair on my face until I was 24), I found myself equipped with the upgrowing moustaches and eyebrows, and the sarcastic nostrils of the operatic fiend whose airs (by Gounod) I had sung as a child, and whose attitudes I had affected in my boyhood. Later on, as the generations moved past me, I . . . began to perceive that imaginative fiction is to life what the sketch is to the picture or the conception to the statue.

Thus G.B.S., more or less explicitly, traces his own roots. Yet, it is well worth noting that what he finally *became*, seems to him to have been as *innate,* as the intended reincarnation of Shakespeare referred to above. His teacher, he says, "puzzled me with her attempts to teach me to read; for I can remember no time at which a page of print was not intelligible to me, and can only suppose that I was born literate." However, he thought of a number of professional choices: "As an alternative to being a Michelangelo I had dreams of being a Badeali (note, by the way, that of literature I had no dreams at all, any more than a duck has of swimming)."

He also calls himself "a born Communist" (which, we hasten to say, means a Fabian Socialist), and he explains the peace that comes with the *acceptance of what one seems to be made to be;* the "born Communist... knows where he is, and where this society which has so intimidated him is. He is cured of his MAUVAISE HONTE. ..." Thus "the complete outsider" gradually became his kind of complete insider: "I was," he said, "outside society, outside politics, outside sport, outside the Church"—but this "only within the limits of British barbarism. ... The moment music, painting, literature, or science came into question the positions were reversed: it was I who was the Insider."

As he traces all of these traits back into childhood, Shaw becomes aware of the fact that only a *tour de force* could have integrated them all:

> ... If I am to be entirely communicative on this subject, I must add that the mere rawness which so soon rubs off was complicated by a deeper strangeness which has made me all my life a sojourner on this planet rather than a native of it. Whether it be that I was born mad or a little too sane, my kingdom was not of this world: I was at home only in the realm of my imagination, and at my ease only with the mighty dead. Therefore, I had to become an actor, and create for myself a fantastic personality fit and apt for dealing with men, and adaptable to the various parts I had to play as author, journalist, orator, politician, committee man, man of the world, and so forth.

"In this," so Shaw concludes significantly, "I succeeded later on only too well." This statement is singularly illustrative of that faint disgust with which older men at times review the inextricable identity which they had come by in their youth—a disgust which in the lives of some can become mortal despair and inexplicable psychosomatic involvement.

The end of his crisis of younger years, Shaw sums up in these words: "I had the intellectual habit; and my natural combination of critical faculty with literary resource needed only a clear comprehension of life in the light of an intelligible theory: in short, a religion, to set it in triumphant operation." Here the old Cynic has circumscribed in one sentence what the identity formation of any human being must add up to. To translate this into terms more conducive to discussion in ego-psychological and psychosocial terms: Man, to take his place in society, must acquire a "conflict-free," habitual use of a dominant *faculty*, to be elaborated in an *occupation;* a limitless *resource*, a feedback, as it were, from the immediate *exercise* of this occupation, from the *companionship* it provides, and from its *tradition;* and finally, an intelligible *theory* of the processes of life which the old atheist, eager to shock to the last, calls a religion. The Fabian Socialism to which he, in fact, turned is rather an *ideology*, to which general term we shall adhere, for reasons which permit elucidation only at the end of this paper.

II. Genetic: Identification and Identity

1

The autobiographies of extraordinary (and extraordinarily self-perceptive) individuals are a suggestive source of insight into the development of identity. In order to find an anchor point for the discussion of the universal genetics of identity, however, it would be well to trace its development through the life histories or through significant life episodes of "ordinary" individuals—individuals whose lives have neither become professional autobiographies (as did Shaw's) nor case histories. . . . I will not be able to present such material here; I must, instead, rely on impressions from daily life, from participation in one of the rare "longitudinal" studies of the personality development of children (Child Guidance Study, Institute of Child Welfare, University of California), and from guidance work with mildly disturbed young people.

Adolescence is the last and the concluding stage of childhood. The adolescent process, however, is conclusively complete only when the individual has subordinated his childhood identifications to a new kind of identification, achieved in absorbing sociability and in competitive apprenticeship with and among his age-mates. These new identifications are no longer characterized by the playfulness of childhood and the experimental zest of youth: with dire urgency they force the young individual into choices and decisions which will, with increasing immediacy, lead to a more final self-definition, to irreversible role pattern, and thus to commitments "for life." The task to be performed here by the young person and by his society is formidable; it necessitates, in different individuals and in different societies, great variations in the duration, in the intensity, and in the ritualization of adolescence. Societies offer, as individuals require, more or less sanctioned intermediary periods between childhood and adulthood, institutionalized *psychosocial moratoria,* during which a lasting pattern of "inner identity" is scheduled for relative completion.

In postulating a "latency period" which precedes puberty, psychoanalysis has given recognition to some kind of *psychosexual moratorium* in human development, a period of delay which permits the future mate and parent first to "go to school" (i.e., to undergo whatever schooling is provided for in his technology) and to learn the technical and social rudiments of a work situation. It is not within the confines of the libido theory, however, to give adequate account of a second period of delay, namely, adolescence. Here the sexually matured individual is more or less retarded in his psychosexual capacity for intimacy and in the psychosocial readiness for parenthood. This period can be viewed as a *psychosocial moratorium* during which the individual through free role experimentation may find a niche in some section of his society, a niche which is firmly defined and yet seems to be uniquely made for him. In finding it the young adult gains an assured sense of inner continuity and social sameness which will bridge what he *was* as a child and what he is *about to become,* and will reconcile his *conception of himself* and his *community's recognition* of him.

If, in the following, we speak of the community's response to the young individual's need to be "recognized" by those around him, we mean something beyond a mere recognition of achievement; for it is of great relevance to the young individual's identity formation that he be responded to, and be given function and status as a person whose gradual growth and transformation make sense to those who begin to make sense to him. It has not been sufficiently recognized in psychoanalysis that such recognition provides an entirely indispensable support to the ego in the specific tasks of adolescing, which are: to maintain the most important ego defenses against the vastly growing intensity of impulses (now invested in a matured genital apparatus and a powerful muscle system); to learn to consolidate the most important "conflict-free" achievements in line with work opportunities; and to resynthesize all childhood identifications in some unique way, and yet in concordance with the roles offered by some wider section of society—be that section the neighborhood block, an anticipated occupational field, an association of kindred minds, or, perhaps (as in Shaw's case) the "mighty dead."

2

Linguistically as well as psychologically, identity and identification have common roots. Is identity, then, the mere sum of earlier identifications, or is it merely an additional set of identifications? The limited usefulness of the *mechanism of identification* becomes at once obvious if we consider the fact that none of the identifications of childhood (which in our patients stand out in such morbid elaboration and mutual contradiction) could, if merely added up, result in a functioning personality. True, we usually believe that the task of psychotherapy is the replacement of morbid and excessive identifications by more desirable ones. But as every cure attests, "more desirable" identifications, at the same time, tend to be quietly subordinated to a new, a unique Gestalt which is more than the sum of its parts. The fact is that identification as a mechanism is of limited usefulness. Children, at different stages of their development, identify with those *part aspects* of people by which they themselves are most immediately affected, whether in reality or fantasy. Their identifications with parents, for example, center in certain overvalued and ill-understood body parts, capacities, and role appearances. These part aspects, furthermore, are favored not because of their social acceptability (they often are everything but the parents' most adjusted attributes) but by the nature of infantile fantasy which only gradually gives way to a more realistic anticipation of social reality. The final identity, then, as fixed at the end of adolescence is superordinated to any single identification with individuals of the past: it includes all significant identifications, but it also alters them in order to make a unique and a reasonably coherent whole of them.

If we, roughly speaking, consider introjection-projection, identification, and identity formation to be the steps by which the ego grows in ever more mature interplay with the identities of the child's models, the following psychosocial schedule suggests itself:

The mechanisms of *introjection and projection* which prepare the basis for later identifications, depend for their relative integration on the satisfactory mutuality (Erikson, 1951) between the *mothering adult(s) and the mothered child.* Only the experience of such mutuality provides a safe pole of self-feeling from which the child can reach out for the other pole: his first love "objects."

The fate of *childhood identifications,* in turn, depends on the child's satisfactory interaction with a trustworthy and meaningful hierarchy of roles as provided by the generations living together in some form of *family.*

Identity formation, finally, begins where the usefulness of identification ends. It arises from the selective repudiation and mutual assimilation of childhood identifications, and their absorption in a new configuration, which, in turn, is dependent on the process by which a *society* (often through subsocieties) *identifies the young individual,* recognizing him as somebody

who had to become the way he is, and who, being the way he
is, is taken for granted. The community, often not without
some initial mistrust, gives such recognition with a (more or
less institutionalized) display of surprise and pleasure in making the acquaintance of a newly emerging individual. For the
community, in turn, feels "recognized" by the individual who
cares to ask for recognition; it can, by the same token, feel
deeply—and vengefully—rejected by the individual who does
not seem to care.

3

While the end of adolescence thus is the stage of an overt
identity *crisis*, identity *formation* neither begins nor ends with
adolescence: it is a lifelong development largely unconscious
to the individual and to his society. Its roots go back all the
way to the first self-recognition: in the baby's earliest exchange
of smiles there is something of a *self-realization coupled with a
mutual recognition.*

All through childhood tentative crystallizations take place
which make the individual feel and believe (to begin with the
most conscious aspect of the matter) as if he approximately
knew who he was—only to find that such self-certainty ever
again falls prey to the *discontinuities of psychosocial development*
(Benedict, 1938). An example would be the discontinuity between the demands made in a given milieu on a little boy and
those made on a "big boy" who, in turn, may well wonder why
he was first made to believe that to be little is admirable, only
to be forced to exchange this effortless status for the special
obligations of one who is "big now." Such discontinuities can
amount to a crisis and demand a decisive and strategic repat-
terning of action, and with it, to *compromises* which can be com-
pensated for only by a consistently accruing sense of the social
value of such increasing commitment. The cute or ferocious,
or good small boy, who becomes a studious, or gentlemanly,
or tough big boy must be able and must be enabled—to combine both sets of values in a recognized identity which permits

him, in work and play, and in official and in intimate behavior to be (and to let others be) a big boy *and* a little boy.

The community supports such development to the extent to which it permits the child, at each step, to orient himself toward a complete *"life plan"* with a hierarchical order of roles as represented by individuals of different age grades. Family, neighborhood, and school provide contact and experimental identification with younger and older children and with young and old adults. A child, in the multiplicity of successive and tentative identifications, thus begins early to build up expectations of what it will be like to be older and what it will feel like to have been younger—expectations which become part of an identity as they are, step by step, verified in decisive experiences of psychosocial "fittedness."

4

The *critical phases* of life have been described in psychoanalysis primarily in terms of instincts and defenses, i.e., as "typical danger situations" (Hartmann, 1951). Psychoanalysis has concerned itself more with the encroachment of psychosexual crises on psychosocial (and other) functions than with the specific crisis created by the maturation of each function. Take for example a child who is learning to speak: he is acquiring one of the prime functions supporting a sense of individual autonomy and one of the prime techniques for expanding the radius of give-and-take. The mere indication of an ability to give intentional sound-signs immediately obligates the child to *"say* what he wants." It may force him to *achieve* by proper verbalization the attention which was afforded him previously in response to mere gestures of needfulness. Speech not only commits him to the kind of voice he has and to the mode of speech he develops; it also *defines him* as one responded to by those around him with changed diction and attention. They, in turn, expect henceforth to be understood by him with fewer explanations or gestures. Furthermore, a spoken word is a *pact:* there is an irrevocably committing aspect to an utterance remembered by others, although the child may have to learn early that certain commitments (adult ones to a child) are subject to change without notice, while others (his) are not. This intrinsic relationship of speech, not only to the world of communicable facts, but also to the social value of verbal commitment and uttered truth is strategic among the experiences which support (or fail to support) a sound ego development. It is this psychosocial aspect of the matter which we must learn to relate to the by now better known *psychosexual* aspects represented, for example, in the autoerotic enjoyment of speech; the use of speech as an erotic "contact"; or in such organ-mode emphases as eliminative or intrusive sounds or uses of speech. Thus the child may come to develop, in the use of voice and word, a particular combination of whining or singing, judging or arguing, as part of a new element of the future identity, namely, the element "one who speaks and is spoken to in such-and-such-a-way." This element, in turn, will be related to other elements of the child's developing identity (he is clever and/or good-looking and/or tough) and will be compared with other people, alive or dead, judged ideal or evil.

It is the ego's function to integrate the psychosexual and psychosocial aspects on a given level of development, and, at the same time, to integrate the relation of newly added identity elements with those already in existence. For earlier crystallizations of identity can become subject to renewed conflict, when changes in the quality and quantity of drive, expansions in mental equipment, and new and often conflicting social demands all make previous adjustments appear insufficient, and, in fact, make previous opportunities and rewards suspect. Yet, such developmental and normative crises differ from imposed, traumatic, and neurotic crises in that the process of growth provides new energy as society offers new and specific opportunities (according to its dominant conception and institutionalization of the phases of life). From a genetic point of view, then, the process of identity formation emerges as an *evolving configuration*—a configuration which is gradually established by successive ego syntheses and resyntheses throughout childhood; it is a configuration gradually integrating *constitutional givers, idiosyncratic libidinal needs, favored capacities, significant identifications, effective defenses, successful sublimations; and consistent roles.*

5

The final assembly of all the converging identity elements at the end of childhood (and the abandonment of the divergent ones)[1] appears to be a formidable task: how can a stage as "abnormal" as adolescence be trusted to accomplish it? Here it is not unnecessary to call to mind again that in spite of the similarity of adolescent "symptoms" and episodes to neurotic and psychotic symptoms and episodes, adolescence is not an affliction, but a *normative crisis,* i.e., a normal phase of increased conflict characterized by a seeming fluctuation in ego strength, and yet also by a high growth potential. Neurotic and psychotic crises are defined by a certain self-perpetuating propensity, by an increasing waste of defensive energy, and by a deepened psychosocial isolation; while normative crises are relatively more reversible, or, better, traversable, and are characterized by an abundance of available energy which, to be sure, revives dormant anxiety and arouses new conflict, but also supports new and expanded ego functions in the searching and playful engagement of new opportunities and associations. What under prejudiced scrutiny may appear to be the onset of a neurosis, often is but an aggravated crisis which might prove to be self-liquidating and, in fact, contributive to the process of identity formation.

It is true, of course, that the adolescent, during the final stage of his identity formation, is apt to suffer more deeply than he ever did before (or ever will again) from a diffusion of roles; and it is also true that such diffusion renders many an adolescent defenseless against the sudden impact of previously latent malignant disturbances. In the meantime, it is important to emphasize that the diffused and vulnerable, aloof and uncommitted, and yet demanding and opinionated personality of

---

[1] William James speaks of an abandonment of "the old alternative ego," and even of "the murdered self" (1896).

the not-too-neurotic adolescent contains many necessary elements of a semideliberate role experimentation of the "I dare
you" and "I dare myself" variety. Much of this apparent diffusion thus must be considered *social play* and thus the true genetic successor of childhood play. Similarly, the adolescent's
ego development demands and permits playful, if daring, experimentation in fantasy and *introspection*. We are apt to be
alarmed by the "closeness to consciousness" in the adolescent's perception of dangerous id contents (such as the Oedipus complex) and this primarily because of the obvious hazards
created in psychotherapy, if and when we, in zealous pursuit
of our task of "making conscious," push somebody over the
precipice of the unconscious who is already leaning out a little
too far. The adolescent's leaning out over any number of preci-
pices is normally an experimentation with experiences which
are thus becoming more amenable to ego control, provided
they can be somehow communicated to other adolescents in
one of those strange codes established for just such experiences—and provided they are not prematurely responded to
with fatal seriousness by overeager or neurotic adults. The same
must be said of the adolescent's "fluidity of defenses," which
so often causes raised eyebrows on the part of the worried clinician. Much of this fluidity is anything but pathological; for
adolescence is a crisis in which only fluid defense can overcome
a sense of victimization by inner and outer demands, and in
which only trial and error can lead to the most felicitous avenues of action and self-expression.

In general, one may say that in regard to the social play
of adolescents prejudices similar to those which once concerned the nature of childhood play are not easily overcome.
We alternately consider such behavior irrelevant, unnecessary,
or irrational, and ascribe to it purely regressive and neurotic
meanings. As in the past the study of children's spontaneous
games was neglected in favor of that of solitary play,[2] so now
the mutual "joinedness" of adolescent clique behavior fails to

---

[2] For a new approach see Anna Freud's and Sophie Dann's report on
displaced children (1951).

be properly assessed in our concern for the individual adolescent. Children and adolescents in their presocieties provide for one another a sanctioned moratorium and joint support for free experimentation with inner and outer dangers (including those emanating from the adult world). Whether or not a given adolescent's newly acquired capacities are drawn back into infantile conflict depends to a significant extent on the quality of the opportunities and rewards available to him in his peer clique, as well as on the more formal ways in which society at large invites a transition from social play to work experimentation, and from rituals of transit to final commitments: all of which must be based on an implicit mutual contract between the individual and society.

6

Is the sense of identity conscious? At times, of course, it seems only too conscious. For between the double prongs of vital inner need and inexorable outer demand, the as yet experimenting individual may become the victim of a transitory extreme *identity consciousness* which is the common core of the many forms of "self-consciousness" typical for youth. Where the processes of identity formation are prolonged (a factor which can bring creative gain) such preoccupation with the "self-image" also prevails. We are thus most aware of our identity when we are just about to gain it and when we (with what motion pictures call "a double take") are somewhat surprised to make its acquaintance; or, again, when we are just about to enter a crisis and feel the encroachment of identity diffusion—a syndrome to be described presently.

An increasing sense of identity, on the other hand, is experienced preconsciously as a sense of psychosocial well-being. Its most obvious concomitants are a feeling of being at home in one's body, a sense of "knowing where one is going," and an inner assuredness of anticipated recognition from those who count. Such a sense of identity, however, is never gained nor maintained once and for all. Like a "good conscience," it is constantly lost and regained, although more lasting and more economical methods of maintenance and restoration are evolved and fortified in late adolescence.

Like any aspect of well-being or for that matter, of ego synthesis, a sense of identity has a preconscious aspect which is available to awareness; it expresses itself in behavior which is observable with the naked eye; and it has unconscious concomitants which can be fathomed only by psychological tests and by the psychoanalytic procedure. I regret that, at this point, I can bring forward only a general claim which awaits detailed demonstration. The claim advanced here concerns a whole series of criteria of psychosocial health which find their specific elaboration and relative completion in stages of development preceding and following the identity crisis. This is condensed in Figure 9.1

Identity appears as only one concept within a wider conception of the human life cycle which envisages childhood as a *gradual unfolding of the personality through phase-specific psychosocial crises:* I have, on other occasions (Erikson, 1950a,b), expressed this *epigenetic principle* by taking recourse to a diagram which, with its many empty boxes, at intervals may serve as a check on our attempts at detailing psychosocial development. (Such a diagram, however, can be recommended to the serious attention only of those who can take it *and* leave it.) The diagram (Figure 9.1), at first, contained only the double-lined boxes along the descending diagonal (I,1—II, 2—III,3—IV,4—V,5—VI,6—VII,7—VIII,8) and, for the sake of initial orientation, the reader is requested to ignore all other entries for the moment. The *diagonal* shows the sequence of psychosocial crises. Each of these boxes is shared by a criterion of relative psychosocial health and the corresponding criterion of relative psychosocial ill-health: in "normal" development, the first must persistently outweigh (although it will never completely do away with) the second. The sequence of stages thus represents a successive development of the component parts of the psychosocial personality. Each part exists in some form (verticals) before the time when it becomes "phase-specific," i.e., when "its" psychosocial crisis is precipitated both by the

	1.	2.	3.	4.	5.	6.	7.	8.
I. INFANCY	Trust vs. Mistrust				Unipolarity vs. Premature Self-Differentiation			
II. EARLY CHILDHOOD		Autonomy vs. Shame, Doubt			Bipolarity vs. Autism			
III. PLAY AGE			Initiative vs. Guilt		Play Identification vs. (oedipal) Fantasy Identities			
IV. SCHOOL AGE				Industry vs. Inferiority	Work Identification vs. Identity Foreclosure			
V. ADOLESCENCE	Time Perspective vs. Time Diffusion	Self-Certainty vs. Consciousness	Role Experimentation vs. Negative Identity	Anticipation of Achievement vs. Work Paralysis	Identity vs. Identity Diffusion	Sexual Identity vs. Bisexual Diffusion	Leadership Polarization vs. Authority Diffusion	Ideological Polarization vs. Diffusion of Ideals
VI. YOUNG ADULT					Solidarity vs. Social Isolation	Intimacy vs. Isolation		
VII. ADULTHOOD							Generativity vs. Self-Absorption	
VIII. MATURE AGE								INTEGRITY VS. Disgust, Despair

individual's readiness and by society's pressure. But each component comes to ascendance and finds its more or less lasting
solution at the conclusion of "its" stage. It is thus *systematically
related* to all the others, and all depend on the proper development at the proper *time* of each; although individual make-up
and the nature of society determine the rate of development
of each of them, and thus the *ratio* of all of them. It is at the
end of adolescence, then, that identity becomes phase-specific
(V,5), i.e., must find a certain integration as a relatively conflict-
free psychosocial arrangement—or remain defective or con-
flict-laden.

With this chart as a blueprint before us, let me state first
which aspects of this complex matter will *not* be treated in this
paper: for one, we will not be able to make more definitive the
now very tentative designation (in *vertical* 5) of the precursors
of identity in the infantile ego. Rather, we approach childhood
in an untraditional manner, namely, from young adulthood
backward—and this with the conviction that early development
cannot be understood on its own terms alone, and that the
earliest stages of childhood cannot be accounted for without a
unified theory of the whole span of preadulthood. For the infant (while he is not spared the chaos of needful rage) does
not and cannot build anew and out of himself the course of
human life, as the reconstruction of his earliest experience ever
again seems to suggest. The smallest child lives in a community
of life cycles which depend on him as he depends on them, and
which guide his drives as well as his sublimations with consistent
feedbacks. This verity necessitates a discussion of the psychoanalytic approach to "environment" to which we shall return
toward the end of this paper.

A second systematic omission concerns the psychosexual
stages. Those readers who have undertaken to study the diagrams of psychosexual development in *Childhood and Society*
(1950a) know that I am attempting to lay the ground for a
detailed account of the dovetailing of psychosexual and psychosocial epigenesis, i.e., the two schedules according to which
component parts, present throughout development, come to
fruition in successive stages. The essential inseparability of

these two schedules is implied throughout this paper, although only the psychosocial schedule, and in fact only one stage of it, is brought into focus.

What traditional source of psychoanalytic insight, then, *will* we concern ourselves with? It is: first pathography; in this case the clinical description of *identity diffusion*. Hoping thus to clarify the matter of identity from a more familiar angle, we will then return to the over-all aim of beginning to "extract," as Freud put it, "from psychopathology what may be of benefit to normal psychology."

III. PATHOGRAPHIC: THE CLINICAL PICTURE OF IDENTITY DIFFUSION

Pathography remains the traditional source of psychoanalytic insight. In the following, I shall sketch a syndrome of disturbances in young people who can neither make use of the institutionalized moratorium provided in their society, nor create and maintain for themselves (as Shaw did) a unique moratorium all of their own. They come, instead, to psychiatrists, priests, judges, and (we must add) recruitment officers in order to be given an authorized if ever so uncomfortable place in which to wait things out.

The sources at my disposal are the case histories of a number of young patients who sought treatment following an acutely disturbed period between the ages of sixteen and twenty-four. A few were seen, and fewer treated, by me personally; a larger number were reported in supervisory interviews or seminars at the Austen Riggs Center in Stockbridge and at the Western Psychiatric Institute in Pittsburgh; the largest number are former patients now on record in the files of the Austen Riggs Center. *My composite sketch* of these case histories will remind the reader immediately of the diagnostic and technical problems encountered in adolescents in general (Blos, 1953) and especially in any number of those young borderline cases (Knight, 1953) who are customarily diagnosed as pre-schizophrenias, or severe character disorders with paranoid, depressive, psychopathic, or other trends. Such well-established diagnostic signposts will not be questioned here. An attempt will be made, however, to concentrate on certain common features representative of the common life crisis shared by this whole group of patients as a result of a (temporary or final) inability of their egos to establish an identity: for they all suffer from *acute identity diffusion*. Obviously, only quite detailed case presentations could convey the full necessity or advisability of such a "phase-specific" approach which emphasizes the life task shared by a group of patients as much as the diagnostic criteria which differentiate them. In the meantime, I hope that my composite sketch will convey at least a kind of impressionistic plausibility. The fact that the cases known to me were seen in a private institution in the Berkshires, and at a public clinic in industrial Pittsburgh, suggests that at least the two extremes of socioeconomic status in the United States (and thus two extreme forms of identity problems) are represented here. This could mean that the families in question, because of their extreme locations on the scale of class mobility and of Americanization, may have conveyed to these particular children a certain hopelessness regarding their chances of participating in (or of successfully defying) the dominant American manners and symbols of success (G. H. Mead, 1934, chapters 8 and 9; for a recent psychoanalytic approach to Role and Status see Ackerman, 1951). Whether, and in what way disturbances such as are outlined here also characterize those more comfortably placed somewhere near the middle of the socioeconomic ladder, remains, at this time, an open question.

1. TIME OF BREAKDOWN

A state of acute identity diffusion usually becomes manifest at a time when the young individual finds himself exposed to a combination of experiences which demand his simultaneous commitment to *physical intimacy* (not by any means always overtly sexual), to decisive *occupational choice,* to energetic *competition*, and to *psychosocial self-definition*. A young college girl, previously overprotected by a conservative mother who is trying

to live down a not-so-conservative past, may, on entering college, meet young people of radically different backgrounds,
among whom she must choose her friends and her enemies;
radically different mores especially in the relationship of the
sexes which she must play along with or repudiate; and a commitment to make decisions and choices which will necessitate
irreversible competitive involvement or even leadership. Often,
she finds among very "different" young people, a comfortable
display of values, manners, and symbols for which one or the
other of her parents or grandparents is covertly nostalgic, while
overtly despising them. Decisions and choices and, most of all,
successes in any direction bring to the fore conflicting identifications and immediately threaten to narrow down the inventory of further tentative choices; and, at the very moment when
time is of the essence, every move may establish a binding prec-
edent in psychosocial self-definition, i.e., in the "type" one
comes to represent in the types of the age-mates (who seem so
terribly eager to type). On the other hand, any marked *avoidance of choices* (i.e., a moratorium by default) leads to a sense
of outer *isolation* and to an *inner vacuum* which is wide open for
old libidinal objects and with this for bewilderingly conscious
incestuous feelings; for more primitive forms of identification;
and (in some) for a renewed struggle with archaic introjects.
This regressive pull often receives the greatest attention from
workers in our field, partially because we are on more familiar
ground wherever we can discern signs of regression to infantile
psychosexuality. Yet, the disturbances under discussion here
cannot be comprehended without some insight into the specific nature of transitory adolescent regression as an attempt
to postpone and to avoid, as it were, a psychosocial foreclosure.
A state of paralysis may ensue, the mechanisms of which appear
to be devised to maintain a state of minimal actual choice and
commitment with a maximum inner conviction of still being
the chooser. Of the complicated presenting pathology only a
few aspects can be discussed here.

2. THE PROBLEM OF INTIMACY

The chart shows "Intimacy vs. Isolation" as the core conflict
which follows that of "Identity vs. Identity Diffusion." That

many of our patients break down at an age which is properly considered more preadult than postadolescent, is explained by the fact that often only an attempt to engage in intimate fellow-ship and competition or in sexual intimacy fully reveals the latent weakness of identity.

True "engagement" with others is the result and the test of firm self-delineation. As the young individual seeks at least tentative forms of playful intimacy in friendship and competition, in sex play and love, in argument and gossip, he is apt to experience a peculiar strain, as if such tentative engagement might turn into an interpersonal fusion amounting to a loss of identity, and requiring, therefore, a tense inner reservation, a caution in commitment. Where a youth does not resolve such strain he may isolate himself and enter, at best, only stereotyped and formalized interpersonal relations; or he may, in repeated hectic attempts and repeated dismal failures, seek intimacy with the most improbable partners. For where an assured sense of identity is missing even friendships and affairs become desperate attempts at delineating the fuzzy outlines of identity by mutual narcissistic mirroring: to fall in love then often means to fall into one's mirror image, hurting oneself and damaging the mirror. During lovemaking or in sexual fantasies, a loosening of *sexual identity* threatens: it even becomes unclear whether sexual excitement is experienced by the individual or by his partner, and this in either heterosexual or homosexual encounters. The ego thus loses its flexible capacity for abandoning itself to sexual and affectual sensations, in a fusion with another individual who is both partner to the sensation and guarantor of one's continuing identity: fusion with another becomes identity loss. A sudden collapse of all capacity for mutuality threatens, and a desperate wish ensues to start all over again, with a (quasi-deliberate) regression to a stage of basic bewilderment and rage such as only the very small child knew.

It must be remembered that the counterpart of intimacy is *distantiation*, i.e., the readiness to repudiate, to ignore, or to destroy those forces and people whose essence seems dangerous to one's own. Intimacy with one set of people and ideas would not be really intimate without an efficient repudiation of another set. Thus, weakness or excess in repudiation is an intrinsic aspect of the inability to gain intimacy because of an incomplete identity: whoever is not sure of his "point of view" cannot repudiate judiciously.

Young persons often indicate in rather pathetic ways a feeling that only a merging with a "leader" could save them—an adult who is able and willing to offer himself as a safe object for experimental surrender and as a guide in the relearning of the very first steps toward an intimate mutuality and a legitimate repudiation. To such a person the late adolescent wants to be an apprentice or a disciple, a follower, sex mate or patient. Where this fails, as it often must from its very intensity and absoluteness, the young individual recoils to a position of strenuous introspection and self-testing which, given particularly aggravating circumstances or a history of relatively strong autistic trends, can lead him into a paralyzing borderline state. Symptomatically, this state consists of a painfully heightened sense of isolation; a disintegration of the sense of inner continuity and sameness; a sense of over-all ashamedness; an inability to derive a sense of accomplishment from any kind of activity; a feeling that life is happening to the individual rather than being lived by his initiative; a radically shortened time perspective; and finally, a basic mistrust, which leaves it to the world, to society, and indeed, psychiatry to prove that the patient does exist in a psychosocial sense, i.e., can count on an invitation to become himself.

3. DIFFUSION OF TIME PERSPECTIVE

In extreme instances of delayed and prolonged adolescence an extreme form of a disturbance in the *experience of time* appears which, in its milder form, belongs to the psychopathology of everyday adolescence. It consists of a sense of great urgency and yet also of a loss of consideration for time as a dimension of living. The young person may feel simultaneously very young, and in fact babylike, and old beyond rejuvenation. Protests of missed greatness and of a premature and fatal loss of useful potentials are common among our patients as they are among adolescents in cultures which consider such protestations romantic; the implied malignancy, however, consists of a decided disbelief in the possibility that time may bring change, and yet also of a violent fear that it might. This contradiction often is expressed in a general slowing up which makes the patient behave, within the routine of activities (and also of therapy) as if he were moving in molasses. It is hard for him to go to bed and to face the transition into a state of sleep, and it is equally hard for him to get up and face the necessary restitution of wakefulness; it is hard to come to the hour, and hard to leave it. Such complaints as, "I don't know," "I give up," "I quit," are by no means mere habitual statements reflecting a mild depression: they are often expressions of the kind of despair which has been recently discussed by Edward Bibring (1953) as a wish on the part of the ego "to let itself die." The assumption that life could actually be made to end with the end of adolescence (or at tentatively planned later "dates of expiration") is by no means entirely unwelcome, and, in fact, can become the only pillar of hope on which a new beginning can be based. Some of our patients even require the feeling that the therapist does not intend to commit them to a continuation of life if (successful) treatment should fail to prove it really worth while; without such a conviction the moratorium would not be a real one. In the meantime, the "wish to die" is only in those rare cases a really suicidal wish, where "to be a suicide" becomes an inescapable identity choice in itself. I am thinking here of a pretty young girl, the oldest of a number of daughters of a mill worker. Her mother had repeatedly expressed the thought that she would rather see her daughters dead than become prostitutes; at the same time she suspected "prostitution" in the daughters' every move toward companionship with boys. The daughters were finally forced into a kind of conspiratorial sorority of their own, obviously designed to elude the mother, to experiment with ambiguous situations and yet probably also to give one another protection from men. They were finally caught in compromising circumstances. The authorities, too, took it for granted that they intended to prostitute themselves, and they were sent to a variety of institutions where they were forcefully impressed with the kind of "recognition" society had in store for them. No appeal was possible to a mother who, they felt, had left them no choice; and much good will and understanding of social workers was sabotaged by circumstances. At least for the oldest girl (and this, because of a number of reasons) no other future was available except that of another chance in another world. She killed herself by hanging after having dressed herself up nicely, and having written a note which ended with the cryptic words "Why I achieve honor only to discard it. . . ."

Less spectacular but not less malignant forms and origins of such "negative identities" will be taken up later.

4. DIFFUSION OF INDUSTRY

Cases of severe identity diffusion regularly also suffer from an acute upset in the sense of workmanship, and this either in the form of an inability to concentrate on required or suggested tasks, or in a self-destructive preoccupation with some one-sided activities, i.e., excessive reading. The way in which such patients sometimes, under treatment, find the one activity in which they can reemploy their once lost sense of workmanship, is a chapter in itself. Here, it is well to keep in mind the stage of development which precedes puberty and adolescence, namely, the elementary school age, when the child is taught the prerequisites for participation in the particular technology of his culture and is given the opportunity and the life task of developing a sense of workmanship and work participation. The school age significantly follows the oedipal stage: the accomplishment of real (and not only playful) steps toward a place in the economic structure of society permits the child to reidentify with parents as workers and tradition bearers rather than as sexual and familial beings, thus nurturing at least one concrete and more "neutral" possibility of becoming like them. The tangible goals of elementary practice are shared by and with age-mates in places of instruction (sweathouse, prayer house, fishing hole, workshop, kitchen, schoolhouse) most of which, in turn, are geographically separated from the home, from the mother, and from infantile memories: here, however, wide differences in the treatment of the sexes exist. Work goals, then, by no means only support or exploit the suppression of infantile instinctual aims; they also enhance the functioning of the ego, in that they offer a constructive activity with actual tools and materials in a communal reality. The ego's tendency to turn passivity into activity here thus acquires a new field of manifestation, in many ways superior to the mere turning of passive into active in infantile fantasy and play; for now the inner need for activity, practice, and work completion is ready to meet the corresponding demands and opportunities in social reality (Hendrick, 1943; Ginsberg, 1954).

Because of the immediate oedipal antecedents of the beginnings of a work identity, the diffusion of identity in our young patients reverses their gears toward oedipal competitiveness and sibling rivalry. Thus identity diffusion is accompanied not only by an inability to concentrate, but also by an excessive awareness as well as an abhorrence of competitiveness. Although the patients in question usually are intelligent and able and often have shown themselves successful in office work, in scholastic studies, and in sports, they now lose the capacity for work, exercise, and sociability and thus the most important vehicle of social play, and the most significant refuge from formless fantasy and vague anxiety. Instead infantile goals and fantasies are dangerously endowed with the energy emanating from matured sexual equipment and of vicious aggressive power. One parent, again, becomes the goal, the other, again, the hindrance. Yet, this revived oedipal struggle is not and must not be interpreted as exclusively or even primarily a sexual one: it is a turn toward the earliest origins, an attempt to resolve a diffusion of early introjects and to rebuild shaky childhood identifications—in other words, a wish to be born again, to learn once more the very first steps toward reality and mutuality, and to acquire the renewed permission to develop again the functions of contact, activity, and competition.

A young patient, who had found himself blocked in college, during the initial phase of his treatment in a private hospital nearly read himself blind, apparently in a destructive overidentification with father and therapist both of whom were professors. Guided by a resourceful "painter in residence" he came upon the fact that he had an original and forceful talent to paint, an activity which was prevented by advancing treatment from becoming self-destructive overactivity. As painting proved a help in the patient's gradual acquisition of a sense of identity of his own, he dreamed one night a different version of a dream which previously had always ended in panicky awakening. Now he fled, from fire and persecution, into a forest which he had sketched himself; and as he fled into it, the charcoal drawing turned into live woods, with an infinite perspective.

5. THE CHOICE OF THE NEGATIVE IDENTITY

The loss of a sense of identity often is expressed in a scornful and snobbish hostility toward the roles offered as proper and desirable in one's family or immediate community. Any part aspect of the required role, or all parts, be it masculinity or femininity, nationality or class membership, can become the main focus of the young person's acid disdain. Such excessive contempt for their backgrounds occurs among the oldest Anglo-Saxon and the newest Latin or Jewish families; it easily becomes a general dislike for everything American, and an irrational overestimation of everything foreign. Life and strength seem to exist only where one is not, while decay and danger threaten wherever one happens to be. This typical case fragment illustrates the superego's triumph of depreciation over a young man's faltering identity:

> A voice within him which was disparaging him began to increase at about this time. It went to the point of intruding into everything he did. He said, "if I smoke a cigarette, if I tell a girl I like her, if I make a gesture, if I listen to music, if I try to read a book—this third voice is at me all the time—'You're doing this for effect; you're a phony.' " This disparaging voice in the last year has been rather relentless. The other day on the way from home to college, getting into New York on the train, he

went through some of the New Jersey swamplands and the poorer sections of the cities, and he felt that he was more congenial with people who lived there than he was with people on the campus or at home. He felt that life really existed in those places and that the campus was a sheltered, effeminate place.

In this example it is important to recognize not only an overweening superego, overclearly perceived as an inner voice, but also the acute identity diffusion, as projected on segments of society. An analogous case is that of a French-American girl from a rather prosperous mining town, who felt panicky to the point of paralysis when alone with a boy. It appeared that numerous superego injunctions and identity conflicts had, as it were, shortcircuited in the obsessive idea that every boy had a right to expect from her a yielding to sexual practices, popularly designated as "French."

Such estrangement from national and ethnic origins rarely leads to a complete denial of *personal identity* (Piers and Singer, 1953), although the angry insistence on being called by a particular given name or nickname is not uncommon among young people who try to find a refuge from diffusion in a new name label. Yet, confabulatory reconstructions of one's origin do occur: a high-school girl of Middle-European descent secretly kept company with Scottish immigrants, carefully studying and easily assimilating their dialect and their social habits. With the help of history books and travel guides she reconstructed for herself a childhood in a given milieu in an actual township in Scotland, apparently convincing enough to some descendants of that country. Prevailed upon to discuss her future with me, she spoke of her (American-born) parents as "the people who brought me over here," and told me of her childhood "over there" in impressive detail. I went along with the story, implying that it had more inner truth than reality to it. The bit of reality was, as I surmised, the girl's attachment, in early childhood, to a woman neighbor who had come from the British Isles; the force behind the near-delusional "truth" was the paranoid form of a powerful death wish (latent in all severe identity crises) against her parents. The semideliberateness of the delusion was indicated when I finally asked the girl how she had m anaged to marshal all the details of life in Scotland. "Bless you, sir," she said in pleading Scottish brogue, "I needed a past."

On the whole, however, our patients' conflicts find expression in a more subtle way than the abrogation of personal identity: they rather choose a *negative identity*, i.e., an identity perversely based on all those identifications and roles which, at critical stages of development, had been presented to the individual as most undesirable or dangerous, and yet, also as most real. For example, a mother whose first-born son died and who (because of complicated guilt feelings) has never been able to attach to her later surviving children the same amount of religious devotion that she bestows on the memory of her dead child may well arouse in one of her sons the conviction that to be sick or dead is a better assurance of being "recognized" than to be healthy and about. A mother who is filled with unconscious ambivalence toward a brother who disintegrated into alcoholism may again and again respond selectively only to those traits in her son which seem to point to a repetition of her brother's fate, in which case this "negative" identity may take on more reality for the son than all his natural attempts at being good: he may work hard on becoming a drunkard and, lacking the necessary ingredients, may end up in a state of stubborn paralysis of choice. In other cases the negative identity is dictated by the necessity of finding and defending a niche of one's own against the excessive ideals either demanded by morbidly ambitious parents or seemingly already realized by actually superior ones: in both cases the parents' weaknesses and unexpressed wishes are recognized by the child with catastrophic clarity. The daughter of a man of brilliant showmanship ran away from college and was arrested as a prostitute in the Negro quarter of a Southern city; while the daughter of an influential Southern Negro preacher was found among narcotic addicts in Chicago. In such cases it is of utmost importance to recognize the mockery and the vindictive pretense in such role playing; for the white girl had not really prostituted herself, and the colored girl had not really become an addict—yet. Needless to say, however, each of them had put herself into a marginal social area, leaving it to law enforcement officers and to psychiatric agencies to decide what stamp to put on such behavior. A corresponding case is that of a boy presented to a psychiatric clinic as "the village homosexual" of a small town. On investigation, it appeared that the boy had succeeded in assuming this fame without any actual acts of homosexuality except one, much earlier in his life, when he had been raped by some older boys.

Such vindictive choices of a negative identity represent, of course, a desperate attempt at regaining some mastery in a situation in which the available positive identity elements cancel each other out. The history of such a choice reveals a set of conditions in which it is easier to derive a sense of identity out of a *total* identification with that which one is *least* supposed to be than to struggle for a feeling of reality in acceptable roles which are unattainable with the patient's inner means. The statement of a young man, "I would rather be quite insecure than a little secure," and that of a young woman, "At least in the gutter I'm a genius," circumscribe the relief following the total choice of a negative identity. Such relief is, of course, often sought collectively in cliques and gangs of young homosexuals, addicts, and social cynics.

A relevant job ahead of us is the analysis of snobbism which, in its upper-class form, permits some people to deny their identity diffusion through a recourse to something they did not earn themselves, namely, their parents' wealth, background, or fame. But there is a "lower lower" snobbism too, which is based on the pride of having achieved a semblance of nothingness. At any rate, many a late adolescent, if faced with continuing diffusion, would rather *be nobody or somebody bad, or indeed, dead—and this totally, and by free choice—than be not-quite-somebody.* The word *total* is not accidental in this connection, for I have endeavored to describe in another connection (1953) a human proclivity to a "totalistic" reorientation when, at critical stages of development, reintegration into a relative "wholeness" seems impossible. . . .

6. TRANSFERENCE AND RESISTANCE

What I can say here about the therapeutic problems encountered with the patients described must be restricted to an attempt at relating to the concepts of identity and diffusion such matters of therapeutic technique as have been elaborated by workers in the field of borderline cases.[3]

On facing therapy, some of the patients under discussion here undergo a phase of particular malignancy. While the depth of regression and the danger of acting out must, of course, guide our diagnostic decisions, it is important to recognize, from the start, a mechanism present in such turn for the worse: I would call it the "rock-bottom attitude." This consists of a quasi-deliberate giving in on the part of the patient to the pull of regression, a radical search for the rock-bottom—i.e., both the ultimate limit of regression and the only firm foundation for a renewed progression.[4] The assumption of such a deliberate search for the "baseline" means to carry Ernst Kris's "regression in the service of the ego" to an extreme: the fact that the recovery of our patients sometimes coincides with the discovery of previously hidden artistic gifts, suggests further study of this point (Kris, 1952).

The element of deliberateness added here to "true" regression is often expressed in an all-pervasive mockery which characterizes the initial therapeutic contact with these patients; and by that strange air of sadomasochistic satisfaction, which makes it often hard to see and harder to believe, that their self-depreciation and their willingness to "let the ego die" harbors a devastating sincerity. As one patient said: "That people do not know how to succeed is bad enough. But the worst is that they do not know how to fail. I have decided to fail well." This almost "deadly" sincerity is to be found in the patients' very determination to *trust nothing but mistrust,* and yet to watch from a dark corner of their mind (and indeed, often from the

[3] I owe new insights in this field to Robert Knight (1953) and to Margaret Brenman (1952).

[4] David Rapaport's ego-psychological approach to "Activity and Passivity" sheds new light on the ego's role in such crises (1967).

corner of an eye) for new experiences simple and forthright enough to permit a renewal of the most basic experiments in trustful mutuality. The therapist, manifestly faced with a mocking and defiant young adult, actually must take over the task of a mother who introduces a baby to life's trustworthiness. In the center of the treatment is the patient's need to redelineate himself, and thus to rebuild the foundations of his identity. At the beginning these delineations shift abruptly, even as violent shifts in the patient's experience of his ego boundary take place before our eyes: the patient's mobility may suddenly undergo a "catatonic" slowdown; his attentiveness may turn into overwhelming sleepiness; his vasomotor system may overreact to the point of producing sensations of fainting; his sense of reality may yield to feelings of depersonalization; or the remnants of his self-assurance may disappear in a miasmic loss of a sense of physical presence. Cautious but firm inquiry will reveal the probability that a number of contradictory impulses preceded the "attack." There is first a sudden intense impulse to completely destroy the therapist, and this, it seems with an underlying "cannibalistic" wish to devour his essence and his identity. At the same time, or in alternation, there occurs a fear and a wish to be devoured, to gain an identity by being absorbed in the therapist's essence. Both tendencies, of course, are often dissimilated or somatized for long periods, during which they find a manifestation (often kept secret) only after the therapeutic hour. This manifestation may be an impulsive flight into sexual promiscuity acted out without sexual satisfaction or any sense of participation; enormously absorbing rituals of masturbation or food intake; excessive drinking or wild driving; or self-destructive marathons of reading or listening to music, without food or sleep.

We see here the most extreme form of what may be called *identity resistance* which, incidentally, far from being restricted to the patients described here, is a universal form of resistance regularly experienced but often unrecognized in the course of some analyses. Identity resistance is, in its milder and more usual forms, the patient's fear that the analyst, because of his particular personality, background, or philosophy, may carelessly or deliberately destroy the weak core of the patient's identity and impose instead his own. I would not hesitate to say that some of the much discussed unsolved transference neuroses in patients, as well as in candidates in training, is the direct result of the fact that the identity resistance often is, at best, analyzed only quite unsystematically. In such cases the analysand may throughout the analysis resist any possible inroad by the analyst's identity while surrendering on all other points; or he may absorb more of the analyst's identity than is manageable within the patient's own means; or he may leave the analysis with a lifelong sense of not having been provided with some essence owed to him by the analyst.

In cases of acute identity diffusion this identity resistance becomes the core problem of the therapeutic encounter. Variations of psychoanalytic technique have in common that the dominant resistance must be accepted as the main guide to technique and that interpretation must be fitted to the patient's ability to utilize it. Here the patient sabotages communication until he has settled some basic—if contradictory —issues. The patient insists that the therapist accept his negative identity as real and necessary (which it is and was) without concluding that this negative identity is "all there is to him." If the therapist is able to fulfill both of these demands, he must prove patiently through many severe crises that he can maintain understanding and affection for the patient without either devouring him or offering himself for a totem meal. Only then can better known forms of transference, if ever so reluctantly, emerge.

These are nothing more than a few hints regarding the phenomenology of identity diffusion as reflected in the most outstanding and immediate transferences and resistances. Individual treatment, however, is only one facet of therapy in the cases under discussion. The transferences of these patients remain diffused, while their acting out remains a constant danger. Some, therefore, need to undergo treatment in a hospital environment in which their stepping out of the therapeutic relationship can be observed and limited; and in which first

steps *beyond* the newly won bipolar relationship to the therapist
meet with the immediate support of receptive nurses, cooperative fellow patients, and helpful instructors in a sufficiently wide
choice of activities.

7. SPECIFIC FACTORS IN FAMILY AND CHILDHOOD

In the discussion of patients who have a relevant pathogenic
trend in common, we are apt to ask what their parents have in
common. I think that one may say that a number of the mothers
in our case histories have in common three outstanding traits.
First, a pronounced status awareness, of the climbing and pre-
tentious, or of the "hold-on" variety. They would at almost any
time be willing to overrule matters of honest feeling and of
intelligent judgment for the sake of a facade of wealth, propriety, and "happiness": they, in fact, try to coerce their sensitive
children into a pretense of a "natural" and "glad-to-be-
proper" sociability. Secondly, they have the special quality of
a penetrating omnipresence; their very voices and their softest
sobs are sharp, plaintive, or fretful, and cannot be escaped
within a considerable radius. One patient, all through childhood, had a repetitive dream of a pair of flapping scissors flying
around a room: the scissors proved to symbolize his mother's
voice, cutting, and cutting off.[5] These mothers love, but they
love fearfully, plaintively, intrusively; they are themselves so
hungry for approval and for recognition that they burden their
young children with complicated complaints, especially about
the fathers, and they plead with the children to justify by their
existence their mother's existence. They are highly jealous and
highly sensitive to the jealousy of others; in our context it is
especially important that the mother is intensely jealous of any

[5] This example illustrates well the balance which must be found in the
interpretation given to such patients between *sexual symbolism* (here castration) which, if overemphasized by the therapist, can only increase the patient's sense of being endangered; and the *representation of dangers to the
ego* (here the danger of having the thread of one's autonomy cut off) the
communication of which is more urgent, more immediately beneficial, and
a condition for the safe discussion of sexual meanings.

sign that the child may identify primarily with the father, or, worse, base his very identity on that of the father. It must be added that whatever these mothers are, they are more so toward the patient; the conclusion is inescapable that these patients, in turn, have, from the beginning, deeply hurt their mothers by shying away from them, and this because of an utter intolerance of extreme temperamental differences. These differences, however, are only extreme expressions of an essential affinity: by which I mean to imply that the patient's excessive tendency to withdraw (or to act impulsively) and the mother's excessive social intrusiveness have in common a high degree of social vulnerability. Behind the mother's persistent complaints, then, that the father failed to make a woman out of her, is the complaint, deeply perceived by both mother and child, that the patient failed to make a mother out of her.

The fathers, while usually successful, and often outstanding in their particular fields, do not stand up against their wives at home because of an excessive mother dependence on them, in consequence of which the fathers also are deeply jealous of their children. What initiative and integrity they have either surrenders to the wife's intrusiveness or tries guiltily to elude her: in consequence of which the mother becomes only the more needy, plaintive, and "sacrificial" in her demands upon all or some of her children.

Of the relationship of our patients to their brothers and sisters I can only say that it seems to be more symbiotic than most sibling relationships are. Because of an early identity hunger, our patients are apt to attach themselves to one brother or sister in a way resembling the behavior of twins (Burlingham, 1952): except that here we have one twin, as it were, trying to treat a non-twin as a twin. They seem apt to surrender to a total identification with at least one sibling in ways which go far beyond the "altruism by identification" described by Anna Freud (1936). It is as if our patients surrendered their own identity to that of a brother or sister in the hope of regaining a bigger and better one by some act of merging. For periods they succeed; the letdown which must follow the breakup of the artificial twinship is only the more traumatic. Rage and paralysis follow the sudden insight that there is enough identity only for one, and that the other seems to have made off with it.

The early childhood histories of our patients are, on the whole, remarkably bland. Some infantile autism is often observed early but usually rationalized by the parents. Yet one has the general impression that the degree of malignancy of the acute identity diffusion in late adolescence depends on the extent of this early autism, which will determine the depth of regression and the intensity of the encounter between new identity fragments and old introjects. As to particular traumata in childhood or youth, one item seems frequent, namely, a severe physical trauma either in the oedipal period or in early puberty—and this in connection with a separation from home. This trauma may consist of an operation or a belatedly diagnosed physical defect; it may be an accident or a severe sexual traumatization. Otherwise the early pathology conforms with that expected as typical for the dominant psychiatric diagnosis given.

8. THE THERAPEUTIC DESIGN

I promised a composite sketch, and a sketch I have presented. Again, only the detailed presentation of a few cases could elucidate the relation of ego weakness to congenital proclivities, on the one hand, and to the educative deficiency of families and classes, on the other. In the meantime, the most immediate clarification of the ego's relationship to its "environment" ensues from the study of the young patient's recovery in a hospital setting, i.e., the study of his determined "oneliness" (as a young woman patient put it); of his tendency to exploit and provoke the hospital environment; of his growing ability to utilize it; and finally, of his capacity to leave this kind of institutionalized moratorium and to return to his old or new place in society. The hospital community offers the clinical researcher the possibility of being a participant observer not only in the individual patient's personal treatment, but also in the "therapeutic design" which is to meet the legitimate demands of patients who share a life problem—here identity diffusion.

It stands to reason that such a common problem receives elucidation, as the hospital community plans on meeting the specific requirements of those who failed in it: in this case the
hospital becomes a planfully institutionalized world-between-
worlds, which offers the young individual support in the re-
building of those most vital ego functions, which—as far as he
ever built them—he has relinquished. The relationship to the
individual therapist is the cornerstone for the establishment of
a new and honest mutuality of function which must set the
patient's face toward an ever so dimly perceived and ever so
strenuously refuted future. Yet, it is the hospital community in
which the patient's first steps of renewed social experimentation take place. The privileges and obligations of such a community immediately demand his subjection to and his initiation
in a communal design which will also strive to meet his and his
fellow patients' needs—and incidentally, also, those of the staff:
for it stands to reason that a communal setting such as a hospital is characterized not only by the identity needs of those who
happen to be the patients, but also of those who choose to
become their brothers' (and sisters') keepers. The discussion
of the ways in which professional hierarchy distributes the functions, the rewards, and the status of such keepership (and thus
opens the door for a variety of countertransferences and
"cross-transferences" which, indeed, make the hospital a fac-
simile of a home) is entering the literature on the subject of
hospital morale (i.e., Bateman and Dunham, 1948; Schwartz
and Will, 1953). From the point of view of this paper, such
studies prepare for discussion also the danger of the patient's
choosing the very role of a patient as the basis of his crystalliz-
ing identity: for this role may well prove more meaningful than
any potential identity experienced before.

9. ONCE MORE: THE DIAGRAM

Diagrams have a quiet coerciveness all their own. Especially
a diagram which has neither been completed nor discarded
becomes a conceptual Harvey: one converses with it unawares.
In therapeutic work, one tries to ignore the embarrassing fact

that now and again the diagram looks over one's shoulder, as
it were, and makes a suggestion; nor do the patients appreciate
such atmospheric interferences. Only as I concluded this impressionistic survey of some of the main features of identity
diffusion, did it occur to me to "locate" them on the chart:
and it cannot be denied that they clarify previously vague parts
of the diagram and suggest specific expansions of theory. Insisting, then, that in principle Harveys should remain expendable, we will briefly outline what this one can teach us.

The original chart showed only the diagonal, i.e., the successive achievement (or failure) of the main components of
relative psychosocial health. However, it bore the legend:
"Above the diagonal there is space for a future elaboration of
the precursors of each of these solutions, all of which begin
with the beginning; below the diagonal there is space for the
designation of the derivatives of these solutions in the maturing
personality."

Because all the *verticals* "begin with the beginning," one
hesitates to enter even tentative terms into the top boxes. Yet,
work with borderline cases (adolescent, juvenile, and infantile)
suggests that the infantile frontier, to which they have all regressed, is that of a basic mistrust in their *self-delineation* and
of a basic doubt in the possibility of any relationship of *mutuality*. The chart, tentatively, assumes that a successful struggle
on the earliest psychosocial frontier of infancy (i.e., the trust-
mistrust frontier), if well guided by a favorable maternal environment, leads to a dominant sense of *Unipolarity* (I, 5) by
which is meant something like a dominant sense of the goodness of individual existence. This, I believe, deserves to be differentiated from the narcissistic omnipotence ascribed to this
age. While as yet vulnerably dependent on direct, continuous,
and consistent maternal support, an actual sense of the reality
of "good" powers, outside and within oneself, must be assumed
to arise. Its negative counterpart is a diffusion of contradictory
introjects and a predominance of fantasies which pretend to
coerce hostile reality with omnipotent vengeance. Once
gained, however, the psychosocial foundation of unipolarity
subsequently permits *Bipolarization* (II, 5) or what, in id terms,

has been called the cathexis of objects. This permits an outgoing experimentation with powerful but loving individuals who retain consistent reality, even though they may go before they come, deny before they give, seem indifferent before they, again, become attentive. In transitory or lasting forms of autism, the child can be seen to shy away from or to despair of such bipolarization, always in search of an illusory good "oneliness."

Subsequent *Play* and *Work Identifications* (III, 5 -IV, 5) with powerful adults and with older and younger age-mates need no further discussion here; the literature on the preschool and school stage amply illustrates the gains and the defeats of these more obviously psychosocial periods.

It is the horizontal (V) which contains the *derivatives of earlier relative achievements which now become part and parcel of the struggle for identity.* It is necessary to emphasize (and possible to illustrate briefly) the principle, according to which early relative achievements (diagonal) when considered at a later stage (any horizontal below the diagonal) must be reviewed and renamed in terms of that later stage. Basic Trust, for example, is a good and a most fundamental thing to have, but its psychosocial quality becomes more differentiated as the ego comes into the possession of a more extensive apparatus, even as society challenges and guides such extension.

To begin, then, with the pathology just described: *Time Diffusion* (V, 1) or a loss of the ego's function of maintaining perspective and expectancy is related to the *earliest crises in life* (I, 1), and this because of the fact that the experience of temporal cycles and of time qualities are inherent in and develop from the initial problems of mounting need tension, of delay of satisfaction, and final unification with the satisfying "object." As tension increases, future fulfillment is anticipated in "hallucinatory" images; as fulfillment is delayed, moments of impotent rage occur in which anticipation (and with it, the future) is obliterated; the perception of an approaching potential satisfaction, again, gives time a highly condensed quality of intense hope and feared disappointment. All of this contributes temporal elements to the formation of basic trust, i.e., the inner conviction that—after all—sufficient satisfaction is sufficiently predictable to make waiting and "working" worth while. Whatever the original inventory of time qualities are, our most malignantly regressed young people are clearly possessed by general attitudes which represent something of a mistrust of time as such: every delay appears to be a deceit, every wait an experience of impotence, every hope a danger, every plan a catastrophe, every potential provider a traitor. Therefore, time must be made to stand still, if necessary by the magic means of catatonic immobility—or by death. These are the extremes which are manifest in few, and latent in many cases of identity diffusion; yet, every adolescent, I would believe, knows at least fleeting moments of being at odds with time itself. In its normal and transitory form, this new kind of mistrust quickly or gradually yields to outlooks permitting and demanding an intense investment in a future, or in a number of possible futures. If these, to us, seem often quite "utopian" (i.e., based on expectations which would call for a change in the laws of historical change as we know them), we must, for the moment, postpone any judgment of value. The adolescent—or some adolescents—may need, at all costs, an outlook with a perspective worth an investment of energy. The actual realizability of such an outlook may be a matter of later learning and adjusting, and often a matter of historical luck.

In the following, I shall let each step on the chart lead to a few suggestive *social considerations* which were only briefly touched on in the foregoing. To envisage a future, the young adult may also need that something which Shaw called "a religion" and "a clear comprehension of life in the light of an intelligible theory." I indicated at the beginning that we would call this something-between-a-theory-and-a-religion, an *ideology*, a term highly conducive to misunderstanding. At this point let me stress only the *temporal* element in world views which might be called ideological: they are grouped around *a utopian simplification of historical perspective* (salvation, conquest, reform, happiness, rationality, technological mastery) in accordance with newly developing identity potentials. Whatever else ideology is (Mannheim, 1949; Schilder, 1951b), and whatever transitory or lasting social forms it takes, we will tentatively view it here and discuss it later—*as a necessity for the growing ego* which is involved in the succession of generations, and in adolescence is committed to some new synthesis of past and future: a synthesis which must include but transcend the past, even as identity does.

We proceed to *Identity Consciousness* (V, 2) the ancestors of which are *Doubt* and *Shame* (II, 2). They counteract and complicate the sense of autonomy, i.e., the acceptance of the psychosocial fact of being, once and for all, a separate individual, who actually and figuratively must stand on his own feet. Here, I beg to quote myself (1946):

> Shame is an emotion insufficiently studied [see, however, Piers and Singer, 1953], because in our civilization it is so early and easily absorbed by guilt. Shame supposes that one is completely exposed and conscious of being looked at: in one word, self-conscious. One is visible and not ready to be visible; which is why we dream of shame as a situation in which we are stared at in a condition of incomplete dress. Shame is early expressed in an impulse to bury one's face, or to sink, right then and there, into the ground. But this, I think, is essentially rage turned against the self. He who is ashamed would like to force the world not to look at him, not to notice his exposure. He would like to destroy the eyes of the world. Instead he must wish for his own invisibility. . . . Doubt is the brother of shame. Where shame is dependent on the consciousness of being upright and exposed, doubt, so clinical observation leads me to believe, has much to do with a consciousness of having a front and a back—and especially a "behind." . . . This basic sense of doubt in whatever one has left behind forms a substratum for later and more verbal forms of compulsive doubting; which finds its adult expression in paranoiac fears concerning hidden persecutors and secret persecutions threatening from behind and from within the behind.

Identity Consciousness then is a new edition of that original *doubt*, which concerned the trustworthiness of the training adults and the trustworthiness of the child himself—only that in adolescence, such self-conscious doubt concerns the reliability and reconcilability of the whole span of childhood which is now to be left behind. The obligation now to achieve an identity, not only distinct but also distinctive, is apt to arouse a painful overall *ashamedness,* somehow comparable to the original shame (and rage) over being visible all around to all-knowing adults—only that such potential shame now adheres to one's identity as a being with a *public history,* exposed to *age-mates* and *leaders.* All of this, in the normal course of events, is outbalanced by that *Self-Certainty,* which comes from the accrued sense of an ever increased identity at the conclusion of each previous crisis, a certainty now characterized by an increasing sense of independence from the family as the matrix of childhood identifications.

Among the societal phenomena corresponding to this second conflict there is a universal trend toward some form of *uniformity* (and sometimes to special uniforms or distinctive clothing) through which incomplete self-certainty, for a time, can hide in a group certainty, such as is provided by the badges as well as the sacrifices of investitures, confirmations, and initiations. Even those who care to differ radically must evolve a certain uniformity of differing (Snobs, Zoot-suiters). These and less obvious uniformities are supported by the institution of comprehensive *shaming* among peers, a judgmental give-and-take and free banding together which leaves only a few "holding the bag" in painful (if sometimes creative) isolation.

The matter of the choice of a *Negative Identity* (V,3) as against *Free Role Experimentation* has been discussed. The position of these terms on the chart signifies their obvious connection with the earlier conflict (III,3) between free *Initiative* (in reality, fantasy, and play) and oedipal guilt. Where the identity crisis breaks through to the oedipal crisis and beyond it, to a crisis of trust, the choice of a negative identity remains the only form of initiative, complete denial of guilt or complete denial of ambition the only possible ways of managing guilt. On the other hand, the normal expression of relatively guilt-free initiative at this stage is a kind of disciplined role experimentation which follows the unwritten codes of adolescent subsocieties.

Of the social institutions which undertake to channel as they encourage such initiative, and to provide atonement as they appease guilt, we may point here, again, to *initiations* and *confirmations:* they strive, within an atmosphere of mythical timelessness, to combine some form of sacrifice or submission with an energetic guidance toward sanctioned and circumscribed ways of action—a combination which assures the development in the novice of an optimum of compliance with a maximum sense of fellowship and free choice. This ego aspect of the matter (namely, the achievement of a sense of a choice as a result of ritual regimentation) as yet awaits study and integration with the better explored sexual aspects of initiation rites and related rituals, official or spontaneous. Armies, of course, utilize this potentiality.

As we approach the middle region of the chart, we find that a more detailed discussion of the terms used has already been offered. Extreme *Work Paralysis* (V,4) is the logical sequence of a deep sense of inadequacy (regressed to a sense of basic mistrust) of one's general equipment. Such a sense of inadequacy, of course, does not usually reflect a true lack of potential: It may, rather, convey the unrealistic demands made by an ego ideal willing to settle only for omnipotence or omniscience; it may express the fact that the immediate social environment does not have a niche for the individual's true gifts; or it may reflect the paradoxical fact that an individual in early school life was seduced into a specialized precocity which early outdistanced his identity development. All of these reasons, then, may exclude the individual from that experimental competition in play and work through which he learns to find and to insist on *his* kind of achievement and work identity.

Social institutions support the strength and the distinctiveness of work identity by offering those who are still learning and experimenting a certain *status-of-the-moratorium,* an apprenticeship or discipleship characterized by defined duties, sanctioned competitions, and special freedoms, and yet potentially integrated with the hierarchies of expectable jobs and careers, castes and classes, guilds and unions.

In Box V,5 we again meet the diagonal, and the over-all focus of this paper; crossing it we enter the area of psychosocial elements which are not derivatives but precursors of future psychosocial crises. The first such element (V,6) is *Sexual Identity vs. Bisexual Diffusion,* the most immediate precursor of *Intimacy vs. Isolation.* Here the sexual mores of cultures and classes make for immense differences in the psychosocial differentiation of masculine and feminine (M. Mead, 1949), and in the age, kind, and ubiquity of genital activity. These differences can obscure the common fact discussed above, namely, that the development of psychosocial intimacy is not possible without a firm sense of identity. Bisexual diffusion can lead young adults toward two deceptive developments. Induced by special mores, or otherwise seduced, they may foreclose their identity development by concentrating on early genital activity without intimacy; or, on the contrary, they may concentrate on social or intellectual status values which underplay the genital element, with a resulting permanent weakness of genital polarization with the other sex. Different mores (Kinsey, Pomeroy, and Martin, 1948) demand from some the ability to postpone genital activity, and from others, the early ability to make it a "natural" part of life: in either case, special problems ensue which may well impair true heterosexual intimacy in young adulthood.

Social institutions here offer ideological rationales for a *prolongation of the psychosexual moratorium* in the form of complete sexual abstinence, in the form of genital activity without social commitment, or in the form of sexual play without genital engagement (petting). What a group's or an individual's "libido economy" will stand for, depends to some extent on the identity gain which accrues from such preferred sexual behavior.

The study of horizontal V of the chart, then, reveals certain systematic consistencies in the described elements of identity diffusion, and in those of identity formation. As pointed out parenthetically, these consistencies correspond to certain social institutions, which (in ways still to be elucidated) support the ego needs and ego functions subsumed under the term *identity.* In fact, the two remaining boxes of horizontal V (which at any rate are marginal to this clinical section) cannot be approached at all without a discussion of social institutions. The prime institution which awaits clarification here is that system of ideals which societies present to the young individual in the explicit or implicit form of an *ideology*. To ideology we may, in tentative summary, ascribe the function of offering youth (1) an overly clear perspective of the future, encompassing all foreseeable time, and thus counteracting individual "time diffusion"; (2) an opportunity for the exhibition of some uniformity of appearance and action counteracting individual identity consciousness; (3) inducement to collective role and work experimentation which can counteract a sense of inhibition and personal guilt; (4) submission to leaders who as "big brothers" escape the ambivalence of the parent–child relation; (5) introduction into the ethos of the prevailing technology, and thus into sanctioned and regulated competition; and (6) a seeming correspondence between the internal world of ideals and evils, on the one hand, and, on the other, of the outer world with its organized goals and dangers in real space and time: a geographic–historical framework for the young individual's budding identity.

I am aware of having, in the conclusion of a pathographic sketch, "sketched in" some references to phenomena which are the domain of social science. I can justify this only with the assumption that clinical work, in cutting through the immense diversity of individual pathology in order to arrive at some workable generalities, may well come upon an aspect of matters institutional which the historical and the economic approach has necessarily neglected. Here, however, we must first attempt to bring some order into the terminological household of our own field, and this especially where it overlaps with areas of social science.

IV. Societal: Ego and Environment

1

It has not escaped the reader that the term *identity* covers much of what has been called the self by a variety of workers, be it in the form of a self-concept (G. H. Mead, 1934), a self-system (H. S. Sullivan, 1953), or in that of fluctuating self-experiences described by Schilder (1951a), Federn (1952), and others.[6] Within psychoanalytic ego psychology, Hartmann, above all, has circumscribed this general area more clearly when in discussing the so-called *libidinal cathexis of the ego in narcissism,* he comes to the conclusion that it is rather a self which is thus being cathected. He advocates a term *"self-representation,"* as differentiated from "object representation" (1951a). This self-representation was, less systematically, anticipated by Freud in his occasional references to the ego's "attitudes toward the self" and to fluctuating cathexes bestowed upon this self in labile states of "self-esteem" (Freud, 1914). In this paper, we are concerned with the *genetic continuity* of such a self-representation—a continuity which must lastly be ascribed to the work of the ego. No other inner agency could accomplish the selective accentuation of significant identifications throughout childhood; and the gradual integration of self-images in anticipation of an identity. It is for this reason that I have called identity, at first, ego identity. But in brashly choosing a name analogous to "ego ideal," I have opened myself to the query as to what the relationship of these two concepts is.

Freud assigned the *internalized perpetuation* of cultural influences to the functions of the "superego or ego ideal" which was to represent the commands and the prohibitions emanating from the environment and its traditions. Let us compare two statements of Freud's which are relevant here.

> The super-ego of the child is not really built up on the model of the parents, but on that of the parents' super-ego; it takes over the same content, it becomes the vehicle of tradition and of all the age-long values which have been handed down in this way from generation to generation. You may easily guess what

---

[6] Here, as in previous publications, I refrain from referring to more comprehensive modifications of psychoanalytic theory (Dollard, Fromm, and Kardiner) because I am as yet unable to establish the convergencies and divergencies between that which they have stated systematically, and that which I am trying to formulate.

great help is afforded by the recognition of the super-ego in understanding the social behavior of man, in grasping the problem of delinquency, for example, and perhaps, too, in providing us with some practical hints upon education. . . . Mankind never lives completely in the present. The *ideologies of the super-ego* perpetuate the past, the traditions of the race and the people, which yield but slowly to the influence of the present and to new developments, and, so long as they work through the super-ego, play an important part in man's life [1933; emphasis added].

Freud, it is to be noted here, speaks of the "ideologies of the super-ego," thus giving the superego ideational content; yet he also refers to it as a "vehicle," i.e., as a part of the psychic system through which ideas work. It would seem that by ideologies of the superego Freud means the superego's specific contributions to the archaic, to the magic in the inner coerciveness of ideologies.

In a second statement Freud acknowledges the social side of the ego ideal. "The ego-ideal is of great importance for the understanding of group psychology. Besides its individual side, this ideal has a social side; it is also the common ideal of a family, a class, or a ration" (1914).

It would seem that the terms *superego* and *ego ideal* have come to be distinguished by their different relation to phylogenetic and to ontogenetic history. The superego is conceived as a more archaic and thoroughly internalized representative of the evolutionary principle of morality, of man's *congenital proclivity* toward the development of a primitive, categorical conscience. Allied with (ontogenetically) early introjects, the superego remains a rigidly vindictive and punitive inner agency of "blind" morality. The ego ideal, however, seems to be more flexibly bound to the ideals of the particular *historical period* and thus is closer to the ego function of reality testing.

Ego identity (if we were to hold on to this term and to this level of discourse) would in comparison be even closer to *social reality* in that as a subsystem of the ego it would test, select, and integrate the self-representations derived from the psychosocial crises of childhood. It could be said to be characterized by the more or less *actually attained but forever to-be-revised* sense of the reality of the self within social reality; while the imagery of the ego ideal could be said to represent a set of *to-be-strived-for but forever not-quite-attainable ideal* goals for the self.

However, in using the word *self* in the sense of Hartmann's self-representation, one opens the whole controversy to a radical consideration. One could argue that it may be wise in matters of the ego's perceptive and regulative dealings with its self to reserve the designation "ego" for the subject, and to give the designation "self" to the object. The ego, then, as a central organizing agency, is during the course of life faced with a changing self which, in turn, demands to be synthesized with abandoned and anticipated selves. This suggestion would be applicable to the *body ego*, which could be said to be the part of the self provided by the attributes of the organism, and, therefore, might more appropriately be called the body self. It concerns the ego ideal as the representative of the ideas, images, and configurations, which serve the persistent comparison with an *ideal self*. It, finally, would apply to what I have called *ego identity*. What could consequently be called the *self-identity* emerges from all those experiences in which a sense of temporary self-diffusion was successfully contained by a renewed and ever more realistic self-definition and social recognition. *Identity formation thus can be said to have a self-aspect, and an ego aspect.* It is part of the ego in the sense that it represents the ego's synthesizing function in meeting one of its frontiers, namely, the actual social structure of the environment and the image of reality as transmitted to the child during successive childhood crises. (The other frontiers would be the id, and the demands made on the ego by our biological history and structure; the superego and the demands of our more primitively moralistic proclivities; and the ego ideal with its idealized parent images.) Identity, in this connection, has a claim to recognition as the adolescent ego's most important support, in the task of containing the postpubertal id, and in balancing the then newly invoked superego as well as the again overly demanding ego ideal.

Until the matter of ego vs. self is sufficiently defined to permit a terminological decision, I shall use the bare term *identity* in order to suggest a social function of the ego which results, in adolescence, in a relative psychosocial equilibrium essential to the tasks of young adulthood.

2

The word *psychosocial* so far has had to serve as an emergency bridge between the so-called "biological" formulations of psychoanalysis and newer ones which take the cultural environment into more systematic consideration.

The so-called basic *biological* orientation of psychoanalysis has gradually become a habitual kind of *pseudobiology,* and this especially in the conceptualization (or lack thereof) of man's "environment." In psychoanalytic writings the terms *outer world* or *environment* are often used to designate an uncharted area which is said to be outside merely because it fails to be inside—inside the individual's somatic skin, or inside his psychic systems, or inside his self in the widest sense. Such a vague and yet omnipresent "outerness" by necessity assumes a number of ideological connotations, and, in fact, assumes the character of a number of world images: sometimes "the outer world" is conceived of as reality's conspiracy against the infantile wish world; sometimes as the (indifferent or annoying) fact of the existence of other people; and then again as the (at least partially benevolent) presence of maternal care. But even in the recent admission of the significance of the "mother–child relationship," a stubborn tendency persists to treat the mother–child unit as a "biological" entity more or less isolated from its cultural surroundings which then, again, become an "environment" of vague supports or of blind pressures and mere "conventions." Thus, step for step, we are encumbered by the remnants of juxtapositions which were once necessary and fruitful enough: for it was important to establish the fact that moralistic and hypocritical social demands are apt to crush the adult and to exploit the child. It was important to conceptu-alize certain intrinsic antagonisms between the individual's and society's energy households. However, the implicit conclusion that an individual ego could exist against or without a specifi-cally human "environment," i.e., social organization, is sense-less; and as for its "biological" orientation, such an implicit assumption threatens to isolate psychoanalytic theory from the rich ecological insights of modern biology.

It is, again, Hartmann (1951b) who opens the way to new considerations. His statement that the human infant is born preadapted to an "average expectable environment" implies a more truly biological as well as an inescapably societal formu-lation. For not even the very best of mother–child relationships could, by themselves, account for that subtle and complex "mi-lieu" which permits a human baby not only to survive but also to develop his potentialities for growth and uniqueness. Man's ecology includes among its dimensions constant natural, histor-ical, and technological readjustment; which makes it at once obvious that only a perpetual social metabolism and a constant (if ever so imperceptible) restructuring of tradition can safe-guard for each new generation of infants anything approaching an "average expectability" of environment. Today, when rapid technological changes have taken the lead, the matter of estab-lishing by scientific means and of preserving in flexible forms an "average expectable" continuity in child rearing and educa-tion has, in fact, become a matter of human survival.

The specific kind of preadaptedness of the human infant (namely, the readiness to grow by predetermined steps through institutionalized psychosocial crises) calls not only for one basic environment, but for a whole chain of such successive environ-ments. As the child "adapts" in spurts and stages, he has a claim, at any given stage reached, to the next "average expect-able environment." In other words, the human environment must permit and safeguard a series of more or less discontinu-ous and yet culturally and psychologically consistent steps, each extending further along the radius of expanding life tasks. All of this makes man's so-called biological adaptation a matter of life cycles developing within their community's changing history. Consequently, a psychoanalytic sociology faces the task of conceptualizing man's environment as the persistent endeavor of the older and more adult egos to join in the organizational effort of providing an integrated series of average expectable environments for the young egos.

3

In a recent paper which thoughtfully, yet somewhat sweepingly reviews efforts at approaching the relation of culture and personality, Hartmann, Kris, and Loewenstein state: "Cultural conditions could and should be viewed also with the question in mind which and what kind of opportunities for ego functions in a sphere free from conflict they invite or inhibit" (1951). In regard to the possibility of studying the reflection of such "cultural conditions" in the psychoanalysis of individuals, the writers seem less encouraging. They state: "Analysts too are aware of differences of behavior caused by cultural conditions; they are not devoid of that common sense which has always stressed these differences, but their impact on the analytic observer tends to decrease as work progresses and as available data move from the periphery to the center, that is from manifest behavior to data, part of which is accessible only to an analytic investigation." The present paper ventures to suggest that rather central problems of ego development, which are, indeed, "accessible only to an analytic investigation," demand that the psychoanalyst's awareness of cultural differences go well beyond that "common sense" which the three authors (being themselves outstanding cosmopolitans) seem to find sufficient in this particular area of observation, while they would assuredly urge a more "analyzed" common sense in other areas.

In order to approach this whole matter psychoanalytically, it may well be necessary for the individual psychoanalyst to ask himself what particular configuration of drives, defenses, capabilities, and opportunities led him into the choice of this ever-expanding field. Some search in this area may clarify the fact that some of the most heated and stubborn answers to the

question of what psychoanalysis is or is *not* originate in another
question of great urgency, namely: what psychoanalysis *must be*
(or *must remain or become*) to a particular worker because a
particular psychoanalytic "identity" has become a cornerstone
of his existence as a man, a professional, and a citizen. I am
not denying here the necessity, in a suddenly expanding and
unexpectedly popular field, to define the original sources of
its inspiration and the fundamentals of its specific propriety.
Yet, psychoanalysis, in its young history, has offered rich opportunities for a variety of identities: it gave new function and
scope to such divergent endeavors as natural philosophy and
Talmudic argument; medical tradition and missionary teaching; literary demonstration and the building of theory; social
reform and the making of money. Psychoanalysis as a movement has harbored a variety of world images and utopias which
originated in the various states of its history in a variety of
countries, and this as a result of the simple fact that man, in
order to be able to interact efficiently with other human beings,
must, at intervals, make a *total orientation out of a given stage of
partial knowledge.* Individual students of Freud thus found their
identity best suited to certain early theses of his which promised
a particular sense of psychoanalytic identity, and with it, an
inspiring ideology. Similarly, overstated antitheses to some of
Freud's tentative and transient theses have served as bases for
professional and scientific identities of other workers in the
field. Such identities easily find elaboration in ideological
schools and in irreversible systematizations which do not permit of argument or change.

    In speaking of scientific proof and scientific progress in a
field which deals directly with the immediate needs of men, it
is necessary to account not only for methodological, practical,
and ethical factors, but also for the necessity of a professional
identity backed by an ideological quasi synthesis of the available
orientations. Sooner or later, then, training analyses must encompass the varieties of professional identity formation in can-
didates-for-training while theoretical teaching must throw light
also on the ideological background of principal differences in

what is felt to be most practical, most true, and most right at various stages of this developing field.

4

The discussion of "professional identities" has necessarily led us beyond identity formation proper, to its derivatives in later, truly adult stages. I will make one more step into adulthood, before returning, in conclusion, to the problem of ideological polarization as an aspect of the societal processes which meets a necessity of adolescent ego development.

I have already implied a hypothesis which goes beyond that of Hartmann, Kris, and Loewenstein, who state that "cultural conditions could and should be viewed *also* [emphasis added] with the question in mind which and what kind of opportunities for ego functions in a sphere free from conflict they invite or inhibit." It may well be that the relationship between the organized values and institutional efforts of societies, on the one hand, and the mechanisms of ego synthesis, on the other, is more systematic; and that, at any rate, from a psychosocial point of view, basic social and cultural processes can *only* be viewed as the joint endeavor of adult egos to develop and maintain, through joint organization, a maximum of conflict-free energy in a mutually supportive psychosocial equilibrium. Only such organization is likely to give consistent support to the young egos at every step of their development.

I have characterized the psychosocial gains of adult ego development with the terms Intimacy, Generativity, and Integrity (VI,6— VII,7—VIII,8 on the chart). They denote a postadolescent development of libidinal cathexes in *intimate engagements;* in parenthood or other forms of *"generating";*[7] and, finally, in the most *integrative experiences* and values accrued from a lifetime. All of these developments have ego aspects and social aspects; in fact, their very alternatives (Isolation, VI,6—Self-Absorption, VII,7—and Despair, VIII,8)

---

[7] See the concern over personal children, patients', and germinating ideas in Freud's "Irma Dream" [chapter 8].

can be held in check only by the individual's fitting participation in social endeavors which "invite opportunities for ego functions in spheres free from conflict." The older generation thus needs the younger one as much as the younger one depends on the older; and it would seem that it is in the sphere of this mutuality of drives and interest throughout the development of the older as well as the younger generations that certain basic and universal values such as love, faith, truth, justice, order, work, etc., in all of their compensatory power and defensive strength, become and remain important joint achievements of individual ego development and of the social process. In fact, as our clinical histories begin to reveal, these values provide indispensable support for the ego development of the growing generations, in that they give some specific superindividual consistency to parental conduct (although *kinds* of consistency—including consistent kinds of being inconsistent —vary with value systems and personality types).

The intrinsic complication and the peculiar social pathology adhering to the *verbal conventions* and *formal institutions* which communicate and perpetuate social values periodically call for special societal processes which will recreate the "average expectability" of the environments either through ceremonial rededication, or through systematic reformulation. In both cases, selected leaders and elites feel called upon to demonstrate a convincing, a "charismatic" kind of generalized generativity, i.e., a superpersonal interest in the maintenance and the rejuvenation of institutions. In recorded history, some such leaders are registered as "great"; they, it seems, are able, out of the deepest personal conflicts to derive the energy which meets their period's specific needfulness for a resynthesis of the prevalent world image. At any rate, only through constant rededication will institutions gain the active and inspired investment of new energy from their young members. More theoretically stated: only by maintaining, in its institutionalized values, meaningful correspondences to the main crises of ego development, does a society manage to have at the disposal of its particular group identity a maximum of the conflict-free energy accrued from the childhood crises of a majority of its young members.[8]

Before briefly applying this general assumption to ideology, I must ask the reader to take one more look at the chart. In boxes V,6—V,7—and V,8 he will find whatever indication I can give of the precursors in adolescence of what later on is Intimacy, Generativity, and Integrity. The struggle for *Sexual Identity*, V,6, while, at first, consumed with the question as to what kind of a male or female one is, through the selective search for *Intimacy*, VI,6, approaches the problem of a choice of a future coparent. The clarification, through a firmer identity formation, of one's status as a *follower* (of some) and a *leader* (of others) V,7, permits the early development of a responsibility toward younger agemates which, although an important social phenomenon in its own right, is a precursor of the sense of responsibility for the next generation *(Generativity)* VII,7. Finally, some form of *Ideological Polarization*, V,8, some breakdown of the multiplicity of values into a few which coerce commitment, must be part and parcel of this gradual reversal of roles, through which the "identified" individual becomes a figure of identification for the young. Such polarization, however, cannot fail eventually to become a critical part of the problem of *Integrity*, VIII,8: a matter which we saw reflected in Shaw's statement: that he "succeeded only too well" in living the public identity "G.B.S.," i.e., in the polarization of his propensities for acting like an actor on the stage of life, and for acting as a reformer in social reality.

---

[8] In this paper, I cannot do more than approach the possible relation of the problem of identity to ideological processes; and I can only parenthetically list possible analogous correspondences between stages of psychosocial development in the individual and major trend, of social organization. The problem of Basic Trust (and Basic Mistrust) seems to have such a correspondence with the institutionalization of a faith and an evil in organized religion or other forms of moral world imagery; the problem of Autonomy (versus Shame and Doubt) with the delineation of individual rights and limitations in the basic principles of law and justice; the problem of Initiative (versus Guilt) with the encouragements and limitations emanating from the dominant ethos of production; and the problem of workmanship with the predominant techniques of production and their characteristic division of labor.

5

Shaw, of course, was a studiedly spectacular man. But, to extend a Shavianism quoted above: a clown is often not only the best but also the most sincere part of the Great Show. It is, therefore, worth while at this point to review the words chosen by Shaw to characterize the story of his "conversion": "I was *drawn into* the Socialist *revival* of the early eighties, among Englishmen *intensely serious* and *burning with indignation* at very *real* and very *fundamental evils* that affected *all the world.*" The words here italicized convey to me the following implications. "Drawn into": an ideology has a compelling power. "Revival": it consists of a traditional force in the state of rejuvenation. "Intensely serious": it permits even the cynical to make an investment of sincerity. "Burning with indignation": it gives to the need for repudiation the sanction of righteousness. "Real": it projects a vague inner evil on a circumscribed horror in reality. "Fundamental": it promises participation in an effort at basic reconstruction of society. "All the world": it gives structure to a totally defined world image. Here, then, are the elements by which a group identity harnesses in the service of its ideology the young individual's aggressive and discriminative energies, and encompasses, as it completes it, the individual's identity. Thus, identity and ideology are two aspects of the same process. Both provide the necessary condition for further individual maturation and, with it, for the next higher form of identification, namely, the *solidarity linking common identities.* For the need to bind irrational self-hate and irrational repudiation makes young people, on occasion, mortally compulsive and conservative even where and when they seem most anarchic and radical; the same need makes them potentially "ideological," i.e., more or less explicitly in search of a world image held together by what Shaw called "a clear comprehension of life in the light of an intelligible theory."

As far as Fabian Socialists are concerned, Shaw seems fully justified in using terms characterizing an ideology of marked intellectual brilliance. More generally, an ideological system is a coherent body of shared images, ideas, and ideals which (whether based on a formulated dogma, an implicit *Weltan-schauung*, a highly structured world image, a political creed, or a "way of life") provides for the participants a coherent, if systematically simplified, over-all orientation in space and time, in means and ends.

The word *ideology* itself has somewhat of a bad name. By their very nature ideologies contradict other ideologies as "inconsistent" and hypocritical; and an over-all critique of ideology characterizes its persuasive simplifications as a systematic form of collective hypocrisy (Mannheim, 1949). For it is true that the average adult, and, in fact, the average community, if not acutely engaged in some ideological polarization, are apt to consign ideology to a well-circumscribed compartment in their lives, where it remains handy for periodical rituals and rationalizations, but will do no undue harm to other business at hand. Yet, the fact that ideologies are simplified conceptions of what is to come (and thus later can serve as rationalizations for what has come about) does not preclude the possibility that at certain stages of individual development and at certain periods in history, ideological polarization, conflict, and commitment correspond to an inescapable inner need. Youth needs to base its rejections and acceptances on ideological alternatives vitally related to the existing range of alternatives for identity formation.

Ideologies seem to provide meaningful combinations of the oldest and the newest in a group's ideals. They thus channel the forceful earnestness, the sincere asceticism, and the eager indignation of youth toward that social frontier where the struggle between conservatism and radicalism is most alive. On that frontier, fanatic ideologists do their busy work and psychopathic leaders their dirty work; but there, also, true leaders create significant solidarities. All ideologies ask for, as the prize for the promised possession of a future, uncompromising commitment to some absolute hierarchy of values and some rigid principle of conduct: be that principle total obedience to tradition, if the future is the eternalization of ancestry; total resignation, if the future is to be of another world; total martial discipline, if the future is to be reserved for some brand of armed superman; total inner reform, if the future is perceived as an advance edition of heaven on earth; or (to mention only one of the ideological ingredients of our time) complete pragmatic abandon to the processes of production and to human teamwork, if unceasing production seems to be the thread which holds present and future together. It is in the totalism and exclusiveness of some ideologies that the superego is apt to regain its territory from identity: for when established identities become outworn or unfinished ones threaten to remain incomplete, special crises compel men to wage holy wars, by the cruelest means, against those who seem to question or threaten their unsafe ideological bases.

We may well pause to ponder briefly the over-all fact that the technological and economic developments of our day encroach upon all traditional group identities and solidarities such as may have developed in agrarian, feudal, patrician, or mercantile ideologies. As has been shown by many writers, such over-all development seems to result in a loss of a sense of cosmic wholeness, of providential planfulness, and of heavenly sanction for the means of production (and destruction). In large parts of the world, this seems to result in a ready fascination with totalistic world views, views predicting milleniums and cataclysms, and advocating self-appointed mortal gods. Technological centralization today can give small groups of such fanatic ideologists the concrete power of totalitarian state machines [1954].

Psychoanalysis has made some contributions to the understanding of these developments especially in so far as they reflect the universal anxieties, inner dependencies and vulnerabilities adhering to the common fact of human childhood. Psychoanalysis can also help to understand the fact that even in civilized beings the superego's paternalistic-primitive simplicity may call for an irrational trust in superpolice chiefs on earth, now that the heavenly discipline which encompassed earlier world images seems to have lost its convincing firmness. However, the application of the psychoanalytic instrument to the questions as to how man changes in his depth as he changes the expanses of his environment, and as to who is affected (and how, and how deeply), by technological and ideological changes (Erikson, 1954)—these questions must await better formulations of the ego's relationship to work techniques, to the technological "environment," and to the prevalent division of labor.

6

In a recent seminar in Jerusalem[9] I had an opportunity to discuss with Israeli scholars and clinicians the question of what the identity of an "Israeli" is, and thus to envisage one extreme of contemporary ideological orientations. Israel fascinates both her friends and her enemies. A great number of ideological fragments from European history have found their way into the consciousness of this small state; and many of the identity problems which have occupied a century and a half of American history are being faced in Israel within a few years. A new nation is established on a distant coast (which does not seem to "belong" to anybody) out of oppressed minorities from many lands, a new identity based on imported ideals which are libertarian, puritanic, and messianic. Any discussion of Israel's manifold and most immediate problems sooner or later leads to the extraordinary accomplishments and the extraordinary ideological problems posed by the pioneer Zionist settlers (now a small minority) who make up what is known as the Kibbutz movement. These European ideologists, given—as it were—a *historical moratorium* created by the peculiar international and national status of Palestine, first in the Ottoman Empire and then in the British mandate, were able to establish and to fortify a significant *utopian bridgehead* for Zionist ideology. In his "homeland," and tilling his very home soil, the "ingathered" Jew was to overcome such evil identities as result from eternal wandering, merchandising, and intellectualizing (Erikson, 1950a) and was to become *whole* again in body and mind, as well as in nationality. That the Kibbutz movement has created

[9] Organized by Professors S. Eisenstadt and C. Frankenstein of the Hebrew University. The initial impressions presented here are mine.

a hardy, responsible, and inspired type of individual, nobody could deny, although certain details of its educational system (such as the raising of children, from the very beginning, in Children's Houses, and the rooming together of boys and girls through the high school years) are under critical scrutiny, both in Israel and abroad. The fact is, however, that in Israel a utopia was established on a frontier exposed all around, under conditions reminiscent of those faced by the Mormons. This historical fact is the only possible framework for judging the rationale and the rationalizations of the style of life which ensued. For no doubt, these pioneers (comparable to this country's settlers, who, in turn, utilized the historical moratorium offered by the discovery of an empty continent, for the establishment of a new "way of life") provided a new nation, sprung up overnight, with a historical ideal. A legitimate question, however, and one not too foreign to this country's historians, concerns the relationship of a revolutionary elite to those who subsequently crowd into and thrive on the lands occupied and on the gains made.[10] In Israel, the by now somewhat exclusive elite of Kibbutzniks faces that incomparably larger part of the population which represents an ideologically all but indigestible mixture: the masses of African and Oriental immigrants, powerful organized labor, the big city dwellers, the religious orthodoxy, the new state bureaucracy—and then, of course, the "good old" mercantile class of middlemen. Furthermore, the more uncompromising part of the Kibbutz movement has not failed to place itself between the two worlds to both of which Zionism maintains strong historical bonds: American and British Jewry (which bought much of the Kibbutz land from Arab absentee landlords) and Soviet Communism, to which the (shall we say) communalistic Kibbutz movement[11] felt ideologically close only to be repudiated by Moscow as another form of deviationism.

[10] We may state tentatively that the elites which emerge from historical change are groups which out of the deepest common identity crisis manage to create a new style of coping with the outstanding danger situations of their society.

[11] I.e., relative communism within the individual community, which, however, in its relation to the economy, rather represents a capitalist cooperative.

The Kibbutz movement thus is one example of a modern ideological utopia which freed unknown energies in youths who considered themselves as of one "people," and created a (more or less explicit) group ideal of pervading significance—if of quite unpredictable historical fate in an industrial world. However, Israel is, undoubtedly, one of the most ideology-conscious countries that ever existed; no "peasants" nor workmen ever argued more about the far-reaching meanings of daily decisions. The subtler meanings of ideology for identity formation can probably be fathomed best by comparing highly verbal ideologies with those transitory systems of conversion and aversion which exist in any society, in that no-man's land between childhood and adulthood more or less derisively called adolescence—exist as the most meaningful part of a young person's or a young group's life, often without the knowledge, or indeed, curiosity, of the adults around them. It must be assumed that much of the spontaneous polarization of tastes, opinions, and slogans which occupy the arguments of youths, and much of the sudden impulse to join in destructive behavior, are loose ends of identity formation waiting to be tied together by some ideology.

7

In the pathographic section of this paper I have pointed to the *total choice* of a negative identity in individuals who could achieve such escape on the basis of autistic and regressive proclivities.

The escape of many gifted if unstable young individuals into a private utopia or, as another patient put it, a "majority of one," might not be necessary were it not for a general development to which they feel unable to submit, i.e., the increasing demand for standardization, uniformity, and conformity which characterizes the present stage of this our individualistic civilization. In this country, the demand for large-scale conformity has not developed into explicit totalitarian ideologies; it has associated itself with the total dogmas of churches and with the stereotypes of businesslike behavior, but, on the whole, shuns political ideology. We appreciate as we study the capacity of our youth to manage the identity diffusion of an industrial democracy with simple trustfulness, with playful dissonance, with technical virtuosity, with "other-minded" solidarity (Riesman, 1950)—and with a distaste for ideological explicitness. What exactly the implicit ideology of American youth (this most technological youth in the world) is—that is a fateful question, not to be lightly approached in a paper of this kind. Nor would one dare to assess in passing the changes which may be taking place in this ideology and in its implicitness, as a result of a world struggle which makes a military identity a necessary part of young adulthood in this country.

It is easier to delineate that malignant turn toward a *negative group identity* which prevails in some of the youth especially of our large cities, where conditions of economic, ethnic, and religious marginality provide poor bases for positive identities: here negative group identities are sought in spontaneous clique formations ranging all the way from neighborhood gangs and jazz mobs, to dope rings, homosexual circles, and criminal gangs. Clinical experience can be expected to make significant contributions to this problem. Yet, we may well warn ourselves against an uncritical transfer of clinical terms, attitudes, and methods to such public problems. Rather, we may come back to a point made earlier: teachers, judges, and psychiatrists, who deal with youth, come to be significant representatives of that strategic act of "recognition" (the act through which society "identifies" its young members and thus contributes to their developing identity) which was described at the beginning of this paper. If, for simplicity's sake or in order to accommodate ingrown habits of law or psychiatry, they diagnose and treat as a criminal, as a constitutional misfit, as a derelict doomed by his upbringing, or—indeed—as a deranged patient, a young person who, for reasons of personal or social marginality, is close to choosing a negative identity, that young person may well put his energy into becoming exactly what the careless and fearful community expects him to be—and make a total job of it.

It is hoped that the theory of identity, in the long run, can contribute more to this problem than to sound a warning.

Summary

In my attempt to circumscribe the problem of identity I have been "all over the map." I do not propose to leave the matter in this condition: as far as is possible, studies taking into account the specific dynamic nature of selected media (life history, case history, dream life, ideology) will follow. In the meantime, and in summary: identity, in outbalancing at the conclusion of childhood the potentially malignant dominance of the infantile superego, permits the individual to forgo excessive self-repudiation and the diffused repudiation of otherness. Such freedom provides a necessary condition for the ego's power to integrate matured sexuality, ripened capacities, and adult commitments. The histories of our young patients illustrate the ways in which aggravated identity crises may result from special genetic causes and from specific dynamic conditions. Such studies, in turn, throw new light on those more or less institutionalized rites and rituals, associations, and movements through which societies and subsocieties grant youth a world between childhood and adulthood: a psychosocial moratorium during which extremes of *subjective experience,* alternatives of *ideological choice,* and potentialities of *realistic commitment* can become the subject of social play and of joint mastery.

References

Ackerman, N. W. (1951), "Social role" and total personality. *Amer. J. Orthopsychiat.,* 21:1–17.

Bateman, J. F., & Dunham, H. W. (1948), The state mental hospital as a specialized community experience. *Amer. J. Psychiat.,* 105:445–449.

Benedict, R. (1938), Continuities and discontinuities in cultural conditioning. *Psychiatry,* 1:161–167.

Bibring, E. (1953), The mechanism of depression. In: *Affective Disorders,* ed. P. Greenacre. New York: International Universities Press, pp. 13–48.

Blos, P. (1953), The contribution of psychoanalysis to the treatment of adolescents. In: *Psychoanalysis and Social Work,* ed. M. Heiman. New York: International Universities Press.

Brenman, M. (1952), On teasing and being teased: And the problem of "moral masochism." *The Psychoanalytic Study of the Child,* 7:264–285. New York: International Universities Press.

Burlingham, D. (1952), *Twins.* New York: International Universities Press.

Erikson, E. H. (1946), Ego development and historical change. *The Psychoanalytic Study of the Child,* 2:359–396. New York: International Universities Press.

———— (1950a), *Childhood and Society.* New York: Norton. London: Imago, 1951.

———— (1950b), Growth and crises of the "healthy personality." In: *Symposium on the Healthy Personality,* Supplement II to the transactions of the fourth conference on *Problems of Infancy and Childhood,* ed. M. J. E. Senn. New York: Josiah Macy, Jr. Foundation.

———— (1953), On the sense of inner identity. In: *Health and Human Relations.* New York: The Blakiston Company.

———— (1954), Wholeness and totality. In: *Totalitarianism,* Proceedings of a conference held at the American Academy of Arts and Sciences, March, ed. C. J. Friedrich. Cambridge, MA: Harvard University Press.

Federn, P. (1952), *Ego Psychology and the Psychoses.* New York: Basic Books.

Freud, A. (1936), *The Ego and the Mechanisms of Defense.* New York: International Universities Press, 1946.

Freud, A. in collaboration with Dann, S. (1951), An experiment in group upbringing. *The Psychoanalytic Study of the Child,* 6:127–168. New York: International Universities Press.

Freud, S. (1914), On narcissism: An introduction. *Collected Papers,* 4:55. London: Hogarth Press, 1948.

———— (1926), Ansprache an die Mitglieder des Vereins B'nai B'rith. In: *Gesammelte Werke*, 17:49–53. London: Imago Publishing Co., 1941.

———— (1932), *New Introductory Lectures on Psychoanalysis*. Lecture 31: The anatomy of the mental personality. New York: W. W. Norton, 1933.

Ginsburg, S. W. (1954), The role of work. *Samiksa*, 8(1).

Hartmann, H. (1951a), Comments on the psychoanalytic theory of the ego. In: *The Psychoanalytic Study of the Child*, 5:74–96. New York: International Universities Press.

———— (1951b), Ego psychology and the problem of adaptation. In: *Organization and Pathology of Thought*, ed. D. Rapaport. New York: Columbia University Press.

———— Kris, E., & Loewenstein, R. M. (1951), Some psychoanalytic comments on "culture and personality." In: *Psychoanalysis and Culture*, ed. G. B. Wilbur & W. Muensterberger. New York: International Universities Press.

———— ———— ———— (1949), Notes on the theory of aggression. In: *The Psychoanalytic Study of the Child*, 3/4:9–36. New York: International Universities Press.

Hendrick, I. (1943), Work and the pleasure principle. *Psychoanal. Quart.*, 12:311–329.

James, W. (1896), The will to believe. *New World*, 5.

Kinsey, A. C., Pomeroy, W. B., & Martin, C. E. (1948), *Sexual Behavior in the Human Male*. Philadelphia: W. B. Saunders.

Knight, R. P. (1953), Management and psychotherapy of the borderline schizophrenic patient. *Bull. Menninger Clin.*, 17:139–150.

Kris, E. (1952), On preconscious mental processes. In: *Psychoanalytic Explorations in Art*. New York: International Universities Press, pp. 303–318.

Mannheim, K. (1949), *Utopia and Ideology*. New York: Harcourt, Brace.

Mead, G. H. (1934), *Mind, Self & Society*. Chicago: University of Chicago Press.

Mead, M. (1949), *Male and Female*. New York: William Morrow.

Newcomb, T. M., et al., eds. (1953), *Readings in Social Psychology*. New York: Henry Holt & Co.

Piers, G., & Singer, M. B. (1953), *Shame and Guilt*. Springfield, Ill.: Charles C Thomas, 1953.

Rapaport, D. (1950), *Emotions and Memory*, 2nd ed. New York: International Universities Press.

———— (1967), Some metapsychological considerations concerning activity and passivity. In: *The Collected Papers of David Rapaport*, ed. M. M. Gill. New York: Basic Books, pp. 530–568.

Riesman, D. (1950), *The Lonely Crowd*. New Haven: Yale University Press.

Schilder, P. (1951a), *The Image and Appearance of the Human Body*. New York: International Universities Press.

———— (1951b), *Psychoanalysis, Man and Society*. New York: W. W. Norton.

Schwartz, M. S., & Will, G. T. (1953), Low morale and mutual withdrawal on a mental hospital ward. *Psychiatry*, 16:337–353.

Shaw, G. B. (1952), *Selected Prose*. New York: Dodd, Mead & Co.

Sullivan, H. S. (1953), *The Interpersonal Theory of Psychiatry*. New York: W. W. Norton.

10.

The Nature of Clinical Evidence

ERIK H. ERIKSON

1

The letter which invited me to this symposium puts into the
center of my assignment the question, *"How does a . . . clinician
really work?"* It gives me generous latitude by inquiring about
the psychotherapist's reliance on *intuition* ("or some other version of personal judgment") or on *objectified tests* ("relatively
uniform among clinicians of different theoretical persuasions"). And it concludes: "To the extent that intuition plays
a role, in what way does the clinician seek to discipline its operation: by his conceptual framework? by long personal experience?" This emphasizes, within the inquiry of how a clinician
works, the question of how he thinks.

Such an invitation is a hospitable one, encouraging the
guest, as it were, to come as he is. It spares the clinician whatever temptation he might otherwise feel to claim inclusion in
the social register of long established sciences by demonstrating
that he, too, can behave the way they do. He can state from
the outset that all four: intuition and objective data, conceptual
framework and experience are acceptable as the corners of the
area to be staked out; but also, that in one lecture he can offer

245

no more than phenomenological groundwork of a markedly personal nature.

The invitation in my case is addressed to a psychotherapist of a particular "persuasion": my training is that of Freudian psychoanalyst, and I help in the training of others—in the vast majority physicians—in this method. I shall place vocation over persuasion and try to formulate how the nature of clinical evidence is determined by a clinician's daily task. If I, nevertheless, seem to feel beholden to Freud's conceptual system—that is, a system originated around the turn of this century by a physician schooled in physicalist physiology—the reason is not narrowly partisan: few will deny that from such transfer of physicalistic concepts to psychology new modes of clinical thinking have developed in our time.

Clinical, of course, is an old word. It can refer to the priest's ministrations at the deathbed as well as to medical ministrations to the sick. In our time and in the Western world, the scope of the clinical is expanding rapidly to include not only medical but also social considerations, not only physical well-being but also mental health, not only matters of cure but also of prevention, not only therapy but also research. This means that clinical work is now allied with many brands of evidence and overlaps with many methodologies. In the Far East, the word *clinical* is again assuming an entirely different historical connotation, insofar as it concerns mind at all: in Communist China the "thought analyst" faces individuals considered to be in need of reform. He encourages sincere confessions and self-analyses in order to realign thoughts with "the people's will." There is much, infinitely much to learn about the ideological implications of concepts of mental sickness, of social deviancy, and of psychological cure. Yet, I feel called upon to speak of the nature of evidence gathered in the psychotherapeutic encounter.

Let me briefly review the elements making up the clinical core of medical work as the encounter of two people, one in need of help, the other in the possession of professional methods. Their *contract* is a therapeutic one: in exchange for a fee, and for information revealed in confidence, the therapist promises to act for the benefit of the individual patient, within the ethos of the profession. There usually is a *complaint*, consisting of the description of more or less circumscribed pain or dysfunction, and there are *symptoms*, visible or otherwise localizable. There follows an attempt at an *anamnesis*, an etiological reconstruction of the disturbance, and an *examination*, carried out by means of the physician's naked senses or supported by instruments, which may include laboratory methods. In evaluating the evidence and in arriving at diagnostic and prognostic inferences (which are really the clinical form of a *prediction)*, the physician *thinks clinically*—that is, he scans in his mind different *models* in which different modes of knowledge have found condensation: the *anatomical* structure of the body, the *physiological* functioning of body parts, or the *pathological* processes underlying classified disease entities. A clinical prediction takes its clues from the complaint, the symptoms, and the anamnesis, and makes inferences based on a rapid and mostly preconscious cross-checking against each other of anatomical, physiological, and pathological models. On this basis, a *preferred method of treatment* is selected. This is the simplest clinical encounter. In it the patient lends parts of himself to an examination and as far as he possibly can, ceases to be a person, i.e., a creature who is more than the sum of its organs.

Any good doctor knows, however, that the patient's complaint is more extensive than his symptom, and the state of sickness more comprehensive than localized pain or dysfunction. As an old Jew put it (and old Jews have a way of speaking for the victims of all nations): "Doctor, my bowels are sluggish, my feet hurt, my heart jumps—and you know, Doctor, I myself don't feel so well either." The treatment is thus not limited to local adjustments; it must, and in the case of a "good" doctor automatically does, include a wider view of the complaint, and entail corresponding *interpretations* of the symptom to the patient, often making the "patient himself" an associate observer and assistant doctor. This is especially important, as subsequent appointments serve a *developing treatment-history*, which step by step verifies or contradicts whatever predictions had been made and put to test earlier.

This, then, for better or for worse, is the traditional core of the clinical encounter, whether it deals with physical or with mental complaints. But in the special case of the *psychothera-peutic encounter,* a specimen of which I intend to present and to analyze presently, three items crowd out all the others, namely, *complaint, anamnesis,* and *interpretation.* What goes on in the therapist's mind between the verbal complaint addressed to him and the verbal interpretation given in return—this, I take it, is the question to be examined here. But this means: in what way can the psychological clinician make his own perception and thought reliable in the face of the patient's purely verbal and social expression, and in the absence of nonverbal support-ive instruments? At this point I am no longer quite so sure that the invitation to "tell us how a . . . clinician really works" was so entirely friendly, after all. For you must suspect that the psychotherapist, in many ways, uses the setting and the termi-nology of a medical and even a laboratory approach, claiming recourse to an anatomy, a physiology, and a pathology of the mind, without matching the traditional textbook clarity of med-ical science in any way. To put it briefly, the element of subjec-tivity, both in the patient's complaints and in the therapist's interpretations, may be vastly greater than in a strictly medical encounter, although this element is in principle not absent from any clinical approach.

Indeed, there is no choice but to put subjectivity in the center of an inquiry into evidence and inference in such clini-cal work as I am competent to discuss. The psychotherapist shares with any clinician the Hippocratic fact that hour by hour he must fulfill a *contract* with individuals who offer themselves to cure and study. They surrender much of their most personal inviolacy in the expectation that they will emerge from the encounter more whole and less fragmented than when they entered it. The psychotherapist shares with all clinicians the further requirement that even while facing most intimate and emotional matters, he must maintain intellectual inner contact with his conceptual models, however crude they may be. But more than any other clinician the psychotherapist must include in his field of observation a *specific self-awareness* in the very act of perceiving his patient's actions and reactions. I shall claim that there is a core of *disciplined subjectivity* in clinical work—and this both on the side of the therapist and of the patient—which it is neither desirable nor possible to replace altogether with seemingly more objective methods—methods which originate, as it were, in the machine-tooling of other kinds of work. How the two subjectivities join in the kind of disciplined understanding and shared insight which we think are operative in a cure—that is the question.

2

First, a word about "history taking," as the anamnesis is called today. In clinics, this is often done by "intake" workers, as if a patient, at the moment of entering treatment, could give an objective history of his sickness, and could reserve until later a certain fervent surrender to "the doctor." In the treatment proper, of course, much of this history will be reported again in significant moments. Whether or not the psychotherapist will then choose to dwell on the patient's past, however, he will enter his life history and join the grouping of individuals already significant in it. Therefore, without any wish to crowd him, I think I would feel methodologically closest to the historian in this symposium.

R. G. Collingwood defines as an historical process one "in which the past, so far as it is historically known, survives in the present." Thus being "itself a process of thought . . . it exists only in so far as the minds which are parts of it know themselves for parts of it." And again: "History is the life of mind itself which is not mind except so far as it *both lives in historical process and knows itself as so living*" (Collingwood, 1956).

However, it is not my task to argue the philosophy of history. The analogy between the clinician and the historian as defined by Collingwood to me centers in the case-historian's function in the art of history taking, of becoming part of a life history. Here the analogy breaks down; it could remain relevant only if the historian were also a kind of clinical statesman, correcting events as he records them, and recording changes as he directs them. Such a conscious clinician-historian-statesman may well emerge in the future.

Let me restate the psychotherapeutic encounter, then, as an historical one. A person has declared an emergency and has surrendered his self-regulation to a treatment procedure. Besides having become a subjective *patient*, he has accepted the role of a formal *client*. To some degree, he has had to interrupt his autonomous life history as lived in the un-self-conscious balances of his private and his public life in order, for a while, to "favor" a part-aspect of himself and to observe it with the diagnostic help of a curative method. "Under observation," he becomes self-observant. As a patient he is inclined, and as a client often encouraged, to historicize his own position by thinking back to the onset of the disturbance, and to ponder what world order (magic, scientific, ethical) was violated and must be restored before his self-regulation can be reassumed. He participates in becoming a *case*, a fact which he may live down socially, but which, nevertheless, may forever change his view of himself.

The clinician, in turn, appointed to judge the bit of interrupted life put before him, and to introduce himself and his method into it, finds himself part of another man's most intimate life history. Luckily he also remains the functionary of a healing profession with a systematic orientation, based on a coherent world image—be it the theory that a sick man is beset by evil spirits or under the temptation of the devil, the victim of chemical poisons or of faulty heritage, racked by inner conflicts, or blinded by a dangerous ideology. In inviting his client to look at himself with the help of professional theories and techniques, the clinician makes himself part of the client's life history, even as the client becomes a case in the history of healing.

In northern California I knew an old Shaman woman who laughed merrily at my conception of mental disease, and then sincerely—to the point of ceremonial tears told me of her way

of sucking the "pains" out of her patients. She was as convinced of her ability to cure and to understand as I was of mine.
While occupying extreme opposites in the history of American
psychiatry, we felt like colleagues. This feeling was based on
some joint sense of the historical relativity of all psychotherapy:
the relativity of the patient's outlook on his symptoms, of the
role he assumes by dint of being a patient, of the kind of help
which he seeks, and of the kinds of help which are eagerly
offered or are available. The old Shaman woman and I disagreed about the locus of emotional sickness, what it "was,"
and what specific methods would cure it. Yet, when she related
the origin of a child's illness to the familial tensions existing
within her tribe, when she attributed the "pain" (which had
got "under a child's skin") to his grandmother's sorcery (ambivalence), I knew she dealt with the same forces, and with the
same kinds of conviction, as I did in my professional nook. This
experience has been repeated in discussions with colleagues
who, although not necessarily more "primitive," are oriented
toward different psychiatric persuasions.

The disciplined psychotherapist of today finds himself heir
to medical methods and concepts, although he may decide to
counteract these with a determined turn to existential or social
views concerning his person-to-person encounter in the therapeutic setting. At any rate, he recognizes his activities as a function of life-historical processes, and concludes that in his sphere
one makes history as one records it.

3

It is in such apparent quicksand that we must follow the tracks
of clinical evidence. No wonder that often the only clinical
material which impresses some as being at all "scientific" is
the more concrete evidence of the auxiliary methods of psychotherapy—neurological examination, chemical analysis, sociological study, psychological experiment, etc.—all of which,
strictly speaking, put the patient into nontherapeutic conditions of observation. Each of these methods may "objectify"

some matters immensely, provide inestimable supportive evidence for *some* theories, and lead to independent methods of cure in *some* classes of patients. But it is not of the nature of the evidence provided in the psychotherapeutic encounter itself.

To introduce such evidence, I need a specimen. This will consist of my reporting to you what a patient *said* to me, how he *behaved* in doing so, and what I, in turn, *thought* and *did*—a highly suspect method. And, indeed, we may well stand at the beginning of a period when consultation rooms (already airier and lighter than Freud's) will have, as it were, many more doors open in the direction of an enlightened community's resources, even as they now have research windows in the form of one-way screens, cameras, and recording equipment. For the kind of evidence to be highlighted here, however, it is still essential that, for longer periods or for shorter ones, these doors be closed, soundproof, and impenetrable.

By emphasizing this I am not trying to ward off legitimate study of the setting from which our examples come. I know only too well that many of our interpretations seem to be of the variety of that given by one Jew to another in a Polish railroad station. "Where are you going?" asked the first. "To Minsk," said the other. "To Minsk!" exclaimed the first, "you say you go to Minsk so that I should believe you go to Pinsk! You are going to Minsk anyway—so why do you lie?" There is a widespread prejudice that the psychotherapist, point for point, uncovers what he claims the patient "really," and often unconsciously, had in mind, and that he has sufficient Pinsk–Minsk reversals in his technical arsenal to come out with the flat assertion that the evidence is on the side of his claim. It is for this very reason that I will try to demonstrate what method there may be in clinical judgment. I will select as my specimen the most subjective of all data, a dream-report.

A young man in his early twenties comes to his therapeutic hour about midway during his first year of treatment in a psychiatric hospital and reports that he has had the most disturbing dream of his life. The dream, he says, vividly recalls his state of panic at the time of the "mental breakdown" which had caused him to interrupt his studies for missionary work abroad and enter treatment. He cannot let go of the dream; it seemed painfully real on awakening; and even in the hour of reporting, the dream-state seems still vivid enough to threaten the patient's sense of reality. He is afraid that this is the end of his sanity.

The Dream: "There was a big face sitting in a buggy of the horse-and-buggy days. The face was completely empty, and there was horrible, slimy, snaky hair all around it. I am not sure it wasn't my mother." The dream report itself, given with wordy plaintiveness, is as usual followed by a variety of seemingly incidental reports of the events of the previous day which, however, eventually give way to a rather coherent account of the patient's relationship with his deceased grandfather, a country parson. In fact, he sees himself as a small boy with his grandfather crossing a bridge over a brook, his tiny hand in the old man's reassuring fist. Here the patient's mood changes to a deeply moved and moving admission of desperate nostalgia for the rural setting in which the values of his Nordic immigrant forebears were clear and strong.

How did the patient get from the dream to the grandfather? Here I should point out that we consider a patient's "associations" our best leads to the meaning of an as yet obscure item brought up in a clinical encounter, whether it is a strong affect, a stubborn memory, an intensive or recurring dream, or a transitory symptom. By associated evidence we mean everything which comes to the patient's mind during and after the report of that item. Except in cases of stark disorganization of thought, we can assume that what we call the synthesizing function of the ego will tend to associate what "belongs together," be the associated items ever so remote in history, separate in space, and contradictory in logical terms. Once the therapist has convinced himself of a certain combination in the patient of character, intelligence, and a wish to get well, he can rely on the patient's capacity to produce during a series of therapeutic encounters a sequence of themes, thoughts, and affects which seek their own concordance and provide their own cross-references. It is, of course, this basic synthesizing trend in clinical material itself which permits the clinician to observe with "free-floating attention," to refrain from undue interference, and to expect sooner or later a confluence of the patient's search for curative clarification and his own endeavor to recognize and to name what is most relevant, that is, to give an *interpretation*.

At the same time, everything said in an hour is linked with the material of previous appointments. It must be understood that whatever insight can result from one episode will owe its meaning to the fact that it clarifies previous questions and complements previous half-truths. Such *evidential continuity* can be only roughly sketched here; even to account for this one hour would take many hours. Let me only mention, then, the seemingly paradoxical fact that during his previous hour the patient had spoken of an increased well-being in his work and in his life, and had expressed trust in and even something akin to affection for me.

As to the rest of the hour of the dream-report I listened to the patient, who faced me in an easy chair, with only occasional interruptions for the clarification of facts or feelings. Only at the conclusion of the appointment did I give him a resume of what sense his dream had made to me. It so happened that this interpretation proved convincing to us both and, in the long run, strategic for the whole treatment. (These are the hours we like to report.)

As I turn to the task of indicating what inferences helped me to formulate one of the most probable of the many possible meanings of this dream-report, I must ask you to join me in what Freud has called "free-floating attention," which—as I must now add—turns inward to the observer's ruminations even as it attends the patient's "free associations" and which, far from focusing on any one item too intentionally, rather waits to be impressed by recurring themes. These themes will, first faintly but ever more insistently, signal the nature of the patient's message and its meaning. It is, in fact, the gradual establishment of strategic intersections on a number of tangents that eventually makes it possible to locate in the observed phenomena that central core which comprises the "evidence."

4

I will now try to report what kinds of considerations will pass through a psychotherapist's mind, some fleetingly, others with persistent urgency, some hardly conscious in so many words, others nearly ready for verbalization and communication.

Our patient's behavior and report confront me with a therapeutic crisis, and it is my first task to perceive where the patient stands as a client, and what I must do next. What a clinician must do first and last depends, of course, on the setting of his work. Mine is an open residential institution, working with severe neuroses, some on the borderline of psychosis or psychopathy. In such a setting, the patients may display, in their most regressed moments, the milder forms of a disturbance in the sense of reality; in their daily behavior, they usually try to entertain, educate, and employ themselves in rational and useful ways; and in their best moments, they can be expected to be insightful and to do proficient and at times creative work. The hospital thus can be said to take a number of calculated risks, and to provide, on the other hand, special opportunities for the patient's abilities to work, to be active, and to share in social responsibilities. That a patient will fit into this setting has been established in advance during the "evaluation period." The patient's history has been taken in psychiatric interviews with him and perhaps with members of his family; he has been given a physical examination by a physician and has been confronted with standardized tests by psychologists who perform their work "blindly," that is, without knowledge of the patient's history; and finally, the results have been presented to the whole staff at a meeting, at the conclusion of which the patient himself was presented by the medical director, questioned by him and by other staff members, and assigned to "his therapist." Such preliminary screening has provided the therapist with an over-all diagnosis which defines a certain range of *expectable mental states,* indicating the patient's special danger points and his special prospects for improvement. Needless to say, not even the best preparation can quite predict what depths and heights may be reached once the therapeutic process gets under way.

The original test report had put the liability of our patient's state into these words: "The tests indicate borderline psychotic features in an inhibited, obsessive–compulsive character. However, the patient seems to be able to take spontaneously adequate distance from these borderline tendencies. He seems, at present, to be struggling to strengthen a rather precarious control over aggressive impulses, and probably feels a good deal of anxiety." The course of the treatment confirmed this and other test results. Thus, a dream-report of the kind just mentioned, in a setting of this kind, will first of all impress the clinical observer as a diagnostic sign. This is an "anxiety dream." Such a dream may happen to anybody, and a mild perseverance of the dream state into the day is not pathological as such. But this patient's dream appears to be only the visual center of a severe affective disturbance: no doubt if such a state were to persist, it could precipitate him into a generalized panic such as brought him to our clinic in the first place. The report of this horrible dream which intrudes itself on the patient's waking life now takes its place beside the data of the tests and the range and spectrum of the patient's moods and states as observed in the treatment, and shows him on the lowest level attained since admission, i.e., relatively closest to an *inability* "to take adequate distance from his borderline tendencies."

The first "prediction" to be made is whether this dream is the sign of an impending collapse, or, on the contrary, a potentially beneficial clinical crisis. The first would mean that the patient is slipping away from me and that I must think, as it were, of the emergency net; the second, that he is reaching out for me with an important message which I must try to understand and answer. I decided on the latter alternative. Although the patient acted as if he were close to a breakdown, I had the impression that, in fact, there was a challenge in all this, and a rather angry one. This impression was, to some extent, based on a comparison of the present hour and the previous one when the patient had seemed so markedly improved. Could it be that his unconscious had not been able to tolerate this very improvement? The paradox resolves itself if we consider that cure means the loss of the right to rely on therapy; for the cured patient, to speak with Saint Francis, would not so much seek to be loved as to love, and not so much to be consoled as to console, to the limit of his capacity. Does the dream-report communicate, protesting somewhat too loudly, that the patient is still sick? Is his dream sicker than the patient is? I can explain this tentative diagnostic conclusion only by presenting a number of inferences of a kind made very rapidly in a clinician's mind, and demonstrable only through an analysis of the patient's verbal and behavioral communications and of my own intellectual and affective reactions.

5

The experienced dream interpreter often finds himself "reading" a dream-report as a practitioner of medicine scans an X ray. Especially in the cases of wordy or reticent patients or of lengthy case reports, a dream often lays bare the stark inner facts.

Let us first pay attention to the dream images. The main item is a large face without identifying features. There are no spoken words, and there is no motion. There are no people in the dream. Very apparent, then, are omissions. An experienced interpreter can state this on the basis of an implicit inventory of dream configurations against which he checks the individual dream production for present and absent dream configurations. This implicit inventory can be made explicit as I have myself tried to do in a publication reviewing Freud's classic first analysis of a "dream specimen" (Erikson, 1954). The dream being discussed, then, is characterized by a significant omission of important items present in most dreams: motion, action, people, spoken words. All we have instead is a motionless image of a faceless face, which may or may not represent the patient's mother.

But in trying to understand what this image "stands for," the interpreter must abandon the classic scientific urge (leading to parsimonious explanation in some contexts but to "wild" interpretation in this one) to look for the one most plausible explanation. He must let his "free-floating" clinical attention and judgment lead him to all the *possible* faces which may be condensed in this one dream face and then decide what *probable meaning* may explain their combined presence. I will, then, proceed to relate the face in the dream to all the faces in my patient's hierarchy of significant persons, to my face as well as those of his mother and grandfather, to God's countenance as well as to the Medusa's grimace. Thus, the probable meaning of an empty and horrible face may gradually emerge.

First myself, then the patient's facial and tonal expression reminded me of a series of critical moments during his treatment when he was obviously not quite sure that I was "all there" and apprehensive that I might disapprove of him and disappear in anger. This focused my attention on a question which the clinician must consider when faced with any of his patient's productions, namely, his own place in them.

While the psychotherapist should not force his way into the meanings of his patient's dream images, he does well to raise discreetly the masks of the various dream persons to see whether he can find his own face or person or role represented. Here the mask is an empty face, with plenty of horrible hair. My often unruly white hair surrounding a reddish face easily enters my patients' imaginative productions, either in the form of a benevolent Santa Claus or that of a threatening ogre. At that particular time, I had to consider another autobiographic item. In the third month of therapy, I had "abandoned" the patient to have an emergency operation which he, to use clinical shorthand, had ascribed to his evil eye. At the time of this dream-report I still was on occasion mildly uncomfortable—a matter which can never be hidden from such patients. A sensitive patient will, of course, be in conflict between his sympathy, which makes him want to take care of me, and his rightful claim that I should take care of him—for he feels that only the therapist's total presence can provide him with sufficient identity to weather his crises. I concluded that the empty face

had something to do with a certain tenuousness in our relationship, and that one message of the dream might be something
like this: "If I never know whether and when you think of
yourself rather than attending to me, or when you will absent
yourself, maybe die, *how can I have or gain what I need most—a
coherent personality, an identity, a face?"*

Such an indirect message, however, even if understood
as referring to the immediate present and to the therapeutic
situation itself, always proves to be "overdetermined," that is,
to consist of a *condensed code* transmitting a number of other
messages, from other life situations, seemingly removed from
the therapy. This we call *"transference."* Because the inference
of a "mother transference" is by now an almost stereotyped
requirement, and thus is apt to lead to faulty views concerning
the relationship of past and present, I have postponed, but not
discarded, a discussion of the connection between the patient's
implied fear of "losing a face" with his remark that he was not
sure the face was not his mother's. Instead, I put first his fear
that he may yet lose himself by losing me too suddenly or too
early.

6

Clinical work is always research in progress, and I would not
be giving a full account of the clinician's pitfalls if I did not
discuss in passing the fact that this patient's dream happened
to fit especially well into my research at the time. This can be a
mixed blessing for the therapeutic contract. A research-minded
clinician—and one with literary ambitions, at that—must always
take care lest his patients become footnotes to his favorite thesis
or topic. I was studying in Pittsburgh and in Stockbridge the
"identity crises" of a number of young people, college as well
as seminary students, workmen and artists. My purpose was to
delineate further a syndrome called *identity-confusion*, a term
which describes the inability of young people in the late 'teens
and early twenties to establish their station and vocation in life,
and the tendency of some to develop apparently malignant
symptoms and regressions (Erikson, 1959). Such research must

reopen rather than close questions of finalistic diagnosis. Perhaps there are certain stages in the life cycle when even seemingly malignant disturbances are more profitably treated as
aggravated life crises rather than as diseases subject to routine
psychiatric diagnosis. Here the clinician must be guided by the
proposition that if he can hope to save only a small subgroup,
or, indeed, only one patient, he must disregard existing statisti-
cal verdicts. For one new case, understood in new ways, will
soon prove to be "typical" for a whole class of patients.

But any new diagnostic impression immediately calls for
epidemiological considerations. What we have described as a
therapeutic need in one patient, namely, to gain identity by
claiming the total presence of his therapist, is identical with *the
need of young people anywhere* for ideological affirmation. This
need is aggravated in certain critical periods of history, when
young people may try to find various forms of "confirmation"
in groups that range from idealistic youth movements to criminal gangs (Erikson, 1962).

The young man in question was one among a small group
of our patients who came from theological seminaries. He had
developed his symptoms when attending a Protestant seminary
in the Middle West where he was training for missionary work
in Asia. He had not found the expected transformation in
prayer, a matter which both for reasons of honesty and of inner
need, he had taken more seriously than many successful believers. To him the wish to gaze through the glass darkly and to
come "face to face" was a desperate need not easily satisfied
in some modern seminaries. I need not remind you of the
many references in the Bible to God's "making his face to shine
upon" man, or God's face being turned away or being distant.
The therapeutic theme inferred from the patient's report of
an anxiety dream in which a face was horribly unrecognizable
thus also seemed to echo relevantly this patient's religious scru-
ples at the time of the appearance of psychiatric symptoms—the common denominator being a *wish to break through
to a provider* of *identity*.

This trend of thought, then, leads us from the immediate
clinical situation (and a recognition of my face in the dream

face) to the developmental crisis typical for the patient's age (and the possible meaning of facelessness as "identity-confusion"), to the vocational and spiritual crisis immediately preceding the patient's breakdown (and the need for a divine face, an existential recognition). The "buggy" in the dream will lead us a step further back into an earlier identity crisis—and yet another significant face.

The horse and buggy is, of course, an historical symbol of cultural change. Depending on one's ideology, it is a derisive term connoting hopelessly old-fashioned ways, or it is a symbol of nostalgia for the good old days. Here we come to a trend in the family's history most decisive for the patient's identity crisis. The family came from Minnesota, where the mother's father had been a rural clergyman of character, strength, and communal esteem. Such grandfathers represent to many today a world of homogeneity in feudal values, "masterly and cruel with a good conscience, self-restrained and pious without loss of self-esteem." When the patient's parents had moved from the north country to then still smog-covered Pittsburgh, his mother especially had found it impossible to overcome an intense nostalgia for the rural ways of her youth. She had, in fact, imbued the boy with this nostalgia for a rural existence and had demonstrated marked disappointment when the patient, at the beginning of his identity crisis (maybe in order to cut through the family's cultural conflict), had temporarily threatened to become somewhat delinquent. The horse and buggy obviously is in greatest ideological as well as technological contrast to the modern means of locomotor acceleration, and, thus, all at once a symbol of changing times, of identity-confusion, and of cultural regression. Here the horrible motionlessness of the dream may reveal itself as an important configurational item, meaning something like being stuck in the middle of a world of competitive change and motion. And even as I inferred in my thoughts that the face sitting in the buggy must *also* represent the deceased grandfather's, also framed by white hair, the patient spontaneously embarked (as reported above) on a series of memories concerning the past when his grandfather had taken him by the hand to acquaint

him with the technology of an old farm in Minnesota. Here
the patient's vocabulary had become poetic, his description
vivid, and he had seemed to be breaking through to a genuinely
positive emotional experience. Yet as a reckless youngster he
had defied this grandfather shortly before his death. Knowing
this, I sympathized with his tearfulness which, nevertheless, remained strangely perverse, and sounded strangled by anger, as
though he might be saying: "One must not promise a child
such certainty, and then leave him."

Here it must be remembered that all "graduations" in
human development mean the abandonment of a familiar position, and that all growth—that is, the kind of growth endangered in our patients—must come to terms with this fact.

We add to our previous inferences the assumption that the
face in the dream (in a *condensation* typical for dream images)
also "meant" the face of the grandfather who is now dead
and whom as a rebellious youth the patient had defied. The
immediate clinical situation, then, the history of the patient's
breakdown and a certain period in his adolescence are all
found to have a common denominator in the idea that the
patient wishes to *base his future sanity on a countenance of wisdom
and firm identity* while, in all instances, he seems to fear that his
anger may have destroyed, or may yet destroy, such resources.
The patient's desperate insistence on finding security in prayer
and, in fact, in missionary work, and yet his failure to find
peace in these endeavors belongs in this context.

It may be necessary to assure you at this point that it is the
failure of religious endeavor, not religiosity or the need for
reverence and service, which is thereby explained. In fact, there
is every reason to assume that the development of a sense of
fidelity and the capacity to give and to receive it in a significant
setting is a condition for a young adult's health, and of a young
patient's recovery.

7

The theme of the horse and buggy as a rural symbol served to
establish a possible connection between the nostalgic mother

and her dead father; and we now finally turn our attention to
the fact that the patient, half-denying what he was half-sug-
gesting, said, "I am not sure it wasn't my mother." Here the
most repetitious complaint of the whole course of therapy must
be reviewed. While the grandfather's had been, all in all, the
most consistently reassuring countenance in the patient's life,
the mother's pretty, soft, and loving face had since earliest
childhood been marred in the patient's memory and imagination by moments when she seemed absorbed and distorted by
strong and painful emotions. The tests, given before any his-
tory-taking, had picked out the following theme: "The mother-
figure appears in the Thematic Apperception Tests as one who
seeks to control her son by her protectiveness of him, and by
'self-pity' and demonstrations of her frailty at any aggressive
act on his part. She is, in the stories, 'frightened' at any show
of rebelliousness, and content only when the son is passive
and compliant. There appears to be considerable aggression,
probably partly conscious, toward this figure." And indeed, it
was with anger as well as with horror that the patient would
repeatedly describe the mother of his memory as utterly exas-
perated, and this at those times when he had been too rough,
too careless, too stubborn, or too persistent.

We are not concerned here with accusing this actual
mother of having behaved this way; we can only be sure that
she appeared this way in certain retrospective moods of the
patient. Such memories are typical for a certain class of patients, and the question whether this is so because they have
in common a certain type of mother or share a typical reaction
to their mothers, or both, occupies the thinking of clinicians.
At any rate many of these patients are deeply, if often unconsciously, convinced that they have caused a basic disturbance
in their mothers. Often, in our time, when corporal punishment and severe scolding have become less fashionable, parents resort to the seemingly less cruel means of presenting
themselves as deeply hurt by the child's willfulness. The "violated" mother thus tends to appear more prominently in images of guilt. In some cases this becomes an obstacle in the
resolution of adolescence—as if a fundamental and yet quite

impossible restitution were a condition for adulthood. It is in keeping with this trend that the patients under discussion here, young people who in late adolescence face a breakdown on the borderline of psychosis, all prove to be partially regressed to the earliest task in life, namely, the acquisition of a sense of basic trust strong enough to balance that sense of basic mistrust to which newborn man (most dependent of all young animals and yet endowed with fewer inborn instinctive regulations) is subject in his infancy. We all relive earlier and earliest stages of our existence in dreams, in artistic experience, and in religious devotion, only to emerge refreshed and invigorated. These patients, however, experience such partial regression in a lonely, sudden, and intense fashion, and most of all with a sense of irreversible doom. This, too, is in this dream.

The mother's veiled presence in the dream points to a complete omission in all this material: there is no father either in the dream or in the associated themes. The patient's father images became dominant in a later period of the treatment and proved most important for the patient's eventual solution of his spiritual and vocational problems. From this we can dimly surmise that in the present hour the grandfather "stands for" the father.

On the other hand, the recognition of the mother's countenance in the empty dream face and its surrounding slimy hair suggests the discussion of a significant symbol. Did not Freud explain the Medusa, the angry face with snake-hair and an open mouth, as a *symbol of the feminine void,* and an expression of the masculine horror of femininity? It is true that some of the patient's memories and associations (reported in other sessions in connection with the mother's emotions) could be easily traced to infantile observations and ruminations concerning "female trouble," pregnancy, and postpartum upsets. Facelessness, in this sense, can also mean inner void, and (from a male point of view) "castration." Does it, then, or does it not contradict Freudian symbolism if I emphasize in this equally horrifying but entirely empty face a representation of facelessness, of loss of face, of lack of identity? In the context of the "classical" interpretation, the dream image would be primarily symbolic of a sexual idea which is to be warded off, in ours a representation of a danger to the continuous existence of individual identity. Theoretical considerations would show that these interpretations do not exclude each other. In this case a possible controversy is superseded by the clinical consideration that a symbol to be interpreted must first be shown to be immediately relevant. It would be futile to use sexual symbolism dogmatically when acute interpersonal needs can be discerned as dominant in strongly concordant material. The sexual symbolism of this dream was taken up in due time, when it reappeared in another context, namely that of manhood and sexuality, and revealed the bisexual confusion inherent in all identity conflict.

8

Tracing one main theme of the dream retrospectively, we have recognized it in four periods of the patient's life—all four premature graduations which left him with anger and fear over what he was to abandon rather than with the anticipation of greater freedom and more genuine identity: the present treatment and the patient's fear that by some act of horrible anger (on his part or on mine or both) he might lose me and thus his chance to regain his identity through trust in me; his immediately preceding religious education—and his abortive attempt at finding through prayer that "presence" which would cure his inner void; his earlier youth—and his hope to gain strength, peace, and identity by identifying himself with his grandfather; and, finally, early childhood—and his desperate wish to keep alive in himself the charitable face of his mother in order to overcome fear, guilt, and anger over her emotions. Such redundancy points to a central theme which, once found, gives added meaning to all the associated material. The theme is: "Whenever I begin to have faith in somebody's strength and love, some angry and sickly emotions pervade the relationship, and I end up mistrusting, empty, and a victim of anger and despair."

You may be getting a bit tired of the clinician's habit of speaking for the patient, of putting into his mouth inferences which, so it would seem, he could get out of him for the asking. The clinician, however, has no right to test his reconstructions until his trial formulations have combined into a comprehensive interpretation which feels right to him, and which promises, when appropriately verbalized, to feel right to the patient. When this point is reached, the clinician usually finds himself compelled to speak, in order to help the patient in verbalizing his affects and images in a more communicative manner, and to communicate his own impressions.

If according to Freud a successful dream is an attempt at representing a wish as fulfilled, the attempted and miscarried fulfillment in this dream is that of finding a face with a lasting identity. If an anxiety dream startling the dreamer out of his sleep is a symptom of a derailed wish-fulfillment, the central theme just formulated indicates at least one inner disturbance which caused the miscarriage of basic trust in infancy.

It seemed important to me that my communication should include an explicit statement of my emotional response to the dream-report. Patients of the type of our young man, still smarting in his twenties under what he considered his mother's strange emotions in his infancy, can learn to delineate social reality and to tolerate emotional tension only if the therapist can juxtapose his own emotional reactions to the patient's emotions. Therefore, as I reviewed with the patient some of what I have put before you, I also told him without anger, but not without some honest indignation, that my response to his account had included a feeling of being attacked. I explained that he had worried me, had made me feel pity, had touched me with his memories, and had challenged me to prove, all at once, the goodness of mothers, the immortality of grandfathers, my own perfection, and God's grace.

The words used in an interpretation, however, are hard to remember and when reproduced or recorded often sound as arbitrary as any private language developed by two people in the course of an intimate association. But whatever is said, a therapeutic interpretation, while brief and simple in form, should encompass a *unitary theme* such as I have put before you, a theme common at the same time to a dominant trend

in the patient's relation to the therapist, to a significant portion
of his symptomatology, to an important conflict of his childhood, and to corresponding facets of his work and love life.
This sounds more complicated than it is. Often, a very short
and casual remark proves to have encompassed all this; and
the trends *are* (as I must repeat in conclusion) very closely
related to each other in the patient's own struggling mind, for
which the traumatic past is of course a present frontier, perceived as acute conflict. Such an interpretation, therefore, joins
the patient's and the therapist's modes of problem solving.

Therapists of different temperament and of various persuasions differ as to what constitutes an interpretation: an impersonal and authoritative explanation, a warm and fatherly
suggestion, an expansive sermon or a sparse encouragement
to go on and see what comes up next. The intervention in
this case, however, highlights one methodological point truly
unique to clinical work, namely, the disposition of the clinician's "mixed" feelings, his emotions and opinions. The evidence is not "all in" if he does not succeed in using his own
emotional responses during a clinical encounter as an evidential source and as a guide in intervention, instead of putting
them aside with a spurious claim to unassailable objectivity. It is
here that the prerequisite of the therapist's own psychoanalytic
treatment as a didactic experience proves itself essential, for
the personal equation in the observer's emotional response
is as important in psychotherapy as that of the senses in the
laboratory. Repressed emotions easily hide themselves in the
therapist's most stubborn blind spots.

I do not wish to make too much of this, but I would suggest
in passing that some of us have, to our detriment, embraced an
objectivity which can only be maintained with self-deception. If
"psychoanalyzed" man learns to recognize the fact that even
his previously repudiated or denied impulses may be "right"
in their refusal to be submerged without a trace (the traces
being his symptoms), so he may also learn that his strongest
ethical judgments are right in being persistent even if modern
life may not consider it intelligent or advantageous to feel
strongly about such matters. Any psychotherapist, then, who

throws out his ethical sentiments with his irrational moral anger, deprives himself of a principal tool of his clinical perception. For even as our sensuality sharpens our awareness of the orders of nature, so our indignation, admitted and scrutinized for flaws of sulkiness and self-indulgence, is, in fact, an important tool both of therapy and of theory. It adds to the investigation of what, indeed, has happened to sick individuals a suggestion of where to look for those epidemiological factors that should and need not happen to anybody. But this means that we somehow harbor a model of man which could serve as a scientific basis for the postulation of an ethical relation of the generations to each other; and that we are committed to this whether or not we abrogate our partisanship in particular systems of morality.

A certain combination of available emotion and responsive thought, then, marks a therapist's style and is expressed in minute variations of facial expression, posture, and tone of voice. The core of a therapeutic intervention at its most decisive thus defies any attempt at a definitive account. This difficulty is not overcome by the now widespread habit of advocating a "human," rather than a "technical" encounter. Even humanness can be a glib "posture," and the time may come when we need an injunction against the use in vain of this word *human,* too.

9

What do we expect the patient to contribute to the closure of our evidence? What tells us that our interpretation was "right," and, therefore, proves the evidence to be as conclusive as it can be in our kind of work? The simplest answer is that this particular patient was amused, delighted, and encouraged when I told him of my thoughts and of my anger over his unnecessary attempts to burden me with a future which he could well learn to manage—a statement which was not meant to be a therapeutic "suggestion" or a clinical slap on the back, but was based on what I knew of his inner resources as well as of the use he made of the opportunities offered in our clinical community.

The patient left the hour—to which he had come with a sense of dire disaster—with a broad smile and obvious encouragement. Otherwise, only the future would show whether the process of recovery had been advanced by this hour.

But then, one must grant that the dream experience itself was a step in the right direction. I would not want to leave you with the impression that I accused the patient of pretending illness, or that I belittled his dream as representing sham despair. On the contrary, I acknowledged that he had taken a real chance with himself and with me. Under my protection and the hospital's he had hit bottom by chancing a repetition of his original breakdown. He had gone to the very border of unreality and had gleaned from it a highly condensed and seemingly anarchic image. Yet that image, while experienced as a symptom, was in fact a kind of creation, or at any rate a condensed and highly meaningful communication and challenge, to which my particular clinical theory had made me receptive. A sense of mutuality and reality was thus restored, reinforced by the fact that while accepting his transferences as meaningful, I had refused to become drawn into them. I had played neither mother, grandfather, nor God (this is the hardest), but had offered him my help as defined by my professional status in attempting to understand what was behind his helplessness. By relating the fact that his underlying anger aroused mine, and that I could say so without endangering either myself or him, I could show him that in his dream he had also confronted anger in the image of a Medusa—a Gorgon which, neither of us being a hero, we could yet slay together.

The proof of the correctness of our inference does, of course, not always lie in the patient's immediate assent. I have, in fact, indicated how this very dream experience followed an hour in which the patient had assented too much. Rather, the proof lies in the way in which the communication between therapist and patient "keeps moving," leading to new and surprising insights and to the patient's greater assumption of responsibility for himself. In this he is helped, if hospitalized, by the social influences of the "therapeutic community," and by well-guided work activities all of which would have to be taken into account, if I were concerned here with the nature of *the therapeutic process* rather than with that of clinical evidence. But it is important to remember that only in a favorable social setting, be it the private patient's private life or the hospitalized patient's planned community, can the two main therapeutic agents described here function fully: the insight gained into the pathogenic past, and the convincing presence of a therapeutic relationship which bridges past and future.

10

I may now confess that the initial invitation really requested me to tell you "how a *good* clinician works." I have replaced this embarrassing little word with dots until now when I can make it operational. It is a mark of the good clinician that much can go on in him without clogging his communication at the moment of therapeutic intervention, when only the central theme may come to his awareness. Since a clinician's identity as a worker is based (as is anybody else's) on decisive learning experiences during the formative years of his first acquaintance with the field of his choice, he cannot avoid carrying with him some traditional formulations which may range in their effect from ever helpful clarifications to burdening dogmatisms. In a good clinician, such formulations have become a matter of implicit insight and of a style of action. On the other hand, he must also be able to call his ruminations to explicit awareness when professional conferences permit their being spelled out—for how else could such thinking be disciplined, shared, and taught? Such sharing and teaching, in turn, if it is to transcend clinical impressionism, presupposes a communality of conceptual approaches. I cannot give you today more than a suggestion that there is a systematic relationship between clinical observation on the one hand and, on the other, such conceptual points of view as Freud has introduced into psychiatry: a *structural* point of view denoting a kind of anatomy of the mind, a *dynamic* point of view denoting a kind of physiology of mental forces, a *genetic* point of view reconstructing the growth of the mind and the stages marking its strengths and its dangers, and finally, an *adaptive* point of view (Rapaport and Gill, 1959). But even as such propositions are tested on a wide front of inquiry (from the direct observation of children and perception experiments to "metapsychological" discussion), it stands to reason that clinical evidence is characterized by an immediacy which transcends formulations ultimately derived from mechanistic patterns of thought.

The "points of view" introduced into psychiatry and psychology by Freud are, at this time, subject to a strange fate. No doubt, they were the bridges by which generations of medical clinicians could apply their anatomical, physiological, and pathological modes of thinking to the workings of the mind. Probably also, the neurological basis of behavior was thus fruitfully related to other determinants; I myself cannot judge the fate of Freud's neurological assumptions as such. A transfer of concepts from one field to another has in other fields led to revolutionary clarifications and yet eventually also to a necessary transcendence of the borrowed concepts by newer and more adequate ones. In psychoanalysis, the fate of the "points of view" was preordained: since on their medical home ground they were based on visible facts such as organs and functions, in the study of the mind they sooner or later served improper reifications, as though libido or the death instinct or the ego really existed. Freud was sovereignly aware of this danger, but always willing to learn by giving a mode of thought free reign to see to what useful model it might lead. He also had the courage, the authority, and the inner consistency to reverse such a direction when it became useless or absurd. Generations of clinical practitioners cannot be expected to be equally detached or authoritative. Thus it cannot be denied that in much clinical literature the clinical evidence secured with the help of inferences based on Freud's theories has been increasingly used and slanted to verify the original theories. This, in turn, could only lead to a gradual estrangement between theory and clinical observation.

I should, therefore, say explicitly which of the traditional psychoanalytic concepts have remained intrinsic to my clinical way of thinking. I would say that I have to assume that the patient is (to varying degrees) *unconscious* of the meaning which I discern in his communications, and that I am helping him by making fully conscious what may be totally repressed, barely conscious, or simply cut off from communication. By doing so, however, I take for granted an effective wish on his part (with my help) to see, feel, and speak more clearly. I would also assume a *regressive trend,* a going back to earlier failures in order to solve the past along with the present. In doing so, however, I would not give the past a kind of fatalistic dominance over the present: for the temporal rear can be brought up only where the present finds consolidation. I would also acknowledge the power of *transference,* i.e., the patient's transfer to me of significant problems in his past dealings with the central people in his life; but I would know that only by playing my role as a new person in his present stage of life can I clarify the inappropriateness of his transferences from the past. In this past, I would consider libidinal attachments and relationships of dependence and of abandonment of paramount importance: but I would assume, in line with everything that we have learned about human development, that these relationships were not disturbed only by a *libidinal disbalance.* Such disbalance, in fact, is part of a *missed mutuality* which kept the child from realizing his potential strength even as the parent was hindered in living up to his potentialities by the very failure of mutuality in relation to this child. You will note, then, that in naming the rock-bottom concepts of repression and regression, transference and libido, I have tried to keep each linked with the observation and experience of the clinical encounter as a new event in the patient's life history. You would find other clinical workers similarly groping for a position which permits them to honor the therapeutic contract as they use and advance the theory of the field. At the end, the therapist's chosen intervention and the patient's reactions to it are an integral part of the evidence provided in the therapeutic encounter. It is from such experience that the psychotherapist goes back to his drawing board, back to his models of the mind, to the blueprints of intervention and to his plans for the wider application of clinical insight.

11

I have given you an example which ends on a convincing note, leaving both the patient and the practitioner with the feeling that they are a pretty clever pair. If it were always required to clinch a piece of clinical evidence in this manner, we should have few convincing examples. To tell the truth, I think that we often learn more from our failures—if indeed we can manage to review them in the manner here indicated. But I hope to have demonstrated that there is enough method in our work to force favorite assumptions to become probable inferences by cross-checking the patient's diagnosis and what we know of his type of illness and state of physical health; his stage of development and what we know of the "normative" crisis of his age-group; the coordinates of his social position and what we know of the chances of a man of his type, intelligence, and education in the social actuality of our time. This may be hard to believe unless one has heard an account of a *series of such encounters* as I have outlined here, the series being characterized by a progressive or regressive shift in all the areas mentioned: such is the evidence used in our clinical conferences and seminars.

Much of clinical training, in fact, consists of the charting of such series. In each step, our auxiliary methods must help us work with reasonable precision and with the courage to revise our assumptions and our techniques systematically, if and when the clinical evidence should show that we overestimated or underestimated the patient or ourselves, the chances waiting for him in his environment, or the usefulness of our particular theory.

In order to counteract any subjectivity and selectivity, whole treatments are now being sound filmed so that qualified secondary observers can follow the procedure and have certain items repeated many times over, sometimes in slow motion.

This will be important in some lines of research, and advantageous in training. Yet, it confronts a second observer or a series of observers with the task of deciding on the basis of their reactions, whether or not they agree with the judgments of the original observer made on the basis of his unrecordable reactions. Nor does the nature of clinical evidence change in such new developments as group psychotherapy, where a therapist faces a group of patients and they face one another as well, permitting a number of combinations and variations of the basic elements of a clinical encounter. Clinical evidence, finally, will be decisively clarified, but not changed in nature, by a sharpened awareness (such as now emanates from sociological studies) of the psychotherapist's as well as the patient's position in society and history.

The relativity implicit in clinical work may, to some, militate against its scientific value. Yet, I suspect, that this very relativity, truly acknowledged, will make the clinicians better companions of today's and tomorrow's scientists than did the attempts to reduce the study of the human mind to a science identical with traditional natural science. I, therefore, have restricted myself to giving an operational introduction to the clinician's basic view which asserts that scientists may learn about the nature of things by finding out what they can do *to* them, but that the clinician can learn of the true nature of man only in the attempt to do something *for* and *with* him. I have focused, therefore, on the way in which clinical evidence is grounded in the study of what is *unique* to the *individual* case —including the psychotherapist's involvement. Such uniqueness, however, would not stand out without the background of that other concern, which I have neglected here, namely the study of what is *common* to verifiable *classes* of cases.

REFERENCES

Collingwood, R. G. (1956), *The Idea of History*. New York: Oxford University Press.
Erikson, E. H. (1954), The dream specimen of psychoanalysis. *J. Amer. Psychoanal. Assn.*, 2:5–56.

———— (1959), Identity and the Life Cycle. *Psychological Issues,* Monogr. 1. New York: International Universities Press.

———— (1962), Youth: Fidelity and diversity. *Daedalus,* 91:5–27.

Rapaport, D., & Gill, M. M. (1959), The points of view and assumptions of metapsychology. *Internat. J. Psycho-Anal.,* 40:153–162.

11.

The Galilean Sayings and the Sense of "I"

ERIK H. ERIKSON

1

Thomas Jefferson, newly inaugurated as president, spent many solitary evenings in the White House studying the gospels in various languages. He marked each passage "line for line," wondering whether or not it spoke to him with the true voice of Jesus, for he was interested only in "the genuine precepts of Jesus himself." "I am a Christian," he asserted, "in the only sense in which he wished anyone to be: sincerely attached to his doctrines in preference to all others; ascribing to himself every *human* excellence; and believing that he never claimed any other." Finally he cut the passages apart and pasted together those which passed his judgment, collecting them under the title of "The Philosophy of Jesus of Nazareth," with a subtitle dedicating this work to the American Indians. I do not intend to pursue here Jefferson's principles of selection: to mention only two omissions, there was no resurrection and there were no miracles, healing or otherwise. But there was, indeed, the Sermon on the Mount.

When I discussed this very private preoccupation of an American president in my 1973 Jefferson Lectures and described his search as one seeking the "authentic," I was not aware of (or not aware of the implications of) the fact that

277

there had emerged in more recent times a whole school of theologians who had developed a method called "form criticism" in order to discern with a certain methodological rigor which of the early sayings of Jesus could reasonably be considered "authentic." This work originated in Germany in the writings of Martin Dibelius (1919), Rudolf Bultmann (1921), and, later, Joachim Jeremias (1947). In this country, however, it has been most vividly reported by Norman Perrin of Chicago, who studied with Jeremias in Germany. His book *Rediscovering the Teaching of Jesus* (1967) persuaded me to review some of Jesus' sayings in the first, the Galilean, part of his ministry, when this unknown rabbi addressed the strangely "mixed" populace of his native region. Would the fact of their authenticity throw some additional light on the singular and ever so far-reaching power of those words—words that had been passed on by word of mouth before they were collected in written accounts, and then (if in a later form) had become some of the most consistently remembered in history?

To begin, however, I must take a certain exception to the term *authentic*, if, indeed, it is meant to convey more than the probable historicity of some words, because it might seem to suggest that the gospel writers' variations of these sayings are somehow "inauthentic." Now the gospels themselves are a creative art form, characterized by a certain freedom of improvisation in reporting a sequence of lively and colorful episodes, each describing within a native setting the encounters of Jesus and the Galilean populace. But all this paperwork (as it were) was done during the latter part of the first century, decades after Jesus' death, and, in fact, it reviews his reported words in the light of his death and resurrection, which are reported as having taken place in the second part of his ministry—that is, in Judaea, in Jerusalem. By then, the purpose of the gospels obviously was to provide a testamental backbone for growing Christian communities in and way beyond Palestine—communities such as Jesus himself had never witnessed. All of this development had an authenticity of its own, in the form of a new tradition of ritualizations and of worship suited to the individual writers' revelatory idiosyncrasies, to the social trends of the day, and to the receptivity and concerns of readers at that historical moment. That all such traditional ritualization sooner or later is apt to lead to some dead ritualisms is a subject to which we will return repeatedly. But in its beginnings it all has its own historical "authenticity."

Maybe I emphasize all this because I must in my own small way make use of some psychoanalytical license in reflecting on a few of Jesus' sayings and in pointing to an inner logic which to me, as a modern person and a psychoanalyst in the Judaeo-Christian orbit, makes their authentication, well, authentic. To do so, however, I will first have to locate Jesus and the Galilee of his time in the geography and history of Judaism, and I will then have to coordinate that historical pursuit with a more contemporary search—one concerning a vital phenomenon that lies on the borderline of psychology and of theology. I am referring to the sense of "*I*" which is that most obvious and most elusive endowment of creatures with consciousness—and language. This phenomenon has been treated by some psychologists, and I will at a proper time refer to some early remarks made by Freud. William James (in his *Principles of Psychology*) approached the problem from a privileged point of view, namely, that of the professional thinker:

> Whatever I may be thinking of, I am always at the same time more or less aware of *myself*, of my *personal existence*. At the same time it is I who am aware; so that the total self of me, being as it were duplex, partly known and partly knower, partly object and partly subject, must have two aspects discriminated in it, of which for shortness we may call one the *Me* and the other the *I*. The I, or "pure ego," is a very much more difficult subject of inquiry than the Me. It is that which at any moment *is* conscious, whereas the Me is only one of the things which it is conscious *of*. In other words, it is the *Thinker*, and the question immediately comes up *what* is the thinker?

In reading this I hear somebody murmur, "I think, therefore I am (I think)." But what we are concerned with in these pages is the sense of *I* of all human beings (including the thinkers) who can join others in a sense of the *We* only by dint of a shared

language which, in turn, must fit the way in which the prevailing
world view influences not only the general outlook of all individuals in a given region but especially their readiness for a
new revelatory voice. The *I,* after all, is the ground for the
simple verbal assurance that each person is a center of awareness in a universe of communicable experience, a center so
numinous that it amounts to a sense of being alive, and more,
of being the vital condition of existence. At the same time, only
two or more persons sharing a corresponding world image as
well as language can, for moments, merge their *I*'s into a *We.*
I will, then, report later what I have been able to discern of the
particular temporal and spatial dimensions on which depend
the relative clarity of the sense of *I,* or, indeed, the peculiar
dread which can impair it.

To return now to biblical times, let me merely suggest here
two questions. What may be the relation of all this to Moses'
report that when he asked God for his name he received the
answer: *"I am that I am"*? And what may be the relation of
all this to the fact that Jesus, the messenger, is (authentically)
reported to have introduced rather than ended a number of
his sayings with "Amen, but I say unto you"?

In the gospels, the ministry of Jesus begins as a provincial
Galilean event. How he is reported to have spoken, and to
whom and in what places, all suggest the Galilean landscape.
The parables, in fact—generally considered to be his most authentic art form—clearly reflect the fertile agricultural countryside and the thriving fishing industry on Galilee's sea. It is from
those shores that Jesus recruited his first disciples—men who,
we thus learn, by no means joined him because they were hungry or wayward, but who, when recruited imperiously on the
edge of the sea, at once followed his itinerary "all through
Galilee." That his sayings traveled far, and quickly so, is made
more probable by the fact that Galilee is a province in Palestine's north. It is crossed by well-traveled highways that in Jesus'
day carried caravans of traders as well as streams of pilgrims
south—either along the Mediterranean shore or down the traversable strip of land along the Jordan river to Jerusalem—and

brought back trade on the way north and northeast in the direction of Damascus. Accordingly (and according to Matthew) all of Jesus' healing and teaching is pictured as being done as he walked along ways and byways, stopping only for an occasional wish to be alone with himself or with his disciples.

The beautiful and fertile countryside, transversed by interregional roads, is only the geographic basis for a region of extremes, each of which can be praised or blamed for the fact that Galilee first listened to Jesus. Extreme conditions could prevail everywhere in Palestine when (anybody's) rioting armies were let loose. And yet there were peaceful, sedentary populations in Greek cities, for example, or in the countryside populated by Jewish landowners: a few were wealthy, but most were "small-holders," some of whom were busy with family handicrafts such as carpentry or pottery, and some of whom employed hirelings or owned slaves. Among all these there was a population frequenting the synagogues, praying and learning the word. And then there was a haplessly migratory mass, often looking for work, such as unemployed hands and laborers—and younger sons. But Galilee, just because it was removed from the centers of Roman power, was also the "cradle" of Zealotism—movements of pious terrorists, waiting for their time, which always ended with a mass sacrifice of young lives. And then, again, there were those who felt defeated in all national (and that meant, of course, religious and national) matters who leaned toward all kinds of messianic movements and, naturally, were at first and long thereafter considered by some to be "unlettered rabble"—a natural audience for Jesus' preaching. The gospels retrospectively give their own descriptions of the social atmosphere of the ministry. They may describe Jesus and his disciples ambling through the fields on the sabbath or up the hills and down the valleys on a "workday," into clusters of villages and out again to neighboring countrysides, finding the level of faith too low for his ministry only near Nazareth, where Jesus "came from." And there was always the Sea of Galilee, either on calm days when he sat on a boat so as better to address the crowd ashore or miraculously to feed all those who had followed him, or, on occasions of severe storms, when it invited other miracles. Thus, curing and teaching, he was forever followed by a large crowd, including such figures as tax collectors and prostitutes who might not have felt welcome elsewhere. And from these crowds emerged, ever again, an individual help-seeker (a leper, a blind man, a man "possessed") or a seeker for help for relatives at home (a centurion, a president of a synagogue, a Canaanite woman). And, indeed, Jesus went into their houses to assist the sick (Peter's mother-in-law, say, who had a fever). But even when he was in a house, it was soon crowded—so much so that in one, some friends lowered a paralyzed man, tied to a bed, into Jesus' presence through a hole in the roof. (We will discuss later what Jesus said.) But on occasion he demanded the right to go up into the hills to pray by himself, or, indeed, to go up a hill and "take his seat" in order to speak to those who began to hear what he was saying: and it was on such an occasion that he delivered the Sermon on the Mount, followed by the Lord's Prayer, that incomparable variation of the Jewish Kaddish. To the crowds, however, he spoke in parables: was it (as the controversy goes) in order to hide the deeper truth from them or, rather, to teach it to them in an art form they would understand?

Here I must—as I will now and then—take recourse to the old Luther Bible which so often, in his German, seems to solve poetically what cannot so easily be decided intellectually. The gospel writers are unsure (perhaps because they want so badly to belong to those who understood the full meaning of Jesus' words) whether or not Jesus means to ascribe to the crowds some ability to sense the meaning of what he is saying by way of the parables. Matthew has Jesus say (to the disciples, to be sure):

> This is why I speak to them in parables, because seeing they do not see, and hearing they do not hear, nor do they understand. With them indeed is fulfilled the prophecy of Isaiah which says: "You shall indeed hear but never understand, and you shall indeed see but never perceive. For this people's heart has grown dull, and their ears are heavy of hearing, and their eyes they

have closed, lest they should perceive with their eyes, and hear with their ears, and understand with their heart, and turn for me to heal them." But blessed are your eyes, for they see, and your ears, for they hear. Truly, I say to you, many prophets and righteous men longed to see what you see, and did not see it, and to hear what you hear, and did not hear it [Matthew 13:13-17].

I will not go here into the various translations of Jesus' words. Luther—who in creating the first German Bible rejuvenated the image of Jesus as he renewed the German language—resolves it all by suggesting that the parables, even if they do not make crowds "understand," can make them "hear with hearing ears" and "see with seeing eyes" ("mit hoerenden Ohren und sehenden Augen"). Indeed, what else could be the purpose of such a special form of narration, if not that it can make you sense—its sense?

According to Matthew, however, the sayings were of less interest to the crowds than were the cures and the miracles, while Jesus seemed to feel driven by his compassion to cure as many as possible even where he also seemed to indicate that he regretted the excessive demand on his time for dramatic "signs" of the Kingdom's arrival. Furthermore, when we hear, as we will, some of the (authenticated!) words which accompanied his cures, it becomes clear that his declaration of being a shepherd of lost sheep expressed the intention to heal his contemporaries way beyond the mere undoing of the diseases or the misfortunes of some. And, indeed, his sayings, some of which at the time must have had a poetic form (maybe, in their native Aramaic, even some rhyming), were addressed to the malaise of faith which was then a national symptom reflecting the political (and in Judaism this was almost identical with the religious) conditions of that time.

The episodic art form of gospels such as St. Matthew's, then, one-sided as each may be, conveys the combination in Jesus' ministry of an extensive capacity to address the wide variety of groups found in Galilee, and yet to be, potentially, in contact with each individual encountered. In this connection, a scene stands out which I, as a psychoanalyst, felt I had good reason to quote in my Jefferson lectures, and this especially because Jefferson had omitted it from *his* authentic data. It is the story of a woman who had lost not only her blood for twelve years but also all her money on physicians, none of whom had helped her at all. Finding herself in a big crowd surrounding Jesus, she did not dare to, or could not, approach him directly, but she pressed in behind him and touched his garment.

> And straightway the fountain of her blood was dried up; and she felt in her body that she was healed of that plague. And Jesus, immediately knowing in himself that virtue had gone out of him, turned him about in the press, and said, "Who touched my clothes?" And his disciples said unto him, "Thou seest the multitude thronging thee, and sayest thou, 'Who touched me?'" And he looked round about to see her that had done this thing. But the woman fearing and trembling, knowing what was done in her, came and fell down before him, and told him all the truth [Mark 5:29–34].

This illustrates Jesus' selective responsiveness to one person reaching out for him in a big crowd. What he then said to her—that will open up a whole new subject to us.

But now we have to leave Galilee. For at a certain point in Jesus' ministry there comes, in all three synoptic gospels, a decisive announcement according to which Jesus, "on leaving these parts, . . . came into the region of Judaea and the Transjordan" (Mark 10:1); or having "finished this discourse," he "left Galilee" (Matthew 19:1); or more goal-specifically: "As the time approached when he was to be taken up to heaven, he set his face resolutely toward Jerusalem" (Luke 9:51). His sacrifice of the Galilean style of ministry, then (Jesus is now thirty-three years old), is based on a clear-cut decision that he had to challenge—yes, nonviolently—the "powers that be" in Jerusalem. What followed was the Passion that eventually led to his being called Christ and made the Cross the acclaimed symbol of the church to come. With this part of the story, variably elaborated as it is in the gospels, we will not deal in these pages. Yet, we point to an additional justification for our concentration on the Galilean part of the ministry in one of the very last words of the Passion story. Mark (14:28) reports that Jesus and the disciples, right after the last supper, went out to the Mount of Olives, where he added to all his sad predictions of the disciples' impending betrayal a most touchingly intimate remark: "But after I am raised up I will go before you into Galilee." His reported reference to the resurrection may not be authentic; but this statement suggests on his part or on that of the witnesses what may well have been a feeling shared with them by the earthly Jesus, namely, that Galilee was home.

2

I have now circumscribed my overall theme: it is the relationship of Jesus' Galilean sayings to what we call the human sense of *I*, in general; and more specifically, what aspects of these sayings may have promised a pervasive healing quality for the historical and religious malaise of Jesus' time. I will admit that beside and beyond this Galilean moment in human evolution I wonder whether such reflections may throw some light on other great sayings in that millennium, such as those attributed to Lao Tse, and their role in Taoist religion. For, incidentally, the Reign or even the Way seems to be a more persuasive designation for what in English is called the Kingdom; and, indeed, the first Christians did refer to their vision as the New Way.

In order to be able to approach the Galilean sayings in their historical setting, however, we must go beyond their Galilean time and place. We have noted that Galilee in all the insularity of its countryside and its seashore nonetheless served as a highway to Jerusalem and beyond to the Hellenistic world and Rome. We must now follow this highway into metropolitan Judaea and review some of the history which gave it its place in the wider world. And on the way we must here and there approach the problem of the human *I* in its relation to the dimensions of the world image suggested by past history and by contemporary historical change.

I have suggested that the sense of *I* is one of the most obvious facts of existence—indeed, maybe *the* most obvious—and that it is, at the same time, one of the most elusive; wherefore psychologists are apt to consider it a philosophical rather than a psychological concern. I will discuss later how my teacher, Sigmund Freud, managed (almost) to ignore it. But it is true, of course, that this subjective sense dwells on the very border of our conscious existence, though no doubt its health is dependent on such qualities of our psychosocial life as our sense of identity. In the Bible, the most direct reference to the human *I* is in the form of an inner light, that is, of a luminosity of awareness. The original Galilean saying is reported in Matthew's account: "Nor do men light a lamp and put it under a bushel, but on a stand, and it gives light to all in the house" (5:15). "The eye is the lamp of the body. So, if your eye is sound, your whole body will be full of light, but if your eye is not sound, your whole body will be full of darkness. If, then, the light in you is darkness, how great is the darkness!" (6:22). And, indeed, our sense of *I* gives to our sensory awareness a numinous center. It is no wonder, then, that our most eloquent recent witness for the inner light is a blind man, Jacques Lusseyran, who lost his eyesight through an accident at the age of seven and a half. He later wrote (in "The Blind in Society"):

> Barely ten days after the accident that blinded me, I made the basic discovery . . . I could not see the light of the world any more. Yet the light was still there. . . . I found it *in myself* and what a miracle!—it was intact. This "in myself," however, where was that? In my head, in my heart, in my imagination? . . . I felt how it wanted to spread out over the world. . . . The source of light is not in the outer world. We believe that it is only because of a common delusion. The light dwells where life also dwells: within ourselves. . . . The second great discovery came almost immediately afterwards. There was only one way to see the inner light, and that was to love.

This numinosity, however, seems lost when it is too eagerly concentrated on for its own sake, as if one light were asked to illuminate another. No wonder that dictionaries avoid the matter! I have before me a psychological dictionary which does not even mention *I.* My thesaurus, in turn, refers first to a "self-designating pronoun" and then to "the spiritual personality"—and nothing in between.

Actually, writers who take the sense of *I* seriously will first of all ask what is the *I*'s counterplayer. They may indeed begin with the second pronoun, *you,* and end with the soul's sense of a divine *Thou.* To my developmental orientation the most telling "map" depicting the development of the sense of *I* would be the whole list of personal pronouns, from *I* to *They,* as each one first gets to be pronounced and understood correctly in childhood, and then as it is meaningfully experienced and reexperienced throughout life. The beginnings of the sense of *I* itself, one should think, can only emerge in a newborn out of the counterplay with a sensed *You* in the maternal caretaker—whom we shall call the Primal Other; and it seems of vital importance that this Other, and, indeed, related Others, in turn experience the new being as a *presence* that heightens *their* sense of *I.* It is this interplay, I think, that helps the original sense of *I* gradually face another fundamental counterplayer, namely, *my Self*—almost an Inner Other. But the original interplay of *You* and *I* remains the model for a mutual recognition throughout life, up to a finite expectation to which St. Paul gave the explicitly religious form of an ultimate meeting now only vaguely sensed beyond "a glass, darkly" (the Ultimate Other, then).

Now, one glance at the list of all personal pronouns reveals a whole developmental program in their sequence: for while *I* and *you* form the original dyad, this dyad soon turns into a number of triads as a series of *hes* or *shes* (and, indeed, a world of *its*) become additional counterplayers within varied connotations: paternal, fraternal, sororal, and so on. And as this happens, the plural concepts *we, you,* and *they* become both verbal necessities and the bearers of important emotional involvements. Thus, the system of pronouns, beginning with *I* and *you,* is built into a ground plan ready to unfold in stages; and one can well see how each of them, once learned, serves a widening experience as it includes, on every stage, new counterplayers.

Take, for example, the necessity—especially in any patriarchal and monotheistic system—to transfer some of the earliest forms of a sense of *I* from their maternal origin to strongly paternal and eventually theistic relationships. Or consider the crisis of adolescence as a transfer of the identity elements formed in childhood and youth to the productive milieu in which one expects to find one's psychosocial identity. Or, again, how the sense of *we* acquired in one's family of origin ("my kind") must be extended to the family and the community one marries into—and, indeed, to one's own new family in which one must help to generate new beings with their own sense of *I*.

Throughout this establishment of new boundaries of *We, Ourselves*, dictated as it is by the realities and the ideology of work and production, there also emerges a gradual demarcation of the decisive borderlines beyond which live those definitely other Others—those *they*s and *them*s whom one has learned to repudiate or to exclude as foreign, if not nonhuman altogether. These habitual rejections, in turn, have helped to give a clearer outline to one's own "true Self" or to those variant "selves" which are either proudly or fatalistically accepted as a self-description within the contemporary world of roles. And yet, throughout all these critical stages with all their involvements, there remains for the *I* a certain existential solitariness which, in these pages, we depict as seeking love, liberation, salvation. So we now return to such geographic and historical conditions as provide in any given period the basis for an ideological orientation in the widest sense of a Way of Life—the essential bridge between all *I*'s and their *We*'s.

When Jesus and his disciples crossed into Judaea, they abruptly entered a country in a most vulnerable condition. True, it was ready to view them as (possibly dangerous) outsiders, for Galilee's name in the exclusively Jewish population of Judaea was, in fact, "Galilee of the Gentiles," whose "north country" Aramaic was made fun of and whose strong admixture of militant zealots was feared by Romans and Jews alike. One of the predominant facts in Judaea was a precarious deal between the representatives of Rome, the occupying power, and the temple's Jewish aristocracy—a deal to keep Jerusalem safe enough to be forever hostess of the temple, the religious empire's sacred center and the central geographic reference of a people, the larger part of which was already living in the enclaves of a widespread Diaspora reaching to Rome, to Alexandria, and to Mesopotamia.

As we now approach such unique space-time configurations as *Diaspora*—configurations which can have quite ambiguous connotations for a nation's sense of existence—we might briefly reconsider the spatial sense established by the all-important fact in American history of a *frontier*. As an overall gestalt, the frontier gradually moved westward and northward until it joined the Pacific Ocean, and yet it still figures in many life plans and ventures, as well as, of course, memories—not to speak of habitual media themes. Let us not overlook, in passing, the configuration of immigration which for so long—as it does in Israel today—expressed the eagerness of the new homecomers to have "made it," no matter what may have made them leave where they came from. "Frontier" has obviously played a significant role in the implicit images of "new deals" as well as the explicit slogan of a "new frontier." The same is true (or, significantly, *has* been true) for the American imagery of fear, which always assumed that armies are *ex*-peditionary forces expected to fight on *foreign* fronts and not meant to wait for a potential enemy ever to *in*-vade. The personal sense of fate which depends on such shared space–time configurations can consist of the simplest of all defensive attitudes, such as who can do what to me—and what can I do to them if they do it. Radical changes in such habitual expectability and the totally new threat of total nuclear vulnerability are absorbed only very, very slowly into either the individual sense of existence or, indeed, the psychosocial and national identity. They demand and are in fact waiting for nothing less than a kind of revelatory reorientation of the whole world image as based on the acceptance of the undeniable facts of developing technology and on the capacity for new modes of ethical adaptation.

We come to the conclusion, then, that whatever a people's geographic and historical setting, its majority (or its leading aristocracy) must be assured of the reliability of a number of dominant space–time qualities which, in fact, correspond to the requirements of a sense of *I*, even if they cohere in a collective *We*. Among these we have mentioned a sense of *numinosity*; we now add a choice of *action*, of a *central position*, as well as a guarantee of *continuity* in time, and all marked by strong *boundaries*—a concept which will prove indispensable to a comparison of the vulnerable peripheries of the Judaic territory and the firm and all-inclusive circumscription of Jehovah's world, not to speak of the possible impact of both on the sense of *I* and the sense of *We*. When describing a group's space–time, then, we must emphasize configurations which seem to enhance all these qualities or, obversely, threaten inactivation, peripherality, discontinuity, and so on.

As we now return to ancient Israel, the reader will wonder with me whether there has ever been a nation more lacking in all such guarantees—except in the form of prophetic promises uttered in the name of a national god—than was Judaea in Jesus' time.

In the Palestinian homeland as a whole, Galilee was then one of the components of a tetrarchy, that is, a dynastic division between the three sons of King Herod the Great, who died around the time of Jesus' birth. Now Galilee was—very relatively speaking—safely in the hands of one son who managed to rule it until A.D. 39 (although he had John the Baptist killed for reasons of personal pique and may have been suspicious of Jesus as a potential successor). The second, the northeastern part, remained in the hands of another son until A.D. 34. Archelaus, however, the son in possession of Judaea, had been deposed by the Romans already, in the year 6; and since then, Jerusalem had been governed by that precarious deal between a Roman procurator (at that time, Pontius Pilate, as you may have heard) and the priestly aristocracy that "owned" the new temple on the site on which Solomon had built the old one almost a thousand years before. I would underline *deal* as one of the disturbing elements in the Jewish national identity of the day, for it was both religiously and politically demeaning—and Jesus, "the King," was of course to be its victim, as an alleged danger to the Pax Romana. Speaking of national identity, it must, incidentally, be assumed that Jesus and the Romans conversed in what was then the official language, namely, Greek.

But then, there are other circumstances as yet to be italicized. All of Palestine was, as it had been for a thousand years, a *buffer nation* between successively contending empires and a geographic *corridor* for great nations—such as Syria, Egypt, and Persia—seeking to "get at" each other. Thus, its very location, which made the small Jewish nation at times conspicuously important, also made it permanently vulnerable, and most of the major events of its history attested to this. A thousand and a half years before, much of the nation had lived in Egypt, from which, thanks to Jehovah and Moses, it had been brought back: the great *Exodus*. There were then again, as there had been more than two millennia earlier, some great kings and great prophets. But there also were incomprehensible interruptions such as the Assyrian and Babylonian *exiles* and *captivities* (in the eighth and sixth centuries B.C.), as well as alternating *occupations* by the Persian and Greek empires and their contending dynastic heirs. Now and again the most unthinkable would happen, namely, that a foreign ruler or general would *intrude* upon the temple's holiest of holies, which only the hereditary high priest should enter once a year on the Day of Atonement to express the nation's confessional commitment to Jehovah. But those few times were deeply remembered.

For one century, however, and from the middle of the second to that of the first century B.C., the Jewish nation had lived in independence, and this after Judas Maccabaeus and his brothers had led a revolt against the occupying Syrians whose king had desecrated the temple and attempted to introduce Hellenic cults. The Maccabaeans made the high priest king and restored a joined territory as great as that of David's and Solomon's. A generation later, however, the rule of these Hasmonaeans (that was their family name) appeared to be bogged down in power struggles. Yet the Romans did not take over until 63 B.C., when Pompey—apparently invited by Palestinian factions—conquered Jerusalem, and, in his turn, entered the holy of holies. It was then that Herod became King of Judaea; he was a Jew by religion, flamboyantly Greek in style,

Roman in allegiance, and unpredictably cruel in personality. Passionately interested in architecture, he began to renovate the temple in 20 B.C. It was there in Jesus' time, and it was to survive until A.D. 70—which, after one more national uprising, marked the end of the ancient kind of Jewish nationhood and of the religious center.

Even such a sketch of Palestine's history makes it vividly clear that the Hebrew nation had to survive and to learn to live with a number of devastating time-and-space configurations. In spite of a venerable past untiringly celebrated in the holy writings, the living historical memory suggested a territorial condition which had made the nation alternately vulnerable to foreign powers and all their actions—as emphasized above. In spite of a most intensive history of singular heroism there was, all in all, a complete *inactivation* of defense; and the freedom of the one symbol of central locus and inner autonomy, namely, the temple, was granted only by the consent of the empire on whose *periphery* it existed. The enumerated conditions of this existence obviously violate every dimension of that sense of *I* which any collective must provide; and one could conclude that such a nation had no identity with a chance of survival in centuries to come.

It is here, however, that we must, at last, turn to Jehovah, who had remained (and was yet to remain) the guardian of those people who would continue to develop, even beyond their final national defeat, a lasting sense of ethnic and religious identity and, in fact, of some lasting moral mission, nurtured rather than famished by the very fact of their dispersion among other nations.

This brings us to the dimensions of monotheism, the religious heritage in Jesus' upbringing. Here we must consider its ethical power as well as its daily condition at the time. No doubt monotheism provided strength to the Jews because it permitted them to accept even disaster as a genuine aspect of what must be Jehovah's plan—and pact. Speaking of the significance of the sense of *I*, we have quoted "I am that I am" (Exodus 3:14). Leif Boman has noted that the word for *being (hayah)*, which is used in connection with Jehovah's very name, has a very active quality. There seems to be, in fact, an identity of being, and becoming, and even of acting and speaking: "For he spoke, and it came to be. He commanded, and it stood forth" (Psalms 33:9). And Jehovah's *hayah* is the people's *hayah:* "Obey my voice, and I will be your God, and you shall be my people" (Jeremiah 7:23). And Jehovah is "everlasting" as well as everywhere: "the Creator of the ends of the earth" (Isaiah 40:28). Thus, divine reality of being becomes a worldwide actuality in its total effectiveness.

Furthermore, Jehovah, once the first *among* the gods, eventually becomes the *first* and the *last*—"so that men from the rising and the setting sun may know that there is none but I . . . I make the light, I create darkness, author alike of prosperity and trouble. I, the Lord, do all these things" (Isaiah 45:6–7).

"Prosperity *and* trouble." Whatever the native word here translated as "trouble," it stands for the price of having been chosen and rooted: " 'I will plant then upon their land, and they shall never again be plucked up out of the land, which I have given them,' says the Lord your God" (Amos 9:15); and to be in their own "house," secure in the generational progression:

[F]rom the time that I appointed judges over my people Israel; and I will give you rest from all your enemies. Moreover the Lord declares to you that the Lord will make you a house. When your days are fulfilled and you lie down with your fathers, I will raise up your offspring after you, who shall come forth from your body, and I will establish his kingdom. He shall build a house for my name, and I will establish the throne of his kingdom for ever. I will be his father, and he shall be my son. When he commits iniquity, I will chasten him with the rod of men, with the stripes of the sons of men; but I will not take my steadfast love from him, as I took it from Saul, whom I put away from before you [2 Samuel 7:11–15].

For such actuality in eternity, both messianic promises and apocalyptic threats become confirmations both of being chosen and of having actively, knowingly, chosen judgment as well as salvation. It can also be sealed, in prayers and in rituals, with "Amen: so it *is*."

Here, of course, man's evolutionary capacity for guilt becomes a pointed part of his sense of existence; and, as creation and procreation become one actuality, so the experience of the Father in monotheism recapitulates the experience of the father in ontogeny. In suggesting that here, too, the most obvious must be taken at its word, I do not mean to reduce such faith to its infantile roots. For the literal believer could well respond with the assertion that human childhood, besides being an evolutionary phenomenon, may well have been created so as to plant in the child at the proper time the potentiality for a comprehension of the Creator's existence, and a readiness for his revelations. And, indeed, the way the father can be experienced in childhood can make it almost impossible *not* to believe deep down in (and indeed to fear as well as to hope for) a fatherly spirit in the universe.

And here the eternal covenant goes right to the heart of matters which are central to the physical and emotive existence of the *I*. Certainly any sense of *I* includes a few basic regions of bodily existence which must be centrally "mine" because they guarantee the core and the extension of my existence: one such center in the *I* space is the heart and one, certainly, the genitals. No wonder, then, that Jehovah as God of a patriarchy takes possession of the region of the penis, so that "my covenent be in your flesh an everlasting covenant" (Genesis 17:13). And more specifically:

> This is my covenant, which you shall keep, between me and you and your descendants after you: Every male among you shall be circumcised. You shall be circumcised in the flesh of your foreskins, and it shall be a sign of the covenant between me and you. He that is eight days old among you shall be circumcised; every male throughout your generations, whether born in your house, or bought with your money from any foreigner who is not of your offspring [Genesis 17:10–12].

Deuteronomy (10:16), in turn, pronounces the pointed warning, "Circumcise therefore the foreskin of your heart, and be no longer stubborn."

Thus one could say much about the development in childhood of a father-bound conscience—intensified as it is in a patriarchal and monotheistic setting. Our main interest in this context, however, is some clarification regarding Jehovah's integrative power in a post- and precatastrophic political timespace. And as we have just seen, Jehovah is in the center of individual existence, even as he is in the religious center: "Then the nations will know that I, the Lord, sanctify Israel, when my sanctuary is in the midst of them for evermore" (Ezekiel 37:28). But this means that he is in the center of a conscience which, within a network of ritual commitments, can feel affirmative and confirmed, choosing the chosen, and, even at the height of Jehovah's wrath, certain of a "kingdom-to-come."

In the scriptures two messianic world images were attached to Jehovah's name which were to play a great role in the evolution of an existential meaning for man: that of God's reign and that of the "son of man." Both were charged with defining (but by all means abstaining from overdefining) the boundaries between history and a "transhistorical" reality (when "all the world will rejoice in the knowledge of Jahweh"); between David's royal territory and Jehovah's universal empire; and between godly, royal, and "ordinary" sonhood, that is, God's dynastic covenant with David and his house and his individual covenant with each Jew. Most nebulous, of course, were the various emphases on the dramatic form (messianic or apocalyptic, salvational or judgmental) which such a New Day or Golden Age would take—not to speak of the human form in which God's servant and messenger would appear: was he to be a king or an anointed Lord (Chrystos Kyrios)—that is, was he a royal or a priestly figure—or both? As Isaiah's God puts it: "It is too light a thing that you should be my servant to raise up the tribes of Jacob and to restore the preserved of Israel; I will give you as a light to the nations, that my salvation may reach to the end of the earth" (Isaiah 49:6). And who or what "remnant of Israel" will survive the apocalypse?

As to the "son of man," it has persistent if persistently ambiguous connotations all the way from an almost evolutionary emergence in Daniel's prophetic dream of a vaguely human shape ("one like a son of man" or "a man-like figure" [Daniel 7:13]) emerging from a pack of superreal beastly creatures; or a human being (ben ādaṁ) sitting at God's right; or, finally, something we cannot afford to omit here, namely, an Aramaic way of simply saying *I*. All of these meanings seem to converge on a transcendent sense of awareness lodged in an earthly human shape, and we will find something of all of them projected by the reporters and historians of that time on Jesus' reference to himself as the son of man.

3

But we should now add a few words on the dangers that can befall yearly and daily ritualizations of such an overwhelming belief in a tough, a central, cosmic power's benevolence. Here I must introduce a term which I find indispensable in any attempt to locate in the social process a phenomenon which corresponds to compulsivity in the individual; I call it "ritualism" (*Toys and Reasons*). The greatest ritualizations can eventually become repetitive and the minutest daily rituals compulsive—whereupon devotion to revered images can become idolism, adherence to detailed laws can become legalism, and reliance on dogma can become dogmatism. This is particularly so under conditions felt to be of danger to the very nature of things; and this, in Jesus' time, may well have been the loss of national power and of cultural consistency under the impact of Hellenization. Under such conditions, then, creative enrichment through live rituals can give place to a superconscientious preoccupation with ritualistic details dominated by a compulsive scrupulosity apt to deaden the renewal and rejuvenation which is the essence of an inventive ritual life. Here one may want to consider how much of the creative life of a great nation had in Judaism been totally absorbed by the religious system: consider only the fact that Jehovah's very sanctified presence, and with it all ritual themes, were soon to be forbidden subjects

for representative art, and this at a time when the arts of other
nations flowered exactly in their images of the divine. By the
same token, musical performance and poetic as well as fictional
literature were restricted to religious subjects. The ritualization
of daily or yearly life, then, was mainly concerned with the
confirmation of the word as contained in the scriptures and a
scrupulous search for their correct interpretation.

The great yearly holidays celebrated at the temple in Jerusalem, when pilgrims doubled the population, were no doubt
occasions of ritual self-transcendence and of national renewal,
but the services in the synagogues spread over the countryside
had turned more to textual preoccupation with the wording of
the scriptures, even as the daily and weekly prayers were (as
Jesus was to point out) occasions demonstrating one's righteousness: under such conditions "isms" are apt to dominate
behavior, and, indeed, there is the word *sabbatism*. All of these
concerns with strictness in ritual life are, of course, a potential
found in all institutions that have outlived the ideological conditions of their origins.

But there was, and is, in the Jewish community a ritualization of everyday life which must have played a great role in the
survival of Judaism. I am referring to family life, as embedded
in a process significantly formulated by Klausner (in his Hebrew *Jesus of Nazareth*), who speaks of "a unifying tendency
which broke down the dividing wall between religion and daily
life, making daily life an essential part of religion and religion
an essential part of daily life. That which was holy was not
thereby profaned but was brought down to earth, while the
secular life was transformed into the sacredness of a religious
duty." But not even Klausner, at this point, mentions a "phenomenon" in Jewish daily life which both confirmed and com-
pensated for the credal emphasis on a dominating masculinity
of Being. How the *Jewish mother*, in daily and weekly life, in
Palestine and throughout the Diaspora, continued to play the
role of a most down-to-earth goddess of the hearth—that would
call for an intimate cultural history which is grounded in some
special chapters of the Old Testament and yet also represents
one of the most consistent trends in Jewish history. In Christian

mythology it was to be glorified in the counterpart to the Passion, namely, the Nativity. In our context, the specific nature of motherhood is really mandatory for any balanced historical account, for the very basis of any sense of *I* originates in the infant's first interplay with that primal, that maternal *Other*, and certainly continues to be nourished by persistent contact with her.

Now, as to the outstanding subgroups in religious life which considered themselves the caretakers of the messianic age to come: temple life and temple politics were dominated by the Sadducees, a party of the priestly aristocracy, who, as we have noted, shared the maintenance of a precarious Pax Romana with the occupying power. The biggest religious "party" was that of the Pharisees, much closer to the people, who cultivated the old ways but were interested in adaptations. For both these reasons they showed a direct and critical interest in Jesus' ministry. On their "left" were the Zealots, who believed in political change by faith-inspired force; one of Jesus' disciples belonged to them. True religious rebirth, however, was cultivated with no concessions by the religious sects who had withdrawn to lonely parts of the country to await the rejuvenation of ancient religiosity: the Essenes and the residents of Qumran. About both we have learned much in recent decades, especially from the Dead Sea Scrolls.

But there was only one man, a carpenter and rabbi baptized by John the Baptist, who, as we had begun to describe, spoke to the crowds of ordinary people with an "authority" that permitted him to *start* with "Amen"; to continue, "but I say unto you . . ."; and then to say it.

"Authentic" sayings, we said. According to the form critics, this means the "earliest form" known of such a saying that can plausibly be traced to Mark (the first gospel, later independently used by Matthew and Luke) and/or to the even earlier collection of sayings called Q (for the German *Quelle*, meaning "source")—if, furthermore, the occurrence of such a form can be shown to be "neither possible nor probable" in ancient Judaism or in the early Church. As we will see (our first example will consist of exactly five words), sayings which survive such a

scrutiny are of immense simplicity, especially if seen against
the background of the spatial and temporal sweep of the world
imagery of much of the preceding Judaic religiosity *and* of the
gospels to follow. But such simplicity, we will claim, is of their
essence. At the same time, however, the gospels' specific art
form permits us, as we have already seen, at least to imagine
these simple sayings as spoken within the context of a most
vivid encounter. Here let me go back to the story of the woman
who was cured of a persistent flow of blood. This example, in
its healing aspects, can be seen immediately to be as close to
our day and work as it seems to have surprised the Galilee of
that day. For, to permit myself a professional and even theoretical response, it makes good sense in modern terms that Jesus,
in the midst of a thick throng, should have felt the touch of
the desperate woman, and felt it as an acute loss of a powerful
quantity of something vital. For this is comparable to and, indeed, is a parabolic representation of a certain interplay or
mutual "transfer" of energy (Freud called it libido, that is, love-
energy) which is assumed to take place and must be understood—as "transference"—in any therapeutic situation. But
now, what *did* Jesus say, having been "touched" in this manner?
"Your faith has healed you." The King James version is "My
daughter, thy faith hath made thee whole"—which underlines
the loving as well as the holistic character of all healing. At any
rate, he acknowledges the woman's aptitude for trust and her
determination to reach him as an essential counterpart to his
capacity to help her. Nor is this the only time that Jesus specifies
this "interpersonal" and active condition. There was a blind
beggar (Mark 10:46–52) seated at the roadside, shouting for
the "son of David." Jesus first "activated" him by having somebody call to him, thus inducing him to throw off his cloak,
spring up, and come to *him.* Then Jesus said, "Your faith has
made you well." And there were the four friends, already mentioned (Mark 2:1–5), who were trying to bring a paralyzed man
on a stretcher through the door of the house in which Jesus
was teaching. Unable to get through, they broke open the roof
"over the place where Jesus was" and lowered the stretcher
through. This time, Mark says, when Jesus saw *their* faith, he

said to the sick man, "My son, your sins are forgiven"—a rabbi's claim to the right of absolution which resulted in a bit of theological argument from some lawyers: "Why does the fellow talk like that?"

But now to the question of authenticity. Here Norman Perrin declares himself not prepared to argue for the total authenticity of any of these healing narratives. He is only ready to claim that "the emphasis upon the faith of the patient, or his friends, in that tradition is authentic." That is, studies have shown that "faith is never demanded" in either the rabbinic tradition or in Hellenistic stories.

This brings us to the definition of two of the criteria on the basis of which the scholars involved are willing to make a decision for or against authenticity. One is the principle of "dissimilarity" which, as we saw, differentiates the sayings quoted from corresponding Judaic and Hellenistic contexts. The other is the principle of "coherence" which connects a number of stories and suggests an authentic element in all of them even if this element could be more definitely specified in only one or the other. Such "coherence" is, of course, most convincing if it illustrates what Bultmann conservatively called a new "disposition of mind."

It will be clear that Jesus' therapeutic formula is only one of many sayings, all cohering in a basic orientation (to be illustrated further) which emphasizes the individual's vital core in the immediate present rather than in dependence on traditional promises and threats of a cosmic nature. If I relate this to the sense of *I*, it will appear to be simplistic, and certainly too "superficial" for a psychoanalyst. Yet, as we have said, to be active (as well as central, continuous, and whole), or at any rate not to feel inactivated (or peripheral and fragmented), is one of the most essential dimensions of a sense of *I*. I would consider Jesus' emphasis on the patient's propensity for an active faith, then, not only a therapeutic "technique" applied to incapacitated individuals but an ethical message for the bystanders as part of a population which at that time must have been weakened in its sense of being the master—or unsure of a faith that could promise to become master—of its collective fate. And as for the enduring meaning of this saying let me here note that this orientation reasserted itself in the history of psychotherapy with Freud's decision to make the hysterical patient *work* for recovery by letting his or her own inner voice direct "free associations" in search of the underlying conflicts instead of merely submitting to hypnosis.

And—to pursue our second concern—what did Freud say about the human sense of *I*? Certainly, in his search for a scientific psychology he did not wish to be sidetracked into man's age-old claim to a soul—which all too often has seemed to become a "narcissistic" center of human self-illusion. He concentrated on the means by which man's consciousness may be made useful in the process of calling to mind what to mankind's vast detriment had become denied and repressed in ontogeny and phylogeny. And so he emphasized what he called the human *Ich*—the right word for *I* in German, but always (and sometimes questionably) translated into English as *ego*. And it is true that the *Ich* as ego to him became a primarily unconscious inner organization of experience on which human adaptation and sanity depend: the "ego gives mental processes an order in time and submits them to reality testing." Therefore, if it is disturbed its control must be restored by insight; but where is insight located? Freud cautiously claims that "On this ego [*an diesem Ich*] hangs consciousness"—a phenomenon, then, "on the periphery of the ego."

But here we face an issue of vast importance in the understanding of Freud's original concepts. If Freud himself in the early days of theory-formation uses the term *Ich* alternately for a conscious surface phenomenon and for a largely unconscious ordering of experience, one cannot blame his translators for refusing to make themselves responsible for a decision as to when the context might suggest *I* rather than *ego*. Freud himself, however, wonders aloud what right he has to narrow down the importance of a conscious sense of *I*. "At first we are inclined greatly to reduce the value of the criterion of being conscious since it has shown itself so untrustworthy," he claims; and then he must admit, "But we should be doing it an injustice. As may be said of our life, it is not worth much, but it is

all we have. Without the illumination thrown by the quality
of consciousness, we should be lost in the obscurity of depth-
psychology; but we must attempt to find our bearings afresh."
Here again, the translator has given in to Freud's usual tendency *not* to overdo the significance of a numinous sense of
aliveness. For the word translated as *illumination* is *die Leuchte*,
a word denoting, indeed, luminosity, and this in the two senses
of the Galilean saying, that is, a *Leuchter*—a lamp—and a
Leuchte, i.e., a luminous quality, a shining light. This whole
"skeptical" remark, then, in which our consciousness, whatever
its worth, is compared with life itself, is in all its caution not
too far from the psalmist's acknowledgment of a light given by
the creator to the apple of the eye.

And while Freud remains, as it were, religiously scientific
because he is determined to pursue his mission, which is to
find a truly analytical method to study human obsession
(whether "evil" or "sick"), he comes, in the statement quoted,
as close as he may wish to the saying, "but when thine eye is
evil, thy body also is full of darkness" (Luke 11:34, King James
version); except that he continues to pursue the darkness behind consciousness, attempting to reveal some structural divisions in man's psyche—that is, besides the ego, the superego,
and, finally, the id, an inner caldron of drives and passions.

Here, as far away from the *I* as we can get, another Galilean
saying seems to have expressed a "new disposition" most decisive for a self-aware human attitude. When challenged by some
Pharisees who saw his disciples sit down to a meal without washing their hands properly and without seeming concerned about
"the washing of pots and cups and vessels of bronze," Jesus
says tough things, as Mark reports it, about their "teaching as
doctrines the precepts of men," thus "making void the word
of God through your tradition." Mark continues: "And he
called the people to him again, and said to them, 'Hear me,
all of you, and understand: there is nothing outside a man
which by going into him can defile him; but the things which
come out of a man are what defile him' " (Mark 7:14–16). And
later, Jesus added for the sake of his questioning disciples:

"Do you not see that whatever goes into a man from outside cannot defile him, since it enters, not his heart but his stomach, and so passes on?" (Thus he declared all foods clean.) And he said, "What comes out of a man is what defiles a man. For from within, out of the heart of man, come evil thoughts, fornication, theft, murder, adultery, coveting, wickedness, deceit, licentiousness, envy, slander, pride, foolishness" [Mark 7:18–22].

Our form critics, I presume, would not underwrite as authentic the exact list of evils emanating from within, although every believer in the id must acknowledge them. But as to Jesus' simple insistence on the fate of what comes in (*es geht den natuerlichen Gang,* Luther puts it: it takes the natural course), Perrin declares it most authentic, and, in fact, "the most radical statement in the whole Jesus tradition," "completely without parallel" in rabbinic or sectarian Judaism. It seems to do away with many deeply ingrained distinctions between clean and unclean which serve the phobic avoidances and the compulsive purifications by daily and weekly ritualisms—at the time probably reinforced in Pharisaic circles by their disdain for the intrusion into Jewish life of Hellenic mores. By then, of course, Jesus had publicly demonstrated not only his unorthodox daily habits but also the liberality of his choice of table fellows. In calling the inner caldron the "heart" of man, however, he certainly points to an *inner* seat of passionate conflict from which emerge the multiple temptations by which the sense of *I* is ruefully inactivated and which it therefore can experience as an inner chaos—an id. And yet, the *I* can possibly manage some of them only by that radical awareness which Jesus here demands.

I have now come dangerously close to claiming that the authentic Jesus does, indeed, make sensible sense in terms of our present-day pursuits. So it is time to present a saying which puts exorcism more explicitly into the (literally) widest actuality in which the Galilean Jesus felt he was operating—that is, the Kingdom: "But if it is by the finger of God that I cast out demons, then the kingdom of God has come upon you" (Luke 11:20). Luther renders this *den Teufel austreiben,* that is, "to cast out the devil," and continues: *so kommt je das Reich Gottes zu Euch,* that is, "and so, every time, the reign of God comes upon you." The saying itself is said to have "high claims on authenticity," even if Matthew speaks of God's "spirit" rather than "finger"—but then the gospel writers often modify what in the original version seems to them to be a bit extreme. I like the finger, however, because it continues the theme of touch which was so prominent in the episode with the woman; except that here, of course, it is the finger of God which is operative through Jesus' action and makes the Kingdom—well, how shall we put it—come? have come? forever coming? For here we seem to have some play with time appearing in special contrast to those grand prophetic predictions of the Kingdom as some final act in history such as decisive redemption. And if the Kingdom is so vague in its temporal boundaries, *where* is it? This question Jesus answers in another context: "Behold, the kingdom of God is in the midst of you" (Luke 17:21). The Greek original, *entos hymōn,* presumably can mean "between you" as well as "within you," for Luther's translation, *inwendig in Euch,* claims just that.

In all these forms, the saying is considered "absolutely characteristic of oral tradition." Thomas, in fact, in his Gnostic way, presents an apparently independent parallel: "The kingdom is within you and it is without you. If you will know yourselves, then you will be known and you will know that you are the sons of the Living Father" (Thomas 3). And again, being asked by the Pharisees (to trick him, no doubt) when the kingdom was coming, Jesus answered: "The kingdom of God is not coming with signs to be observed" (Luke 17:20). This could be seen to contradict the first saying we quoted where Jesus, in fact, refers to his own observable act of healing; but Luther, again, seems to be on the right track, for he translates "not coming with signs to be observed" as *kommt nicht mit ausserlichen Gebaerden;* it does not "come with extraneous gestures."

If I may say in my own words what I understand all this to mean: these quotations make it clear that Jesus speaks of the Kingdom as an experience of inner as well as interpersonal actualization open to every individual who accepts his mediation. Since Jehovah, as we saw, is a god whose very being is action, such initiative, it seems, is now certified as a property of human existence—if through Jesus' mediation. For to be the voice announcing such an actuality as a potential in the here and now of every individual—that, it seems, is the essence of Jesus' ministry: "if it is by the finger of God that I . . ." We have seen that one of the conditions for the realization of such a potential is faith, which, of course, includes repentance. But, again, it is an individual decision to become aware of universal sin in one's own personal form which, of course, also means to acknowledge these universal potentials in one's neighbor. All of which implies that the "kingdom" is no longer (if it ever was) a static territory or a predictable time span: it is a dominion (*malkuth shamayim*) in motion, a Coming, a Way—a fulfillment in the present which contains an anticipation of a future.

Why do I repeat here what has been said often and better? I wish, of course, to relate it to the concept of an *I*-time, for which I have postulated, among others, the qualities of activity and wholeness, and to which I must now add that of *centrality*, a being present in the center of events. Thus, repentance as an active choice (and the Greek word for it is *metanoia*, translated by Luther as *Umkehr*—"turnabout") makes one central to one's life-space. With all the pain of penitence inherent in the word, one need not be inactivated by bad conscience, nor banned by divine judgment; and this seems to be a step toward the alertness of the sense of *I*, which is also implied in that repeated encouragement: "Be aware! Be Wakeful! Watch!"

Having related some sayings concerned with the boundaries of adult existence, we turn to one which focuses on the beginnings of human life: childhood. Mark 10 refers to an episode when the disciples rebuked some people who brought their children ("even infants," according to Luke) to Jesus so that they might be touched by him. Indignantly, he said: " 'Let the children come to me, do not hinder them; for to such belongs the kingdom of God. Truly, I say to you, whoever does not receive the kingdom of God like a child shall not enter it.' And he took them in his arms and blessed them, laying his hands upon them" (Mark 10:14–16). A variation of this saying is offered by Matthew (18:3): "Unless you turn and become

like children" . . . suggesting a turn like a positive "metanoia."
Perrin places this saying among a special dozen which exhibit
the radical and total character of the challenge of Jesus, and
among these he calls it, "*the* most memorable and most pregnant." We will cite it as the first of a series of intergenerational
expositions, the most fully carried through being the parable
of the Prodigal Son. But there a father greets his delinquent
young son's repentance as a return from death, and thus reminds us of all the maldevelopments that can blight childhood.
Here, the saying under consideration is a total affirmation of
the radiant potentials of childhood. This is the more aston-
ishing as today we consider ourselves the discoverers of childhood, its defenders against all those history-wide negative
attitudes which permitted proud and righteous as well as
thoughtless adults to treat children as essentially weak or bad
and in dire need of being corrected by stringent methods, or
as expendable even to the point of being killed.

A detrimental counterpart of these attitudes is, of course,
a more modern sentimentalization of childhood as an utterly
innocent condition to be left pampered and unguided. In view
of these and other trends, and especially of the Judaic concentration on bookish learning for spiritual improvement, Jesus'
saying seems simply revolutionary. But it must be seen that he
refers to an adult condition in which childlikeness has not been
destroyed, and in which a potential return to childlike trust has
not been forestalled. What is suggested, then, is a preservation
and reenactment of the wonder of childhood: the "innocent
eye" and ear. Consider in this connection the series of sayings
commending the "seeing eyes" and "hearing ears" which can
comprehend the parables tacitly.

Keeping in mind the patriarchal days in which this was
said, one cannot help noticing, on Jesus' part, an unobtrusive
integration of maternal and paternal tenderness. And, indeed,
if we ask what reassurance for the individual *I* may be hidden
in this and the following intergenerational sayings, it is, I think,
the confirmation of *continuity* of the stages of development.
The adult must not feel that the step of faith expected of him
demands his leaving the child or, indeed, his youth behind

him: on the contrary, only the continuation into maturity of true childlikeness guarantees his faith. Perrin, in this context, speaks of the child's ready trust and instinctive obedience; and I have held in my own writings that the strength of infancy is basic trust, developed in the interaction of the budding *I* with the "primal Other," namely, the maternal person (or persons). This continues into adulthood as a mutuality between growing perceptiveness and a discernible order in the universe. As to an "instinctive obedience," this, too, calls for a correspondence with the pedagogic instinct in adults. But this is the point, and probably was the point in Jesus' time: the imposition of a merely compelling obedience, with disregard of the child's natural tendency to conform, can almost guarantee inner ambivalence leading either to rebellious negation or to that widespread compulsiveness of adjustment which then is apt to find an expression in personal scrupulosity and shared ritualisms—which Jesus preached against as dangerous to faith.

4

As we now turn from sayings which have served primarily to clarify dimensions of the sense of *I* to some others concerned also with intergenerational matters, we begin with the shortest example of another of Jesus' art forms: the parable. Here, the storyteller gives away the nature of parables by asking what the contemporary generation of adults may be *comparable* to; and then selects a concrete scene that could take place any day in a Galilean town.

> But to what shall I compare this generation? It is like children sitting in the market places and calling to their playmates, "We piped to you, and you did not dance; we wailed, and you did not mourn." For John came neither eating nor drinking, and they say, "He has a demon"; the Son of man came eating and drinking, and they say, "Behold, a glutton and a drunkard, a friend of tax collectors and sinners!" Yet wisdom is justified by her deeds [Matthew 11:16–19].

What is here called "calling" obviously means berating, because these children complain that the other children will not "dance to their piping" and in answer to their wailing will not beat their chests in mourning. In other words, they will not play the more demanding complementary parts of the game. This description, then, is meant to bring home to his listeners what Jesus thinks they are doing with him and with John the Baptist, his mentor and baptismal initiator. It is noteworthy that Jesus, when referring to John, always speaks of him with loving respect as an absolutely necessary step in his own revelatory mission—a fact played down by the early church, which rests its whole case on the absolute uniqueness of Jesus' mission. At any rate, here, in addition, Jesus proclaims John's historical right to emphasize radical asceticism in *his* part of the story, while Jesus insists on the legitimacy of his own ritual use of a joyous table-fellowship in which he—so shockingly for his times—includes tax collectors and sinners of all kinds who are not welcome at anybody else's table or, for that matter, inside anybody else's house. Thus, as it were, he demonstrates the historical relativity of all forms of daily ritualization, emphasizing that nobody has a right to compel others to dance to his piping or, indeed, to make them compulsively mourn—provided, of course, that whatever rituals one does choose reflect one's function in the "coming."

I know that I again repeat the obvious in all its simplicity, and this, as before, in order to point to its importance for one of the dimensions of the sense of *I*. Here it is the choice or the sense of one's participation in whatever ritualization seems to express the meaning of the historical and transhistorical moment. I have already mentioned the importance for basic trust of the early feeding situation of the human infant, including that meeting of eye to eye which, it is increasingly clear, is an important source of the sense of *I*—and of a primal *We*. This, I believe, adds to the experience of ritualized meals, besides the shared gratitude for the selection and preparation of the food served, the joy of shared companionship as expressed in the natural exchange of special glances and smiles. This, of course, is an age-old Judaic ritualization which finds its most exalted expression in the expectation of a heavenly table-fellow-ship with "many from East and West"—and all of them with Abraham, Isaac, and Jacob. Here, indeed, each *I* finds its im-mortal place among the dining *We*.

But now, one word about the conclusion of this saying: "Yet wisdom is justified by her deeds." Maybe this speaks for itself. Luke has it as "justified by all her children"—meaning, maybe, that a wise gamesmanship will have the approval of all the "children." It will be felt to be the Way. The saying's tenderness toward children is matched by Jesus' direct appeal to God as Abba, an Aramaic term comparable to daddy or papa, used only by very small children and, of course, not to be found in the Old Testament where, in fact, even the use of the appella-tion "Father" is rare. It is at Gethsemane, right after Jesus had assured the disciples that he and they would all go back to Galilee again, that in a prostrate appeal for God's decision regarding his earthly fate Jesus is said to have addressed God as "Abba" (Mark 14:36).

And now, to the most outstanding example of the use of "Father" as a direct appeal, which is, of course, the Lord's Prayer. Its authentic "directness, brevity, and intimacy," in Per-rin's words, is all the more convincing in that it is a version of the traditional Kaddish which prays that God "may establish his kingdom . . . speedily." Besides its convincing poetic form, one word seems to vouch for the genuineness in Luke's version of the Lord's Prayer, which goes back to Q: only in Aramaic can the same word (*hobā*) mean "debt" and "sin" (even as the word *Schuld* in German can mean "guilt" and "debt"). To Matthew, however, the word *Father* does not seem to be sufficient in its intimate immediacy, and he adds "who art in heaven"—a good example of editorial embellishments of the original sayings—and here, in our terms, a certain distantiation instead of a confirmation of the immediacy which seems con-cordant in the "authentic" sayings. The prayer, of course, con-tains, in all its brevity, the principle expressed later in the "golden rule"—that is, a promised complementarity of forgiv-ing and being forgiven which makes unnecessary what is typical

in the tradition before and after Jesus, namely, the vindictive
threat of a negative outcome in the case of a negative attitude.

As to the sense of *I*, "Abba," besides its radical diminution
of a patriarchal, punitive threat, seems to add to the many
possible meanings of fatherhood a sure dimension of "*my* father." In fact, it has, within a severe patriarchal setting, an
implication of a maternal "touch." The "my" in all this also
increases the sense of being selected and confirmed in one's
sonship, and thus, again, a generational continuity as well as
an affirmation of paternal care. This is especially important
where the generational links of "biological" paternity are considered to be the earthly condition of "the Way."

To see Abba in fatherly (or, as I shall claim, parental)
action, we must finally turn to some of the parables which are
lost-and-found stories. As pointed out, no parable can be declared "authentic" in its totality by our form critics; nor can
we claim for sure the designation "Galilean," except in the
sense that wherever a parable appears in the gospels its essence
must have originated in the treasure of Jesus' early talks. Here
is a short one (originating in Q) which once more reminds us
of the setting in which parables were apt to "happen":

> Now the tax collectors and sinners were all drawing near to hear
> him. And the Pharisees and the scribes murmured saying, "This
> man receives sinners and eats with them." So he told them this
> parable: "What man of you, having a hundred sheep, if he has
> lost one of them, does not leave the ninety-nine in the wilder-
> ness, and go after the one which is lost, until he finds it? And
> when he has found it, he lays it on his shoulders, rejoicing.
> And when he comes home, he calls together his friends and his
> neighbors, saying to them, 'Rejoice with me, for I have found
> my sheep which was lost.' Just so, I tell you, there will be more
> joy in heaven over one sinner who repents than over ninety-
> nine righteous persons who need no repentance" [Luke
> 15:1–7].

To illustrate the inventiveness some of the parables can
evoke in different gospel writers, let us compare St. Thomas's
Gnostic version:

> Jesus said: "The Kingdom is like a shepherd who had a hundred sheep. One of them went astray, which was the largest. He left behind ninety-nine, he sought for the one until he found it. Having tired himself out, he said to the sheep: 'I love thee more than ninety-nine' " [Thomas 107].

Here we see Thomas making sense out of the parable by appointing the lost sheep the largest of the hundred and therefore a logical object both of the shepherd's search and of his love.

There has been much discussion as to the danger the shepherd exposed the vast majority of the *non*lost sheep to by following that single lost one: or did he, maybe, as Jeremias suggests, pursue it only after the others were safely in their fold? My group-psychological orientation makes me feel that there is *some* safety in mere numbers for animals with *some* herd instinct. But it is obviously difficult not to wonder by what right God or Jesus may pay such exclusive attention to one nearly lost creature—unless, of course, it reminds us of ourselves.

This brings us to the story of the "Prodigal Son," which immediately follows in Luke 15:11. One must have tried to paraphrase such a parable to realize how essential is every detail. So here it is, in full:

> And he said, "There was a man who had two sons; and the younger of them said to his father, 'Father, give me the share of property that falls to me.' And he divided his living between them. Not many days later, the younger son gathered all he had and took his journey into a far country, and there he squandered his property in loose living. And when he had spent everything, a great famine arose in that country, and he began to be in want. So he went and joined himself to one of the citizens of that country, who sent him into his fields to feed swine. And he would gladly have fed on the pods that the swine ate; and no one gave him anything. But when he came to himself he said, 'How many of my father's hired servants have bread enough and to spare, but I perish here with hunger! I will arise and go to my father, and I will say to him, "Father, I have sinned against heaven and before you; I am no longer worthy to be called your

son; treat me as one of your hired servants.'' ' And he arose and
came to his father. But while he was yet at a distance, his father
saw him and had compassion, and ran and embraced him and
kissed him. And the son said to him, 'Father, I have sinned
against heaven and before you; I am no longer worthy to be
called your son.' But the father said to his servants, 'Bring
quickly the best robe, and put it on him; and put a ring on his
hand, and shoes on his feet; and bring the fatted calf and kill
it, and let us eat and make merry; for this my son was dead, and
is alive again; he was lost, and is found.' And they began to
make merry.

   "Now his elder son was in the field; and as he came and
drew near to the house, he heard music and dancing. And he
called one of the servants and asked what this meant. And he
said to him, 'Your brother has come, and your father has killed
the fatted calf, because he has received him safe and sound.'
But he was angry and refused to go in. His father came out and
entreated him, but he answered his father, 'Lo, these many years
I have served you, and I never disobeyed your command; yet
you never gave me a kid, that I might make merry with my
friends. But when this son of yours came, who has devoured
your living with harlots, you killed for him the fatted calf!' And
he said to him, 'Son, you are always with me, and all that is mine
is yours. It was fitting to make merry and be glad for this your
brother was dead, and is alive; he was lost, and is found' "
[Luke 15:11–32].

The two distinct parts of the parable make us alternately
sympathize with the lost son and with the older one who was
so concerned over all the excessive attention to his younger
brother. Yet the parable is so evenly constructed that we can
end up only realizing that both brothers are at odds within us,
too. Incidentally, the whole setting must have felt quite ordinary to listeners of that day, since it was apparently quite common then (and quite legal) for younger sons to ask their fathers
for their share and to seek their fortunes in, say, a Levantine
city. So the really outstanding item is the young man's delinquent disposition and the accident of a famine which made it
necessary for him to become dependent on a foreign master
who forced him to become a swineherd. Strangely, even to be

a shepherd in those days would have put him in the category of an outcast or of a "gentile sinner"—the kind of person that Jesus associated with so liberally but was "rightfully" despised by such Pharisee-like personalities as the older brother. Whether or not the father knew of all his younger son's misfortunes, the highly ritualized welcome immediately established the fact that the son's loss of status did not count with the father. Where Luke's text speaks of the approaching boy's "distance" at the moment when his father espied him, incidentally, the King James version makes him as yet "a great way off," which suggests that the father had begun to look out for him and that the immediate welcome he arranged had long been planned, from the kiss of forgiveness to the robe of an honored guest, from the ring of special status to the fatted calf.

Even lengthy parables can be summarized in a brief saying. I think the last dozen words of the Prodigal Son will do: "Your brother was dead, and is alive; he was lost, and is found." Again, then, the "Way" is "within" and "amidst you." And the Abba was steadfast in loving both these sons—so different in familial status and in personality. Almost like a mother, some readers may be tempted to say, and, indeed, as one reviews this parable's theme of the healing of the generational process, one cannot help asking: was there, in this earthly vision of the comparison, no mother, either dead or alive? And if alive, was she not called to say hello, too? But a parable is not a case history or even history; and as to the implied comparison with God, it must be remembered that in all the masculinity dictated by the patriarchal "system" and the rules of language, the dominating quality of the deity was that of a pervasive spirit, out of bounds for any personal characterization: "I am that I am."

And so the parable's meaning, in its patriarchal and monotheistic setting, is the father's overall parental care and above all his forgiveness which permits him to take special chances with the lost ones—that is, to take chances with those who took chances—so as to let them find both themselves and him. The story of the Prodigal Son thus reaffirms generational and existential continuity, confirmed by the joy of table fellowship.

And, too, the parables are apt to deal with the power of potential growth—for example, in the tiny mustard seed:

> And he said, "With what can we compare the kingdom of God, or what parable shall we use for it? It is like a grain of mustard seed, which, when sown upon the ground, is the smallest of all the seeds on earth; yet when it is sown it grows up and becomes the greatest of all shrubs, and puts forth large branches so that the birds of the air can make nests in its shade" [Mark 4:30–32].

This text speaks entirely for itself; but Perrin provides an image found in the Jewish literature where birds in the branches of a tall tree symbolize nations finding a common nesting ground in the messianic future. Thus, parables can lead from the simplest and most concrete observations to unlimited implications, always restating in an imagery speaking to the least intellectual of minds the promise of the future which begins in the immediate present.

Jesus' sayings and his parables, then, complement each other in their logic and in their imagery. The parable of the Prodigal Son makes it clear that the father and the sons can find themselves and one another only by gaining their own identity in the very fulfillment of their intergenerational tasks within their cultural and economic matrix (is *that* the missing mother?). And this, as I hope to have indicated, is among the dimensions demanded by every listener's sense of *I*—wherefore in listening the audience becomes tuned to the storyteller's peculiar *caring* about these dimensions. And here, a pervasive peculiarity of Jesus' care seems to be his essential nonviolence, and this in spite of an occasional militancy which, in fact, is a necessary trait for the nonviolent. As he seems to advocate a maximum of work and a minimum of "works," so he demands a maximum of strength but a minimum of violence—whether against the self in the form of debilitating guilt or against others as hatefulness. Let us review, in conclusion, some sayings pertinent to this theme.

In Perrin's discussion of authentic sayings, that about children immediately precedes the following one about overcoming violence:

"But if anyone strikes you on the right cheek, turn to him the other also; and if any one would sue you and take your coat, let him have your cloak as well: and if any one forces you to go one mile, go with him two miles" [Matthew 5:39b–41].

Nothing could be more abruptly (one is tempted to say "violently") demanding than this and similar suggestions of responses to violent challenges: interestingly enough, to those in the know the turning of the left cheek adds the invitation of a special insult to the danger of injury; the offer of the cloak implies total nakedness; and the party that can force you to go one mile is the Roman soldiery. Here, even Perrin is somewhat perplexed and concludes that these are intended to be "vivid examples" which "exceed normal and natural" human tendencies in order to "imitate the reality of God." But here, for once, I must disagree, and this on the basis of having studied the nonviolent tactics of one of Jesus' modern followers, Mahatma Gandhi. Nonviolent behavior must often be shocking in order to shake up the violent opponent's seemingly so normal attitude, to make him feel that his apparently undebatable and spotless advantage in aggressive initiative is being taken away from him and that he is being forced to overdo his own action absurdly. For human violence almost never feels all that "natural," even to the aggressor himself—neither the violence toward children nor that against loved persons nor even that evoked by declared enemies. And here what Freud called the human superego—that is, the self-negating part of the human conscience as developed in childhood—is fortified by the experience of moral as well as physical violence from adults, while in adulthood it can become so oppressive that one can maintain one's self-esteem only by turning the very violence of one's superego against an evil in others which one wishes to deny in oneself. This, then, can lead to the designation of whole groups of others to membership in what I have called a not-quite-human (or quite unhuman) *pseudo-species*, the extermination of which then becomes a service to God.

5

I have now counterposed a few examples of the style and the logic of Jesus of Nazareth's original sayings with some of the dimensions of the human sense of *I*. I did so because I share the belief that the elemental sayings that emerged in the millennium "before Christ," and in Jesus' own short life, all deal with dimensions of human consciousness in a new manner nowadays expressed in the terms of *individuality* and *universality*, that is, a more aware *I* related to a more universal *We*, approaching the idea of one mankind. In my chosen context, however, I could not attempt to look back on the roots of these sayings in the Judaic world; nor could I review some of Freud's dramatic conjectures concerning the archaic and infantile origins of the Mosaic religion—and its gradual self-transcendence through spirituality and intellectuality. As to Jesus' ministry, I had to stop short of the Judaean Passion that followed the Galilean period after Jesus' decision to confront militantly but nonviolently the violence latent in the political and spiritual deals between the Roman and the priestly establishments by which mortally endangered Israel had learned to live. Here, so one could extend the parable just reported, the son of man took chances not just with the lost ones but also with those who act out so strenuously the roles they find appropriate for their superior identity.

What followed was the crucifixion and the reported resurrection of him who thus became Christ and whose course of life was then creatively mythologized—from the nativity to the ascension. What was then recorded in writing for the Hellenistic world in the services of the mother churches of Christianity developed another kind of authenticity best illustrated by the then emerging victorious symbolisms—such as that of the cross, which, in its utter simplicity, seems to combine the form of homo erectus with his arms all-inclusively extended and that of the son of man dying a deliberately human death under the most vulnerable conditions, only to be resurrected as the savior. Or think of the maternal Madonna who gradually occupied such a shining ceremonial center. The ensuing history of ritual-ization, however, with all its wealth of new social, cultural, and artistic forms, eventually could not escape manufacturing its own kind of compulsive ritualism, including a new pseudo-spe-ciation which permitted the saved species to use even the Chris-tian faith as a rationale for crusades—and murderous hate.

All this must make us even more attentive to the study of the origins and eventual evolution of those simplest revelatory formulations. For their very brevity and simplicity of manifest meaning could never be contrived, and could emerge only when their time had come; even as in subsequent periods they were and had to be experienced with a new immediacy in terms of changing human actualities. In this connection (and to re-turn once more to that question of authenticity) it seems that the least authentic of the reported sayings of Jesus are those which are most concrete or descriptive in their predictions of the forms the kingdom may take, such as those offered so de-finitively in the apocalyptic expectations. Perrin concludes: "Time is thought . . . as opportunity or occasion, as something which is given meaning by that which fills it." This demon-strates, he adds, "the inadequacy of a linear concept of time"—which reminds us once more of Einstein's concept of an *I*-time:

> The experiences of an individual appear to us arranged in a series of events; in this series the single events which we remem-ber appear to be ordered according to the criterion of "earlier" and "later." There exists, therefore, for the individual, an I-time, or subjective time. This in itself is not measurable [Lincoln Barnett, *The Universe and Dr. Einstein*].

But what would Einstein have thought of our main con-cern with Jesus' sayings? With the challenging naivete of genius he makes (in his *Ideas and Opinions*) a number of statements which must interest us most of all, because he associates "the Judaism of the Prophets and Christianity as Jesus Christ taught it" as one body of teaching "capable of curing all the social ills of humanity"—and therefore worthy of being purged of all subsequent additions, "especially those of the priests." In this context Einstein muses that the Jewish God is

> [S]imply a negation of superstition, an imaginary result of its elimination. It is also an attempt to base the moral law on fear, a regrettable and discreditable attempt [*bedauernswert, unruehmlich*]. Yet it seems to me that the strong moral tradition of the Jewish nation has to a large extent shaken itself free from this fear. It is clear also that "serving God" was equated with "serving the living."

And again: "The best of the Jewish people, especially the Prophets and Jesus, contended tirelessly for this." Finally, Einstein extols as a contrast to the emphasis on fear "something which finds splendid expression in many of the Psalms, namely, a sort of intoxicated joy and amazement at the beauty and grandeur of this world." And here he adds a sentence connecting it all with the modernity of mind: "This joy is the feeling from which true scientific research draws its spiritual sustenance."

Einstein's reference to "joy" in this connection might remind us of the role "wonder" played during his childhood in drawing him toward scientific observation, which, as he said on another occasion, turned him from the *I* and the *We* to the *It*—and its revelatory power. For he perceived the fact that "the world of our sense experience is comprehensible as a miracle" which permits him to share "Spinoza's God," "who reveals himself in the orderly harmony of what exists."

What must especially interest us, however, is Einstein's remark, made in passing, concerning the strong tendency in Judaism to "base the moral law on fear"—a tendency which, as we saw, seems to be transcended in the Galilean sayings. We have, of course, suggested that the adoration of Jehovah as a threatening and vengeful god was part of a monotheistic covenant which would eventually compensate for all earthly terror, for it would make historical disasters part of an overall plan designed by an ultimately benevolent, universally caring power. But in its most primitive manifestations this trend must be viewed as another manifestation of that innate human tendency to internalize the morally threatening figures of parental voices and gestures, a tendency which Freud so tellingly called the superego—that is, an inner voice lording it over the sense of *I* and, so it appears from many biblical passages, apt to be "projected" on the monotheistic world order. Here, no future world image can afford to neglect the insights of psychoanalysis which awakened human awareness to the superego's pathogenic inner tyranny in order to heal some of the unconscious sources of unmanageable self-hate as well as the hate of otherness. To do this, the psychoanalytic procedure had to open up the forgotten recesses of childhood, first uncovering a primal source of neurotic suffering and then revealing a treasure of human potentialities, the knowledge of which, as we saw, adds such explicit meaning to Jesus' sayings about children. And here we can, for the adult stages of life, add the deeply religious belief of Einstein, the "childlike" scientist, in the correspondence of the *I*'s searching for orientation in the world, and in "Spinoza's God." A corresponding complementarity, here applied to the symbolic equation of the *I* with an inner eye full of light, can be seen in sayings throughout the centuries—such as Meister Eckhart's "The eye with which we see God is the same as the eye with which God sees us." Hegel, in turn, seems to suggest some caution in an otherwise equally sweeping promise: "Man knows about God only insofar as God knows about himself in man." We have seen how, finally, Freud decided that on the way to more knowledge man must learn to understand the human unconscious as the source of the most destructive and self-destructive drives—an aspect of human nature which Einstein, like Freud, all too soon found associated with the most sublime scientific and technical inventiveness.

Therefore, a brief concluding word about the lasting implications of the militant nonviolence practiced and recommended by Jesus. In my *Gandhi's Truth* I reported how on a visit to India I found myself a guest in a city (Ahmedabad) and in a circle of individuals among whom were some survivors of the first nonviolent adventure engaged in by Gandhi in India—a circumstance which permitted me to study this event in psychoanalytical terms: whereupon it became quite apparent to what extent this Indian prophet, in establishing new, nonviolent principles of political and economic action in his South African days, had knowingly combined elements in his native religion with Jesus' sayings and actions. While Gandhi's personal conflicts seem to have included quite a struggle with a somewhat Western superego, his principles included, besides a readiness for martyrdom, the taking of that daring chance already alluded to in these pages, namely, a conscious and determined projection of the *best* in us, on the (seemingly) *worst* enemy, and a willingness to face him nonviolently. (In British terms of understatement, this was expressed in Gandhi's rather regularly having afternoon tea with the very mill owner against whom he was leading a nonviolent strike.) The setting of this strike may now seem to some of us to be as far removed from our worldwide scene as were the Galilean hills of Jesus' time. And, indeed, any possible solution in human terms of today's biggest threats to humanity would have to come to grips with the danger that human beings will become impotent manipulators in a technically perfect system of destruction and thus participate in the killing of millions of individuals without feeling mortally angry even at one.

In this overwhelming technological context, I must now conclude that we can hardly ignore—for whatever denominational reasons—what as yet can be learned about the basic sayings of our religious tradition and thus about the evolution of human consciousness and conscience. Here, the Galilean sayings must count as an event central to our Judaeo-Christian heritage—a step in human comprehension and self-awareness which is by no means fully expressed in, or restricted to, its ecclesiastic fate.

References

Barnett, L. (1948), *The Universe and Dr. Einstein.* New York: W. Sloane Associates.

Bultmann, R. (1921), *Geschichte der Synoptische Tradition.* Gottingen: Vandenhoeck & Ruprecht. (Engl. transl., *History of the Synoptic Tradition*. Rev. ed. New York: Harper & Row, 1968.)

Dibelius, M. (1919), *Die Formgeschichte des Evangelius*. Tubingen: Mohr. (Engl. trans., *From Tradition to Gospel*. New York: Scribners, 1934.)

James, W. (1890), *The Principles of Psychology*, 2 vols. New York: Henry Holt & Co.

Jeremias, J. (1947), *Die Gleichnisse Jesus*. Zurich: Zvingli. (Engl. trans., *The Parables of Jesus*. New York: Scribners, 1963.)

Perrin, N. (1967), *Rediscovering the Teaching of Jesus*. London: S.C.M. Press.

12.

THE WHITE HOUSE
WASHINGTON

May 13, 1994

Mrs. Joan Erikson
Harwich, Massachusetts 02645

Dear Joan:

Hillary and I were so saddened to hear of Erik's death, and we extend our deepest sympathy to you and your family on your loss.

Throughout his long career, countless people turned to Erik's intelligence and insight to explain what humans could not understand about themselves. His pioneering contributions to psychoanalysis changed the ways in which we see our lives and challenged us to reexamine our relationships to the world around us. His work reflects a remarkable breadth of scholarship. More than that, it reveals an extraordinary level of empathy and compassion. He will be sorely missed.

I hope you can take comfort in the knowledge that Erik made a tremendous difference in our world. Please know that Hillary and I will keep you in our thoughts and prayers.

Sincerely,

Bill Clinton

13.

Erikson, Our Contemporary: His Anticipation of an Intersubjective Perspective

STEPHEN SELIGMAN, D.M.H.

REBECCA SHAHMOON SHANOK, M.S.W., Ph.D.

Erik Erikson's work constitutes a fundamental and independent vision of psychoanalysis. While this vision emerged from the psychoanalytic ego psychological milieu in which Erikson worked, it strains the limits of that tradition, both in its content and its tone; this may help account for its limited acceptance in the American analytic mainstream, in contrast to its widespread influence in other intellectual circles (Wallerstein, 1995). This paper considers Erikson's "way of looking at things" (Erikson, 1950, p. 403) in light of current developments in psychoanalytic thinking, especially the turn to an "intersubjective" point of view that emphasizes the essential place of relationships in motivation, development, and clinical practice. We propose, first, that important potentials that remain only implicit in Erikson's work are clarified and explicated when he is approached from the point of view of the current relational psychology, and that, second, this way of approaching his ideas, in turn, points to directions in which the emerging perspective can be expanded to encompass many of the strongest ideas from ego psychology. Further, we believe that Erikson's insistence on the inclusion of broad social and historical conditions in psychoanalytic psychology challenges adherents to the "two-person" perspective to include a wider array of familial, institutional, and cultural relationships in their project.

Psychoanalytic thinking in the United States has been transformed since Erikson published his essential works in the 1950s and 1960s. The traditional emphasis on drives and the structural model that was dominant during Erikson's day has been fundamentally altered by new paradigms that assert the primacy of relationships. Within this general umbrella, an array of distinctive points of view—object relational, self psychological, neo-Kleinian, social constructivist, and so on—has emerged on the North American psychoanalytic scene in the last decades, animating innovations and controversies at the very heart of the psychoanalytic conception of human nature, of analytic treatment, and of the psychoanalytic identity. Of particular interest is the emergence of an "intersubjective," or relational, perspective that emphasizes the inseparability of the self from its others. Adherents of this viewpoint critique the old "one-person" version of psychoanalysis as ignoring the extent to which development, personality, and clinical interaction all are essentially the outcomes of mutual interaction between two people.

Proponents of the emerging view frequently claim that their model supersedes the earlier analytic models, viewing them as anachronisms. At the same time, loyalists of the "classical" drive and ego psychological viewpoints have reacted with alarm that the most essential elements of analysis are being undermined. This new pluralism has also given rise to controversies about whether psychoanalysis remains a unified discipline, or whether distinctive and incompatible paradigms now require analysts to identify with one or another of these analytic "schools." (See, for example, Greenberg and Mitchell, 1983; Pine, 1990; and Wallerstein, 1992, for a spectrum of views.)

IDENTITY, INSTINCTS, AND INTERSUBJECTIVITY: SYNTHESIZING
EGO PSYCHOLOGICAL AND RELATIONAL CONCEPTS IN A SOCIALLY
ORIENTED PSYCHOANALYTIC VISION

How does Erikson's perspective fit into this situation? Our view
is that Erikson's unique and profound vision anticipates the
current intersubjective turn at the same time that it preserves
much of what is most valuable in the classical approach and
the structural model. Erikson's project was to apply the ego
psychological emphasis on adaptation and integration so as
to integrate the broadest historical, sociological, and political
dimensions into psychoanalysis without losing Freud's radical
insights about the primacy of the body and unconscious symbolic processes.

Erikson located his account of personality and development squarely in the context of relationships. For him, the
individual is inextricable from the social surround, at the most
basic level. His conceptualization of identity locates subjectivity
as essentially constructed in the integration of self-experience
with others. His developmental model gives the highest priority
to the mutual regulation of the potential for development
within the person with the imperatives of both familial others
and the broader culture, to an extent still unparalleled in psychoanalytic theorizing.

Similarly, Erikson's methodological and clinical approach
parallels current developments. He took a relativist view of psychoanalytic knowledge, akin to contemporary social con-
structivism (see for example, Spence, 1982; Hoffman, 1983,
1991; Schafer, 1983; D. B. Stern, 1989). He was consistently
and keenly attentive to the influence of the analyst's personality and historical situation, and he took an inclusive view of
countertransference as an omnipresent and normal part of
clinical and even psychohistorical work.

But rather than supporting the view that thinking in relational terms forces a choice from a "one-person" to a "two-
person" psychology, Erikson's relational approach relocates a
number of the most important ideas from the classical Freudian

edifice so as to strengthen and preserve them. For example, his conception of "zones, modes, and modalities" (Erikson, 1950) remains the most ambitious and successful effort to integrate Freud's discovery of infantile sexuality with the more complex and broad actuality of child development in the familial and cultural context. For him, the physiological does not manifest itself as prior to personal and social meaning and experience, but is inextricably tied up with it. In many ways, Erikson's orientation resembles the transactional systems approach that is currently emerging in both developmental psychology and related fields of psychoanalysis: biological, psychological, and social factors interrelate in a transactional mutual influence system in which each factor takes on its meanings and effects as it interacts with the other factors and whole system (see, for example, Greenspan, 1981; Sameroff, 1983; Sander, 1995; Thelen, 1995). Erikson's reading of Freud encompasses much in the current relational approach, but does not dispense with the omnipresence of the physical, and indeed it goes beyond some current theorizing in its effort to stress the articulations of multiple determinants of meaning in the evolution of each person's experience.

Erikson is thus pursuing, in a very sophisticated and contemporary way, the ego psychological emphasis on adaptation and integration as fundamental aspects of personality functioning and experience. He does not, however, fall into the mechanistic, impersonal, and nonrelational tendencies of the ego psychology proposed by many of its leading proponents (e.g., Hartmann, 1956; see also Jacoby, 1975), which sacrificed the personal experience of subjectivity in an effort to precisely describe psychic structures. Erikson drew on the ego psychological emphasis on synthetic and integrative processes (Nunberg, 1931; Hartmann, 1958), but did so in a way which was both theoretically expansive and experience-near. Erikson vitalized and humanized what is best in ego psychology—the recognition that the integration of multiple perspectives and motivations is an essential human activity.

Overall, then, Erikson's point of view is dialectical and transactional, such that manifestations of the different layers of psychic reality and functioning—ranging from the most primitive domains of the intrapsychic mind to the most global and complex historical developments—are in continuous interplay, influencing one another as they are played out and transformed in the course of each individual's life cycle, as well as in the broader scale of "historical moments" (Erikson, 1975). Even when he did not make it fully explicit, Erikson insisted that the core elements of psychoanalytic psychology—the most private longings, fears, and impulses, and the traces of the relationships within which they were organized—could not be considered without understanding the contexts of actual others and culturally shared forms of meanings within which they are expressed. Erikson's psychoanalytic psychology is thus one that not only permits, but insists upon, the simultaneity of "one-person" and "two-person" approaches, since these perspectives are reflections of an overall process of personal development, interpersonal interaction, cultural systems, and historical change (cf. Ghent, 1989; Hoffman, 1991).

Thus, Erikson's theory advanced the psychoanalytic ego psychology within which it was conceived, and has essential affinities to the current relational view that argues for the inseparability of the individual "self" from its surrounding others. However, while many of these affinities are obvious and explicit, some remain only implicit; as imaginative and independent as he was, Erikson's thinking was constrained in some respects by the limitations of his ego psychological era. For example, his account of identity emphasizes the individual and static side of the experience of subjectivity, rather than the inextricable and dialectical intertwining of self and other that would arise from the fullest explication of that concept, and he rarely refers to European analysts who were his contemporaries with whom he bears striking commonalities, such as Winnicott (1951, 1958, 1967). We (Seligman and Shanok, 1995) have argued elsewhere, and Wallerstein (1995) has explicated, that the fullest possibilities of Erikson's theory are fully realized only when he is reread from the intersubjective perspective.

At the same time, Erikson's thinking challenges the limitations, expansive as they are, of that approach. Following

Freud's most ambitious project for psychoanalysis, Erikson used psychoanalysis in service of the broadest intellectual purposes, pursuing anthropological, religious, historical, and philosophical questions, and he crafted a unique and profound psychoanalytic model that was in turn influenced by and in contact with these other disciplines. Erikson's comprehensive vision suggests that contemporary analysts should not stop at the limits of the two-person dyadic relationship that currently characterizes the intersubjective turn, but, instead, include the array of social systems and historical conditions that influence the individual's psychology, without losing sight of the particular vicissitudes of unconscious mental life. And Erikson's theory suggests the possibility of integrating some of the stronger ego psychological concepts into current relational theorizing, where they have at times been overlooked in the contemporary atmosphere of innovation or shunted to the side by the overly simplistic assumption that concepts which originated in one-person psychologies cannot be usefully revised for inclusion in the relational point of view. Overall, Erikson's capacity to contain multiple perspectives in his profound and original vision suggests that efforts to narrow the psychoanalytic focus, even in service of long overdue and essential theoretical advances, should be scrutinized with the greatest care and skepticism.

INTEGRATING ERIKSON WITH RELATIONAL THEORY: IDENTITY AS AN INTERSUBJECTIVE CONCEPT

In what follows, we will consider four aspects of the Eriksonian "way of looking at things" to further elaborate the convergences and potentials that arise when Erikson's theory is approached in light of current relational orientations: his concept of identity; his reorientation of the role of infantile sexuality and the role of the body in development—that is, his theory of "zones, modes, and modalities"; his epigenetic-developmental model; and his methodological approach to clinical and psychohistorical material.

IDENTITY AS AN INTERSUBJECTIVE CONCEPT

Much contemporary analytic discourse focuses on the problem of subjectivity, with the growing consensus that the mind must be understood as inextricable from its contexts. Despite this emphasis, however, the prevailing theoretical perspectives, taken by themselves, have not fully captured the extraordinary complexity of adult life in contemporary culture.

Reconsidering Erikson's concept of identity in light of contemporary developments—in systems and relational theory, dialectical thinking, and developmental research—offers a generative opportunity to develop a theory of subjectivity and the self that can capture the vital sense of being a person constituted in relationships with others. More than any other single aspect of Erikson's work, the identity concept defined his effort to use analysis as an integrative and comprehensive psychology that serves social and scientific goals without losing the fundamental emphasis on the individual's psychic reality.

Erikson's concept of identity includes a sense of confidence in continuity of the self matched by consistency of one's meaning to others (Erikson, 1950, p. 261). He further described identity as "a configuration gradually integrating constitutional givens, idiosyncratic libidinal needs, favored capacities, significant identifications, effective defenses, successful sublimations, and consistent roles" (Erikson, 1959, p. 116). Thus, identity is the synthetic, adaptive sense of being a person in a complex world, which includes mediations between internal object representations and the external world of current actual relationships, roles, and situations.

Erikson thus proposed the identity concept as an overarching one, in an effort to most fully interpret and exploit the possibilities of Freud's proposal for a psychology of the ego, and, indeed, Erikson often used the term *ego identity* interchangeably with the single word *identity* (see, for example, Erikson, 1959). Embedding his individual psychoanalytic psychology of the individual in historical, sociological, anthropological, and literary constructs, Erikson addressed the complexity of adult experience and advanced the idea that development continues to take place after adolescence. He was thus working to broaden such vital concepts of his day as "libido," "drives," and "the ego" by placing them in a framework that was simultaneously developmental and sociohistorical.

In locating the psychoanalytic subject as inextricable from its objects, Erikson was decisively anticipating current intersubjective approaches. In some respects, however, even this expansive conceptualization was constrained by the limitations of his ego psychological era, even though his eloquent and metaphorical style often challenged those constraints. Erikson often overemphasized the unity and autonomy of the individual at the expense of the more relational and interactional aspects of identity. Much in Erikson's approach has lent itself to readings of the identity concept that have been static, emphasizing sameness and continuity over developmental time and psychic space and neglecting the dynamic complexity of everyday life, especially as it is constituted in contemporary "postmodern" culture. Moreover, Erikson diminished his conceptual range by describing the identity process as a developmental stage, separating it from the matrix of intimate relationships within which identity is established and maintained and from which it is inextricable (Shanok, 1981, 1987, 1993; Franz and White, 1985; Blatt and Blass, 1990; Seligman, 1990; Mitchell, 1991; Seligman and Shanok, 1995).

We have proposed that the identity concept will be most fully elaborated by locating it in a more fully symmetrical transaction between paradoxically and dialectically linked elements of experience, such as individuality and relatedness, internal objects and external others, and continuity and change over time. In addition, the identity concept will be strengthened when it emphasizes the dynamic tension between unity and multiplicity that is typical of subjective experience, especially in light of the extraordinary complexities of contemporary urban life (Seligman and Shanok, 1995).

This perspective also implies a revision of Erikson's postulate that the resolution of intimacy issues *follows* identity formation. Instead, they develop concurrently, as closely interrelated, and as evolving in processes of ongoing reintegration in which both sets of dynamics are intertwined and continually modified (Shanok, 1981, 1987, 1993; Seligman and Shanok, 1995). In the course of adult development, the capacities for identity and intimacy draw upon and organize the outcomes of the previous stages, and continue to evolve and be modified concurrently. Personal identity and intimate relatedness are of a higher order than the stages that follow in Erikson's account of adult development; they are the "envelope" within which subsequent development proceeds as well as within which prior development is organized in adulthood. Our view, then, is that identity is continuous and integrative, rather than merely a developmental stage. Relationships that sustain and actualize the person's "identity" are inseparable from it; individual identity is both rooted in and continually nourished by the relational.

OBJECT RELATIONS THEORIES AND THE IDENTITY CONCEPT

Erikson was exceptional among analysts in his emphasis on the centrality of the transaction between representations of past relationships with the direct experience of actual others in the present. But he nonetheless relied primarily on the ego psychological vocabulary of functions and structures, and did not make much explicit use of the object relational or interpersonal orientations that were emerging at the same time that he was developing his theory, although he shared much with those viewpoints. (In addition to the overall relational focus, for example, Erikson's emphasis on the ubiquity of play as a form of psychic functioning throughout individual development and in cultures finds its closest parallels in Winnicott's [1967, 1971] work.)

Object relations–oriented psychologies are more specific and elaborate in describing the influence of prior relationships, including irrational motivations that were contained in them, in constructing present experience. Mechanisms like projection, identification, and projective identification take on even broader significance when they are understood as the "pathways" for such construction, rather than simply alternative forms of defense (Sandler and Rosenblatt, 1962; Schafer, 1968; Sandler, 1981; Mitchell, 1991).

When internal objects are viewed as traces of the past, the capacity to integrate representations of past experiences with the actuality of present experiences in a more or less synchronous way becomes an important element of identity, involving as it does the simultaneity of past experience with the novelty of the present and the uncertainty of the emerging future. As an aspect of his ongoing effort to integrate object relations and ego psychological orientations, Sandler (1981) has described the processes of "actualization" in which internal representations of past relationships are enacted and mediated in actual current relationships. From this point of view, identity involves the capacity for actualization of earlier relationships in a way that flexibly integrates the drive to repeat and reexperience the past with the novelty of present opportunities. As past experiences are reproduced in the present, their influence and meaning can be transformed as they transact with current actualities and developmental potentials. This is most dramatically illustrated in Erikson's (1958, 1969) comprehensive and profound analyses of the identity crises of Luther and Gandhi, which demonstrate the power of his paradigm to illuminate how individuals mediating and synthesizing intrapsychic, familial, physiological, and cultural factors can generate extraordinary personal solutions as well as moments of great historical significance.

BROADENING CONTEMPORARY VIEWS OF SUBJECTIVITY BY APPLYING THE CONCEPT OF IDENTITY

Overall, then, approaching Erikson's theory from the point of view of contemporary relational theory counters efforts to argue that psychoanalytic concepts which emphasize psychic functions and capacities, such as adaptation and synthesis, are inconsistent with those that emphasize experience, process, and intersubjective interactions. Similarly, this reading of Erikson's identity concept can overcome some of the limitations currently associated with both self psychology and ego psychology, as well as the widespread impression that they are incompatible.

At its most dynamic, identity involves the (more or less) flexible capacity to be influenced by and connected to one's past while being active in and available to the present and the unfolding future, as well as the particular forms and actual relationships within which this synthesis is played out. In other words, the capacity for identity refers to the ability to organize the inner world of representations—including unconscious representations, motivations, and defenses, in relation to the outer world of actual relationships; this includes coordinating the most irrational dimensions of the internal world with the more realistic demands of everyday social life. Thus specified and refined, Erikson's concept of identity provides a profound account of subjective experience in terms of processes of locating self and other representations in intersubjective space. It encompasses inner worlds, outer actualities, and their complex mediations and transactional influence on one another, without dispensing with the importance of bodily experience, unconscious thinking, or irrational motivation.

The Social Embeddedness of the Body: Erikson's Reinterpretation of Instinct Theory

Psychoanalytic instinct theory, especially in its more constricted forms, has reified the analytic conception of the relationship of the body to psychic experience, in a pseudoscientific effort that detaches the dynamism of personality and development from its subjective and intersubjective roots. Taking Erikson's imaginative response to this problem together with the new paradigms proposed by psychoanalytic relational theories provides an important basis for preserving what seems important in psychoanalytic theories of psychic energy while avoiding its many pitfalls.

Erikson boldly reinterpreted Freud's instinct theory in a way that is consistent with contemporary thinking. Rather than positing an autonomous physiological energy prior to other motivations, he sought to integrate the Freudian emphasis on the body with his interest in integrating psychoanalysis with other social sciences. He saw this as advancing the essence of the ego psychological project; his theoretical strategy was more sweeping than that of the other master ego psychological theorists in that he displaced the original drive theory by integrating it with the ego psychological postulate that other motivations and capacities, such as organization, adaptation, and social activity, are basic elements of human nature. In contrast, more conservative theorists, like Hartmann and his colleagues and Anna Freud, proposed the three-system structural model of the mind, with the more adaptive and organized functioning of the ego operating in conflict with the more irrational drives (Arlow and Brenner, 1964; A. Freud, 1936; Hartmann, 1958). (That the tripartite paradigm came to dominate post-World War II American psychoanalysis helps account for Erikson's marginalization there.)

Erikson paid special attention to the role of the body in development, as well as in overall personality functioning. However, he reworked Freud's theory of libidinal phases so as to broaden its base in the entire experience of physical development, rather than in the narrower conception that changes in the libidinally charged zones were the foci and motivators of other developmental changes. Erikson's revision of drive theory included both a content and a formal dimension. He did not assign primacy to sexual pleasure and destructiveness as the basic sources of psychic energy, instead seeing those aims as always playing out with, being defined by, and inseparable from the larger context of the entire body, social relationships and cultural norms. Similarly, he did not accept the physicalistic metaphor of drive discharge as the fundamental psychic motivation. In his most important theoretical monograph, published as the inaugural issue of *Psychological Issues* and introduced by David Rapaport, Erikson (1959) wrote:

> While it was a step of inestimable import when Freud applied contemporaneous concepts of physical energy to psychology, the resultant theory that instinctual energy is transferred, displaced, transformed in analogy to the preservation of energy in physics no longer suffices to help us manage the data that we have learned to observe.

It is here that ego concepts must close a gap. We must find the nexus of social images and of organismic forces—and this is not merely in the sense that here images and forces are, as the saying goes, "interrelated." More than this: the mutual complementation of ethos and ego, of group identity and ego identity, puts a greater common potential at the disposal of both ego synthesis and social organization [p. 23].

Erikson's position has much in common with those of his contemporaries in the British object relations school, who argued that relationship seeking was a primary motivation and that relationships were primary organizers of development and experience (e.g., Fairbairn, 1952; Winnicott, 1958; Bowlby, 1969). The current relational analysts have elaborated on this theoretical position and argue that drive theory has been entirely superseded (e.g., Mitchell, 1993), while some others have proposed positions that integrate elements of the drive theory position without regarding the drives as innate, or primary motivational forces. Several such proposals suggest that the experience of tension associated with particular wishes is a form of mental organization that emerges in the course of development and acquires motivational significance along with other motivations (Loewald, 1980; Sandler, 1981; D. N. Stern, 1985; Kernberg, 1991). Many of these writers, whether relocating or rejecting the drive concept entirely, have instead emphasized the function of affects as a psychobiological function that has both motivational and regulatory functions (Emde, 1980).

Erikson's approach to these issues, then, is in line with the current consensus both in its general orientation and its simultaneous emphasis on affects and relationship contexts. In discussing the question of the aggressive instinct in relation to clinical observations, he wrote:

Here some would say . . . that children are at the mercy of that second primeval power the assumption of which followed the concept of the libido in the psychoanalytic system—namely, an instinct of destruction, of death. I shall not be able to discuss this problem here, because it is essentially a philosophical one,

based on Freud's original commitment to a mythology of primeval instincts. His nomenclature and the discussion which ensued
have blurred the clinical study of a force which will be seen to
pervade much of our material; I refer to the rage which is
aroused whenever action vital to the individual's sense of mastery is prevented or inhibited. What becomes of such rage when
it, in turn, must be suppressed and what its contributions are to
man's irrational enmity and eagerness to destroy, is obviously
one of the most fateful questions facing psychology [1950, p. 68].

Here, Erikson seems to find the Freudian instinct metapsychology burdensome, and suggests, in a tactful way that must
have been conditioned in part by the constraints of his psychoanalytic milieu, that it be put aside in approaching clinical data.
Moreover, his particular view of the aggressive drive here agrees
quite precisely with the contemporary analysts who have understood the emergence of destructiveness as a consequence of
developmental stress, rather than an innate and fundamental
phenomenon (see, for example, Stechler, 1987, and Mitchell,
1993). Also, Erikson anticipated the current emphasis on affects as sources and regulators of personal vitality and activity
in a variety of implicit and explicit ways.

But there is also a more sweeping implication here: on the
one hand, Erikson remained loyal to his Freudian roots and
asserted the central role of the body in development, and in
analysis in general; for him, development is propelled by physiological change over the life cycle, in adulthood as well as childhood. But, unlike the "orthodox" views that reify the
psychological impact of the physical in presenting the isolated
and primary drives as prior to other experience, he embedded
the physical in the interplay of the individual psychology, interpersonal relationships, and the cultural surround.

Once he has staked out this ground, Erikson is left with
the problem of defining another approach, and he does so
immediately in proposing his psychoanalytic developmental
psychology of "zones, modes, and modalities," which appears
only four pages after the just quoted passage from *Childhood
and Society*. Here, Erikson suggests that infantile experience,

including infantile sexuality, was simultaneously a matter of focal zones of sensorimotor sensitivity and activity, correlated senses of bodily experience, and overall ways of relating with significance at physical, intrapsychic, interpersonal, *and* cultural levels. Changes in physical capacities are indeed essential in spurring developmental shifts, but he does not reduce these changes to shifts in the erogenous zones, although he includes them. Instead, he uses the Freudian psychosexual stages to generate metaphors that organize a variety of aspects of the child's experience.

For example, the emergence of muscular control in the second and third years of life is seen as setting the stage for a shift in which experiences are most salient—bowel and bladder training, control and dyscontrol, an interest in the relationship between interior spaces and their contents and exteriors, "holding on vs. letting go," concerns about destructiveness and the durability of objects, "autonomy vs. shame," and so on; these experiences are understandable as part of an overall configuration. Although it is not difficult to see how these patternings are articulated with regard to anal sensation and muscular control, they are not epiphenomenal to it: in contrast to the Freudian metapsychology, where anal erotism is regarded as at the base of the overall developmental pattern, the various issues are regarded by Erikson as equally salient at several levels of the child's experience—the entire body, inanimate objects, control of one's emotions and others in the world, the retention of internal representations of objects, and so on.

In addition, relationships with the most important others, especially parents, follow similar patternings, as do the cultural expectations that provide rationales and meaning systems that give sense to bodily, emotional, and interpersonal experiences. Each culture has its own way of arranging the zone-mode-modality patterns of each developmental phase to suit its particular economic and ideological imperatives, although there is something in each phase's essence that spans cultures and historical periods. At the base of Erikson's epigenetic scheme, then, is a dialectical transaction between culture and biology that cannot be reduced to either pole. The same intertwining that we have described at the complex level of identity is at the center of every developmental phase: Erikson located the personal experience of vitality and force that Freud tried to capture in his drive theory in the creative potentials of human growth and development, the power of culture, and the intricate dynamisms of family life.

Erikson thus posits overarching integrative configurations, like identity, that characterize each developmental phase, and these configurations are forms of organization that cut across biological, psychological, and social levels. In this way, his work anticipates currently emerging applications of systems theories to psychology, including psychoanalysis, that imply that it is the relationships between different elements of various systems, including personalities, that are most essential for understanding them, rather than just the contents of the elements themselves (e.g., Sameroff and Chandler, 1975; Greenspan, 1981; Sameroff and Emde, 1989; Sander, 1995; Thelen, 1995). Linked to research and theorizing in biology, neuroscience, developmental psychology, cognitive science, and other innovative fields, these efforts can be understood as contemporary updates of ego psychology's interest in the organizing principles and forms of adaptation, coordination, integration, and regulation in psychic functioning.

Erikson, of course, shared this interest, and his analyses show great precision and depth in evoking such principles, although this systematic side of his work is sometimes overshadowed by his graceful and painterly prose.[1] While some have regarded the persuasiveness of his writing as an indication of "soft thinking," what is indeed remarkable about Erikson's genius is how his imaginative and integrative orientation captures *both the content and experience of these organizational processes*—a sense of something both underlying and overarching, and often nonverbal: the contours of the forces, pleasures, and anxieties that are at the core of psychoanalytic discourse.

---

[1]Indeed, his own experience as a painter seems quite relevant here, as well as the influence of Joan Erikson (1988), whose ongoing commitment to the significance of nonverbal activity and sensory experience was often gratefully acknowledged by her husband (Erikson, 1950, 1969).

The literary force of Freud's may account, at least in part, for the persistence of the overvaluation of drive theory. Similarly, Erikson is one of the strongest of all psychoanalytic writers, able to capture the dynamic intricacy of the everyday experience of childhood, adulthood, and development in general without sacrificing the depth of psychoanalytic insight. He conveys a sense of energy and force that speaks to what is essential and appealing in libido theory, without treating this force as if it were something ontologically prior to human activity and development. In locating and communicating this dynamism in human growth and activity, Erikson's work suggests a basis on which to preserve what seems important in psychoanalytic theories of psychic energy (what Rapaport [1959] called the dynamic perspective in metapsychology) while avoiding its worst aspects.[2]

ERIKSON'S DEVELOPMENTAL PERSPECTIVE AND CURRENT RELATIONAL AND TRANSACTIONAL MODELS

Freud's emphasis on the drives as the fundamental motivational force was closely intertwined with his reliance on the psychosexual model as an account of child development. Erikson offered a fundamental elaboration and revision of Freud's developmental model that remains among the most imposing to emerge from within psychoanalysis. In so doing, he preserved what was strongest in or outside of Freud's approach, without submitting to some of its more questionable assumptions.

Incorporating his extraordinary child-analytic sensibility with the overall psychosocial–psychoanalytic project that we have described, Erikson went further than other analysts in characterizing development throughout life in terms of the synthesis of individual imperatives (especially but not exclusively

[2]This position is also, as Smelser (this volume, chapter 3) has pointed out, consistent with Marx's (Marx and Engels, ca. 1846) view, most developed in his early writings, that individual psychology arises in social interaction, and it points to some directions for the sometimes avidly sought-after integration of Marxism and psychoanalysis.

those of biological growth and development) with the requirements of the culture for particular personality types and psychosocial aptitudes, as mediated by familial relationships and
other interpersonal and institutional systems. He offered a
more flexible model to capture the ways that the forms and
motivations of each stage of development overlap and persist
throughout the life cycle, while appropriately regarding the
ways in which each phase does indeed have a distinctive character. Erikson pursued a special implication of this view, that
developmental crises—the transitions from one phase to another—were of special importance, and used this perspective
to forge the identity concept. Finally (although this accounting
is not complete), he extended the analytic interest in development through adolescence into adulthood so as to inspire entire subdisciplines related to adult development and
psychohistory.

Erikson's perspective finds much support in a growing consensus that has only recently emerged in both psychoanalytic-
and academic-developmental psychological research: current
researchers generally argue for a developmental systems perspective, and stress the importance of overall relationship contexts and processes in understanding individual factors, such
that the various aspects of any person's development are understood as affecting the others to create complex systems that
have their own integrative and adaptive properties (e.g., Sameroff, 1983; Beebe, Jaffe, and Lachmann, 1993; Beebe, 1995;
Sander, 1995; Stolorow, 1995; Thelen, 1995). In addition to
supporting Erikson's overall insistence on an inclusive and
complex developmental model, a number of more specific current research orientations parallel Erikson's approach. For example, family relationships are increasingly regarded as the
most important subjects for empirical research into socioemo-
tional development (e.g., Main, Kaplan, and Cassidy, 1985;
Sameroff and Emde, 1989), and the effects of genetic and environmental influences in development are understood as inextricable from one another (Plomin, Loehlin, and DeFries,
1985). Such findings have often been taken as supportive of the
overall relational-intersubjective perspective in psychoanalysis

(Emde, 1988; Lachmann and Beebe, 1992; Stolorow, Atwood, and Brandchaft, 1994; Seligman, 1996).

The related domain of observational research about infants and parents has been even more frequently integrated with the new relational approach. Contemporary accounts emphasize how the infant is innately prepared for interpersonal and intersubjective experience, and that infant development cannot be conceptualized without reference to the interpersonal contexts in which it takes place and which give it its vitality and meaning. Moreover, both infant development and caregiving relationships are viewed as systems in which the particular attributes, actions, and experiences of the infant and parents have effects and become meaningful as they emerge and are transformed in the evolving processes of mutual interaction (Sameroff and Chandler, 1975; Greenspan, 1981).

From this perspective, infants are regarded as formidable influences on those who care for them, and on their broader social environments as well (E. H. Erikson and J. M. Erikson, 1953). More specifically, current models describe infants and parents as being involved in processes of mutual regulation in which continuous and rapid signaling, feedback, and response proceed through a variety of modes of cooperative communication. This perspective runs very close to Erikson's own emphasis on social interaction in general, and on mutual influence patterns in particular, as the basic arena in which development proceeds from the beginnings of life forward. Like Erikson, contemporary researchers regard the infant's earliest experiences as social from the beginning, rather than as the solipsistic merger that Freud and many subsequent analysts have posited.

With respect to the current ideological debates within psychoanalysis, infant observation research has generally been understood as providing support for the intersubjective-interpersonal orientation to the therapist–patient relationship. The image of the infant and parent continuously monitoring, influencing, and determining each other's behavior and meaning to one another resembles contemporary schemes that emphasize similar processes of mutual influence and recognition between patient and analyst.

Erikson similarly placed processes of mutual regulation at the very center of his developmental theory, and his use of the term anticipates its current fruitfulness as a paradigm by observational researchers by several decades (see, for example, Erikson, 1950, p. 75, for his usage, and Tronick, 1989, for a more current account). Similarly, even where they do not make it explicit, current infant observers share Erikson's basic interest in how the caretaking environment is both determined by and potentiates the emergence of the infant's emerging physiological and psychosocial capacities (e.g., Sander, 1962; Emde, 1980; D. N. Stern, 1985), a process which was at the heart of Erikson's epigenetic perspective.

ERIKSON'S CLINICAL AND EPISTEMOLOGICAL PERSPECTIVE: AFFINITIES TO CONTEMPORARY APPROACHES

Erikson's methodological and clinical approach similarly has much in common with current developments, although these concerns were not at the center of his best-known contributions. His view of how and what analysts come to know has much in common with the emerging dialectical, constructivist perspective about the creation of psychoanalytic knowledge. Current theorists argue that analytic knowledge is not a matter of uncovering preexisting facts, but of constructing an account that makes sense. Rather than reflecting historical truth, the emerging narrative reflects such factors as the analyst's and patient's personalities and the ideological and cultural contexts within which they are working (Spence, 1982; Schafer, 1983; D. B. Stern, 1989; Hoffman, 1991; Cushman, 1995).

Erikson's essential outlook was similarly relativistic. He considered the maintenance of multiple perspectives to be a cornerstone of psychoanalytic insight, and was a master of synthesizing an array of data from different sources of clinical, historical, and methodological work. His approach to Martin Luther, for example, demonstrated his extraordinary capacity to understand multiple determinants in analyzing how the transaction between familial, psychoneurotic, physiological, and historical factors led to Luther's defiance of the papal Bull and, more broadly, spurred the Protestant Reformation (Erikson, 1958). He applied the same acuity and inclusiveness in his clinical case vignettes.

Erikson never lost sight of the interplay of external givens and individual subjectivity, and was never satisfied with simplified conceptions of reality; he was thus approaching "social facts" with the same psychoanalytic skepticism that he applied to clinical material. His proposal for a distinction between objective "actuality" and subjective "reality" foreshadows current attention to the dialogical construction of what may appear to be "facts" in the psychological field (Erikson, 1964; Hoffman, 1994).

Similarly, in his clinical and psychohistorical work, he was consistently and keenly attentive to the role of the analyst's personality and historical situation in determining interpretations of clinical, biographical, and historical data (this volume, chapter 10). Erikson was exceptionally comfortable considering his own subjectivity and historical location, and his own self-reflections were a critical part of both his clinical and psychohistorical works, notably in his eloquent letter to Gandhi in *Gandhi's Truth* (1969), as well as in his account of the life experiences that shaped his own intellectual development in *Life History and the Historical Moment* (Erikson, 1975). And along similar lines, Erikson (1975) considered countertransference to be a normal and critical part of analytic intervention and inquiry, much like the current intersubjectivists, although with a somewhat different language.

Overall, then, he insisted on the essential importance of self-awareness for analysts. Without harsh or pathologizing judgment, he scrutinized other analysts' work from a similar point of view. For example, Erikson's extraordinary commentary on Freud's reading of the Irma dream (see chapter 8), which stands as one of the great examples of psychoanalytic interpretive writing, includes an analysis of the influence of Freud's own psychology on his approach to this dream that is expansive, precise, and compassionate. Along related lines, in pursuing both his acute perception of the historical–cultural context of clinical work and his special interest in the psychoanalytic psychology of gender, he critiques Freud's insensitivity to Dora's familial and psychosocial situation, calling for a broadened notion of transference that encompasses the patient's psychosocial actuality along with her private fantasies and desires, as they interact with the analyst's personality and social-historical role (Erikson, 1964).

Conclusion

Erikson's imaginative theorizing, then, offers important directions for current innovations, at the same time that it is enhanced when taken together with them. The contemporary emphasis on subjectivity and intersubjectivity calls upon analysis to see itself as a science that studies how experiences and meanings are constructed in social interactions; this does not exclude, of course, interactions that involve unconscious fantasies, wishes, and other of the particular mental phenomena in which analysts have been especially interested. Although he did not explicitly use the language of intersubjectivity, Erikson's theory of motivation, development and personality relies on the same essential postulates, at the same time that it speaks to the ubiquity of both biology and culture in a richer and more inclusive way. Erikson's assertion that the potential of psychoanalysis cannot be fulfilled without understanding how individual experience is determined by the social world and created in social activity is consistent with contemporary relationally oriented developments, and, in some ways, proposes an even more radical and ambitious reading of the psychoanalytic project.

References

Arlow, J. A., & Brenner, C. (1964), *Psychoanalytic Concepts and the Structural Theory*. New York: International Universities Press.

Beebe, B. (1995), Systems models in development and psychoanalysis. Paper presented at the spring meeting, Division of Psychoanalysis (39) of the American Psychological Association, Santa Monica, CA.

———— Jaffe, J., & Lachmann, F. (1993), A dyadic systems view of communication. In: *Relational Perspectives in Psychoanalysis*, ed. N. Skolnick & S. Warshaw. Hillsdale, NJ: Analytic Press, pp. 61–81.

Blatt, S. J., & Blass, R. (1990), Attachment and separateness: A dialectical model of the products and processes of the development throughout the life cycle. *The Psychoanalytic Study of the Child*, 45:107–127.

Bowlby, J. (1969), *Attachment and Loss: Attachment*, Vol. 1. New York: Basic Books.

Cushman, P. (1995), *Constructing the Self, Constructing America: A Cultural History of Psychotherapy*. Reading, MA: Addison-Wesley.

Emde, R. N. (1980), Toward a psychoanalytic theory of affect. In: *The Course of Life: Psychoanalytic Contributions Toward Understanding Personality Development*, Vol. 1, *Infancy and Early Childhood*, ed. S. I Greenspan & G. H. Pollock. DHHS Publication No. [ADM] 80-786. Washington, DC: U.S. Government Printing Office.

———— (1988), Development terminable and interminable: II. Recent psychoanalytic theory and therapeutic considerations. *Internat. J. Psycho-Anal.*, 69:283–296.

Erikson, E. H. (1950), *Childhood and Society*, 2nd ed. New York: Norton, 1963.

———— (1958), *Young Man Luther*. New York: Norton.

———— (1959), Identity and the Life Cycle: Selected Papers. *Psychological Issues*, Monogr. 1. New York: International Universities Press.

———— (1964), Psychological reality and historical actuality. In: *Insight and Responsibility*. New York: Norton, pp. 159–215.

———— (1969), *Gandhi's Truth*. New York: Norton.

———— (1975), *Life History and the Historical Moment*. New York: Norton.

———— Erikson, J. M. (1953), The power of the newborn. *Mademoiselle*, 62:100–102.

Erikson, J. M. (1988), *Wisdom and the Senses: The Way of Creativity.* New York: Norton.

Fairbairn, W. R. D. (1952), *Psychoanalytic Studies of the Personality.* London: Tavistock.

Franz, C. E., & White, K. M. (1985), Individuation and attachment in personality development: Extending Erikson's theory. *J. Personality,* 53(2):224–256.

Freud, A. (1936), *The Ego and the Mechanisms of Defense.* New York: International Universities Press.

Ghent, E. (1989), Credo: The dialectics of one-person and two-person psychologies. *Contemp. Psychoanal.,* 25:169–211.

Greenberg, J., & Mitchell, S. (1983), *Object Relations in Psychoanalytic Theory.* Cambridge, MA: Harvard University Press.

Greenspan, S. I. (1981), *Psychopathology and Adaptation in Infancy and Early Childhood: Principles of Clinical Diagnosis and Preventive Intervention.* New York: International Universities Press.

Hartmann, H. (1956), Notes on the reality principle. In: *Essays on Ego Psychology.* New York: International Universities Press, 1964, pp. 241–267.

———— (1958), *Ego Psychology and the Problem of Adaptation.* New York: International Universities Press.

Hoffman, I. Z. (1983), The patient as interpreter of the analyst's experience. *Contemp. Psychoanal.,* 19:389–422.

———— (1991), Discussion: Toward a social-constructivist view of the psychoanalytic situation. *Psychoanal. Dial.,* 2:287–304.

———— (1994), Dialectical thinking and therapeutic action in the psychoanalytic process. *Psychoanal. Quart.,* 63:187–218.

Jacoby, R. (1975), *Social Amnesia: A Critique of Conformist Psychology from Adler to Laing.* Boston: Beacon Press.

Kernberg, O. F. (1991), A contemporary reading of "On narcissism." In: *Freud's "On Narcissism": An Introduction,* ed. J. Sandler, E. S. Person, & P. Fonagy. New Haven: Yale University Press, pp. 131–148.

Lachmann, F. M., & Beebe, B. (1992), Reformulations of early development and transference: Implications for psychic structure formation. In: *Interface of Psychoanalysis and Psychology.* Washington, DC: American Psychological Association.

Loewald, H. W. (1980), *Papers on Psychoanalysis.* New Haven: Yale University Press.

Main, M., Kaplan, N., & Cassidy, J. (1985), Security in infancy, childhood and adulthood: A move to the level of representation. In: Growing Points of Attachment Theory and Research, ed. I. Bretherton & E. Waters. *Monographs of the Society for Research in Child Development,* Serial No. 209, 50(1–2):66–104.

Marx, K., & Engels, F. (1846), *The German Ideology.* New York: International Publishers, 1947.

Mitchell, S. (1991), Contemporary perspectives on the self: Toward an integration. *Psychoanal. Dial.,* 1:121–147.

——— (1993), Aggression and the endangered self. *Psychoanal. Quart.,* 62:351–382.

Nunberg, H. (1931), The synthetic function of the ego. *Internat. J. Psycho-Anal.,* 12:113–140.

Pine, F. (1990), *Drive, Ego, Object, Self.* New York: Basic Books.

Plomin, R., Loehlin, J. C., & DeFries, H. C. (1985), Genetic and environmental components of "environmental influences." *Developmental Psychol.,* 21:391–402.

Rapaport, D. (1959), A historical survey of psychoanalytic ego psychology. *Psychol. Issues,* 1:5–17.

Sameroff, A. (1983), Developmental systems: Context and evolution. In: *Handbook of Child Psychology: Volume 1. History, Theory and Methods,* ed. P. Mussen. New York: Wiley.

——— Chandler, M. J. (1975), Reproductive risk and the continuum of caretaking casualty. In: *Review of Child Development Research,* Vol. 4, ed. F. D. Horowitz. Chicago: University of Chicago Press, pp. 187–244.

——— Emde, R. N. (1989), *Relationship Disturbances in Early Childhood: A Developmental Approach.* New York: Basic Books.

Sander, L. W. (1962), Issues in early mother-child interaction. *J. Amer. Acad. Child Psychiatry,* 1:141–166.

———— (1995), Identity and the experience of specificity in a process of recognition: Commentary on Seligman and Shanok. *Psychoanal. Dial.*, 5:579–593.

Sandler, J. (1981), Unconscious wishes and human relationships. *Contemp. Psychoanal.*, 17:180–196.

———— Rosenblatt, B. (1962), The concept of the representational world. *The Psychoanalytic Study of the Child*, 17:128–145.

Schafer, R. (1968), *Aspects of Internalization.* New York: International Universities Press.

———— (1983), *The Analytic Attitude.* New York: Basic Books.

Seligman, S. (1990), What is structured in psychic structure?: Affects, internal representations and the relational self. Paper presented at the Spring Meeting of the Division of Psychoanalysis (39), American Psychological Association, Chicago.

———— (1996), Commentary on Peter Wolff's "The irrelevance of infant observations for psychoanalysis." *J. Amer. Psychoanal. Assn.*, 44:430–446.

———— Shanok, R. S. (1995), Subjectivity, complexity and the social world: Erikson's identity concept and contemporary relational theories. *Psychoanal. Dial.*, 5:537–565.

Shanok, R. S. (1981), *Motherhood, Womanhood and the Life Cycle: Fresh Perspectives on the Psychoanalytic and Adult Developmental Literature.* Unpublished master's thesis, Teachers College, Columbia University.

———— (1987), Identity and intimacy issues in middle class married women during the marker processes of pregnancy, adoption and Ph.D. work. *Dissertation Abstracts International*, Volume Issue #4809B (University Microfilms No. 8724093).

———— (1993), Toward an inclusive adult developmental theory: Epigenesis reconsidered. In: *The Course of Life: Psychoanalytic Contributions Toward Understanding Personality Development*, Vol. 6, ed. G. Pollock & S. I. Greenspan. Madison, CT: International Universities Press.

Spence, D. P. (1982), *Narrative Truth and Historical Truth: Meaning and Interpretation in Psychoanalysis.* New York: Norton.

Stechler, G. (1987), Clinical applications of a psychoanalytic systems model of assertion and aggression. *Psychoanal. Inq.*, 7:348–363.

Stern, D. B. (1989), The analyst's unformulated experience of the patient. *Contemp. Psychoanal.*, 25:1–33.

Stern, D. N. (1985), *The Interpersonal World of the Infant.* New York: Basic Books.

Stolorow, R. D. (1995), Dynamic, dyadic, intersubjective systems: An evolving paradigm for psychoanalysis. Paper presented at the spring meeting, Division of Psychoanalysis (39) of the American Psychological Association, Santa Monica, CA.

——— Atwood, G. E., & Brandchaft, B., eds. (1994), *The Intersubjective Perspective.* Northvale, NJ: Aronson.

Thelen, E. (1995), Motor development: A new synthesis. *American Psychologist*, 50:79–95.

Tronick, E. (1989), Emotions and emotional communication in infants. *American Psychologist*, 44:112–119.

Wallerstein, R. S. (1988), The continuum of reality, inner and outer. In: *Fantasy, Myth and Reality: Essays in Honor of Jacob A. Arlow, M.D.*, ed. H. Blum, Y. Kramer, A. K. Richards, & A. D. Richards. New York: International Universities Press, pp. 305–321.

——— (1992), *The Common Ground of Psychoanalysis.* Northvale, NJ: Jason Aronson.

——— (1995), Locating Erikson in contemporary psychoanalysis: Commentary on Seligman and Shanok. *Psychoanal. Dial.*, 5:567–577.

Winnicott, D. W. (1951), Transitional objects and transitional phenomena. In: *Playing and Reality.* New York: Basic Books, pp. 1–25.

——— (1958), The capacity to be alone. *Internat. J. Psycho-Anal.*, 39:416–420.

——— (1967), The location of cultural experience. *Internat. J. Psycho-Anal.*, 48:368–372.

——— (1971), *Playing and Reality.* New York: Basic Books.

14.

Erik H. Erikson's Critical Themes and Voices: The Task of Synthesis

LAWRENCE J. FRIEDMAN

From the publication of *Childhood and Society* in 1950 through the 1970s Erik Homburger Erikson was acknowledged as a major influence in American intellectual life, a figure of great academic distinction whose views on American culture also commanded wide public attention. His wide-ranging approach helped make the immediate postwar decades an unusually hospitable period for interdisciplinary enquiry and maintained the vital role in America of the intellectual as cultural critic, and an examination of his engagement with American society helps throw many of his fundamental intellectual concerns into relief.

By the time he wrote *Childhood and Society* (1950) Erikson had built intimate ties with leading American personality theorists like Henry Murray and John Dollard, pioneering cultural anthropologists such as Margaret Mead and Ruth Benedict, and leaders within the international psychoanalytic community. If the book marked him out as perhaps the most significant post-Freudian thinker, in shifting psychoanalysis decidedly towards social concerns, its critique of American culture was subtle rather than severe. The criticisms deepened in subsequent years as Erikson confronted McCarthyism, developed close friendships with culture critics like David Riesman, Benjamin Spock, and Talcott Parsons, came to engage Reinhold Niebuhr and Paul Tillich, and cultivated ties to innovative theorists in American psychoanalysis like David Rapaport and George Klein. In 1970 Erikson won the Pulitzer Prize and the National Book Award for *Gandhi's Truth,* a volume that looked to the nonviolent Indian leader for alternatives to America's vast nuclear arsenals and its deepening role in the Vietnam War. His photograph appeared in publications ranging from the *New York Times* to *Newsweek.* He completed a decade teaching one of the most popular courses in the history of Harvard University, where he profoundly influenced a new generation of culture critics. Robert Coles, Robert Lifton, Carol Gilligan and Richard Sennett continue to see themselves in Erikson's debt. So does Vice-President Albert Gore.

From Geza Roheim in 1950 to Hetty Zock in 1990, intellectuals and scholars in both Europe and America have sought to explain Erikson's thoughts, to tell us what he "really" meant. Although most have acknowledged that Erikson was a very unsystematic thinker who constantly reformulated his ideas, they have felt compelled to "frame," "distill," or "explain" his contributions. For example, some have described him as a political–cultural "conservative" who insisted (like many other ego psychologists) on the subordination of the self to society and its traditions. Others have disagreed, maintaining that Erikson admired revolutionaries like Luther and Gandhi, who forged broad new identities for themselves and their societies. Most have placed Erikson firmly within psychoanalytic traditions (including an allegiance to drive theory), while others have asserted that he had gradually broken from psychoanalysis (the "Jewish science") in all of its essentials and become a Christian existentialist. There are literally hundreds of publications and dissertations about Erikson. The fullest analyses of his work are Coles (1970), Roazen (1976), and Zock (1990). Coles praises heavily and places Erikson in the reform tradition of the revolutionary leaders he describes. Roazen is more critical; he underscores Erikson's inconsistencies and his political–cultural conservatism. Zock thoroughly delineates his increasing focus on existential concerns.

Interpretations of Erikson's thought have tended to reflect the interpreter's need to explain him in clearer and more precise terms than he provided. There is a significant difference between the Erikson one reads and the Erikson one reads about, with virtually every Erikson interpreter resorting to some degree of reductionism in the interests of order and clarity. My recognition of this problem does not mean that I have been able to avoid it. When I have taught Erikson in my seminar on recent American intellectual history, I have assigned the essays in *Childhood and Society* to illustrate the preoccupation of thinkers immediately after the Second World War with authoritarian–totalitarian social psychology, and his writings of the 1960s and 1970s to underscore the general intellectual preoccupation of those decades with ethnic and gender differences and American militarism. These assignments produced a usable Erikson but also one that simplified the multiple, complex, and "layered" themes in his texts.

Perhaps it is impossible to avoid reducing Erikson's thought so that it serves our needs for order. However, let us make the attempt by underscoring three general topical areas—the nature of American society, the premises and applications of psychoanalysis, and the elements of the human life-cycle—that attracted much of his attention from the 1930s to the 1980s. In all three areas, his thoughts have evolved over time in subtle ways, and it is important to try to determine how he integrated them.

I

When I started a book-length study of Erikson in the spring of 1990, his friend Robert Jay Lifton urged me never to lose sight of his evolving visions of American society because it was among his foremost preoccupations. It was no small matter that when he was naturalized in 1939, six years after migrating from Europe, he changed his surname from Homburger to Erikson. Like Leif Erikson, the Norwegian discoverer of America, he was enchanted by America's possibilities. The severe economic depression that greeted Anna Freud's student when he arrived in Boston seemed less overwhelming than in Europe; he was exhilarated by the energy and hope that President Roosevelt seemed to inspire.

For this young immigrant, there was a fundamental difference between American and European responses to the international economic crisis. In essays of the 1930s and 1940s (revised as chapters for *Childhood and Society*), he compared America both implicitly and explicitly to the totalitarian tragedies of Germany and Russia. The United States was far more open to diverse ethnic and cultural groupings. With its flood of immigrants, America was a society of new beginnings and a more inclusive, pan-human identity. He anticipated Daniel Boorstin by asserting that America's traditions of democracy and social mobility promoted healthy compromise and non-ideological accommodation of disparate interest groups. To be sure, Erikson feared that this spirit of compromise could stifle some of the emotions requisite for healthy psychosocial development. This apprehension paralleled Louis Hartz's worry that liberal capitalist consensus checked political, social, and economic analysis. Like Richard Hofstadter, Erikson also worried about the intensity of American economic competitiveness, the country's work ethic, and its allegiance to productive efficiency over more enduring human values. Indeed, Erikson feared that American wives had come to embrace a puritan morality that provoked mistrust of life and healthy sensuality in their children; they did this to check the aggressive secular orientations of their husbands in the crude marketplace of industrial capitalism. But for Erikson, these ills of America were dwarfed by those brought on in Europe by Hitler and Stalin. He felt that these leaders exploited deep discontent that derived from the more socially stratified and culturally rigid character of the Old World with its capacity for dangerous ideological politics and imbalanced, sometimes gangsterlike, youth rebellion. Whatever their problems, Americans could not produce a Holocaust.

A few months before *Childhood and Society* was published in 1950, Erikson resigned his first and much prized psychology professorship at the University of California. He saw shades of Nazilike thought control in America's emerging McCarthyite climate and refused to sign the University's loyalty oath [see chapter 7]. The next year he joined the staff of the Austen Riggs Center in Stockbridge. He worked there with disturbed American adolescents and planned to write a book on them with a comparative chapter on a German adolescent, Martin Luther. That chapter became the book *Young Man Luther* (1958) and reflected Erikson's continuing need to compare New and Old World cultures. Until the early 1960s, though, he tended to characterize McCarthyism, homebound and puritanical "moms," disturbed adolescents, and other American deficiencies as serious blemishes in a relatively healthy national culture represented by the hopefulness and the pragmatic reform tradition of the New Deal.

By the time of the Cuban missile crisis, however, the negatives had come to outweigh the assets. Erikson became increasingly disenchanted with his adopted country. Above all, he became apprehensive that America's arms race with the Soviet Union could eventually lead to domestic turmoil and nuclear war. Invited by Hubert Humphrey to a private White House function shortly after the Gulf of Tonkin crisis, he warned that the economic and ethical costs of American involvement in Vietnam could destroy the New Deal–Great Society tradition of domestic justice and racial equality. Between 1965 and 1973, Erikson elaborated his concept of "pseudospeciation" as he observed a deepening American presence in Vietnam and a concomitant increase in domestic racial tension. "Pseudospeciation" signified the arrogant placing of one's nation, race, culture, and (or) society ahead of those of others; it was the failure to recognize universal mutuality—that all of humanity was of one species. Erikson spent much of the 1960s studying Gandhi's nonviolent movement for Indian independence as he searched for a viable alternative to elements of "pseudospeciation" that he sensed were increasingly conspicuous in America. (Erikson first used the term "pseudospeciation" in "The Ontogeny of Ritualization in Man" [1966]. He elaborated it in *Gandhi's Truth* [1969], and *Dimensions of a New Identity* [1974a].

His "White House Notes" [1965] detail his visit to the Johnson White House.)

From a broader perspective, it was the combination of McCarthyism, the nuclear perils of the Cold War, the American presence in Vietnam, and the ebbing fortunes of the American civil rights movement that diminished Erikson's enthusiasms for the United States. By 1973, when he lectured before a National Endowment for the Humanities forum on Thomas Jefferson and American identity, he contrasted the national travesties of slaveholding and Indian killing with the fresh, flexible, hopeful, and protean qualities that had drawn him to America in the 1930s. Although there seemed, then, to be a basic shift in Erikson's perspective on America, it can also be characterized as a difference in emphasis. After all, many of the notions that he was advancing during the late 1960s and early 1970s had been implicit in *Childhood and Society*.

II

As Erikson's emphasis in his descriptions of America shifted, it was possible to discern changes in his perspectives on the psychoanalytic profession and its doctrines (his second long-standing topical interest). A wandering artist until the late 1920s, he received psychoanalytic training in Freud's Vienna that gave him a vocation and an orderly daily routine. He worked closely with Anna Freud, his training analyst, and spent time with her father, "the professor." As a result of this experience, Erikson identified firmly for the rest of his life with psychoanalytic tradition, including drive theory. He felt at home with most of Freud's essential formulations and never considered overt rebellion or deviation.

Still, even in his training period in Vienna, Erikson had a somewhat different emphasis than the Freuds. He embraced the new focus on ego psychology but was always uncomfortable with Anna Freud's emphasis on the ego's defenses for coping with everyday problems. From the very start, he was more impressed than the two Freuds with ego strengths and self-confidence—the ways in which the normal, healthy self functioned successfully. Erikson also seemed somewhat more concerned than the Freuds with the effect of society and culture upon inner psyche. Indeed, aboard a ship with his family headed to the New World late in 1933, he showed fellow passenger George Kennan a draft of a psychoanalytic essay on Hitler and German youth that would later appear (much revised) in *Childhood and Society.*

As a research associate at Harvard, Yale, and the University of California during the 1930s and 1940s, Erikson deepened his interest in the psychological strengths of healthy children rather than pursuing the traditional psychoanalytic focus on deficits and defenses among neurotics and psychotics. Wherever he could, he chose to observe and work with children who demonstrated good coping skills. Moreover, his close contacts with Margaret Mead, Gregory Bateson, Ruth Benedict, and others in the early culture and personality movement led him to choose as his essential psychoanalytic focus the way cultural institutions and traditions shaped and were shaped by inner psyches. Sometimes he referred to this as a "configurational" perspective—a way of looking at phenomena like children's block constructions that suggested intersections between the outer society and the inner individual psyche. His shift from psychoanalytic orthodoxy went further. Whereas the Freuds and most of their close followers tended to view religion and other cultural institutions as neurotic crutches, Erikson showed how they could often be useful in promoting strong selfhood.

These differences in emphasis, and Anna Freud's insistence that she could not "understand" Erikson's writings, often gave him a sense of inhabiting the margins of the psychoanalytic profession. Perhaps to compensate, but also with genuine sincerity, he sometimes acted as a figure of the psychoanalytic establishment. In 1965, for example, he denied openly the legitimacy of the American Academy of Psychoanalysis because it was not approved by the American Psychoanalytic Association (Quen and Carlson, 1978, p. 139). At a national psychoanalytic meeting somewhat later, Erikson mocked Jeffrey Masson for his attack on Freud's revised seduction theory. Openly contentious alternatives to the APA and to "the professor" did not merit serious consideration (Masson, 1984, p. 47).

After the late 1950s, however, Erikson became more and more concerned with the way the individual found his place in the moral and ethical order of the world. Appealing less to clinical evidence or even to psychoanalytic theory, his style became increasingly evocative. Some characterized it as prophetic. For Erikson, the revolutionary insights of figures like Luther, Gandhi, Jefferson, and of course, Jesus, derived less from inner psychic or even psychosocial processes than from the decision of a person to take the full burden of his existence upon himself in its relationship to a higher essence. If Erikson continued to perceive that he was amplifying Freud's teachings under changing historical circumstances, he sometimes sounded more like the revolutionary existential prophets that he had researched.

III

With considerable assistance from his wife, Joan, Erikson spent the late 1940s working on the concept of an eight-stage human life-cycle. It overlapped with his two other topical interests, for it was rooted in his observations of American children and in his desire to elaborate Freud's developmental perspective. As his concept emerged, each of life's stages stood for a "crisis" in the developmental process, with a new psychic strength pitted against a new vulnerability. At the same time, each stage was psychosocial, for the crisis was acted out in encounters with other humans, beginning with the infant facing his mother. This mutuality expanded, as one aged, to a "widening radius of social relations."

In *Childhood and Society*, Erikson published the first detailed account of his developmental model: (1) Basic Trust vs. Basic Mistrust (infancy); (2) Autonomy vs. Shame and Doubt (early childhood); (3) Initiative vs. Guilt (play age); (4) Industry vs. Inferiority (school age); (5) Identity vs. Role Confusion (adolescence); (6) Intimacy vs. Isolation (young adulthood); (7) Generativity vs. Stagnation (adulthood); (8) Ego Integrity vs. Despair (old age). Unlike Freud, he emphasized neither infancy nor early childhood, but the fifth, or adolescent identity stage. The first four stages represented efforts to establish and consolidate a personal identity, while the last three stages signaled efforts to retain it in the face of aging and bodily infirmities. For the first time since G. Stanley Hall's 1905 study of adolescence, a major personality theorist was emphasizing that period in the life-cycle. Erikson retained this focus in *Young Man Luther* (1958) as he explored Luther's developmental crisis of adolescence in conjunction with the emergence of the Protestant Reformation.

Erikson continued to discuss adolescent identity issues in the 1960s, especially in conjunction with college-student protests (with which he tended to empathize). However, his major research of that decade, *Gandhi's Truth* (1969), focused on adult life. Erikson tried to explain how the middle-aged Mahatma organized a local labor strike in 1918 which launched his nonviolent crusade against British rule throughout India. Because the adult stages of Erikson's psychosocial life-cycle were the least developed in his work, it is hardly surprising that as his interest in the middle-aged Gandhi developed (and he himself aged), Erikson made *two* major modifications of his eight-stage theory which (among other benefits) allowed him to gain greater insight into the meaning of adulthood.

First, he included within *Insight and Responsibility* (1964a) a crucially important essay, "Human Strength and the Cycle of Generations." In it, he proposed a "schedule of virtues" to correspond with each of the eight stages of the life-cycle: Hope, Will, Purpose, Competence, Fidelity, Love, Care and Wisdom. These virtues were strengths inherent in the human organism that social environments (especially the conduct of adults towards children) could thwart or enhance. They were aspects of an evolving ethical character in the individual (coming into full fruition during adulthood) that was connected explicitly to psychological development. Erikson, with his increasing interest in the existential concerns of adult life, was linking ethical to psychosocial development in each of his eight stages.

In 1965, Erikson presented a paper ("Ontogeny of Ritualization") to the Royal Society of London. (Twelve years later he elaborated this paper in *Toys and Reasons*.) He related a social ritual form to each of his eight psychosocial–ethical stages. At each stage, he postulated, every society orients its members to ways of construing the world through a universal ritual element. At the first or infancy stage of Hope, for example, there was a ritualized *numinous* encounter between mother and infant, followed at each successive stage by the rituals of the *judicious*, the *dramatic*, the *formal*, the *convictional*, the *affiliative*, the *generational*, and the *integral*. The eighth or *integral* ritual saw the old person integrating or becoming living testimony to the wisdom of the society's entire ritual process.

By the middle 1960s, then, just as he was formulating the crucial strands of his biography of middle-aged Gandhi, Erikson had linked his schedule of ethical virtues and social rituals to his eight psychosocial stages. Through the completion of *Gandhi's Truth* and for at least the next decade, he focused on the seventh or "generative" stage when adults were ethically obligated to create and attend to younger generations. In terms of virtues, they were obligated to personally "care" for youth. From the standpoint of ritualization, adults became the "ritualizers" responsible for conducting the whole ritualization process in an authoritative and ethical, but not an authoritarian or moralistic, manner. Through their personal presence and words and deeds, they actualized and authenticated society's genuine, lasting rituals. Having worked out this perspective on the meaning of adult generativity, Erikson was able to articulate Gandhi's essential contributions to younger generations—the example of militant nonviolence as an ethical obligation to redress social injustice and overcome ethnic, nationalistic, and often moralistic tribalism in favor of wider, more inclusive human identities.

Since the mid-1970s, reflecting his own shift from midlife to old age, Erikson focused increasingly on the eighth stage which involved the struggle for personal integrity, moral wisdom, and integration of the ritual process. In 1976 he wrapped up fifteen years of lectures on Bergman's film *Wild Strawberries*

by publishing the extremely thoughtful article "Reflections on
Dr Borg's Life Cycle." Focusing on the old man, Borg, in Bergman's film, Erikson described the quest of old age for integrity
in the face of despair as a process of successfully reliving, integrating, and consolidating all of the prior seven life stages.

Old age, then, was an active and vigorous period for the
self, for society, and for the evolution of human ethics. In the
late 1970s and through the 1980s, Erikson found himself in
closer collaboration than ever before with his wife Joan as they
jointly elaborated aspects of the eighth stage of the life-cycle.
They portrayed "wisdom," the virtue of old age, as a phenomenon that involved more than self-integration and integrity. It
was a "comradeship with men and women of distant times and
of different pursuits who have created orders and objects and
sayings conveying human dignity and love." Indeed, before he
lost his capacity for sustained writing, Erikson had launched a
biography and regular "dialogue" with a young man from a
distant time and place, Jesus [see also chapter 11], who had
also attempted to explicate "the last problems" of life. (For
some of Erikson's most interesting reflections on old age, see
Erikson [1981, 1982, chap. 3]; Hall [1983].)

IV

By now, something of the complexity of Erikson's three long-
standing general topical interests—American society, psychoanalysis, and the human life-cycle—should be apparent.
Through the decades, there were certainly strong continuities
in the way he elaborated each topic. But there were also marked
shifts in his emphasis. In his initial qualified embrace and his
subsequent relative coolness towards America, he was comparing it to other national cultures. From the 1930s through the
1950s, the comparison was largely to European societies, especially Germany. In the course of the 1960s, as he prepared
Gandhi's Truth, India and Hindu culture also became crucial
to his focus. Indeed, the book was in some sense a dialogue on
the future of modern man between Freud the German Jew,

Gandhi the Indian Hindu, and Erikson the Danish-German-American Jew turned Protestant. His extension of psychoanalysis into a perspective that dealt seriously with inner human strengths as well as deficits and outer culture as well as inner personality was so gradual and cautious that it is exceedingly difficult to show how it moved him to embrace questions of ultimate meaning and value. Changes in Erikson's developmental model for human experience were also slow and subtle. It was initially unclear that he was departing from Freud in emphasizing adolescence and adult life over early childhood and outer culture as the equal of inner psyche. A few suspected, however, that the more he amplified his developmental model, the less interested he was in traditional psychoanalytic issues.

It is no easy task to integrate the three aspects of Erikson's intellectual life. Consider the first. Although he embraced the America of Roosevelt as his promising new physical and political home during the 1930s, he continued to regard Freud's Vienna psychoanalytic circle of broad-ranging interdisciplinary thinkers as his intellectual and cultural base. His increasingly critical attitude toward America's warrior qualities in the 1960s and early 1970s may have correlated roughly with his development of a strong ethical dimension in his life-cycle theory and his increasing embrace of questions of ultimate meaning and value. However, elements of all of these were clearly discernible in his June 1950 statement against the loyalty oath to the University of California Committee on Privilege and Tenure [see chapter 7]. Surely, Erikson's increasing concern with existential issues after the late 1950s was compatible with his decision to explicitly couple ethical virtues with his stages of the life-cycle. Suggestions of this existential–ethical merger, however, could be detected in almost every essay in *Childhood and Society*. Logically, Erikson's deepened concern since the mid-1960s with the generative stage responsibility of adults for the well-being of youth (far more than the procreation of children) promoted his critical discussions of the dangers of nuclear war, bellicose tribalism, and the value of militant nonviolence. It is also appropriate to note, however, that he and Joan formulated the life-cycle theory, in which generativity (and its ethical obligation of adults to children) was a stage, during the late 1940s as they reflected on their obligations to their three children in a world shaken in the aftermath of a devastating war and the Holocaust. In 1964 Erikson added a strong element of individual ethical choice and responsibility to each stage of the life-cycle. The next year, he amplified this addition by underscoring the importance of social ritual as the self sought to master the crisis of each stage. Although individual ethical decision is not necessarily incompatible with social ritual, ethical issues were more congruent with Erikson's increasing existential concerns after the late 1950s, while social ritual was closer to his cultural explorations of the 1930s and 1940s that produced *Childhood and Society*.

Clearly, Erikson's three areas of long-standing interest do not fold neatly into each other. In addition, he often had pressing interests that did not overlap clearly with his interests in American and other national cultures, his evolving psychoanalytic perspective, or his changing developmental model. Erikson's considerable historical writing, for example, focused on the role of the revolutionary leader in challenging increasingly untenable social–ideological premises and fashioning new identities for himself and the citizenry of his society. And though his discussion of the leader often involved national culture, psychoanalytic theory, and developmental considerations, Erikson, when he acted as historian-biographer, usually felt that he had another, more pressing task: to demonstrate deep clinical empathy for and understanding of the individual leader's life in the context of its immediate surrounding culture. He treated Luther and Gandhi, for example, in much the same way as he dealt with a hospital patient or an analysand. All else was subordinated to maximizing his clinical effectiveness. Similarly, when Erikson studied the Sioux in the late 1930s and the Yurok in the early 1940s, he was interested in marshaling the skills of anthropological field work through insightful social observations. Although he displayed modest interest in describing Sioux and Yurok ego strengths instead of psychic deficits, he did not consider psychoanalytic theory, national culture, or developmental stages to be his primary focus. One can cite other vital Erikson concerns—the sources of Einstein's scientific and Tagore's literary creativity, psychological issues in the Allied war effort during the early 1940s, or the American civil rights movement of the 1960s—which related only tangentially to his three long-term intellectual preoccupations. My point here is that Erikson had many and frequently changing if intense interests. Therefore, one cannot assess large portions of his writing in terms of his three general areas of intellectual preoccupation.

V

Is it possible to provide a meaningful overview of the ideas of a thinker with three general and evolving, if less than compatible, long-range intellectual concerns as well as a number of intense shorter term preoccupations? When critics have been attentive to at least some of the incompatibilities in Erikson's thought, they have sometimes described him as an unsystematic and often exceedingly vague thinker. He was an artist, it is said, who never entirely made the shift from visual images to precise and logical scholarly writing. On the borders of several callings—psychoanalysis, history, theology, and anthropology—he never felt that he had to satisfy the methodological disciplinary obligations of any of them. It might be better to underscore the eclectic, vague, and often incompatible qualities of Erikson's thought, and to leave it at that, than to conclude (as many critics who recognize the lacunae and vagaries in his thought continue to do) by summing him up with reductionist clarity. However, perhaps we can do better than either the simplistic summations or the emphasis on Erikson's gaps and imprecisions. Neither does justice to the profundity and depth of his mind or the experiential, tentative nature of his language. The mind and the language worked in tandem with an evolving life and temperament. Attention to all four helps us to account for his long-term intellectual concerns as well as his inconsistencies and intellectual incompatibilities.

In 1959 David Riesman (with Talcott Parsons' support) wrote a letter to the dean of Harvard College, McGeorge

Bundy, recommending that he hire Erikson as a professor. Riesman described Erikson as a man with

> [A] modesty so profound as to be trying at times to his friends and colleagues. A psychoanalyst without an MD, a social scientist without even an AB, an artist . . . he has felt a recurrent diffidence about what he could do outside the area of work with patients where he felt more secure and most widely appreciated. His decision that he is willing to come to Harvard indicates that he has attained . . . a greater confidence in his own powers as a teacher and colleague and fellow researcher.

Having come to know Erikson through a decade of summer visits in Bennington and Stockbridge, Riesman was underscoring Erikson's profound problem of self-confidence that appeared to be mending itself. This change was to the good, Riesman concluded, for Erikson would be able to "bring his way of working and his widening curiosities to a group of able and responsible undergraduates and graduate students."

Riesman's appraisal of Erikson as a man with a profound and long-standing (if diminishing) problem of confidence that stood in the way of intellectual dialogue outside a familiar clinical setting was cogent. Erikson's personal papers at the Houghton Library and my interviews with dozens of his closest associates testify to his marked diffidence. It was often coupled with extreme political caution—a reticence to reveal his deficiencies by confronting or offending others. The diffidence and caution were rooted in many factors in his early life. Perhaps the most important were the circumstances of an adopted child who intuited even before he was told that German pediatrician Theodor Homburger was not his real father. He sensed that he had to learn more about his absent Danish parent to make himself whole. As he wandered about Europe as a part-time artist concerned with vague philosophic issues regarding the nature of existence, Erikson was (by his own subsequent admission) deeply disturbed and filled with self-doubts.[1]

---

[1] Erikson's "Autobiographic Notes on the Identity Crisis" (1970) is the fullest published account of his early years. Neither of two revised versions of this essay reveals as much. However, I have relied far more heavily for

It was not until he arrived in Vienna in the late 1920s that his life began to stabilize. He assumed a regular job as an art teacher in a school for the children of Anna Freud's analysands and others. She took him on in a training analysis and gave him the vocation of an early child analyst. At the same time, he married Joan Serson, a bright and creative student of dance and a daughter of devout Canadian Episcopalians. She had the self-confidence and "groundedness" that Erikson lacked. The marriage was an exceedingly close one, and he commenced a life-long habit of looking to Joan for stability and orientation.

With a vocation and the stability that Joan provided, Erikson found a measure of confidence. Before the Vienna Psychoanalytic Society, he chided Anna Freud for a mechanistic perspective on ego defenses that lost sight of the strengths and longings of the whole person. Believing, too, that he had the ability to practice child analysis more successfully and with fewer controls outside of Vienna, and feeling less than comfortable with Hitler coming to power in bordering Germany, Erikson moved with his family to Copenhagen, and then to America. After a spell in Boston he moved in 1936 to Yale.

At the Institute of Human Relations, for the first time since his arrival in America, Erikson came across an organized forum for broad interdisciplinary intellectual exchange. Anthropologists talked with sociologists, psychologists, and psychiatrists. He met John Whiting, Scudder Mekeel, and other interdisciplinary cultural anthropologists and took an interest in their field work. He was also introduced to Margaret Mead and Gregory Bateson and began to investigate Hitler's appeal to youth, American Indian societies, and, more generally, the relationship between psychoanalysis and culture. But Erikson sensed a constricted quality in Institute gatherings—an effort to somehow "tighten," and systematize psychoanalysis through behaviorist psychological assumptions and methods. Consequently,

---

personal and professional biographical data on Erikson's unpublished letters and papers in the Houghton Library and on tape recorded interviews over 1990 and 1991 with Erik and Joan Erikson and their closest friends in the Cambridge-Boston area. Indeed, my entire appraisal of his confidence "problem" and the development of his intellectual dialogues in the rest of this section is based on these sources.

despite the exhilaration over witnessing for the first time sustained interdisciplinary dialogues, he was generally silent and exceedingly cautious politically. Indeed, he often felt like an outsider at the Institute seminars.

Erikson's confidence increased substantially in 1939 when he left Yale to become a research associate at the University of California's Institute of Child Welfare and to practice psychoanalysis in the San Francisco area. In the 1940s, he gained acclaim for published versions of some of the essays that became *Childhood and Society*. Anthropologists Clyde Kluckhohn and Alfred Kroeber, amazed at the depth of his insights into the Sioux and the Yurok, began extensive discussions with Erikson. Mead and Gregory Bateson liked the interdisciplinary culture and personality orientation of all of his early publications, visited with him regularly, and introduced him to Ruth Benedict. Benjamin Spock valued his writing on the connections between childhood and culture and became his close friend, as did the Jungian intellectual, Joseph Wheelwright. By 1950, when his early essays on psychoanalysis and culture were brought together in his first book, Erikson felt more sure of himself as an intellectual among important thinkers than he had in the past. In recognition of the quality of his work, the university psychology department appointed him to a professorship. This meant a great deal to a man who had never received more than a German gymnasium diploma.

As the withdrawn and diffident young man Erikson grew older, gained confidence, and entered into a large array of serious intellectual dialogues, he simultaneously launched his three long-term intellectual preoccupations. *Childhood and Society* included essays on American, German, and Russian national character, an exposition of the eight-stage human life-cycle, and his cautious shift from psychoanalytic orthodoxy through emphasis upon culture and ego strengths, as well as other topics that captivated him.

It goes without saying that the substantial success of this first book at the age of forty-eight further reduced Erikson's timidity. Indeed, it opened rich dialogues with Riesman, David

Rapaport, Reinhold Niebuhr, and other important intellectuals. If he tried to be cautious politically during the 1949 to 1951
struggle against the University of California loyalty oath and
refused to assume a leadership role, he still stuck out as one
of the few in the faculty who risked their careers by continually
refusing to sign the document. Although the university was
still willing to continue his employment, he left on grounds of
principle. When he did, his confidence received another boost,
for he had seven impressive job offers from which to choose. He
accepted Robert Knight's offer to research, teach, and practice
therapy at the Austen Riggs Center, where he quickly emerged
with David Rapaport as the venerated intellectual coleader of
that premier facility. Rapaport ("Mr Metapsychology") detailed to the psychoanalytic profession the profound theoretical import of Erikson's work. By the time Riesman and Parsons
recommended him for a special interdisciplinary professorship
at Harvard in 1959, Erikson's self-confidence was higher than
it had ever been. Moreover, he was eager to add to his circle
of intellectual colleagues on the banks of the Charles River.

For Erikson, it is clear that self-confidence, intellectual exchanges, and innovative writing reinforced each other and
made him less self-protective politically. As a very large circle
of important thinkers and bright young graduate students conversed regularly with Erikson during his Harvard years, he expanded his life-cycle model by adding eight virtues and eight
social rituals, became a serious student of the psychology of
adult life, and completed *Gandhi's Truth*—the most ambitious
of all of his writings.

If Erikson's enhanced confidence went hand in hand with
his expanding intellectual dialogues and his innovative writing,
these factors also help us to explain his intellectual inconsistencies. As the decades progressed, Erikson's initial diffidence became a joyous tolerance of different perspectives. Indeed,
tolerance promoted wider and richer dialogues beyond psychoanalytic and anthropological circles, with theologians like Paul
Tillich and Reinhold Niebuhr, historians like Bruce Mazlish
and John Demos, and India scholars such as Suzanne and Lloyd
Rudolph, Lois and Gardner Murphy, and many more. The

American Academy of Arts and Sciences organized conferences to facilitate some of Erikson's discussions, and Robert Lifton established the annual Wellfleet meeting to provide additional dialogues for him. Erikson's correspondence in the 1960s and 1970s reveals that vast blocs of his time were devoted to a great diversity of intellectual exchanges, organized and spontaneous. Despite old age, he delighted in trading drafts of papers with other thinkers, commenting at conferences, and simply discussing ideas during long walks. In his many discussions, he maintained a language and a focus deeply respectful of the particular interests and experiences of his fellow discussant. Indeed, he openly acknowledged speaking "in different tongues to different audiences." Since he wrote against a background of this rich daily social–intellectual experience, it is small wonder that Erikson's ideas were rarely fully formulated systematically. It was inescapable, for example, that a work like *Gandhi's Truth* would reflect the existential concerns evident in his dialogues with Tillich, the apprehensions of nuclear war voiced in his discussions with Lifton and Brenman-Gibson, the joy for the colors and smells and sounds of India enhanced by exchanges with Pamela Daniels, Sudhir Kakar, and Kamla Chowdry, and the psychoanalytic interests of friends like Robert Wallerstein and George Klein. Since the language with which Erikson carried on each of his dialogues was nearly inseparable from the ideas exchanged, *Gandhi's Truth* consisted of many different tones, textures, and premises.

VI

In view of Erikson's expanding dialogues, it is not surprising that his writings often seemed vague and the three long-term concerns he addressed never folded into each other very well. Since only his unpublished private correspondence makes this fully apparent, one can understand why his ideas were often simplified, misunderstood, and attacked. Indeed, in the course of the 1970s and early 1980s, a guru of the American intellectual community became a somewhat peripheral figure. I shall conclude by offering some conjectures about why this happened.

Within American intellectual culture, widespread recognition often tends to provoke questioning and attack. By 1970 Erikson was perhaps the most sought-out speaker in academia. At this time, a series of attacks erupted. The first came from American feminists, including Kate Millett, Juliet Mitchell, Elizabeth Janeway, and his former teaching assistant Carol Gilligan. As part of his work at the University of California's Institute for Child Welfare in the 1940s, Erikson had observed the play constructions of normal Berkeley children. He found that the constructions closely paralleled the morphology of the sex organs, with boys making erect, intrusive, tall or long assertive structures while girls constructed low, enclosed, inner areas that were closely connected and readily permeable. In *Childhood and Society* and especially in a 1964 issue of *Daedalus,* Erikson developed a biological-psychological-social interpretation of his observations (1964b). Corresponding with their genital organs, boys built powerful outward turning and dominating structures while girls constructed more intricate inward turning structures which were more accessible. Boys patrolled and took charge of outer spaces; girls welcomed other people and objects within the inner spaces that preoccupied them. In an age when life was threatened by the projectiles of nuclear war, Erikson looked to the female disposition for survival, coexistence, and relational alternatives to male assertiveness. Women exhibited the qualities of peace and coexistence that men might choose to discover within themselves.

By the late 1960s and early 1970s, several feminist thinkers dismissed Erikson, as they had Freud, for portraying "deficient castrated womanhood," and for falsely describing learned behavior in a sexist society as inborn. Gilligan's attack came later and was somewhat different. She charged that Erikson had subsumed women in what was essentially a male developmental model. However, the theme of Gilligan's widely heralded *In a Different Voice* (1982)— that men were more dominational and women were more relational—bore a striking resemblance to Erikson's ideas on inner and outer space. Erikson publicly held his ground. He claimed that he was stressing female differences as assets. Moreover, he was not arguing that biology was destiny; social and psychological forces were equally relevant. Still, Erikson smarted privately over the spirited feminist attacks.[2]

In March 1975, Marshall Berman, a political theorist at City College (CUNY), struck what Erikson regarded as a far more devastating blow. Reviewing *Life History and the Historical Moment* on the front page of the New *York Times Book Review,* he attacked Erikson for concealing his Judaism. Berman also mocked the "cosmic chutzpah of his claim to be Erik Erikson, his own father" by repudiating his legal name of Erik Homburger in 1939 and renaming himself as his own son (the ultimate self-made man). Although Erikson had established his reputation by emphasizing the need to face honestly all personal identity issues, Berman claimed he was actually insecure and arrogant and could not face the problem of identity in his own life. Erikson was not what he seemed (Berman, 1975).

Berman's essay may have damaged Erikson's reputation like nothing before. Privately, Erikson wrote letters to friends countering Berman's account of his religious upbringing and his name change. Paul Roazen, a former student in Erikson's graduate seminar at Harvard in the mid-1960s, received one of these letters but saw validity in Berman's charge of duplicity. Indeed, Roazen totally rewrote his draft of *Erik H. Erikson: The Power and Limits of a Vision* (1976) to underscore Erikson's tendency to slide over complex theoretical issues and to revise significantly some of his early publications without indicating the change to his readers. Roazen also accused Erikson of a subtle conservative political bias where Erikson emphasized the "ingenious" adaptation of the self to the surrounding culture. Howard Kushner (1977, 1979) wrote two articles that accentuated Roazen's charges and echoed a claim that Joel Kovel (1974) had made even before the Berman review: that Erikson was an apologist for "the established order." But such a charge

---

[2]Jean Strouse (*Women and Analysis,* Boston: G. K. Hall, 1985, pp. 291–340) prints a somewhat revised edition of Erikson's 1964b *Daedalus* essay and his 1974b response to feminist criticism. Hopkins (1980) provides an overview of the controversy over Erikson's theory and adds further criticism.

did not lead neoconservative intellectuals to embrace Erikson. On the contrary, David Gutmann (1974) scored him in *Commentary* for shifting from a favorable portrayal of America in the first edition of *Childhood and Society* to one unduly critical of its racist traditions and its role in the Vietnam War.

Amidst these harsh attacks, Erikson had his defenders. John Munder Ross, Karolyn Gould, and Mark Gerzon wrote to the *New York Times Book Review* to criticize Berman. David Riesman urged Kushner to modify his attacks on Erikson's alleged conservatism. Others talked privately of the simplicities and overkill of the attacks. However, none felt obligated to wage the sort of systematic and prolonged defense of Erikson that had traditionally occupied followers of other leading psychoanalytic thinkers, and one can understand why. Unlike Freud, Heinz Kohut, or other major psychoanalysts, Erikson had never organized a movement to elaborate, propagate, and defend his ideas. Rather, he had simply maintained separate and highly idiosyncratic conversations with different creative thinkers. These associates never came together save for a gathering at Robert Lifton's Wellfleet cottage or an occasional American Academy of Arts and Sciences conference. Erikson's rapport with each always involved its own particular issues and its unique types of communication. His letters to Robert Coles, for example, differed fundamentally in content and style from those to Lifton. Because there was no cohesive Eriksonian movement like there had been a Freudian, Jungian, or Kohutian movement, it would have been difficult to conduct an organized defense or effective efforts to ostracize Gilligan or Roazen for their "infidelities." Erikson's close associates never even considered these traditional warfare techniques of the psychoanalytic profession.

Perhaps because there has been no Eriksonian movement, with specific followers assigned the task of precise and sustained doctrinal elaboration of his ideas, original Erikson publications have remained the major sources for his thought. As he aged and wrote less, dated and unrevised texts constituted his primary literary legacy. To be sure, there were developmental

psychologists, psychoanalysts, educators, theologians, psycho-
historians, and even a few literary critics who invoked Erikson's
concepts to give theoretical shape to their own writings. But
most of these works simplified, diminished, and transformed
Erikson's richly multilayered expressions and ideas into dull
textbooklike lessons. It is difficult to believe that many of these
publications, particularly the one-dimensional Eriksonian psy-
chobiographies and the mechanical enumerations of the eight
stages of his life-cycle, could draw bright young students to
Erikson's original works.

Finally, it may be that Erikson's diminished reputation was
partially grounded in the decline of those interdisciplinary values in academia that had helped to give his writings wide cur-
rency. He had gained prominence during the 1950s and 1960s,
perhaps the high decades of interdisciplinary scholarship in
recent American history. Much as *Childhood and Society* and
Young Man Luther combined many disciplines, so did Riesman's
The Lonely Crowd, Richard Hofstadter's *The Age of Reform,* David
Potter's *People of Plenty,* and Leo Marx's *The Machine in the
Garden.* By the 1970s and 1980s creative scholarship was being
produced, more and more, by satisfying the tenets of specific
academic disciplines. Even blatantly interdisciplinary work had
to meet specific disciplinary-based criteria in traditional academic units. At Harvard, for example, there was no longer a
Department of Social Relations to offer refuge to those, like
Riesman and Erikson, who did not fit into a single academic
speciality area. In the late 1980s, the Sociology Department
into which Riesman had been moved had refused to tenure
Paul Starr. Starr's monumental cultural, historical, and economic study, *The Social Transformation of American Medicine,*
had failed to satisfy the department's specific disciplinary criteria. Thirty years after Riesman and Talcott Parsons had convinced McGeorge Bundy to hire Erik Erikson because he was
different from most scholars and ranged broadly over many
disciplines, it was difficult to believe that Harvard would do
so again.

REFERENCES

Berman, M. (1975), Review of E. H. Erikson, *Life History and the Historical Moment. NY Times Book Rev.,* March 30.

Coles, R. (1970), *Erik H. Erikson: The Growth of His Work.* Boston, Toronto: Little, Brown.

Erikson, E. H. (1950), *Childhood and Society.* New York: Norton.

—— (1958), *Young Man Luther.* New York: Norton.

—— (1964a), *Insight and Responsibility.* New York: Norton.

—— (1964b), The inner and the outer space: Reflections on womanhood. *Daedalus,* 92: 582–606.

—— (1965), White House notes. Erikson Papers, Houghton Library.

—— (1966), The ontogeny of ritualization in man. *Philosoph. Trans. Roy. Soc. London,* Series B, 251:337–349, 772.

—— (1968), Womanhood and the inner space. In: *Identity: Youth and Crisis.* New York: Norton, pp. 261–294.

—— (1969), *Gandhi's Truth.* New York: Norton.

—— (1970), Autobiographic notes on the identity crisis. *Daedalus,* 99:730–759.

—— (1974a), *Dimensions of a New Identity.* New York: Norton.

—— (1974b), Once more the inner space: Letter to a former student. In: *Women and Analysis,* ed. J. Strouse. Boston: G. K. Hall, pp. 320–340.

—— (1975), *Life History and the Historical Moment.*

—— (1976), Reflections on Dr. Borg's life cycle. *Daedalus,* 105:2 (Spring):1–31.

—— (1977), *Toys and Reasons: Stages in the Ritualization of Experience.* New York: Norton.

—— (1981), On generativity and identity. *Harvard Ed. Rev.,* 51:249–269.

—— (1982), *The Life Cycle Completed.* New York: Norton.

Gilligan, C. (1982), *In a Different Voice.* Cambridge, MA: Harvard University Press.

Gutmann, D. (1974), Erik Erikson's America. *Commentary,* 58:60–64.

Hall, E. (1983), A conversation with Erik Erikson. *Psychol. Today.* June:22ff.

Hopkins, L. B. (1980), Inner space and outer space: Identity in contemporary females. *Psychiatry,* 43:1–11.

Kovel, J. (1974), Erik Erikson's psychohistory. *Soc. Policy,* 4:60–64.

Kushner, H. I. (1977), Pathology and adjustment in psychohistory: A critique of the Erikson model. *Psychocultural Rev.,* Fall:493–506.

———— (1979), Americanization of the ego. *Can. Rev. Amer. Studies,* 10:95–101.

Masson, J. (1984), The persecution and expulsion of Jeffrey Masson. *Mother Jones,* 9: (December) 47.

Quen, J. M., & Carlson, E. T., Eds. (1978), *American Psychoanalysis: Origins and Development.* New York: Brunner/Mazel.

Riesman, D. (1959), Letter of June 2 to McGeorge Bundy: Erikson Papers, Houghton Library.

Roazen, P. (1976), *Erik H. Erikson: The Power and Limits of a Vision.* New York: Free Press.

Zock, H. (1990), *A Psychology of Ultimate Concern: Erik H. Erikson's Contribution to the Psychology of Religion.* Atlanta, GA: Rodopi.

15.

Epilogue

LEO GOLDBERGER, Ph.D.

My first personal encounter with Erik Erikson was at a tea hosted by Norman Rockwell, who had served on the Board of Trustees of the Austen Riggs Center while Erik Erikson worked there throughout the fifties. It was sometime in the mid- to late sixties and the tea was in honor of Erikson who was on one of his regular visits to the Berkshires; the Riggs staff, along with a few of their guests (which included me and my friend, the late George Klein), were invited. I still have a vivid image of the imposing silver-haired Erikson sitting in a comfortable easy chair, surrounded by an adoring cluster of Riggs fellows who hung on his every word. Though eager to meet him, I stayed instead in another part of the living room, enjoying a conversation with our host, the other famous celebrity. Near the end of the tea party, while Erikson was circulating around the room, I was finally introduced to him by our mutual friend, George Klein, who made a point of mentioning my Danish backgound to Erikson. (I was raised and schooled in Denmark before immigrating to these shores shortly after the war years.) It was clear that Erikson instantly viewed me as a "compatriot"; the feeling was, of course, mutual as I had read of his Danish parentage and felt an emotional tie to him. The Danish component of his "identity" obviously meant a great deal to him. I sensed that there might even have been a hint of envy of my knowledge

379

of Danish, a language he had never learned. We chatted at some length, among other things about his unsuccessful attempt to obtain a work permit in Denmark in the early thirties.

Later, in 1971, when a group of analysts and psychologists, including myself, concerned about the stagnant atmosphere within psychoanalysis, intitiated a series of publications to encourage innovative and interdisciplinary studies (which eventuated in the quarterly, *Psychoanalysis and Contemporary Thought*), Erik H. Erikson was on the editorial advisory board. Erikson was the quintessential integrator of ideas from a wide array of disciplines and sources, from the natural and social sciences to the disciplines of history, literary criticsm, theology, and continental philosopy. He was not one to pause at the so-called great divide separating the positivistic and the hermeneutic landscape of knowledge. Like Freud, Erikson was challenged by the big picture, addressing man's ultimate, philosophical concerns while maintaining his clinical focus on individual pathology and the healing process.

Erikson rejected the disjunction between mind-as-meaning and mind-as-mechanism; his writings traversed phenomenology, abstractions, interpretation, and evolution-based speculation. He left to others the task of situating and coordinating the conceptual scaffold he created within the broader realm of psychoanalytic ego psychology. Thus, he refrained from the endless debate on such issues as whether psychoanalysis is or is not a "true" science. In a similar vein, he never became caught up in the critical debates ushered in by postmodernism, questioning the very notion of the "self," the conception of "development" as a linear stage sequence, or the assumption of essential gender differences. And although Erikson employed the "narrative approach" par excellance to convey his insights, he did not find it necessary to explicate his rationale for embracing "narratology" or acknowledge his "constructionist" leanings in his identity concept. As an artist, social philosopher, and clinician, his interests lay in other directions—exemplified so beautifully in his elegant style of writing, with its carefully crafted mosaics of evocative prose and multilayered meanings. And his brilliant writings struck just the right chords at the precise historical moments when his refreshing perspective was most needed. His theories and visionary insights met the need felt by so many of us for an alternative to the increasingly outmoded dogma of orthodox Freudians and their self-styled heirs. By contrast, Erikson—though still positing a *somatic order* as the bedrock for his developmental theory—nevertheless brought to the fore the contingencies of culture and history in a synthesis that visualized a complex, contextual interweaving of individuals, generations, and larger historical trends. His vision was optimistic in its central emphasis on the innate adaptive powers of integration and synthesis of the ego—derived from his evolutionary notion of the species-specific capacity for rejuvenation and renewal. Despite the Holocaust, the nuclear threat, racism, tribal and religious wars around the globe, he maintained his faith that mankind would ultimately counterpose the destructive aspects of *pseudospeciation* with an inclusive human identity and universal ethic. Paradoxically, Erikson's marginalized status in each of the fields from which he drew his knowledge was in no way a setback to his becoming one of the most influential, respected, and frequently cited writers across the interdisciplinary spectrum. Today, within the academic discipline of psychology, for example, there is hardly an introductory, developmental, or personality textbook in psychology that does not have a special "treatment" of Erik Erikson's theories, usually including a brief biography, a photo, and a chart depicting the Eight Stages of Man. His classic papers on ego identity and the Irma dream, included in the present volume, are still a "must" on every psychoanalytic candidate's reading list, while a perusal of the current psychological literature suggests that Erikson's stage theory is alive and well in that it still generates ideas, research questions, and theoretical modifications (especially as it relates to gender issues and the priority Erikson accorded autonomy over intimacy).

While Erikson was one of the major figures of our time, gaining wide public recognition for his "unique and fertile understanding of how man pursues his own humanity by confronting himself—and society—in a continual quest for identity," (Woodward, 1970, p. 84) he was also simply, "Erik," to many of us, whether we knew him well or just casually. He was an endearingly unpompus person—or to use Harry Stack's Sullivan's famous phrase—he was "more human than otherwise." Some anecdotes will illustrate:

When George Klein died in 1971, I was quite moved by a phone call I received from Erikson expressing sorrow at George's untimely death and by his genuine concern that the unfinished manuscript George was working on not be left unpublished: "It is too important!" he asserted. In fact, Klein's posthumous book, *Psychoanalytic Theory: An Exploration of Essentials* was, finally, published in 1976 by International Universities Press, shepherded by Merton Gill and myself. Klein's indebtedness to Erikson is readily apparent throughout the book. He explicated the essentially *social* nature of Erikson's identity concept, pointing out that when properly understood, "identity" conveys a sense of "we-ness," a "we-go," as Klein termed it. Erikson was decidedly not confined to a "one-person psychology," and, as Seligman and Shanok suggest in the present volume, he anticipated the "intersubjective" perspective in psychoanalysis—just as he anticipated many other trends current today.

During the turbulent years of the student revolution, perhaps sometime in the early seventies, I ran into Erikson in the Riggs lunchroom and after some brief chitchat he asked me, with his characteristic curiosity and empathic attention, what I was teaching these days at New York University. My answer was: 'Freud, but it's not going too well, my students want to read *you*, Erikson, instead." "Isn't that interesting," he reflected, "At Harvard, where I'm lecturing on my own ideas, they clamor for Freud instead." "What is the moral of this?" he asked rhetorically, "Youth needs to rebel!"

Many years later, when Erikson returned to Riggs for a summer month, before going on to the Cape, I asked him what he planned to do for the month. In a low, confiding tone of voice he said he had offered to give a seminar on a topic to be chosen by the fellows, but to his surprise they wanted him to do Kohut's self psychology. I was of course a bit stunned on hearing this, wondering what on earth possessed the fellows to show such poor judgment, not to take advantage of Erikson doing Erikson. I expressed my dismay to him. "Well what can you do?" he said wearily, with a touch of hurt but not anger. "You know, these are young people. The real problem is that I'm not that familiar with Kohut's writings myself and at my age, I'm not so sure I want to spend the time catching up." I'm afraid I didn't find out what Erikson's seminar focused on that summer, but I'm pretty sure it wasn't Kohut.

On several other occasions, he invoked his age as an excuse for not doing something. For example, when asked why he at times failed to answer his voluminous mail, he answered with gusto: "Having reached the age of seventy, I believe I've earned the right to distinguish between shit and gold—and most of the mail I receive is shit!"

Yet another occasion—perhaps on Erikson's last visit to Riggs —I asked him what he was currently working on. In reply he said something like: "For many years now I had wanted to end my work with a psychohistory of Kierkegaard (his Danish "compatriot" as he had sometimes referred to him in print), but unfortunately I don't know any Danish and I've gotten too old to learn it. Of course, as I'm sure you know, it's essential to know Danish to fully grasp Kierkegaard's difficult text and to read about his historical context—so I am working on a study of Jesus instead." Taken aback by this unexpected shift from Kierkegaard to Jesus, I could only respond, "But don't you need to know Hebrew, Aramaic, Babylonian and Latin to research the life of Jesus?" "No," he said, "The literature on the historical Jesus is rich and of the highest quality. It is available in German or English and I have already become totally immersed in it." In 1981 with the publication of Erikson's "The Galilean Sayings and the Sense of I," reprinted in the present volume, I was left in awe of his impressive scholarship on Jesus. If only he had known Danish, imagine how he might have situated Kierkegaard's psychohistorical drama! And one can only wonder about the determinants of Erikson's lifelong preoccupation with Kierkegaard (the "psychoanalytic theologian," as Ernest Becker called him in *The Denial of Death*), aside from the obvious Danish connection. Certainly, what has clearly emerged in Erikson's oeuvre is his evolving conception, not just of an inherently *social* ego identity, but of a *transcendental* one, marking Erikson the "theological psychoanalyst," cast in a Kierkegaardian mold, at least in terms of the existential character of his philosophical outlook.

An early champion of Erikson, Robert Coles, in his (1970) essay, "The Measure of Man" wrote: "Erikson seems to have realized from the beginning of his career that in science and in history what is called 'truth' constantly changes, since no 'fact' is immune to new information. What remains much longer is a viewpoint, or a manner of inquiry." One can only say "Amen" to this and hope that Erikson's manner of psychoanalytic inquiry—his "Way of Looking at Things"—which he once characterized as constituting "a very special admixture of laboratory conditions, methdological climate, and personal ideological involvement" will continue to inform generations to come.

REFERENCES

Coles, R. (1970), The measure of man. *The New Yorker,* Nov 16:64.

Woodward, K. (1970), Psychoanalyst Erik Erikson and the search for identity. Cover Story. *Newsweek,* Dec. 21.

Bibliography[1]

ERIK H. ERIKSON

Die Zukunft der Aufklaerung und die Psychoanalyse. *Z. psychoanal. Paedag.*, 4:201–216, 1930.

In English: Psychoanalysis and the Future of Education. *Psychoanal. Quart.*, 4:50–68, 1935.

Bilderbuecher. *Z. psychoanal. Paedag.*, 5:13–19, 1931.

Triebschicksale im Schulaufsatz. *Z. psychoanal. Paedag.*, 5:417–445, 1931.

Book Review: *Psychoanalysis for Teachers and Parents*, by Anna Freud. *Psychoanal. Quart.*, 5:291–293, 1936.

Configurations in Play—Clinical Notes. *Psychoanal. Quart.*, 6:139–214, 1937.

Dramatic Productions Test. In: *Explorations in Personality*, ed. Henry A. Murray and others. New York: Oxford University Press, 1938, pp. 552–582.

On Play Therapy : eds. A Panel Discussion with Maxwell Gitelson and others. *Amer. J. Orthopsychiat.*, 8:466–524, 1938.

Observations on Sioux Education. *J. Psychol.*, 7:101–156, 1939.

Problems of Infancy and Early Childhood. In: *Cyclopedia of Medicine*. Philadelphia: Davis and Company, 1940, pp. 714–730.

Studies in the Interpretation of Play: 1. Clinical Observation of Play Disruption in Young Children. *Genet. Psychol. Monogr.*, 22:557–671, 1940.

[1] Most of these entries were derived from a listing maintained by Mrs. Helen Linton, the librarian at the Austen Riggs Center, Stockbridge, MA and for which we are most appreciative. Although the bibliography includes all of Erik Erikson's major writings, it is by no means exhaustively complete nor does it include unpublished, archival materials that pertain to Erikson at the Hougton Library and elsewhere.

On Submarine Psychology. Committee on National Morale (for the Coordinator of Information) 1940. Unpublished.

On the Feasibility of Making Psychological Observations in Internment Camps. Committee on National Morale (for the Coordinator of Information) 1940. Unpublished.

Concerning the Interrogation of German Prisoners of War. Committee on National Morale (for the Coordinator of Information) 1940. Unpublished.

Further Explorations in Play Construction., *Psychol. Bull.*, 38:748, 1941.

Comments on Hitler's Speech of September 30, 1942. Council on Inter-Cultural Studies, 1942. Unpublished.

Hitler's Imagery and German Youth. *Psychiatry*, 5:475–493, 1942.

Revised in: *Personality in Nature, Society and Culture*, ed. Clyde Kluckholn & Henry A. Murray. New York: Alfred A. Knopf, 1948.

Observations on the Yurok: Childhood and World Image. Monograph, Univ. of Calif. Publ. Amer. Archeol. Ethnol., 35:257–301, 1943.

Plans for the Veteran with Symptoms of Instability. Stanford, CA: In: *Community Planning for Peacetime Living*, ed. Louis Wirth. Stanford, CA: Stanford University Press, 1945.

Childhood and Tradition in Two American Indian Tribes. In: *The Psychoanalytic Study of the Child*, 1:319–350. New York: International Universities Press, 1945.

Ego Development and Historical Change. In: *The Psychoanalytic Study of the Child*, 2:359–396. New York: International Universities Press, 1946.

Childhood and Society. New York: Norton, 1950, 400 pp. Second, enlarged edition, 1963.

Growth and Crisis of the "Healthy Personality" (With Joan M. Erikson). In: *Symposium on the Healthy Personality*, ed. Milton J. E. Senn. (Prepared for the White House Conference 1950.) New York: Josiah Macy, Jr. Foundation, 1950, pp. 91–146.

Statement to the Committee on Privilege and Tenure of the University of California Concerning the California Loyalty Oath. *Psychiatry*, 141:244–245, 1951.

Sex Differences in the Play Configurations of Preadolescents. *Amer. J. Orthopsychiat.*, 21:667–692, 1951.

Cross-Cultural Patterns in the Adjustment and Maladjustment of Children, I. Deviations from Normal Child Development with Reference to Cross-Cultural Patterns. II. Etiology of Maladjustment in the Environment of the Child. *Scandinavian Seminar on Child Psychiatry and Child Guidance*. Geneva, World Health Organization, 1952. (Abstract)

Remarks Made at an Interagency Conference at Princeton, New Jersey, September 21–25, 1951. In: *Healthy Personality Development in Children: As Related to Programs of the Federal Government*. New York: Josiah Macy, Jr. Foundation, 1952.

The Power of the Newborn (with Joan M. Erikson). *Mademoiselle*, 61:100–102, 1953.

On the Sense of Inner Identity. In: *Health and Human Relations*. Report of a Conference held at Hiddensen, Germany, August 2–7, 1951. New York: The Blakiston Company, 1953, pp. 124–143.

Identity and Young Adulthood. Presented at the 33th Anniversary of the Institute of the Judge Baker Guidance Center, Boston, May 1953.

Wholeness and Totality—A Psychiatric Contribution. In: *Totalitarianism, Proceedings of a Conference Held at the American Academy of Arts and Science*, ed. Carl J. Friedrich, March, 1953. Cambridge, MA: Harvard University Press, 1954. pp. 156–171.

The Dream Specimen of Psychoanalysis. *J. Amer. Psychoanal. Assoc.*, 2:5–56, 1954. Also in: *Psychoanalytic Psychiatry and Psychology, Clinical and Theoretical Papers, Austen Riggs Center*, Vol. I. ed. Robert P. Knight & Cyrus R. Friedman. New York: International Universities Press, 1954, pp. 131–170.

Identity and Totality: Psychoanalytic Observations on the Problems of Youth. *Human Development Bulletin*, Fifth Annual Symposium. Chicago: The Human Development Student Organization, 1954, pp. 50–82.

Freud's "The Origins of Psychoanalysis." *Internat. J. Psycho-Anal.*, 36:1–15, 1955.

The Problem of Ego Identity. *J. Amer. Psychoanal. Assn.*, 4:54–121, 1956.

The First Psychoanalyst. *Yale Review*, 46:40–62, 1956. Also in: *Freud and the Twentieth Century*, ed. Benjamin Nelson. London: George Allen & Unwin, 1957.

Ego Identity and the Psychosocial Moratorium. In: *New Perspectives for Research on Juvenile Delinquency*. Washington, DC: Children's Bureau, U.S. Department of Health, Education and Welfare, 1956, pp. 1–23.

The Confirmation of the Delinquent (with Kai T. Erikson). *Chicago Review*, 10:15–23, 1957.

Identity and the Psychosocial Development of the Child. In: *Discussions on Child Dvelopment*, Proceedings of the Third Meeting of the Child Study Group, World Health Organization, Vol. 3. New York: International Universities Press, 1958.

Young Man Luther, A Study in Psychoanalysis and History. New York: Norton, 1958.

The Nature of Clinical Evidence. *Daedalus*, 87:65–87, 1958. Also in: E. Erikson, *Insight and Responsibility*. New York: Norton, 1964.

Identity and the Life Cycle: Selected Papers. *Psychological Issues*, Monogr. 1. 1959. New York: International Universities Press, 1959.

Late Adolescence. In: *The Student and Mental Health*, ed. Daniel H. Funkenstein. The World Federation for Mental Health and the International Association of Universities, 1959.

Youth and the Life Cycle, an Interview. *Children*, 7:2. U.S. Department of Health, Education and Welfare, Washington, DC: 1950.

Indentity and Uprootedness in Our Time. In: *Uprooting and Resettlement*, Eleventh Annual Congress. *Bull. World Fed. Ment. Health*, Vienna, 1958.

Psychosexual Stages in Child Development. In: *Discussions on Child Development*, ed. J. M. Tanner & Barbara Inhelder. World Health Organization Study Group, 4, 1959.

The Roots of Virtue. In: *The Humanist Frame*, ed. Julian Huxley. New York: Harper & Brothers, 1961.

Childhood and Society. In: *Children of the Caribbean*. San Juan: The Commonwealth of Puerto Rico, Printing Division. 1961, pp. 18–29. Also, Postscripts to the Conference, pp. 151–154.

Introduction. In: *Emotional Problems of the Student*, by Graham B. Blaine and Charles C. McArthur. New York: Appleton-Century-Crofts, 1961.

Youth: Fidelity and Diversity, *Daedalus*, 91:5–27, 1962.

Reality and Actuality. *J. Amer. Psychoanal. Assn.*, 10:451–473, 1962.

The Golden Rule and the Cycle of Life (The George W. Gay lecture on Medical Ethics, 1961). *Harvard Med, Alumni Bull.*, 37:2, 1963. Also in: *The Study of Lives*, ed. R. W. White. New York: Appleton-Century-Crofts, 1963.

Editor, *Youth: Change and Challenge*. New York: Basic Books, 1963.

The Inner and Outer Space: Reflections on Womanhood. *Daedalus*, 93:582–606, 1964.

Insight and Responsibility. New York: Norton, 1964.

Memorandum on Identity and Negro Youth. *The Journal of Social Issues*, 20:29–42, 1964.

Psychoanalysis and Ongoing History: Problems of Identity, Hatred and Nonviolence. *Amer. J. Psychiatry*, 122:241–250, 1965.

Concluding Remarks: On the Potential of Women. In: *Women and the Scientific Professions*, ed. Jacquelyn A. Mattfeld & Carol G. Van Aken. The M.I.T. Symposium on American Women in Science and Engineering, Cambridge, MA. M.I.T. Press, pp. 232–245, 1965.

The Concept of Identity in Race Relations: Notes and Queries, *Daedalus*, 95:145–170, 1966.

The Ontogeny of Ritualization in Man. In: *Philosophical Transactions of the Royal Society of London*, 251:147–526, 1966. Revised in: *Psychoanalysis—A General Psychology. Essays in Honor of Heinz Hartmann*, ed. Rudolph M. Lowenstein et. al. New York: International Universities Press, 1966.

Concluding Remarks on Ritualization of Behavior in Animals and Man. In: *Philosophical Transactions of the Royal Society of London*, 251:513–524, 1966.

Words for Paul Tillich. *Harvard Divinity Bull.*, 30:13–15, 1966.

Gandhi's Autobiography: The Leader as a Child. *The American Scholar*, Autumn:632–646, 1966.

Eight Stages of Man. *Internat. J. Psychiatry*, 2:281–300, 1966.

Book review: Thomas Woodrow Wilson, by Sigmund Freud and William C. Bullitt. *N. Y. Rev. Books*, Vol. 8, 1967.

Memorandum on Youth for the Committee on the Year 2000. *Daedalus*, 96:860–870, 1967.

Memorandum on the Military Draft. In: *The Draft: Facts and Alternatives*, ed. Sol Tax. Chicago: University of Chicago Press, 1968, pp. 280–283.

The Human Life Cycle. In: *International Encyclopedia of the Social Sciences*. New York: Crowell-Collier, 1968, pp. 286–292.

Psychosocial Identity. In: *International Encyclopedia of the Social Science*. New York: Crowell-Collier, 1968, pp. 61–65.

Identity: Youth and Crisis. New York: Norton, 1968.

On the Nature of Psycho-Historical Evidence: In Search of Gandhi. *Daedalus*, 97:695–730, 1968.

Insight and Freedom. The T. B. Davie Memorial Lecture on Academic Freedom. U. of Capetown. On Student Unrest and Remarks on Remarks on Receiving the Foneme Prize. Second S.A. 1968. International Convention, Fonene Institute, Milano, 1969. (Unpublished).

On the Nature of Psycho-Historical Evidence: In Search of Gandhi. *Internat. J. Psychiatry*, 8:451–476, 1969.

Gandhi's Truth. New York: Norton, 1969.

Reflections on the Dissent of Contemporary Youth. *Daedalus*, 97:154–76, 1970. Also in: *Internat. J. Psycho-Anal.*, 51:11–22, 1970.

Autobiographic Notes on the Identity Crisis. *Daedalus*, 99:730–759, 1970. Also in *The Twentieth Century Science*, ed. Gerald Holton. New York: Norton, 1972.

Play and Actuality. In: *Play and Development*, ed. Maria Piers. New York: Norton, 1972, pp. 127–160.

Environment and Virtues. In: *Arts of the Environment,* ed. Gyorgy Kepes. New York: Braziller, 1972, pp. 4–77.

On Protest and Affirmation. Address, Class Day, Harvard Medical School. *Harvard Med. Alumni Bull.,* 46:30–32, 1972.

Youth: Fidelity and Diversity. *Humanitas,* 8:2–35, 1972.

By Way of a Memoir. In: *Clinician and Therapist, Selected Papers of Robert P. Knight,* ed. Stuart P. Miller. New York: Basic Book, 1972, pp. vii–xii.

Thoughts on the City for Human Development. *Ekistics,* 35(209):216–220, 1973.

Conversations with Huey P. Newton. In: *In Search of Common Ground,* ed. Kai T. Erikson. New York: Norton, 1973.

Dimensions of a New Identity: The 1973 Jefferson Lectures in the Humanities. New York: Norton, 1974.

Once more the inner space: Letter to a former student. In: *Women and Analysis,* ed. Jean Strouse. Boston: G. K. Hall, pp. 320–340, 1974. New York: Dell, pp. 365–387, 1975.

Life History and the Historical Movement. New York: Norton, 1975.

Toys and Reasons: Stages in the Ritualization of Experience. New York: Norton, 1977.

Psychoanalytic reflections on Einstein's centenary. In: *Albert Einstein: Historical and Cultural Perspectives,* ed. Gerald Holton & Yehuda Elkana. Princeton, NJ: Princeton University Press, pp. 151–173, 1980.

Dorothy Burlingham's School in Vienna (with Joan M. Erikson). *Bull Hampstead Clin.,* 3:91–94, 1980.

Themes of Work and Love in Adulthood, ed. Neil J. Smelser and Erik H. Erikson. Cambridge, MA: Harvard University Press, 1980.

The Galilean Sayings and the Sense of "I." *Yale Rev.,* Spring:321–362, 1981.

On generativity and identity (with Joan M. Erikson). *Harvard Ed. Rev.,* 51:249–269.

The Life Cycle Completed: A Review. New York: Norton, 1982.

Anna Freud-Reflections. *Bull. Hampstead Clin.,* 6:51–54, 1983.

Reflections: On the relationship of adolescence and parenthood. *Adolescent Psychiatry,* 2:9–13, 1983.

Vital Involvement in Old Age: The Experiences of Old Age in Our Time (with Joan M. Erikson and Helen Q. Kivnick). New York: Norton, 1986.

A Way of Looking at Things: Selected Papers from 1930 to 1980, ed. Stephen Schlein. New York: Norton, 1987.

ABOUT THE LIFE AND WORK OF ERIK ERIKSON*

Albin, M., ed. (1980), *New Directions in Psychohistory: The Adelphi Papers in Honor of Erik H. Erikson.* Lexington, MA: Lexington Books.

Andersen, D. C. (1993), Beyond rumor and reductionism: A textual response to Erik H. Erikson. Special Issue: Erik H. Erikson. *Psychohist. Rev.,* 22:35–68.

Capps, D., Capps, W. H., & Bradford, M. G., eds. (1977), *Encounters with Erikson: Historical Interpretation and Religious Biography.* Missoula, MT: Scholars Press.

——— Browning, D. S., eds. (1983), *Life Cycle Theory and Pastoral Care.* Philadelphia: Fortress Press.

Bruner, J. (1987), The artist as analyst. A review of *A Way of Looking at Things: Selected Papers from 1930–1980,* by E. Erikson. *N.Y. Rev. Books,* Dec. 3:8–13.

Coles, R. (1970), *Erik H. Erikson: The Growth of His Work.* Boston: Little Brown.

Evans, R. (1964), *Dialogue with Erik Erikson: With Reactions from Ernest Jones.* Northvale, NJ: Jason Aronson, 1995.

Gross, F. L. (1987), *Introducing Erik Erikson: An Invitation to His Thinking.* Lanham, MD: University Press of America.

Gutmann, D. (1974), Erik Erikson's America. *Commentary,* 58:60–64.

Hall, E. (1983), A conversation with Erik H. Erikson. *Psychol. Today,* June:22ff.

Hopkins, L. B. (1980), Inner space and outer space: Identity in contemporary females. *Psychiatry,* 43:1–11.

Johnson, R. A. (1977), *Psychohistory and religion: The Case of Young Man Luther.* Philadelphia: Fortress Press.

*Compiled by the editors.

Knowles, R. T. (1986), *Human Development and Human Possibility: Erikson in the Light of Heidegger*. Lanham, MD: University Press of America.

Kotre, J. (1984), *Outliving the Self: Generativity and the Interpretation of Lives*. Baltimore: Johns Hopkins University Press.

Kovel, J. (1974), Erik Erikson's psychohistory. *Soc. Policy*, 4:60–64.

Kushner, I. H. (1977), Pathology and adjustment in psychohistory: A critique of the Erikson model. *Psychocult. Rev.*, Fall:493–506.

——— (1993), Taking Erikson's identity seriously: Psychoanalysing the psychohistorian. Special Issue: Erik H. Erikson. *Psychohist. Rev.*, 22:7–34.

Mullen, R. E. (1976), *Being Between*. Pasadena, CA: JCK.

Roazen, P. (1976), *Erik H. Erikson, an Introduction*. New York: St. Martin's Press.

Wallulis, J. (1990), *The Hermeneutics of Life History: Personal Achievement and History in Gadamer, Habermas, and Erikson*. Evanston, IL: Northwestern University Press.

Woodward, K. (1970), Psychoanalyst Erik Erikson and the search for identity. Cover story. *Newsweek*, Dec. 21.

Wright, J. E., Jr (1982), *Erikson, Identity and Religion*. New York: Seabury Press.

Zock, H. (1990), *A Psychology of Ultimate Concern: Erik Erikson's Contribution to the Psychology of Religion*. Atlanta, GA: Rodopi Press.

Name Index

Ackerman, N. W., 197
Aprahamian, M., 10
Arlow, J. A., 336
Arrien, A., 79–80
Atwood, G. E., 343

Banton, R., 69
Barnett, L., 317–318
Bateman, J. F., 214
Bateson, G., 24, 359, 368, 369
Becker, E., 383
Beebe, B., 342, 343
Benedict, R., 24, 187, 353, 359, 369
Benveniste, D., 25
Bergman, I., 362–363
Berliner, H., 9
Berman, M., 373
Bibring, E., 201
Blass, R., 332
Blatt, S. J., 332
Blos, P., 196
Boman, L., 292–293
Boorstin, D., 356
Bowlby, J., 337
Bradford, M .G., 69
Branch, T., 72
Brandchaft, B., 343
Brenman, M., 4, 9, 208n, 371
Brenner, C., 336
Breuer, J., 124
Brill, A. A., 126n
Bultmann, R., 278, 300

Bundy, M., 366–367, 375
Bunyan, J., 75
Burlingham, D., 3, 212

Campbell, J., 75
Capps, D., 69
Capps, W. H., 6–7, 69
Caputo, P., 73
Carlson, E. T., 359
Cassidy, J., 342
Cavell, M., 6
Chandler, M. J., 340, 343
Chowdry, K., 371
Clinton, B., 10, 323
Colby, K., 146–147
Coles, R., 52–53, 57, 72, 354, 374, 384
Collingwood, R. G., 17, 249
Cushman, P., 344

Daniels, P., 371
Dann, S., 191n
Davis, W., 74
de Bell, D., 9
de Marneffe, D., 87
DeFries, H. C., 342
Demos, J., 370
Descartes, R., 34–35, 36, 38, 41
Dewey, J., 101
Dibelius, M., 278
Dollard, J., 223n, 353
Dunham, H. W., 214

Eckhart, M., 319

395

Subject Index

399